The Origins of Global Humanitarianism

Whether lauded and encouraged or criticized and maligned, action in solidarity with culturally and geographically distant strangers has been an integral part of European modernity. Traversing the complex political landscape of early modern European empires, this book locates the historical origins of modern global humanitarianism in the recurrent conflict over the ethical treatment of non-Europeans that pitted religious reformers against secular imperial networks. Since the sixteenth-century beginnings of European expansion overseas and in marked opposition to the exploitative logic of predatory imperialism, these reformers – members of Catholic orders and, later, Quakers and other reformist Protestants – developed an ideology and a political practice in defense of the rights and interests of distant "others." They also increasingly made the question of imperial injustice relevant to growing "domestic" publics in Europe. A distinctive institutional model of long-distance advocacy crystallized out of these persistent struggles, becoming the standard weapon of transnational activists.

Peter Stamatov is currently Associate Professor of Sociology at Yale University. His work has appeared in *The American Sociological Review, Theory and Society*, and *Contemporary Sociology*, as well as in Hungarian and Brazilian scholarly journals. He is a past winner of the Bendix Prize of the Comparative Historical Section of the American Sociological Association and was a recipient of Cátedra de Excelencia (Excellence Chair) at the Universidad Carlos III de Madrid.

CAMBRIDGE STUDIES IN SOCIAL THEORY, RELIGION AND POLITICS

Editors

David C. Leege, University of Notre Dame

Kenneth D. Wald, University of Florida, Gainesville

Richard L. Wood, University of New Mexico

The most enduring and illuminating bodies of late-nineteenth-century social theory – by Marx, Weber, Durkheim, and others – emphasized the integration of religion, polity, and economy through time and place. Once a staple of classic social theory, however, religion gradually lost the interest of many social scientists during the twentieth century. Recent phenomena such as the emergence of Solidarity in Poland; the dissolution of the Soviet empire; various South American, Southern African, and South Asian liberation movements; the Christian Right in the United States; and Al Qaeda have reawakened scholarly interest in religiously based political conflict. At the same time, fundamental questions are once again being asked about the role of religion in stable political regimes, public policies, and constitutional orders. The Cambridge Studies in Social Theory, Religion and Politics series produces volumes that study religion and politics by drawing on classic social theory and more recent social scientific research traditions. Books in the series offer theoretically grounded, comparative, empirical studies that raise "big" questions about a timely subject that has long engaged the best minds in social science.

Titles in the Series

Paul A. Djupe and Christopher P. Gilbert, *The Political Influence of Churches*

Joel S. Fetzer and J. Christopher Soper, *Muslims and the State in Britain, France, and Germany*

Jonathan Fox, *A World Survey of Religion and the State*

Anthony Gill, *The Political Origins of Religious Liberty*

Brian J. Grim and Roger Finke, *The Price of Freedom Denied: Religious Persecution and Conflict in the Twenty-First Century*

Kees van Kersbergen and Philip Manow, editors, *Religion, Class Coalitions, and Welfare States*

Ahmet T. Kuru, *Secularism and State Policies toward Religion: The United States, France, and Turkey*

Pippa Norris and Ronald Inglehart, *Sacred and Secular: Religion and Politics Worldwide*

Peter Stamatov, *The Origins of Global Humanitarianism: Religion, Empires, and Advocacy*

The Origins of Global Humanitarianism

Religion, Empires, and Advocacy

PETER STAMATOV

Yale University

CAMBRIDGE
UNIVERSITY PRESS

CAMBRIDGE
UNIVERSITY PRESS

32 Avenue of the Americas, New York, NY 10013-2473, USA

Cambridge University Press is part of the University of Cambridge.

It furthers the University's mission by disseminating knowledge in the pursuit of education, learning, and research at the highest international levels of excellence.

www.cambridge.org
Information on this title: www.cambridge.org/9781107021730

© Peter Stamatov 2013

First published 2013
Reprinted 2014

A catalog record for this publication is available from the British Library.

Library of Congress Cataloging in Publication data
Stamatov, Peter, 1967–
The origins of global humanitarianism : religion, empires, and advocacy / Peter Stamatov, Yale University.
    pages   cm. – (Cambridge studies in social theory, religion and politics)
Includes bibliographical references and index.
1. Indigenous peoples – Colonization.   2. Europe – Territorial expansion.
3. Europe – Colonies – History.   4. Imperialism – Moral and ethical
aspects – History.   5. Humanitarianism – Religious aspects – Christianity – History.
I. Title.
JV305.S73   2013
361.7'509–dc23   2013017439

ISBN 978-1-107-02173-0 Hardback

... for the growing good of the world is partly dependent on unhistoric acts; and that things are not so ill with you and me as they might have been, is half owing to the number who lived faithfully a hidden life, and rest in unvisited tombs.

George Eliot, *Middlemarch*

Contents

Acknowledgments

Let me start by acknowledging the "civilians" from outside of academia who supported me through the long years of research and writing: Gabriel Bravo, Ildikó Krén, Miguel Otero, George Perez, and Laurence Winkworth. And where would I be without the support of my family, Katia, Sako, Zlati, and Philip? The "life-course" of this project coincided with the cruelly brief life of my dog Seven who I still miss enormously.

Rogers Brubaker and Rick Biernacki taught me how to be a sociologist. My interest in the questions this book addresses began to take shape in Budapest of the mid-1990s, in classes taught by Judit Bodnár and István Rév. In Los Angeles I was lucky to be able to discuss ideas with Mabel Berezin, Jon Fox, Robert Gedeon, Mara Loveman, Mick Mann, Eyal Rabinovitch, and Stephanie Limoncelli. Hannah Brückner and Chris Wildeman have been special in New Haven. Thanks also go to colleagues and students at Yale: Julia Adams, Jeff Alexander, Ateş Altınordu, Jen Bair, David Bargueño, Shai Dromi, Phil Gorski, Andy Junker, Alondra Nelson, Sam Nelson, Jensen Sass, Rachel Sherman, Sam Stabler, Luke Wagner, and Jonathan Wyrtzen. In Budapest, again, I had long conversations with Stefan Detchev, João Gonçalves, and Jon Stewart. And then my *familia madrileña* adopted me: Juan Díez Medrano, Juan Fernández, Roberto Garvía, Marga Torre, and Celia Valiente. I'm also indebted to Angela Alonso, Rossi Guentcheva, Maartje Jensen, and Damon Mayrl.

I would like to acknowledge the staff of several libraries that made my research possible: the UCLA Research Library; the former Social Science Library at Yale; Kati Deseő and Hédi Erdős at the, again, former library of Collegium Budapest; the Friends' Library in London; the British Library; and the María Moliner Library of the Universidad Carlos III de Madrid. Eric Crahan at Cambridge University Press believed in the project and gave it its title. I thank also Lew Bateman, Susan Thomas, and Shaun Vigil.

Research funding provided by the following institutions is gratefully acknowledged: the Collegium Budapest Institute for Advanced Studies, the Griswold Fund of the Whitney Humanities Center at Yale, the University of California Institute for Global Conflict and Cooperation, the Social Science Research Council, and Yale University. This book is being published with the generous assistance of the Frederick W. Hilles Publication Fund of Yale University.

Introduction

Distant strangers matter. Our lives continue to be centered on the intimacy of face-to-face relationships with family, friends, and loved ones. At the same time, we are constantly exposed to initiatives and organizations that try to get us interested in the fate of geographically and culturally distant people. An established not-for-profit industry working for the welfare of such distant populations is a ubiquitous presence in the public spaces of contemporary Western societies. If nothing else, its appeals for donations intrude with some regularity into our everyday lives. So do the images of distant people in distress whom we are urged to support.

Should we decide to express our support, we are given a menu of choices. We can do that in different ways – through practices individual or collective, public or private, organized or spontaneous. Sometimes the instigator is an explicitly political organization that orchestrates lobbying, advocacy, or public protests. In other cases, what we do is limited to transfers of cash or donations in kind to distressed populations. Concern for distant strangers can also express itself in practices of selective consumption, such as the boycotts of products that are thought to cause suffering, or the preferential consumption of other products, the proceeds of which are seen as enhancing these strangers' welfare. At a minimum, we may develop a sustained interest in media reports of distant suffering and injustice.

Why and how did such practices become an integral part of modern life? This is the general question this book addresses. It explains our persisting involvement of various degrees and forms with the fate of humans at a distance as the end result of complex historical processes. These processes culminated with the crystallization of an enduring institutional model of political practice that I call long-distance advocacy. It is this model that forms the institutional backbone of contemporary humanitarian engagement with distant strangers. And the central argument I make here is that the model emerged from the struggles of religious actors in the course of European imperial expansion overseas.

Members of distinctively activist religious organizations, starting with the Catholic mendicant orders in the sixteenth century, were the pioneers who "invented" the institutional model of long-distance advocacy. They did not do this intentionally. In the course of their evangelizing work in overseas possessions of Iberian empires, however, such religious specialists became increasingly preoccupied with an issue they could ill afford to disregard: the harsh and inhumane treatment to which European settlers submitted new imperial "others" in the Caribbean and in America. Moved to protect the welfare of new and potential converts to Christianity, they engaged in various political activities, appealing to the heads of political and religious authorities in Europe: the monarchs in Spain and Portugal and the pope in Rome.

This series of denunciations of the abuses of Iberian imperialism was the first milestone in the history of early modern long-distance advocacy. Later, members of Protestant organizations, most notably Quakers, took the same road in their effort to abolish the enslavement and trade of Africans in European colonies. The international antislavery movement that they initiated ushered in a crucial stage in the history of long-distance advocacy in which it acquired its distinctively modern organizational patterns. For this was a movement that, especially in its British version, involved for the first time a critical mass of lay supporters for a distant cause – that of ending the colonial slave trade. So enduring and so influential was the antislavery movement that it diffused a model of action and thought that is still with us today.

HISTORY'S TENTACLES

The approach I choose, then, is to understand the current state of affairs through a historical lens: as the outcome of deep historical processes, of causal forces in the past and of cumulative developments that have all combined to shape of our current social world. I have chosen this approach deliberately – as an analytically fruitful way to enrich our conversation on the social foundations of moral involvement.

There are several possible ways to approach the larger question of how and why people engage in activities oriented meaningfully toward the well-being of geographically and culturally distant strangers. Thus the question of the moral relevance of distance – and of how people at a distance should and do matter morally – has been addressed by political philosophers who have produced important arguments about compassion and indifference, about universalisms and particularisms, about moral cosmopolitanism and parochialisms.[1]

---

[1] See, for example, Joseph A. Amato, *Victims and Values: A History and a Theory of Suffering* (New York: Praeger, 1990); Lawrence Blum, "Compassion," in *Explaining Emotions*, ed. Amélie Oksenberg Rorty (Berkeley: University of California Press, 1980); Joshua Cohen, ed. *For Love of Country: Debating the Limits of Patriotism* (Boston: Beacon Press, 1996); Richard Dagger, *Civic Virtues: Rights, Citizenship, and Republican Liberalism* (New York: Oxford University

While these works examine the ideological and philosophical foundations of solidarity and moral affiliation across space, empirically oriented researchers have studied important recent cases of popular mobilization oriented toward the rights of distant populations: instances of what Dieter Rucht has called "distant-issue movements." Representative examples include, the international movement against the apartheid system in South Africa, the movement for solidarity with victims of persecution in Central America, the transnational support for the Zapatista movement in Mexico, the campaigns against sweatshops and for labor rights in the global South, the activities in support of insurgent trade unions in communist Eastern Europe, and the boycott of baby formula for its negative impact on health in the Third World.[2]

Press, 1997); Abram de Swaan, "Widening Circles of Identification: Emotional Concerns in Sociogenetic Perspective," *Theory, Culture & Society* 12, no. 2 (1995); William A. Galston, "Cosmopolitan Altruism," in *Altruism*, ed. Ellen Frankel Paul, Fred D. Miller, Jr., and Jeffrey Paul (Cambridge: Cambridge University Press, 1993); Alan H. Goldman, "The Moral Significance of National Boundaries," *Midwest Studies in Philosophy* 7 (1982); Robert Goodin, "What Is So Special about Our Fellow Countrymen?," *Ethics* 98 (1988); Otto Kallscheuer, "'And Who Is My Neighbor?': Moral Sentiments, Proximity, Humanity," *Social Research* 62, no. 1 (1995); Anthony Pagden, "Stoicism, Cosmopolitanism, and the Legacy of European Imperialism," *Constellations* 7, no. 1 (2000); Thomas Pogge, *World Poverty and Human Rights: Cosmopolitan Responsibilities and Reforms*, 2nd ed. (Cambridge: Polity Press, 2008); Michael Walzer, *Thick and Thin: Moral Argument at Home and Abroad* (Notre Dame: University of Notre Dame Press, 1994).

[2] See Dieter Rucht, "Distant Issue Movements in Germany: Empirical Description and Theoretical Reflections," in *Globalizations and Social Movements: Culture, Power, and the Transnational Public Sphere*, ed. John A. Guidry, Michael D. Kennedy, and Mayer N. Zald (Ann Arbor: University of Michigan Press, 2000). On the anti-apartheid movement, see Donald R. Culverson, *Contesting Apartheid: U.S. Activism, 1960–1987* (Boulder, Colorado: Westview Press, 1999); Wouter Goedertier, "The Quest for Transnational Authority, the Anti-Apartheid Movements of the European Community," *Revue Belge de Philologie & d'Histoire* 89, no. 3/4 (2011); Rob Skinner, *The Foundations of Anti-Apartheid: Liberal Humanitarians and Transnational Activists in Britain and the United States, c.1919–64* (Houndmills: Palgrave Macmillan, 2010); Sarah A. Soule, "Situational Effects on Political Altruism: The Student Divestment Movement in the United States," in *Political Altruism? Solidarity Movements in International Perspective*, ed. Marco Giugni and Florence Passy (Lanham: Rowman & Littlefield, 2001); Håkan Thörn, *Anti-Apartheid and the Emergence of a Global Civil Society* (Basingstoke: Palgrave Macmillan, 2006). On the solidarity movement with Central America, Sharon Erickson Nepstad, *Convictions of the Soul: Religion, Culture, and Agency in the Central America Solidarity Movement* (New York: Oxford University Press, 2004); Christian Smith, *Resisting Reagan: The U.S. Central America Peace Movement* (Chicago: University of Chicago Press, 1996); Gregory L. Wiltfang and Doug McAdam, "The Costs and Risks of Social Activism: A Study of Sanctuary Movement Activism," *Social Forces* 69, no. 4 (1991). On *Zapatismo*, Josee Johnston and Gordon Laxer, "Solidarity in the Age of Globalization: Lessons from the Anti-MAI and Zapatista Struggles," *Theory and Society* 32, no. 1 (2003); Heidy Sarabia, "Organizing 'Below and to the Left': Differences in the Citizenship and Transnational Practices of Two Zapatista Groups," *Sociological Forum* 26, no. 2 (2011). On sweatshops and labor rights, Mark Anner and Peter Evans, "Building Bridges across a Double Divide: Alliances between US and Latin American Labour and NGOs," *Development in Practice* 14, no. 1–2 (2004); Andrew Battista, *The Revival of Labor Liberalism* (Urbana: University of Illinois Press, 2008). On solidarity with Eastern Europe, Natalie Bégin, "Kontakte

Although these two approaches rarely engage in a direct dialogue, there are interesting complementarities and tensions between them. On the one hand, the empirical studies of moral engagement across distance reaffirm the practical validity of the philosopher's concerns. By highlighting concrete political activities, they show how real people are indeed moved by deep questions of morality.[3] On the other hand, they also complicate the moral philosophers' relatively neat discursive universe. Empirical studies remind us that ideas about solidarity and moral affiliation do not exist in a social vacuum. The concrete individuals who subscribe to and act on such ideas and beliefs are situated in concrete political and social contexts, react to particular events, and are exposed to various information flows from communication media. A persistent commitment to one's ethical ideals involves contesting and engaging with organizations or political authorities of various kinds, as well as working to change the general moral climate and prevailing cultural understandings of right and wrong. And, significantly, putting moral ideas to practice means confronting the practical dilemmas and challenges of coordinated collective action: disseminating information, raising consciousness, recruiting adherents, generating and maintaining their commitment, making decisions on tactics, organizing protests and rituals, and facing repression and persecution. Thus next to moral philosophy's analytical precision and conceptual insights, the social scientist's typical preoccupations and sensitivities enrich our understanding of the complex processes through which ideas of moral affiliation across space are activated in concrete practices.

The recognition of this complexity, however, almost by default leads to the standard procedure that had dominated the field of social movement research: the in-depth study of individual cases of public mobilization around distant issues. Only a close investigation of a case can reveal the multiple interlocking processes involved in a complex social phenomenon. At the same time, gains from the knowledge of individual instances come with certain losses. Taken out of the larger comparative context, even the most fine-grained empirical study of one or few individual cases would miss important causal dynamics. Students of social movements have long recognized the complex way in which individual instances of mobilization are interconnected in time and space. The

zwischen Gewerkschaften in Ost und West: Die Auswirkungen von 'Solidarnosc' in Deutschland und Frankreich," *Archiv für Sozialgeschichte* 45 (2005); Kim Christiaens, Idesbald Goddeeris, and Wouter Goedertier, "Inspirées par le Sud? Les mobilisations transnationales Est-Ouest pendant la guerre froide," *Vingtième Siècle* 109 (2011). On the baby formula boycott, James E. Post, "Assessing the Nestlé Boycott: Corporate Accountability and Human Rights," *California Management Review* 27, no. 2 (1985); Kathryn Sikkink, "Codes of Conduct for Transnational Corporations: The Case of the WHO/UNICEF Code," *International Organization* 40, no. 4 (1986).
3 A strong case for the importance of moral commitment in collective action is made by James M. Jasper, *The Art of Moral Protest: Culture, Biography, and Creativity in Social Movements* (Chicago: University of Chicago Press, 1997); Smith, *Resisting Reagan*.

organizational structures that initiate popular mobilization form a relatively autonomous social field. There are important interactions within this field even between units with diametrically opposed political and social agendas, including the spread of distinctive organizational forms. Temporally, mobilization events cluster in waves and cycles as, for example, "spin-off movements" arise out of other instances of mobilization.[4]

These related analytical moves form a part of a more general interest within sociology to understand the temporal interconnectedness of events and, more importantly, establish the causal inferences that can be derived only from this interconnectedness.[5] This is where, for my purposes, history matters. For if we want an answer to the general question of why and how people mobilize to act on behalf of distant strangers, an understanding, however fine-grained, of the conditions and factors that shape individual instances of such mobilization is not sufficient in itself. These individual instances must be placed in a larger historical sequence of developments, which reveals an important causal dynamics.

Consider, for example, a case that brings forth a complex web of organizational and cultural continuities in the long-term history of other-directed popular mobilization. Between 1904 and 1913, a large number of ordinary people were mobilized in Britain to condemn the forced labor and gruesome cruelties inflicted on Africans in the so-called Free Congo State created by Leopold II, the King of Belgians. The Congo Reform Association organized numerous public meetings and set up local auxiliaries, as well as sister movements in the United States, Germany, France, Norway, and Switzerland.

---

[4] See, e.g., Joseph R. Gusfield, "Social Movements and Social Change: Perspectives of Linearity and Fluidity," *Research in Social Movements, Conflict and Change* 4 (1981); Doug McAdam, "'Initiator' and 'Spin-Off' Movements: Diffusion Processes in Protest Cycles," in *Repertoires and Cycles of Collective Action*, ed. Mark Traugott (Durham: Duke University Press, 1995); Peter Stamatov, "The Religious Field and the Path-Dependent Transformation of Popular Politics in the Anglo-American World, 1770–1840," *Theory and Society* 40 (2011); Sidney Tarrow, "Cycles of Collective Action: Between Moments of Madness and the Repertoire of Contention," in *Repertoires and Cycles of Collective Action*, ed. Mark Traugott (Durham: Duke University Press, 1995); "Studying Contentious Politics: From Event-ful History to Cycles of Collective Action," in *Acts of Dissent: New Developments in the Study of Protest*, ed. Dieter Rucht, Ruud Koopmans, and Friedhelm Neidhardt (Lanham: Rowman & Littlefield, 1999); Charles Tilly, *Popular Contention in Great Britain, 1758–1834* (Cambridge, MA: Harvard University Press, 1995); Nancy Whittier, "The Consequences of Social Movements for Each Other," in *The Blackwell Companion to Social Movements*, ed. David A. Snow, Sarah A. Soule, and Hanspeter Kriesi (Malden: Blackwell, 2004); Mayer N. Zald and John D. McCarthy, "Social Movement Industries: Competition and Cooperation Among Movement Organizations," *Research in Social Movements, Conflict and Change* 3 (1980).

[5] Andrew Abbott, *Time Matters: On Theory and Method* (Chicago: University of Chicago Press, 2001); William H. Sewell, Jr., "Three Temporalities: Toward and Eventful Sociology," in *The Historic Turn in the Human Sciences*, ed. Terrence J. McDonald (Ann Arbor: University of Michigan Press, 1996).

Perceptive readers will notice that I am referring to some of the developments covered in Adam Hochschild's moving – and well-deservedly popular – book *King Leopold's Ghost*.[6] When it comes to the discovery and popularization in Europe and America of the Congo issue, Hochschild's account seems to attribute the "heroism" in his book title to two important, complex, and colorful figures involved in the Congo Reform Association: the shipping clerk Edmund Dene Morel and the diplomat Roger Casement. Yet a closer look at the specifics of the mobilization of public opinion qualifies the central importance of these strong individuals and reveals instead how the campaign was deeply embedded in a long-standing and persistent organizational culture of humanitarian mobilization.

Edmund Morel, the chief promoter of the campaign against the Congo atrocities, was not acting alone. He was connected with a group of British merchants trading with West Africa who were critical of British and European imperial policies because of an ideological commitment to free trade. The campaign began to take shape when a somewhat uneasy alliance emerged between these free traders and the head of an older humanitarian organization, H. R. Fox Bourne of the Aborigines Protection Society. The popular outreach that Morel envisioned only became a reality after the Quaker cocoa merchant William Cadbury made a significant financial contribution to the Congo Reform Association in 1905 and facilitated contacts with the Society of Friends, whose long-standing antislavery committee embraced the issue and, in turn, mobilized local Quaker structures. Finally, the true engine of popular mobilization turned out to be evangelical missionaries with firsthand experience of the "heart of darkness" in Leopold's Congo. Not only were they able to shape the official report produced by Roger Casement that authoritatively framed the issue in Britain; using newly available photographic techniques, they provided pictorial proof of the atrocities and, most importantly, organized a series of speaking "atrocity" tours in Britain. The missionaries' lantern slide presentations in churches mobilized wide religious constituencies that provided the backbone of the Congo reform agitation.[7]

This is not to say that the drive and dedication of an individual like Edmund Morel was of no importance. Yet equally – if not more – important was a whole cast of "supporting" characters that did the less visible legwork to produce the popular commitment needed for a campaign like this. And, what is more important for my purposes, all relevant actors were shaped – in various ways – by a long-standing and persistent organizational culture of antislavery

---

[6] Adam Hochschild, *King Leopold's Ghost: A Story of Greed, Terror, and Heroism in Colonial Africa* (Boston: Houghton Mifflin, 1998).

[7] See Kevin Grant, *A Civilised Savagery: Britain and the New Slaveries in Africa, 1884–1926* (New York: Routledge, 2005). Grant's treatment is an insightful correction of earlier accounts that credited Morel as the only significant driving force behind the campaign. See, e.g., Wm. Roger Louis, "The Triumph of the Congo Reform Movement, 1905–1908," *Boston University Papers on Africa* 2 (1966).

humanitarianism. I trace, in the second half of this book, the initial consolidation of this culture around the turn of the nineteenth century out of an international abolitionist network. A century later, this culture was in decline compared to the glory days of antislavery mobilization in the 1830s when a large movement had demanded the immediate abolition of slavery in British colonies. Even at its nadir, however, it continued to exercise important formative effects.

Three overlapping groupings created the Congo atrocities campaign: free traders, Quakers, and evangelical Christians. All three were conditioned by ideological commitments and organizational experience that were the persistent sediment of previous antislavery struggles. Quakers, as we will see, were the pioneers of politicized antislavery. Both the antislavery committee of the Society of Friends and the Aborigines Protection Society, since its foundation in 1837 by Quaker Thomas Hodgkin, were the continuing organizational embodiment of a distinct Quaker humanitarian tradition of long roots. Evangelicals, both from the official Church of England and from nonconformist denominations, were early adopters of antislavery principles and because of their religious and political muscle gradually emerged as the dominant force in the antislavery field. With its emphasis on converting non-Europeans, the evangelical version of humanitarianism was at tension with the humanitarianism of non-conversionist Quakers. Still, the central role of missionaries in the Congo campaign was, in important ways, the result of the close alignment of missions and antislavery since at least the 1820s. Like the Quakers, the free traders – and Morel himself – had deep misgivings about missionary enthusiasm. What is more, they simply did not share the religious concerns of their Quaker and evangelical allies. But in many ways the larger free-trade movement had been influenced by a preexisting culture of antislavery and religious reformism. When it first emerged – and spread internationally – as a coherent political project with the Anti-Corn Law League of the 1840s, its originators copied both the organizational models of the antislavery movement and its typical moralistic framing of a public issue, if only to take advantage of the committed constituencies that powered religious associations at the time.[8]

---

[8] On the Aborigines Protection Society, see Amalie M. Kass and Edward H. Kass, *Perfecting the World: The Life and Times of Dr. Thomas Hodgkin, 1798–1866* (Boston: Harcourt Brace Jovanovich, 1988); Ronald Rainger, "Philanthropy and Science in the 1830's: The British and Foreign Aborigines' Protection Society," *Man* 15, no. 4 (1980); Charles Swaisland, "The Aborigines Protection Society, 1837–1909," *Slavery & Abolition* 21, no. 2 (2000). The increasing identification between missionary evangelicalism and antislavery is discussed by Roger Anstey, "Religion and British Slave Emancipation," in *The Abolition of the Atlantic Slave Trade: Origins and Effects in Europe, Africa, and the Americas,* ed. David Eltis and James Walvin (Madison: University of Wisconsin Press, 1981); Andrew Porter, *Religion versus Empire? British Protestant Missionaries and Overseas Expansion, 1700–1914* (Manchester: Manchester University Press, 2004); C. Duncan Rice, "The Missionary Context of the British Anti-Slavery Movement," in *Slavery and British Society, 1776–1846,* ed. James Walvin (London: Macmillan, 1982); Mary Turner, *Slaves and Missionaries: The Disintegration of Jamaican Slave Society, 1787–1834*

Thus, apart from various situational and proximate causes that lent the Congo atrocities movement its historically specific trajectory, all its relevant actors were also influenced by an important distal factor: the strong organizational culture of antislavery. It is this culture that made them think of distant atrocities as a social problem that had to be addressed urgently. And because of the history of political mobilizations this culture had produced, it provided these actors with the standard tools and technology to address the problem.[9]

HISTORY IN THE PRESENT

Nor has history ceased to matter for later instances of distant-issue mobilization – a fact that has been obscured by a tendency to isolate a post–World War II transnational humanitarianism as a distinctly novel phenomenon with no history. Consider, for example, the rhetoric of a historian describing the "human rights revolution" of the 1970s in the "journal of record" of American historians. According to this account, centered on the pioneering role of Amnesty International, it is at this time that human rights activists "discovered the importance of the fact-finding mission," "devised ways to collect accurate accounts of some of the vilest behavior on earth that no one had bothered to document before," "invented ways to move this information to wherever activists had some chance to shame and pressure the perpetrators," and "learned how to purchase public support through icons and mass media."[10]

As we will see, this sharp rhetoric of invention, discovery, and novelty is misleading. It assigns to distant twentieth-century successors – and, yes, imitators – a credit that is better claimed by some of the protagonists of this book: the Catholic friars of the sixteenth century or Anthony Benezet and Thomas Clarkson two centuries later. The incautious presentism in the phrases excerpted

(Urbana: University of Illinois Press, 1982). On the tensions between the Quaker and evangelical versions of antislavery and humanitarianism, see Zoë Laidlaw, "Heathens, Slaves and Aborigines: Thomas Hodgkin's Critique of Missions and Anti-slavery," *History Workshop Journal* 64, no. 1 (2007). The religious origins of the Anti-Corn Law League are explored by Paul A. Pickering and Alex Tyrell, *The People's Bread: A History of the Anti-Corn Law League* (London: Leicester University Press, 2000); Donald Read, *The English Provinces, c. 1760–1960: A Study in Influence* (New York: St. Martin's Press, 1964), 134–36.

[9] It is hardly incidental that for his next project Hochschild explored the sources of this organizational culture. See Adam Hochschild, *Bury the Chains: Prophets and Rebels in the Fight to Free an Empire's Slaves* (Boston: Houghton Mifflin, 2005). For the centrality of the same organizational tradition in the anti-apartheid movement at an even later stage, see Thörn, *Anti-Apartheid*, 75–76.

[10] Kenneth Cmiel, "The Emergence of Human Rights Politics in the United States," *Journal of American History* 86, no. 3 (1999). A somewhat more temperate account appeared five years later: "The Recent History of Human Rights," *American Historical Review* 109, no. 1 (2004). For another treatment emphasizing uncritically the unprecedented novelty of Amnesty International, see Ann Marie Clark, *Diplomacy of Conscience: Amnesty International and Changing Human Rights Norms* (Princeton: Princeton University Press, 2001).

in the preceding paragraph, however, is indicative of a general scholarly fascination with historical discontinuities in the study of mobilizations around distant issues, often understood as deeply connected with recent processes of "globalization" and "transnationalism."

These discontinuities have been emphasized in different ways. Thus, for example, Peter Evans characterizes transnational networks of alternative globalization as a "new weapon" for the globally underprivileged. Florence Passy draws a strong contrast between a charity-oriented humanitarianism of the past and an organizationally coherent "solidarity movement" that, emerging with the "new middle classes" of the 1960s and their "new social movements," is bold enough to make "genuine" political claims. And even when acknowledging important continuities between the past and present of transnational campaigns, scholars are often tempted to focus on the unprecedented organizational sophistication of contemporary global civic initiatives, thus clearly separating them from historical precedents.[11]

This drift toward a discontinuist analytical framework is perhaps not surprising. Recent cases of public mobilization around the rights of distant strangers are simply more cognitively available than older historical instances that often demand specialized knowledge – and more research hours. Furthermore, these recent cases easily fit the logic of a scholarly attention cycle where, after decades of measuring and predicting the "modernization" of analytically isolated national "societies," social scientists increasingly turned toward interactions cross-cutting previously unproblematic nation-state borders.

Yet there are analytical advantages to be gained from considering the continuities and similarities with the past. Audie Klotz has highlighted, for example, the parallels between the nineteenth-century antislavery movement and the transnational mobilization against apartheid in the 1980s. Both mobilized around a surprisingly similar normative agenda, sought a far-ranging political, economic, and cultural transformation by addressing both national governments and international organizations, recruited constituents across national boundaries, and had an important religious dimension.[12]

---

[11] See Peter Evans, "Fighting Marginalization with Transnational Networks: Counter-Hegemonic Globalization," *Contemporary Sociology* 29, no. 1 (2000); Florence Passy, "Political Altruism and the Solidarity Movement: An Introduction," in *Political Altruism? Solidarity Movements in International Perspective*, ed. Marco Giugni and Florence Passy (Lanham: Rowman & Littlefield, 2001). For accounts sensitive to important continuities, see Margaret E. Keck and Kathryn Sikkink, *Activists Beyond Borders: Advocacy Networks in International Politics* (Ithaca: Cornell University Press, 1998); Ronnie D. Lipschutz, "Reconstructing World Politics: The Emergence of Global Civil Society," *Millennium* 21, no. 3 (1992); Dieter Rucht, "Transnationaler politischer Protest im historischen Längsschnitt," in *Globalisierung, Partizipation, Protest*, ed. Ansgar Klein, Ruud Koopmans, and Heiko Geiling (Opladen: Leske + Budrich, 2001).

[12] Audie Klotz, "Transnational Activism and Global Transformations: The Anti-Apartheid and Abolitionist Experiences," *European Journal of International Relations* 8, no. 1 (2002).

Nor are these similarities surprising if we look at the mechanics of popular support. The general pattern is remarkably uniform: an initial nucleus of "issue entrepreneurs" discover the problem and then turn to preexisting organizations to elicit wider support. This was true for the Congo atrocities campaign in early twentieth-century Britain, for the movements of international solidarity of the 1980s, and – as we will see – for the very beginnings of the politicized antislavery movement in the late eighteenth-century British Empire.[13] Two centuries of technological advances since then have sped up communications and reduced connectivity costs. Yet when it comes to the setting up of the specialized organizations that orchestrate public support for distant issues and the specific activities for which these organizations mobilize supporters, activists continue to use some variation of a set of organizational routines that crystallized in the early nineteenth century.[14]

Furthermore, in both aspects – the initial discovery of an issue and in the orchestration of organizational support – religion continues to play an important role. Religious actors and organizations are prominent among the initiators and carriers of postwar transnational and human rights organizations. Even in a typically "secular" European state like Germany, approximately one-third of organizations providing development aid to the Third World are church-based.[15]

What, then, if we focus not on the discontinuities but on the remarkable persisting patterns that still continue to inform action on behalf of distant strangers? As we will see, the parallels and continuities between older and newer instances of politicized action oriented toward distant strangers become even more striking when we give these older cases the careful attention they deserve. But the point, of course, is not simply to temper the ahistorical enthusiasm for the present with somber reminders of *plus ça change*. No doubt, a lot has changed between now and the early sixteenth century when the analytical narrative of this book starts. Yet highlighting and exploring such continuities and similarities that persist against the grain of historical change is a useful entry point into understanding how our present – and the world as we know it – came to be. They give us a glimpse into the deeper causal processes and

---

[13] On the organizational inception of the Central America solidarity movement and anti-apartheid, see Nepstad, *Convictions of the Soul*; Skinner, *Foundations of Anti-Apartheid*; Smith, *Resisting Reagan*.

[14] Charles Tilly, "Social Movements and National Politics," in *Statemaking and Social Movements: Essays in History and Theory*, ed. Charles Bright and Susan Harding (Ann Arbor: University of Michigan Press, 1984).

[15] Klotz, "Transnational Activism," 59–60; Lowell W. Livezey, "US Religious Organizations and the International Human Rights Movement," *Human Rights Quarterly* 11, no. 1 (1989); Claudia Olejniczak, "Entwicklungspolitische Solidarität: Geschichte und Structure der Dritte Welt-Bewegung," *Forschungsjournal Neue Soziale Bewegungen* 11, no. 3 (1998); Jackie Smith, Ron Pagnucco, and Winnie Romeril, "Transnational Social Movement Organisations in the Global Political Arena," *Voluntas* 5, no. 2 (1994): 130.

structures that cumulatively have shaped our current interest in distant people and our efforts to support and advocate their rights.

THE INSTITUTION OF LONG-DISTANCE ADVOCACY

Where attention to similarities in the long term is most immediately useful is in the recognition that these parallels across time and space are not incidental. The persistent similarities between different campaigns indicate that in each of them the same basic pattern of action gets activated. And, of course, this is not because each time activists decide to mobilize people around a distant issue they independently rediscover the same techniques. Rather – as my brief discussion of the Congo Reform Association suggests – they reproduce, consciously or not, a culturally and cognitively available model that has already been tested in practice.[16]

Analytically, then, concrete instances of mobilization around distant issues can be understood as the reiteration of a distinctive pattern of social interaction. In the theoretical logic of sociological "new institutionalism," such standardized, taken-for-granted patterns or sequences of interactions are defined as institutions – an important and consequential feature of social life. Institutions, in this general sense, are cultural models that define the identities of actors and provide reproducible uniform "scripts" for action.[17]

An interactional pattern becomes an institution – is institutionalized – when it is embedded in social structures such as organizations or in prevalent cultural understandings. Once embedded in this way, its invocation and use in practice are easy, appropriate, and "normal." There is no need for individuals to mobilize specifically in order to ensure the activation of this pattern. Conversely, the non-activation of an institution is considered unusual and may

---

[16] On the serial reproduction of persistent patterns of collective action (described as "repertoires," "technologies of mobilization," or "modular forms"), see Pamela E. Oliver and Gerald Marwell, "Mobilizing Technologies for Collective Action," in *Frontiers in Social Movement Theory*, ed. Aldon D. Morris and Carol McClurg Mueller (New Haven: Yale University Press, 1992); Sidney Tarrow, *Power in Movement: Social Movements and Contentious Politics*, 2nd ed. (Cambridge: Cambridge University Press, 1998); Tilly, *Popular Contention*.

[17] Ronald L. Jepperson, "Institutions, Institutional Effects and Institutionalism," in *The New Institutionalism in Organizational Analysis*, ed. Walter W. Powell and Paul DiMaggio (Chicago: University of Chicago Press, 1991); Ronald L. Jepperson "The Development and Application of Sociological Neoinstitutionalism," in *New Directions in Contemporary Sociological Theory*, ed. Joseph Berger and Morris Jr. Zelditch (Lanham: Rowman & Littlefield, 2002). See also Elisabeth S. Clemens and James M. Cook, "Politics and Institutionalism: Explaining Durability and Change," *Annual Review of Sociology* 25 (1999); Frank R. Dobbin, "Cultural Models of Organization: The Social Construction of Rational Organizing Principles," in *The Sociology of Culture: Emerging Theoretical Perspectives*, ed. Diana Crane (Oxford: Blackwell, 1994); and Lynne G. Zucker, "Organizations as Institutions," *Research in the Sociology of Organizations* 2 (1983). On the importance and consequences of such scripts in social movement participation, see Smith, *Resisting Reagan*, 373–74.

even incur negative sanctions. One can think, then, of the general interactional pattern that gets repeatedly activated in campaigns around distant issues as the institution of "long-distance advocacy" – a sequence of interactions and a set of roles that have achieved a certain degree of permanence and acquired a taken-for-granted quality for their practitioners.

The idea of "long-distance advocacy" as institution borrows from Keck and Sikkink's pioneering work on "transnational advocacy networks;" I want to preserve the felicitous emphasis on the rich variety of politicized practices they were able to capture with their concept of advocacy. As Andrews and Edwards have suggested more recently, the "synthetic" concept of advocacy sharpens the focus by covering conceptually a set of related social phenomena that is typically parceled out by self-segregating research fields studying, respectively, "interest groups," "social movements," or "non-profit organizations."[18] Yet I focus on the general institution, a layer deeper than the concrete network this institution generates, and I define the scale as "long-distance," not "transnational."

As the empirical material of the book will show, I agree wholeheartedly with Keck and Sikkink's emphasis on the inherently networked character of the social carriers of long-distance advocacy. These are unruly groupings of individuals and organizations coming from heterogeneous social and geographical locations to connect and engage in a common political project. But the networked connectedness is only a part, albeit a very important part, of the story. Equally relevant are the concrete practices that the constituent members of the networks engage in. The practices that gradually solidified, as we will see, into a standardized and reproducible script of action provided the interactional cohesion of advocacy networks. If networks emerge, it is because they cohere around a common set of practices that underlie their common project. In other words, networks and action scripts are co-constitutive. By highlighting long-distance advocacy as such institutionalized set of roles and action scripts, I direct attention to the basic cultural and cognitive models and dispositions that make action – and networks – possible.

I also define the scale inherent in this institutional model, as well as the substantive orientation of its practitioners around distant issues, with the admittedly bland qualifier "long-distance." Keck and Sikkink's original concept of transnational activism invokes the world as we know it: a political world

---

[18] Keck and Sikkink, *Activists beyond Borders*; Kenneth T. Andrews and Bob Edwards, "Advocacy Organizations in the U.S. Political Process," *Annual Review of Sociology* 30, no. 1 (2004). In the idiom of the resource mobilization paradigm in the study of social movements, this pattern is comprised of constituents or adherents of social movement organizations (or less clearly institutionalized initiatives) who engage in actions oriented toward the welfare of beneficiaries at a distance. For the distinction between adherents or constituents and beneficiaries, see William A. Gamson, *The Strategy of Social Protest* (Chicago: Dorsey Press, 1975); John D. McCarthy and Mayer N. Zald, "Resource Mobilization and Social Movements: A Partial Theory," *American Journal of Sociology* 82, no. 6 (1977).

divided relatively neatly into serial constitutive units of nation-states "owned" by their nations. The networks they discuss transect this national political topology by connecting individuals in various national contexts. Despite its current pervasiveness, however, this national ordering of global political space is of strikingly recent provenance, having coalesced only in the post-Second World War period. Before that, the political framework of empire often encompassed what after decolonization would emerge as separate "nations" (with their "own" states) into a singular and distance-spanning political unit.[19] In fact, instead of cross-cutting or connecting separate "nations," the first long-advocacy networks that I discuss here were coextensive with empire or connected several imperial settings. In this sense, they are better described not as "transnational" but as "imperial" – or even, with the emergence of a movement against the slave trade in the late eighteenth century, as "trans-imperial." I describe these networks with the generic qualifier "long-distance" not only in order to make the analytical nomenclature more historically accurate, but also to suggest the relative detachment of these networks from nation-centric historical processes.

Earlier, I started by situating my approach against two standard ways in which action on behalf of distant strangers and distant issues has been analyzed: the philosopher's interest of the moral relevance of distance and territory in general and the social scientist's sustained study of individual cases of such action. By defining long-distance advocacy as an institution of Western modernity, I want to bridge conceptually these two analytical extremes of generality and particularity. The cultural model of long-distance advocacy has been long available to be activated in concrete instances. In this sense, it is very close to those human universals that form the preoccupation of moral philosophy. At the same time, despite its widespread availability and recurrent use, this model is not as universal as to be transhistorical. Its activation and use in specific social context is deeply intertwined with the concrete conditions, factors, and actors of that specific historical moment. More than that: long-distance advocacy is a deeply particular and historical social phenomenon in that it developed and emerged as the historically contingent outcome of the formative processes on which this book focuses and, in particular, of the recurrent pattern of religious radicalization in the imperial context.

IMPERIAL TENSIONS AND RELIGIOUS CONFLICT

Institutions, in the sense I use the concept here, are thoroughly enmeshed with history. Despite their persistence, the various institutions that we take for a

---

[19] Frederick Cooper, *Colonialism in Question: Theory, Knowledge, History* (Berkeley: University of California Press, 2005), 153–203; Michael Mann, "Has Globalization Ended the Rise and Rise of the Nation-State?" *Review of International Political Economy* 4, no. 3 (1997); James Muldoon, *Empire and Order: The Concept of Empire, 800–1800* (New York: St. Martin's Press, 1999).

natural part of our lives are not immutable phenomena outside of history, but rather the end result of historically contingent processes. In this sense, each institution, as a standardized sequence of interactions and a set of roles, has a "life course" with a beginning, a distinctive historical trajectory, and – sometimes – an end.[20]

These consideration raise the issue of the origins of institutions: when and how institutions became what they are. The general question, therefore, is when a specific interactional pattern first emerged in its distinctive form and why. The qualification "in its distinctive form" is important here. An institution is a composite phenomenon which consists, analytically speaking, of various elements: practices and roles. These practices and roles, in themselves, may predate the institution. Yet for an institution to be socially and analytically relevant, these practices and roles, be they preexisting or completely novel, must be combined in a distinctively new and enduring way.

The argument of this book is that the institution of long-distance advocacy was created gradually in its distinctive form by religious actors between the sixteenth and eighteenth centuries. Members of Catholic religious orders and then committed Protestants, most notably Quakers, problematized the moral relevance of non-Europeans: both indigenous communities and enslaved Africans. These religious actors engaged in the first sustained activities to defend and represent the interests of geographically and culturally distant populations. Most importantly for my purposes, they gradually developed and systematized a set of advocacy practices that were to become the standard tools in subsequent iterations of an institutionalized interactional pattern: appeals to political and religious authorities for change in policies, political alliances with non-European leaders, dissemination of information about abuses, and, more generally, the spread of ideologies and norms of universal human dignity and peaceful relations with distant non-Europeans.

The elaboration of this distinctive set of advocacy practices, in turn, was the end result of a relational process of political contestation as these religious actors engaged in recurrent conflicts with other imperial actors in the context of European expansion overseas. And an important causal factor for the flaring up of these conflicts – and the subsequent formation and formalization of an institutionalized set of advocacy practices – was a culture of distinctly religious reformism that pushed its carriers, both Catholic and Protestant, toward a politicized confrontation with rival imperial networks.

---

[20] Consider, for example, the contrasting examples of two Western institutions that, today, are in very different points of their "life-cycle": the very "young" institution of same-sex marriage and the institution of polygamy, not only very "old," but by now highly restricted – if not extinct – in the Western world. The literature on institutional change is suggestive of the inherent historicity of an otherwise durable institution. See, e.g., Wolfgang Streeck and Kathleen Thelen, "Introduction: Institutional Change in Advanced Political Economies," in *Beyond Continuity: Institutional Change in Advanced Political Economies*, eds. Wolfgang Streeck and Kathleen Thelen (Oxford: Oxford University Press, 2005).

The deep sources for these developments were the historically specific structures of European overseas expansionism since its beginnings in the sixteenth century. In the course of their expansion into the "New World," Europeans carried with them, among other things, a distinctive separation of institutional sectors that had taken roots in the large area of Western Christendom since the late Middle Ages. First, there was a significant separation between the organizations and networks of political and religious power. Under the Pope – a bishop unencumbered by higher political rule in his own realm of Rome – a relatively independent and tightly organized church covered the area of Western Christianity, monopolized the means of grace, and held in its hand the power to consecrate. Second, a mercantile sector emerged, exemplified by the merchants of the Italian maritime republics who since the fifteenth century allied with Iberian monarchs in overseas expansionary projects. Again, this sector was relatively independent from traditional forms of political power, partly because its members were able to amass their own form of political clout in strong cities outside of monarchical influence.[21]

This separation of political, religious, and commercial spheres meant, in practice, that the expansion project was carried out by distinct if often overlapping and cooperating networks of actors, each with their predominant goals and values. A newer historiography has consistently highlighted the analytical importance of the differentiation of these imperial networks.[22] The interaction between them emerges thus as an important causal dynamics shaping the course of European overseas expansion. As David Abernethy has shown, for example, the synergies between the governance, economic, and religious branches of overseas expansionism account for the success and remarkable durability of the European imperial project between the sixteenth and the mid-twentieth centuries.[23]

---

[21] David B. Abernethy, *The Dynamics of Global Dominance: European Overseas Empires 1415–1980* (New Haven: Yale University Press, 2000); Robert Bartlett, *The Making of Europe: Conquest, Colonization, and Cultural Change, 950–1350* (London: Allen Lane, 1993); Thomas A. Brady, Jr., "The Rise of Merchant Empires, 1400–1700: A European Counterpoint," in *The Political Economy of Merchant Empires*, ed. James D. Tracy (Cambridge: Cambridge University Press, 1991); Michael Mitterauer, *Why Europe? The Medieval Origins of its Special Path* (Chicago: University of Chicago Press, 2010).

[22] Alan Lester, "Imperial Circuits and Networks: Geographies of the British Empire," *History Compass* 4, no. 1 (2006). On the British case, see also John L. Comaroff, "Images of Empire, Contests of Conscience: Models of Colonial Domination in South Africa," *American Ethnologist* 16, no. 4 (1989); Zoë Laidlaw, *Colonial Connections, 1815–45: Patronage, the Information Revolution and Colonial Government* (Manchester, UK: Manchester University Press, 2005); Alan Lester, *Imperial Networks: Creating Identities in Nineteenth-Century South Africa and Britain* (London: Routledge, 2001); Geoffrey A. Oddie, "'Orientalism' and British Protestant Missionary Constructions of India in the Nineteenth Century," *South Asia* 17, no. 2 (1994). For such differentiation in the Iberian imperial context, see Murdo J. MacLeod, "La espada de la Iglesia: Excomunión y la evolución de la lucha por el control político y económico en Chiapas colonial, 1545–1700," *Mesoamérica* 11, no. 20 (1990).

[23] Abernethy, *Dynamics of Global Dominance*.

At the same time, the very fact of the institutional differentiation of these imperial networks provided the conditions for disagreements, conflicts, and contestation between them. While engaged in the same general project, these differentiated actors brought to it their distinctive ideologies and values and thus pursued their distinctive logic of action. The interactional universe of European overseas expansion carried within itself the inherent tensions between the deeply incompatible "value spheres" of modernity identified by Max Weber.[24]

Weber focused in particular on the ways in which the "ultimate" values of historically solidified religious traditions reaching beyond the here and now of the material world stood in tension with the inherently "worldly" exigencies of the economic and political order. In reality, as he noted in regard to the tension between religious and political ethics, these oppositions produced various outcomes depending on the "widely varying empirical stands" of religion: from the "always unavoidable collapse of even the highest relations of tension with the world in favor of compromises and qualifications" to "an active faith revolution" when "humans violate God's will."[25]

The transposition, via differentiated sectoral networks, of these intrinsic tensions into the imperial context provided the structural foundations for the elaboration of the practices that coalesced into the institution of long-distance advocacy. In that context, too, these tensions produced varying empirical configurations of forces across time and space. Religious opposition to networks of imperial governance and economically driven networks of settlers did not uniformly produce "active faith revolutions." In a remarkable stable pattern, however, religious actors did consistently mobilize to contest rival imperial networks over the issue of ethical treatment of non-Europeans. As we will see, from the first assault on exploitative labor practices by Dominicans in 1511 until at least the beginnings of a politicized movement for the abolition of the Atlantic slave trade by Pennsylvania Quakers in the mid-eighteenth century, it was invariably religious actors driven by a distinctively religious ethics – and opposing the actions and values of their imperial rivals – who pioneered the ideological and organizational foundations of political action in defense of distant strangers.

Thus, if the general structural context of empire provided the openings for inter-network conflict, it was the specifically religious orientation of one of the constituent imperial networks that provided the direction and substantive focus of the conflict: the ethics of relations with non-Europeans. This was

---

[24] Max Weber, "Religious Rejections of the World and Their Directions," in *From Max Weber: Essays in Sociology*, ed. H. H. Gerth and C. Wright Mills (New York: Oxford University Press, [1915] 1946).

[25] Ibid., 337. My citations from this translation are slightly modified to reflect better the original meaning of the text. See Weber, *Gesammelte Aufsätze zur Religionssoziologie* (Tübingen: Mohr, 1986), vol. 2, 550.

not, of course, because religious actors were disinterested altruists or early proponents of a universalist doctrine of human diversity and equality as we understand these values today. Rather, the distinctive logic of religion, often in roundabout ways, brought to the fore and problematized the issue of proper relations with "imperial others." For these actors, an acute sense of account-ability to a higher force made the ethical problem of relating to others from a specifically religious vantage point a central focus of their action.

Preoccupation with salvation, with the concrete individual's fate not nec-essarily in the material world of today, but in the grander universe of sacred eternity, is a central element of religious ethics. Salvation – whether one's own or that of others – and the proper ways to ensure it are thus a paramount con-sideration in a distinctively religious logic of action. As again Weber observed in a typically dense passage, "every structuring of salvation in a universalist grace-dispensing organization will feel responsible before God for the souls of all humans or for the souls of those entrusted to it. It will therefore consider itself justified and obliged to oppose – even with reckless force – the endan-germent of these souls when they are led astray in issues of faith, as well as to promote the spread of redeeming means of grace."[26]

This intense concern with salvational status and salvational prospects – whether one's own, of fellow Europeans, or of exploited and abused non-Europeans – unites otherwise disparate contentious religious actors across the spatial and temporal expanse of overseas imperialism. They were roused to action and confronted settlers and administrators on their conviction that exploitative practices and the abuse of non-Europeans imperiled eternal souls and prevented salvation. Thus, for Catholic friars in sixteenth-century Iberian territories, the exploitation of indigenous people became a problem because it prevented the proper evangelization of these prospective Christians. After all, the friars were the officially appointed agents of inevitable conversion; abuses were, if nothing else, an obstacle for the proper fulfillment of their evangelistic duties. For the decidedly non-conversionist Quakers in Pennsylvania two cen-turies later, the toleration of slavery in American colonies and violence against Indians were the sins that jeopardized the eternal prospects of all involved, Europeans and non-Europeans alike.

The problems thus witnessed and defined required action. And act these individuals did, driven by specifically religious interests and considerations. In the process, they inevitably placed themselves in opposition to other imperial networks and this opposition only intensified as their actions became bolder and more radical. At the same time, as the conflict deepened, repeated actions began to solidify in standard action scripts that then could be "applied" to other instances of the same problem. In short, the gradual emergence and consolidation of these advocacy scripts – or the institution of long-distance

---

[26] *Gesammelte Aufsätze*, vol. 2, 550. My translation, amending the text on page 336 in "Religious Rejections."

advocacy – was the end result of repeated and recurrent conflictual inter-actions, the conflicts themselves ignited and fueled by the inherent logic of religion.

THE RELIGIOUS LOGIC OF RADICALIZATION

Stating the formative process in such general terms, however, begs an impor-tant question. Despite the latent tension between competing imperial networks, there was nothing inevitable about the flaring up of conflict between them – as numerous instances of religious complicity with the goals of imperial gover-nance and economic exploitation prove. Why – and when –did religious actors radicalize and initiate such conflict? To understand the origins of the recurrent conflict, we must take into account another important fault line between social groupings: this time, however, not between functionally differentiated networks that transposed their differences onto the imperial context, but rather within religious networks themselves.

By the very virtue of their functional differentiation from other imperial net-works, such religious networks were part of a broader organizational field of religion. While both "lay" observers and analysts are often tempted to flatten "religion" into a presumably consistent sets of belief outlined in the doctrinal statements of religious organizations, the social reality of lived and practiced religion is much more complex – and more interesting – than simply the instan-tiation of officially sanctioned pronouncements. One feature of this complexity is the inherent fractionality of the religious field.

Even when all the participants in the field subscribe to the same religious beliefs, differences in views on various issues are bound to exist. Like all other areas of social life, then, the religious field is necessarily stratified into factions. Yet unlike these other areas, the principles around which this stratification occurs are of distinctive religious nature. And perhaps the most pronounced principle of differentiation would be competing claims around what Weber called "the experiential inequality of charisma" (or what Bourdieu in his inter-pretation of Weberian theory conceives as unequal distribution of specifi-cally religious "capital").[27] Omnipresent in its latent form, this differentiation manifests itself in specifically religious struggles of various kinds and intensity. Within Christianity, such tensions have been at play in different configurations since the very beginnings of its formal separation from Judaism. Well into – and beyond – the early modern period that forms the focus of my investiga-tion here, the trajectory of Western Christianity was punctured by constantly

---

[27] *Gesammelte Aufsätze*, vol. 2, 551; "Religious Rejections," 338. For "religious" and "spiritual" capital, see Pierre Bourdieu, "Genesis and Structure of the Religious Field," *Comparative Social Research* 13 (1991); as well as the insightful development of this theme in Bradford Verter, "Spiritual Capital: Theorizing Religion with Bourdieu Against Bourdieu," *Sociological Theory* 21, no. 2 (2003).

emerging movements that challenged in various ways the religious status quo and attempted to reshape faith and practice.[28]

Most relevant for my purposes is one specific product of these tensions and struggles, whether they erupt in full-fledged conflict or not: the crystallization within religious organizations of inherently activist communities of reformers. It is the representatives of such communities within both Catholic and Protestant organizations that embarked on a collision course with rival imperial networks and developed in the process the typical action scripts of long-distance advocacy. In the Catholic case, they were members of the religious orders – concrete organizational embodiments of a reformist religious culture that, in turn, continued to be shaped by movements for religious reform. In the Protestant case, the leading role in the initiation of a conflict over the issue of colonial slavery was taken up by reformers within the Society of Friends who were guided toward the path of imperial conflict by their program of reforming the ranks of their organization.

Key here is an essential asymmetry deriving from the unequal distribution of Weber's religious charisma – as well as from the intrinsic property of this basic principle of religious stratification that is partially obscured when Bourdieu and followers amend it into "capital." In many ways, religious reform movements such as those embodied in Catholic orders or the one represented by the mid-eighteenth century Quaker "Reformation" are just a manifestation of a more general pattern of "revitalization movements" that seek to resolve a perceived crisis and to restore the religious group and wider society to a precrisis state of lost harmony and perfection.[29] Nevertheless, important aspects of the emergence and functioning of such movements are deeply rooted in the logic of the religious field proper even as they exercise an important influence on other areas of social life.

Like economic stratification, religious stratification is a multidimensional and complex phenomenon. It is not simply a matter of individual possession,

[28] See, e.g., Klaus Koschorke, "Gnosis, Montanismus, Mönchtum: Zur Frage emanzipatorischer Bewegungen im Raum der Alten Kirche," *Evangelische Theologie* 53, no. 3 (1993); Ronald A. Knox, *Enthusiasm: A Chapter in the History of Religion* (New York: Oxford University Press, 1950). On the various religious reform movements in the early modern period, see Ted Campbell, *The Religion of the Heart: A Study of European Religious Life in the Seventeenth and Eighteenth Centuries* (Columbia: University of South Carolina Press, 1991); Mary Fulbrook, *Piety and Politics: Religion and the Rise of Absolutism in England, Württemberg and Prussia* (Cambridge: Cambridge University Press, 1983); Michael A. Mullett, *The Catholic Reformation* (London: Routledge, 1999); *Radical Religious Movements in Early Modern Europe* (London: Allen and Unwin, 1980); John Spurr, *English Puritanism, 1603–1689* (New York: St. Martin's Press, 1998); W. R. Ward, *Christianity under the Ancien Régime, 1648–1789* (Cambridge: Cambridge University Press, 1999).
[29] See Anthony F. C. Wallace, "Revitalization Movements," *American Anthropologist* 58, no. 2 (1956); Michael E. Harkin, "Introduction: Revitalization as History and Theory," in *Reassessing Revitalization Movements: Perspectives from North America and the Pacific Islands*, ed. Michael E. Harkin (Lincoln: University of Nebraska Press, 2004).

in larger or lesser quantity, of a definable property, such as "religious" or "spiritual" capital. Being "more" religious means does not mean simply having more of that which religious "have-nots" lack. "More" religion means also a more intense and "purified" religion, a qualitatively different ethos or habitus, a distinctive way of seeing the world and acting in it that sharply differentiates those whom Weber described as "religious virtuosi" or carriers of an "aristocratism of highest potency": "salvational aristocratism."[30]

This "virtuosity" or "aristocratism" is, of course, the product of relational and interactional processes that, as Bourdieu consistently reminds us, are foundational to all social fields, not just the field of religion. The religious virtuosi's beliefs and practices are of a "higher" quality and consistency not because they partake of some undefined transcendental substance, but because they are conceived and perceived as such in comparison – and often in direct opposition – to "normal" levels of religious engagement that prevail in the field. Although this is a difference in degree, the implications of this relational differentiation manifest themselves in patterns of social action that are sui generis. In such a high level of "religiousness," the intensification and distillation of religious ethical maxims and precepts into their hardest essence can carry religiously determined action to the most extreme, radical, and uncompromising end of the spectrum. Religious "virtuosity" then unlocks the faith's potential to "relativize" and "reject" the world as it appears to the senses, including the taken-for-granted aspects of the political and economic order. In this case, the basic transcendental or "other-worldly" orientation of religion instills in the actor a heightened sense of accountability to a higher force and demands compliance with a religiously imposed moral standard.[31]

It is when individuals of such heightened religious commitment emerged on the imperial scene and unlocked the contestatory potential of their religious outlook that a conflict over the treatment of non-Europeans emerged, pitting them against rival imperial networks. Again, as we will see, this conflictual pattern has been remarkably stable throughout history. It connects as if in a common thread the first denunciation of Spanish abuses by Dominicans in sixteenth-century Hispaniola and the principled stance of Catholic priests, missionaries, and Quakers against violence in Central America as late as the 1980s. In the centuries in-between, the pattern repeated itself many times in both Catholic and Protestant territories as representatives of an intensified religious orientation rose in defense of the rights of subjugated non-Europeans.[32]

---

[30] Weber, "Religious Rejections."
[31] Peter L. Berger, *The Sacred Canopy: Elements of a Sociological Theory of Religion* (Garden City, NY: Doubleday, 1967), 96–100; Christian Smith, "Correcting a Curious Neglect, or Bringing Religion Back In," in *Disruptive Religion: The Force of Faith in Social-Movement Activism*, ed. Christian Smith (New York: Routledge, 1996).
[32] On the role of religious figures in the contestation of Central American violence, see Nepstad, *Convictions of the Soul*; Jorge Caceres Prendes, "Revolutionary Struggle and Church Commitment: The Case of El Salvador," *Social Compass* 30, nos. 2–3 (1983); Smith, *Resisting*

Typically, this was a conflict of two interlocking dimensions; religious activists contested not only secular actors, they also attacked the conciliatory stance of the less-engaged factions of their own religious organization that – unlike them – were more willing to compromise and condone existing practices of exploitation. And if this conflict was the product of the differentiation and tensions, both within the field of empire and within the field of religion proper, it also generated, it turn, something distinctively new. As Georg Simmel observed in his classical treatment, the "positive" function of conflict is that it can strengthen preexisting social bonds or indeed create new ones where none existed by imposing a unity of purpose among contestants on each side. Not only that: such solidarity once created can persist in various forms beyond the duration of the immediate conflict.[33] The same generative dynamics were at play in the religious conflict over the treatment of non-Europeans. Not only did such conflict heighten preexisting tensions between rival networks. Where the religious figures that were the party and initiators of such conflict were able to attract a critical mass of supporters they formed a distinctive community – the very first instances of Keck and Sikkink's "advocacy networks." In turn, this community provided the social setting within which the ideas and values of ethical engagement with imperial "others" were articulated and propagated, while at the same time concrete advocacy practices aiming at changing the existing problematic state of affairs were developed and maintained.[34]

Although this generative conflict has occurred repeatedly through the centuries and has continued to fuel ideological and political struggles, its later iterations have inevitably been influenced by previous instances of such struggles. If what Simmel called the "integrative" function of conflict creates a distinctive community, this community in turn creates its own culture. The ideas and practices that form that culture may acquire a degree of permanence and even a "life" of their own outside of the bounds of the community. This cultural continuity assured, as we will see, that the ideas and practices of long-distance advocacy first articulated by Catholic friars in the sixteenth century continued to be employed by a variety of religious actors. What is more, when in the mid-eighteenth century Quaker reformer Anthony Benezet attempted to initiate his

---

Reagan. Various iterations of the conflictual pattern up to the emergence of the anti-apartheid movement are documented in Basil Amey, "Baptist Missionary Society Radicals," *Baptist Quarterly* 26, no. 8 (1976); Turner, *Slaves and Missionaries*; Mary Killough, "Niels Otto Tank (1800–1864): Moravian Missionary to Suriname and Wisconsin," *Transactions of the Moravian Historical Society* 29 (1996); Geoffrey A. Oddie, *Social Protest in India: British Protestant Missionaries and Social Reforms, 1850–1900* (New Delhi: Manohar, 1979); Skinner, *Foundations of Anti-Apartheid.*

[33] Georg Simmel, *"Conflict" and "The Web of Group-Affiliations"* (New York: Free Press, 1964 [1908]), especially 101.

[34] The processes I describe here conform to the general model of social change outlined by Thomas Rochon in which new ideas and prescriptions for action are created first by "critical communities" and are then disseminated. See Thomas R. Rochon, *Culture Moves: Ideas, Activism, and Changing Values* (Princeton, NJ: Princeton University Press, 1998).

own political campaign for the abolition of the slave trade, he explicitly evoked the example of Bartolomé de las Casas, a central figure of that earlier tradition of religious advocacy.

That such examples and cultural models transcended confessional boundaries is indicative of the influence of such earlier instances on later cases of religious struggles and advocacy. In this sense, the history of long-distance advocacy is cumulative, path-dependent, and even recursive. The institutional model that crystallized out of religious struggles provided a set of "ready-made" tools of action that subsequent adopters could use. At the same time, the very existence, availability, and permanence of the institution encouraged, in subtle ways, actors to embark on a path of political contestation – especially those religious actors who were structurally in a situation of tension and opposition against other imperial actors.

In short, the interactional process of religious radicalization and the institutional model of long-distance advocacy fed into and reinforced each other. If religious conflict "created" long-distance advocacy, familiarity and exposure to the institutional model bred further conflict. The chapters that follow present in more narrative and analytical detail this complex and entangled early history of the emergence of long-distance advocacy. They discuss the consecutive stages of this history, from the very first religious activities in defense of imperial others to the emergence of a durable international network of antislavery activists in the late eighteenth century.

Because of the inherently cumulative dynamics of these developments where later instances of the same conflictual configuration are "contaminated" by earlier precedents, it is useful to start with the relatively less complicated initial instances of religious conflict in which the relevant processes and relations emerged with larger analytical clarity. This is why Chapter 1 sets the stage by describing how the pattern of religious confrontation with the ethics of imperial conquests played out for the first time in the "new" imperial world. The chapter examines the developments on the island of Hispaniola, the first major Spanish overseas possession in the early sixteenth century, where the interactive emergence of a conflictual relationship between imperial networks and the concomitant radicalization of religious actors led to the first articulation of the ideas, practices, and dispositions that would form the core of long-distance advocacy. Chapter 2 traces the repeating occurrence of the same conflictual and generative interactions, as well as the resulting cumulative growth of a "pro-indigenist" network consisting of members of Catholic religious orders. This network that followed as a counterpoint and a counterforce Spanish and Portuguese expansion and state-building into the American mainland and as far as the Philippines became increasingly committed to political activities and developed its own distinct ideology.

Chapter 3 then shifts the focus to a specific exploitative institution that would form the focus of another wave of long-distance advocacy: the enslavement of Africans and their incorporation as forced labor into a thriving plantation-based colonial economy. Driven by the same dynamics that underlay the earlier indigenist religious project, several attempts to problematize, alleviate, and even abolish colonial slavery and the transatlantic slave trade that fueled it sprang from reformist religious movements, both Catholic and Protestant. In fact, Catholic reformers, including members of a new generation of religious orders like Jesuits and Capuchins, carried further the ideological and organizational legacy of indigenist advocacy and consistently outperformed their Protestant equivalents.

It was only with the emergence of movement for the abolition of the British slave trade in the late eighteenth century that the balance tipped in favor of Protestant initiatives and another robust network of activists consolidated. The last three chapters examine the emergence of this influential network. First I discuss in Chapter 4 the actions of a nucleus of reforming Pennsylvania Quakers who conceived and prepared this project in the larger political and cultural context of the British Empire. Again, these developments are best understood as yet another iteration of the established pattern of conflict pitting networks of religious reformers against rival imperial networks. Chapters 5 then outlines the subsequent growth of the network initiated and led by Quakers as well as its subsequent entanglements with a rapidly changing political configuration of empire, situating the antislavery project in its tense interactions with both an increasingly interventionist British imperial state and a growing movement for colonial autonomy. In the final chapter (Chapter 6), I trace the interestingly uneven growth of the network in its next stage. As it spread across the Atlantic and away from its Pennsylvanian origins into Britain and France, it also shifted its center of gravity to London.

Meanwhile, something new emerged: as London activists introduced and experimented with new technologies of mobilization of wider audiences, the institutional model of long-distance advocacy acquired its distinctively modern shape. It was at that point that antislavery activists were able to establish organizational structures and patterns of action that have informed developments of global solidarity ever since. Thus, the late eighteenth century emerges as an important "evolutionary" moment in the history of long-distance advocacy. At the same time, seen in an exceedingly long historical perspective, this moment was prepared by a long arc of religious conflict and advocacy that formed a consistent counterpoint to the geographical expansion of European political and economic power. After the analytical narrative reaches this important formative moment, I outline in the Conclusion the persisting institutional legacy of these development and circle back to some of the considerations raised in the opening pages, focusing on the general question of the relationship between moral considerability and modernity.

I

Caribbean Beginnings, 1511–1520

Since 1493, Hispaniola – or Little Spain, as the Spanish named the island containing today Haiti and the Dominican Republic – was the first far-flung outpost of what was to become a massive empire in America. In the political imagination of the time, any polity was and had to be, by definition, a Christian polity in which private and public affairs were structured along Christian precepts and popular religious observance was regular and intense. All the more so in this newly acquired overseas possession of the "Catholic Monarchs," Isabella of Castile and Ferdinand of Aragon, who had already distinguished themselves in reclaiming the Iberian Peninsula for Christianity by expelling its last Islamic rulers. At least for the sincerely devout Isabella, the "New World" opened by Columbus's voyages offered the remarkable prospect of extending the Christian commonwealth to hitherto unknown parts of the globe and converting their inhabitants.

Yet Hispaniola's distance prevented the immediate establishment of a well-oiled church hierarchy of the kind operating in Spain and other European states. No priests and bishops were appointed. Instead, in a pattern foreshadowing the later Spanish and Portuguese conquest of mainland America, the mendicant orders, the highly mobile activist and ascetic arm of the Catholic Church, were entrusted with the evangelization of indigenous people and the pastoral oversight of European settlers.

The news of Columbus's "discoveries" immediately captured the attention and imagination of Franciscans excited by the prospect of evangelizing new potential recruits to the Christian flock. Two lay brothers from the French province of the order joined Columbus's second voyage in 1493 and by 1502 there were as many as twenty Franciscans on Hispaniola,[1]

[1] See Antonine Tibesar, "The Franciscan Province of the Holy Cross of Española, 1505–1559," *The Americas* 13, no. 4 (1957).

When in 1510 the Dominican order received the authorization to send missionaries to Hispaniola like their Franciscan competition, expectations for an evangelistic success must have been high. Yet the seventeen or so newly arrived Dominicans found themselves in a lawless frontier environment where rapacious Spaniards exploited and abused indigenous people in a decidedly unchristian manner. In fact, so incensed were the Dominicans by the brutal exploitation of indigenous labor by Spanish settlers that in 1511, they entrusted their brother Antonio (or Antón) Montesino with the delivery of a fiery sermon on the Sunday before Christmas that attacked vehemently the Spanish for their abuses. Scandalized, the settlers demanded a retraction. Yet in his next Sunday sermon, Montesino again confronted them and announced the decision of his Order to refuse confession and absolution of their sins unless they mended their ways.

Faced with the Dominicans' intransigence, the Spanish community accused them of subverting royal authority and sent representatives to denounce them in King Ferdinand's court. In response, the king and the hierarchy of the Dominican order banned the friars from preaching on the subject. The Dominicans in Hispaniola, however, dispatched Montesino to present a memorial to the King documenting the atrocities they had witnessed. Pedro de Córdoba, the head of the Dominican community in Hispaniola, returned to Spain, too, to explain the position of the protesting friars to their superiors in the hierarchy of the order.[2]

The Dominicans' protests and the settlers' counterattack resulted in a heated and persisting discussion in Spain and its overseas possessions not only of the treatment of indigenous people, but also, more generally, of the legal and ethical foundations of imperial conquest. Indeed, this confrontation marked the beginnings of a long wave of religiously inspired protest within the Iberian overseas empires. The small Dominican community in Hispaniola formed the first nucleus of what grew to become a larger network of religious activists who, defending the interests of indigenous people within the empire, worked to influence legislation and developed a series of reformist projects. In the process,

---

[2] Bartolomé de las Casas narrates the Montesino episode in his *Historia de las Indias*, vol. III, book 1, critical ed. (Madrid: Alianza, 1994 [1527]), 1757–75; English translation in Casas, *History of the Indies*, trans. Andrée Collard (New York: Harper and Row 1971), 181–89. See also Benno M. Biermann, "Die ersten Dominikaner in Amerika," *Missionswissenschaft und Religionswissenschaft* 32 (1947/48); Anthony Pagden, *The Fall of Natural Man: The American Indian and the Origins of Comparative Ethnology* (Cambridge: Cambridge University Press, 1982), 30–36; Demetrio Ramos, "El hecho de la Conquista de América," *Corpus Hispanorum de Pace* 25 (1984): 36–46; Michael Sievernich, "Anfänge prophetischer Theologie: Antonio de Montesinos Predigt (1511) und ihre Folgen," in *Conquista und Evangelisation: 500 Jahre Orden in Lateinamerika*, ed. Michael Sievernich (Mainz: Matthias-Grünewald-Verlag, 1992); Frank Moya Pons, *Después de Colón: Trabajo, sociedad y política en la economía del oro* (Madrid: Alianza, 1987), 79–98; Lewis Hanke, *The Spanish Struggle for Justice in the Conquest of America* (Dallas: Southern Methodist University Press, 2002 [1949]), 17–22; Miguel Ángel Medina, *Una comunidad al servicio del Indio: La obra de Fr. Pedro de Córdoba, O. P. (1482–1521)* (Madrid: Instituto Pontificio de Teologia, 1983).

there emerged an early version of a cultural model of action that has been, in various configurations, present and influential ever since.

PREDATORY IMPERIALISM AND ITS RELIGIOUS CRITICS

Searching for historical beginnings – for the very first instance of a social phenomenon – is a risky enterprise, if only because the accumulated richness of centuries of human activities is constantly likely to surprise us with earlier and earlier precedents. Indeed, what the Dominicans initiated in Hispaniola and Spain in the early sixteenth century was, in many respects, remarkably similar to earlier instances of a religiously inspired intervention on behalf of conquered people that had been occurring with some frequency in the preceding centuries. If anything, the events of 1511 and the ensuing developments show how persistent, and therefore analytically important, this general configuration of religious confrontation with the politics of conquest was.

The early modern world was, from a European perspective, a world increasingly divided morally. The political and economic ascendancy and expansion of Western Europe was predicated on and, indeed, produced a moral partitioning of space. Increasing individual liberties and rights in the heartland of Europe was coupled with the exploitation and dehumanizing of distant "others."[3]

Religion played an important role in the rise of the West and the concomitant inherently double-faced moral regime of European-dominated modernity. As a "core" of Western European power institutions crystallized in the late medieval period, it spread by conquest first into the immediate periphery of Europe and then into much of the world overseas. Christianity was an integral part of the fabric of this European expansion, not least because it provided important cultural and organizational elements out of which a distinct European identity and a distinct European institutional culture were constructed. The strong position of the Catholic Church in Europe in the period between the eleventh and thirteenth centuries and the Christian identity it forged led to the crystallization of a strong common self-understanding of Western Europeans as distinct from the non-European "heathen" – both in ethno-racial and geographical terms. The Europeans' common Christian culture cast them as a people or race apart from others and naturalized the expectation that Christendom was to expand territorially and extend over the lands of surrounding heathen.[4]

Christianity was thus deeply implicated in the creation and maintenance of a medieval legacy of hardening racism, xenophobia, and persecution against people considered deviant.[5] At the same time, however, religious

---

[3] See Brady, "Merchant Empires."
[4] See Bartlett, *Making of Europe*, esp. pp. 243–55.
[5] See ibid., and R. I. Moore, *The Formation of a Persecuting Society: Power and Deviance in Western Europe, 950–1250* (Oxford: Blackwell, 1987).

thought provided more attenuated conceptual schemes for the understanding of human "otherness." At least since the late Middle Ages, Europeans had a variety of such schemes at their disposal. There was the "low" folkloric vision of the "wild man" or *homunculus* that emphasized the bestial, nonhuman qualities of non-Europeans. Christianity and cannon law, on the other hand, developed more refined classifications of human diversity. Although deriving from the Greek notion of the "barbarian," the medieval notion of the "pagan" moved, however inconclusively, from the original emphasis on different descent and culture toward belief as the main marker of difference. And since the expansionist vision of Christianity allowed for the "convertibility" of the heathen, further finer distinctions were applied to describe different types of pagans and to prescribe different ethical rules for engagement with them. In the influential classification of Tommaso de Vio, Cardinal Cajetan (1469–1534), only those pagans living under a Christian prince or on the territory of the former Roman Empire were subject to Christian legislation and the dominion of the Church, whereas the "true infidels" living elsewhere could not be legitimately waged war against or subjected to Christian authority. Another classification, going back to Aquinas, distinguished between the "vincibly ignorant" Jews, Muslims, and Heretics, whose religious beliefs were a conscious rejection of Christianity, and the "invincibly ignorant" who, by no fault of their own, had never been exposed to the Gospel.[6]

Thus, Christianity played a complex and contradictory in the creation of a morally divided world of Europeans and non-Europeans, of Christian "insiders," and various non-Christian "outsiders." On the one hand, Christianity reinforced ideologies of European superiority which, in turn, justified the exploitative treatment of non-Europeans. At the same time, however, the resources of religion provided the inspiration and the organizational base for a persistent critique of European political and economic expansion. This critique urged humane treatment of the people entering the orbit of European imperialism, if only to facilitate their evangelization and conversion to Christianity.

The first intimations of a religious critique of the exploitation of populations conquered by European powers go as far back as the late eighth century

---

[6] On the different understandings of non-European and non-Christian "others" in the Middle Ages, see Bartlett, *Making of Europe*, 295–96; Felipe Fernández-Armesto, *Before Columbus: Exploration and Colonization from the Mediterranean to the Atlantic, 1229–1492* (Philadelphia: University of Pennsylvania Press, 1987); Joseph Höffner, *Kolonialismus und Evangelium: Spanische Kolonialethik im Goldenen Zeitalter*, 2nd ed. (Trier, Germany: Paulinus-Verlag, 1969), 42–43; Pagden, *Fall of Natural Man*, 19–38; Antonio Rumeu de Armas, "Los problemas derivados del contacto de razas en los albores del Renacimiento," *Cuadernos de historia* 1 (1967); P. E. Russell, "El descubrimiento de las Canarias y el debate medieval acerca de los derechos de los principes y pueblos paganos," *Revista de historia canaria* 36, no. 171 (1978).

when Alcuin of York decried the hasty imposition of tithes on the Saxons conquered by Charlemagne as counterproductive to their evangelization.[7] Better documented in surviving evidence from the early thirteenth century is the more systematic denunciation of the abuses against newly conquered "pagans" in Prussia and the Baltic. Clergymen like the first Catholic bishop of Prussia, the Cistercian Christian, and the papal legate to Livonia (William of Modena), decried the atrocities committed by the Teutonic Knights and the Swordbrothers, the two military orders officially commissioned with the conquest and evangelization of these territories. Their denunciations resulted in a series of papal and imperial bulls affirming, although rather cautiously and ambiguously, the freedom of the conquered population and threatening infractions with ecclesiastical penalties like excommunication.[8]

Led by similar considerations, representatives of the Catholic Church cooperated with royal authorities in efforts to protect indigenous populations from the depredations of European settlers during the fifteenth-century Iberian conquest and colonization of the Canary Islands. As a result, Queen Isabella forbade the enslavement of converted islanders by the conquering feudal lords. When legislation did not eradicate the problem, Franciscans on the islands sought the intervention of the royal court and the Pope. In 1434, at the request of the Spanish bishop of the Canaries, Pope Eugene IV condemned the excessive taxes levied by Spanish lords and threatened to excommunicate those who sold into slavery converts, present and prospective, to Christianity. In 1462, Pius II again authorized the bishop of the Canaries and the archbishop of Toledo and Seville to excommunicate slave scouts who, by enslaving their victims, prevented their conversion to Christianity. After that, clergymen continued to address similar grievances to the royal court.[9]

---

[7] See Donald A. Bullough, "Was There a Carolingian Anti-War Movement?" *Early Medieval Europe* 12, no. 4 (2003): 374; and Erich Maschke, *Der deutsche Orden und die Preußen: Bekehrung und Unterwerfung in der preußisch-baltischen Mission des 13. Jahrhunderts* (Berlin: Emil Ebering, 1928), 5–7.

[8] See Hartmut Boockmann, "Bemerkungen zu den frühen Urkunden über die Mission und Unterwerfung der Prussen," in *Die Ritterorden zwischen geistlicher und weltlicher Macht im Mittelalter*, ed. Zenon Hubert Nowak (Torun: Uniwersytet Mikolaja Kopernika, 1990); "Die Freiheit der Prußen im 13. Jahrhundert," in *Die Abendländische Freiheit vom 10. zum 14. Jahrhundert: Der Wirkungszusammenhang von Idee und Wirklichkeit im europäischen Vergleich*, ed. Johannes Fried (Sigmaringen, Germany: Jan Thorbecke, 1991) and Maschke, *Deutsche Orden*.

[9] Eduardo Aznar Vallejo, "The Conquest of the Canary Islands," in *Implicit Understandings: Observing, Reporting, and Reflecting on the Encounters between Europeans and Other Peoples in the Early Modern Era*, ed. Stuart B. Schwartz (Cambridge: Cambridge University Press, 1994); Rumeu de Armas, "Problemas derivados"; Rafael Torres Campos, *Carácter de la conquista y colonización de las Islas Canarias* (Madrid: Depósito de la Guerra, 1901), pp. 56–64; Dominik Josef Wölfel, "La Curia Romana y la Corona de España en la defensa de los aborígenes Canarios," *Anthropos* 25 (1930).

HISPANIOLA AND THE BEGINNINGS OF EXPLOITATIVE OVERSEAS IMPERIALISM

Thus, by the beginnings of Spanish expansion overseas in the early sixteenth century, there had been a tradition of a distinctively religious opposition to the forces of European political and economic expansionism. When the Dominican community on Hispaniola protested against the exploitation of indigenous people in 1511, they, in a sense, reproduced that very tradition. In many ways, however, Hispaniola was the beginning of something distinctively new. The introduction of Spanish authority there prefigured or, indeed, invented the many distinctive institutions of Iberian expansion into the "New World." The perceived novelty itself of this American world and its inhabitants suggests how different this environment was from the environment of earlier European expansionism that largely stayed within a geography whose limits had been inherited from the Roman Empire.[10]

"Discovered" by Columbus during his first expedition to the Caribbean in 1492, Hispaniola became the first American territorial possession of the Castilian Crown when Columbus's second voyage brought settlers to the island in 1493. Far from being the outcome of a determined policy, these beginnings of Spanish settlement and domination in the Americas resulted from the mismatch between the levity of Columbus's sales pitch for his unsuccessful ventures and the religious and political earnestness of his main business partners, the sovereigns of Castile and Aragon, Isabella and Ferdinand.

When the Catholic majesties financed Columbus's first expedition, the expectation was that it would follow the typical pattern of trade in the Mediterranean and along the African coast by establishing trading outposts in Asia where Spanish woolen cloth would be exchanged for the riches of the Orient. Hispaniola with its friendly inhabitants seemed particularly attractive to Columbus because it was the only island where his expedition found gold deposits. By these standards, however, the expedition was a failure. The cloth Columbus was carrying was lost or spoiled and no commercial profit materialized. To save face, on his way back to Spain in 1493, Columbus composed a letter addressed to the monarchs and his other financial partners that creatively transformed a commercial failure into the promise of wonderful prospects. He had reached, he claimed, Asian islands with great commercial potential,

---

[10] The next sections draw on the work of several historians: Helen Nader, "Desperate Men, Questionable Acts: The Moral Dilemma of Italian Merchants in the Spanish Slave Trade," *Sixteenth Century Journal* 33, no. 2 (2002); Samuel M. Wilson, *Hispaniola: Caribbean Chiefdoms in the Age of Columbus* (Tuscaloosa: University of Alabama Press, 1990); Moya Pons, *Después de Colón*; Carl Ortwin Sauer, *The Early Spanish Main* (Berkeley: University of California Press, 1966); J. H. Elliott, "The Spanish Conquest and Settlement of America," in *The Cambridge History of Latin America*, Vol. 1: *Colonial Latin America*, ed. Leslie Bethell (Cambridge: Cambridge University Press, 1984).

populated by unwarlike people eager to accept Christianity and the sovereignty of the Castilian Queen. The wealth thus generated would suffice to finance the coveted conquest of the holy city of Jerusalem from the Muslims.

Ferdinand and Isabella seized this opportunity to enlarge easily their dominions and wealth while bringing numerous new souls to the fold of Christianity. They immediately claimed sovereignty over the newly discovered islands by publicizing Columbus's letter in several European languages and by securing from Pope Alexander VI the bull *Inter caetera* that delegated to them the authority to evangelize and rule these and any other overseas territories. Columbus was dispatched promptly back to Hispaniola with seventeen ships, 1,200 Europeans, and military support against potential Portuguese attacks on the new Castilian trading post.

Columbus's plan was to exploit to the fullest the terms of the contract with his royal partners and creditors and exercise unrestricted authority over a profitable business enterprise. Well-disposed local inhabitants, the Taínos,[11] would provide tribute and gold under the direction of their leaders, the *caciques*. The Spaniards employed and paid by Columbus would keep the indigenous people under control. Yet again, however, developments on the ground defied the lofty expectations. The Spanish community on Hispaniola was beset by diseases, lack of food, and a remarkably incompetent administration. Columbus's exploration of the neighboring islands of Cuba and Jamaica in 1494 failed to discover the sources of "Asian" riches he had promised the monarchs. Meanwhile, the initially good relations between Europeans and Taínos deteriorated as a Spanish party in search of gold found a reason to punish a *cacique* and his relatives. Another *cacique* and his people attacked the Spaniards who responded with a punitive expedition. In this atmosphere of violence spiraling out of control, the prospects for any profits and riches remained distant. Thus, in 1494, Columbus decided to offer his creditors the only "goods" his expedition had been able to acquire: 500 out of the 1,500 prisoners the Spaniards and their Taíno allies had captured in the course of the hostilities. The 500 were sent to Spain to be sold as slaves; the rest were given as slaves to the Spanish settlers.

Next to gold, slave trafficking had been on Columbus's mind at least since his first journey when he suggested this possibility in his report to the monarchs. There he had envisioned as potential slaves not the peaceful Taínos of Hispaniola, but the warlike Caribs from neighboring islands who, he reported, were engaged, according to his Taíno informants, in idolatry and

[11] Although I use the term Taíno, a nineteenth-century reconstruction, instead of alternatives such "Island Arawaks," there is no agreement on the proper ethnonym for the indigenous population of Hispaniola. See, e.g., Neil L. Whitehead, "The Crises and Transformations of Invaded Societies: The Caribbean (1492–1580)," in *The Cambridge History of the Native Peoples of the Americas*, vol. III: South America, part 1, eds. Frank Salomon and Stuart B. Schwartz (Cambridge: Cambridge University Press, 1999), 867; Sauer, *Early Spanish Main*, 37.

anthropophagy. Columbus's simplistic and misinformed distinction between peaceful Indians and cannibal Caribs would take on a life of its own later when the official designation of an indigenous population as "Caribs" was usually no more than a justification to wage a military expedition against them. Yet not even such a loose distinction could justify the enslavement of the people in this first shipment of slaves to Spain. Ferdinand and Isabella felt uneasy with such treatment of their new Caribbean subjects whom Columbus had initially described as peaceful and eager to adopt Christianity and Castilian power. They temporized and sought the advice of theologians and lawyers as well as more information from Columbus.

The Escalation of Hostilities

During the monarchs' deliberation, the development of an unequal regime in which Spanish overlords increasingly exploited indigenous populations in the Caribbean continued. After the first armed conflicts, Taínos around the Spanish settlement and in the center of the island stopped collaborating and providing food to a Spanish community still ridden with illnesses and starvation. For Columbus, this was a rebellion against the royal authority he had imposed over the island and, therefore, a good reason to launch yet another punitive expedition. For ten months in 1495–96, a force of Spaniards and allied Taínos occupied the interior of Hispaniola and submitted the *caciques* there to their authority. By that time, any remnants of reciprocal good will between Taínos and Spaniards evaporated. The settlers imposed de facto forced labor on local people by compelling them to provide food. To avoid Spanish violence, the Taínos fled to hide in the mountains. At the end of the campaign, Columbus imposed a tribute of gold and cotton that the *caciques* would collect from their people under the threat of Spanish arms.

In March 1496, Columbus left for Spain with two ships carrying 200 Spaniards abandoning the island and 30 Tainos to Spain to plea for more patience and support from the monarchs. The administration of Hispaniola was entrusted to his equally incompetent brother Bartolomé who suppressed violently another uprising against Spanish tribute and abuses. In 1497, however, the discontent among Spanish settlers against the leadership of the Genoese Columbus family erupted in a revolt led by the former majordomo of Christopher Columbus, Francisco Roldán. Roldán and his men took over the western part of the island. Indigenous communities were now assaulted and exploited by two rival Spanish groups. The last remnants of indigenous political organization were destroyed when Bartolomé Columbus attacked the Taínos he thought were allies of the rebellious Roldán, imprisoned the *caciques* Mayobanex and Guarionex, and shipped out the captured prisoners as slaves. Ironically, the destruction of indigenous leaders who had acted as intermediaries between their communities and the Spanish overlords made the collection of tribute even more difficult if not impossible, even if Bartolomé gave up on gold, requesting cotton and cassava instead.

Repartimiento

Remarkably, Christopher had been able to once more reassure the monarchs during his trip to Spain and obtain their renewed commitment to the enterprise. What is more, the Crown was moving toward establishing a truly permanent settlement and issued a letter patent that authorized Columbus to allot land as private property to Spaniards to settle on and cultivate. Columbus returned to the troubled situation of Hispaniola in 1498. The coveted gold was not being produced. Nor was the centralized tribute system working; rather, the settlers were extracting haphazardly food and personal service from indigenous people. In search of profits, Columbus again resorted to enslaving allegedly rebellious Taínos and sent another shipment of slaves to Spain.

The other problem was Roldán and his people, with whom he entered negotiations. In 1499, to secure their loyalty, Columbus gave them the right to settle as free citizens (*vecinos*) and not – as it was initially – as his employees. By that time, however, indigenous servitude had become a basic feature of the colonial society in Hispaniola. Thus, along with the land – and going beyond royal provisions – Roldán's people were given property rights over indigenous communities. After that, it was only natural that similar rights were given to the Spaniards who had remained loyal to Columbus. Each Spaniard was thus assigned a specific community who, under their *caciques*, was to provide for him plants and food, personal service, or labor in the gold mines without any limitations. This certainly went beyond what the monarchs had authorized, Columbus admitted in a letter for them, yet was the only way to save the colony from a disaster. Indeed, this assignment or "distribution" (*repartimiento*) of indigenous communities to the individual Spaniard overlords was to be an enduring institution replicated, after Hispaniola, throughout Spanish America.

By 1499, critics of Columbus's disastrous administration were finally successful in gaining the monarchs' favor. These, in turn, used this opportunity to assert a fuller authority over their overseas possessions. Columbus was deprived of his monopoly as new expeditions of trade and exploration were authorized. Authority over such expeditions was granted to the archdeacon of the cathedral of Seville, Juan Rodríguez de Fonseca, who had been involved in organizing expeditions since Columbus's second voyage. The trips authorized by an increasingly powerful Fonseca began exploring, trading, and eventually raiding for slaves in the American littoral of what was known then as Tierra Firme (first touched by Columbus in 1498), its offshore islands and other Caribbean islands apart from Hispaniola.

At the same time, the royally appointed Francisco de Bobadilla replaced Columbus as governor of Hispaniola. After arriving to the island and sending Columbus and his clique in chains back to Spain in 1500, Bobadilla revived gold production by suspending temporarily, against the monarchs' wishes, the requirement that part of the gold – which they had proclaimed their property – be given over to the royal treasury. Now Spaniards could exploit indigenous people in the gold mines while keeping all the gold and profits for themselves.

Encomiendas and Royal Power

In this period, the level of violence declined as there were no new attacks on Taínos or uprisings. Furthermore, after several years of consultation with theologians, Ferdinand and Isabella issued in 1500 a *cédula real*, a royal letter patent, declaring all Indians free vassals of the Castilian Crown and banning their enslavement, unless it happened in the course of "just war." Yet despite such limitations, the exploitation of indigenous labor was firmly established under the conditions of *repartimiento*.

Exploitation and violence characterized the regime of the next governor, Nicolás de Ovando, who arrived in Hispaniola in 1502 with about 2,000 new Spanish settlers. Having been informed of the prevailing abuses, the monarchs gave Ovando detailed instructions on the humane treatment of the indigenes. Like his predecessors, however, the new governor – a knight of the military order of Alcántara – was all too willing to deploy violence against what he perceived as insubordination. By 1504, several expeditions "pacified" violently the Southeastern and Western parts of the island that at that time still contained tributary yet nominally independent local kingdoms not subsumed under the system of *repartimiento*. The last vestiges of indigenous political organization were thus destroyed. In search of more gold and laborers, Ovando initiated in 1508 the occupation of the island of Puerto Rico. There, too, initial cooperation with indigenous people quickly deteriorated into abusive exploitation as forced labor arrangements were imposed.

At the same time, the Crown continued to assert control over the political and economic arrangements in their overseas possessions. Royal instructions in 1503 ordered that indigenous labor, in modification of the existing *repartimiento* system, be organized under the so-called *encomiendas*. Under terms of the *encomienda*, the power of the Spanish lords over the indigenous community "assigned" to them was reduced, at least on paper. Now Indians were, nominally, free vassals of the Crown "commended" or "entrusted" to individual Spaniards. They were paid minimal wages and were required, at least initially, to work for only a part of the year. The right to seek redress of grievances directly from representatives of the Crown was granted, too, while Spanish *encomenderos* were required to provide for the welfare and Christianization of their charges.

Thus conceived in the spirit of benevolent paternalism, the *encomieda* system served to reduce the anxieties that Ferdinand, and particularly the devout Isabella, had regarding the legality and morality of the exploitative arrangements that emerged in their first overseas possession. At the same time, the *encomiendas* were a tool for the Crown and its governors to exercise control over Spanish settlers as the assignment and reassignment of indigenous laborers to "deserving" Spaniards was at the governor's discretion. Finally, the Crown used the system in order to create the conditions for a pliant and productive labor force to mine the gold they desperately needed for their revenue.[12]

Under these conditions, the abusive and ultimately destructive exploitation of indigenous people continued unabated, despite frequent royal admonitions on the just treatment of their vassals and the limitations of tributary labor to six or eight months of the year. Official policy became even more centered on the extraction of gold and revenue after Isabella's death in 1504. The widowed Ferdinand was deeply involved in political and military maneuvers in his search to secure the succession to the throne and to preserve the powerful position he had enjoyed in the dynastic union of Castile and Aragon. Simultaneously, his de facto minister Fonseca, a cleric with remarkably little interest in matters spiritual, streamlined control over business and administration in the Indies by setting up a new institution: the Casa de Contración in Seville.

Isabella, on her part, had further enabled abuses against Caribbean indigenes by relaxing her initial strictures against their enslavement and authorizing, in 1503, the capture of such "Cannibals" in the islands and the American littoral that resisted the "Sacred Catholic Faith" and persisted in alleged barbarous practices like cannibalism. This instruction encouraged the predatory behavior of traders exploring the region who, from now on, could enslave with impunity by simply defining the people they raided as anthropophagic barbarians. In 1508, at the request of *procuradores* (proctors or agents) of the Hispaniola settlers in Spain, Ferdinand authorized the "importation" of Indians from the neighboring islands, with the provision that they be paid wages and not treated as servants. The capital needed was immediately raised and settlers started slaving raids on Cuba and on the Lucayas (Bahamas) that were probably fully depopulated by 1513. In subsequent years, Ferdinand became even more involved in the emerging trade in slaves by making sure the Crown receive a share from the profits. The importation of enslaved Africans from Spain was also authorized and practiced, although on a smaller scale.

In 1509, Ovando was replaced as governor by Christopher Columbus's son Diego who had been able to receive acknowledgment from the court of

---

[12] The institutional model for *encomienda* in Spanish America came from various Castilian forms of feudal dependency, ultimately descendants of the Roman *commendatio* which established relationship of personal patronage between two individuals. As we will see, *encomenderos* throughout the empire consistently tried to appropriate for themselves the full jurisdiction over the territories and populations entrusted to them and to make their dominion permanent and hereditary. See Robert S. Chamberlain, "Castilian Backgrounds of the Repartimiento-Encomienda," *Contributions to American Anthropology and History* 25 (1939); Mario Góngora, *Studies in the Colonial History of Spanish America* (Cambridge: Cambridge University Press, 1975); Lynne Guitar, "No More Negotiation: Slavery and the Destabilization of Colonial Hispaniola's Encomienda System," *Revista/Review Interamericana* 29, no. 1 (1999); Ruggiero Romano, "Entre encomienda castellana y encomienda indiana: Una vez más el problema del feudalismo americano (siglos XVI-XVII)," *Anuario IEHS* 3 (1988); Silvio A. Zavala, *La encomienda indiana*, 2nd ed. (Mexico City, Mexico: Editorial Porrúa, 1973).

the monopolies and privileges granted initially to his father. The economy of Hispaniola was collapsing at that time. To the frustration of Ferdinand, who was permanently hungry for gold to finance his wars in Europe, gold production was dying out with the exhaustion of the gold deposits and the mortality of exploited indigenous labor. In 1509, Juan de Esquivel, experienced "pacifier" from the wars on Hispaniola in 1504, was dispatched to occupy Jamaica. There again, despite royal admonitions, friendly indigenous occupants were quickly reduced to forced labor. Cuba was subjected to the same treatment in 1511–12. Meanwhile, Ferdinand claimed even more control over the governance of the island by introducing, in 1511, a permanent legal tribunal – the *audiencia* – as a limitation to the power of the governor.

A THIRD IMPERIAL NETWORK

Within a period of less than twenty years since first contact, Spanish political authority was firmly established in the Caribbean. A set of institutions were introduced that were to be replicated widely during the conquest of the American mainland. These included both the institutions through which the imperial center exercised its power (governors and royal *audiencia*) and those that cemented the exploitation of indigenous labor by European settlers (*repartimiento* and *encomienda*).

Meanwhile, the combination of exploitation, starvation, diseases imported from Europe, and armed conflicts decimated the Taíno population. Enslaved Africans and Caribs from the surrounding islands provided forced labor. Along with the implantation of political authority, an unequal racial regime was firmly established where Spanish overlords exploited the labor of non-Europeans.[13] The typical configuration of abusive and predatory imperialism had taken firm shape for the first time in a far-flung European possession overseas.

Another facet of these developments was that two differentiated and occasionally competing networks of actors had simultaneously taken shape and pursued their distinct, if often overlapping, interests: settlers and agents of imperial governance. Settlers attempted to secure as much freedom of action for themselves within a political unit officially subordinate to the Castilian Crown. In the opposite direction, the monarchs consistently tried to impose as much control as possible over the political and economic affairs of the imperial outpost in Hispaniola.

While thus vying for position within the newly opened imperial space, settlers and royal governance shared, nevertheless, an underlying agreement: both networks profited from the unequal racial regime they de facto established and worked for the maintenance of this regime. Both settlers "on the ground" and the monarchs (and their representatives) sought their gains from

---

[13] Guitar, "No More Negotiation"; Noble David Cook, "Sickness, Starvation, and Death in Early Hispaniola," *Journal of Interdisciplinary History* 32, no. 3 (2002); Elliott, "Spanish Conquest."

the exploitation of imperial "others," whether indigenous Caribs or imported enslaved Africans. For European settlers, these imperial others were mostly a source of cheap labor. They were thus driven by an arrogant disposition that excluded any consideration of the dignity or welfare of these human beings. The Crown, it is true, did endorse policies that took seriously, to different degrees, the welfare of the new subjects the overseas expansion had incorporated under its dominion. Yet ultimately, especially after Isabella's death, these new imperial subjects were no more than human sources of revenue and wealth.

When, after Montesino's first sermon in 1511, the Dominicans on Hispaniola began to contest in public this state of affairs, they opposed the imperial regime of inequality and exploitation created and maintained by these two imperial networks. They also brought into play a distinctively religious logic against the exploitative logic that informed the actions of the actors entrenched in the imperial context of Hispaniola. Within the limitations of a decidedly Christian worldview, the Dominicans championed a position in which the exploited "Indians" were not considered a nearly subhuman source of labor and wealth, but souls in need of salvation and, ultimately, fellow human beings whose welfare must be taken seriously.

However rudimentary the ideological articulation of this position, it was a formidable bid into an emerging symbolic struggle. This was an alternative ethical vision of political and economic expansion. Although, at least in the beginning, not questioning the legitimacy of Spanish expansionism, this vision criticized the status quo and held the promise for different, more humane social arrangements in which indigenous people, if not granted full political equality, were considered morally relevant as fully equal human beings.[14]

The articulation of this oppositional vision was intimately connected with another process through which the Dominican critics of the imperial status quo – by the very fact of their protest – emerged as a consequential "third" force in the political and ethical landscape of empire. By confronting and, more generally, interacting with the other two networks of empire, the networks of settlers and of governance, they in fact carved out a distinct corporate identity and distinct interests as a new set of actors who were concerned with the well-being of imperial others while engaging practically in activities to defend their interests.

THE ENDURANCE OF PROTEST

This is another way to understand the significance of the Dominicans' activities in this context: namely, that by invoking a distinctly religious logic in opposition to established imperial actors and interests they developed a set of distinctive practices and orientations. A persistent institutional model of practical

---

[14] See Sievernich, "Anfänge Prophetischer Theologie."

involvement with the welfare of distant strangers began to crystallize with their activities.

Institutional endurance is the key here. For after the initial protests in 1511, the Dominicans were able to persist in maintaining their oppositional stance in various ways. At first, their protests and pleas for humane treatment of indigenous people met with the settlers' staunch resistance. Unable to silence the Dominicans, they dispatched their representatives, including one of the Hispaniola Franciscans, to the royal court to seek an intervention against the subversive activities. In response, the Dominicans, too, sent their representatives to counteract the settlers' lobbying and to work for a reform of the exploitative regime on the island.

Although the initial reaction of the king and the order hierarchy was unfavorable toward the Dominicans, Montesino and de Córdoba as representatives of the Hispaniola Dominicans were able to change things with their memorials and lobbying in Spain. In fact, their activities were compelling enough to force upon the court a public discussion of the ethics of empire. After consulting theologians and lawyers, Ferdinand convoked a learned *junta*, the standard form of political consultation at the time in which the debates of university professors of theology and law – civil and canon – resulted in policy recommendations. The deliberations produced the so-called Laws of Burgos of 1512 that regulated the *encomienda* system with the explicit aim of preventing further abuses.

For the Dominicans, however, these measures did not go far enough. While imposing stricter regulations on the institution of *encomienda*, the Laws of Burgos did not question the legitimacy of the institution itself. That was hardly surprising: several influential courtiers had a stake in the *encomienda* system as absentee owners, and their political clout certainly influenced the emerging legislation. Yet for the protesting Dominicans, the *encomienda* encapsulated all the evils of unjust domination in the Caribbean.[15] Pedro de Córdoba appealed personally to the king for further and more radical legislation. His appeal resulted in yet another *junta* which produced in 1513 the revision of the existing laws through the so-called Instructions of Valladolid.

In addition to the legality of labor arrangements, the Dominican protests forced the issue of the morality of imperial conquest itself on the royal agenda. In 1513, King Ferdinand temporarily suspended further expeditions into the American mainland while a committee of theologians discussed the legality of such operations. The deliberations of the committee resulted in the drafting of the *Requerimiento*, a legal document that the Spaniards had to read to

---

[15] The less-than-enthusiastic response of the Dominicans to the law is captured by Bartolomé de Las Casas's later characterization: "… the theologians and jurists of the council composed seven propositions which, although contaminated by prejudice, could not deny Indians the condition of free men, at least in the first two. As for the rest of the propositions, they smack of the tyranny the informers were striving to maintain." Casas, *History of the Indies*, 190–91.

indigenous people before establishing their authority on their land. The intention was to secure the consent of local people to Spanish authority and conversion to Christianity, while avoiding unjustified violence against them.[16]

Thus, what was, initially, an episode of confrontation between religious
and secular imperial interests deepened into a protracted struggle over legislation and policy. In a continuous conflictual interaction with other networks
of empire, the Dominicans embarked on an enduring project to reform the
exploitative regime of the emerging overseas empire. The acts of political intervention they undertook thus were acquiring a certain degree of permanence.

ENTER LAS CASAS

The first results of the continuing protests were hardly an unqualified success.
It soon became clear that the legalistic procedure of *Requerimiento* did nothing to prevent gratuitous violence against indigenous Americans. Similarly, the
Laws of Burgos and their revision failed to make a significant impact on the situation in Hispaniola. On the one hand, the bureaucrats on the island dragged
their feet and implemented the royal ordinances less than enthusiastically, if at
all. Nor did they receive from the court any significant incentives to comply.
Ferdinand himself was similarly less than enthusiastic about protecting the
welfare of his overseas subjects. A series of orders he issued contradicted the
spirit of the laws and reaffirmed, in particular, the legality of enslavement of
"rebellious" Caribs for labor in the gold mines.[17]

The suspension of further expansion into American mainland was only
temporary. There, after jurisdictional disputes with other "explorers," Vasco
Núñez de Balboa, established his authority over the Spanish colony of Santa
María la Antigua del Darién in 1511. He administered a unusually prosperous settlement by cultivating relatively peaceful relationships with indigenous
communities and not "assigning" them as forced laborers to his minions. All
this changed in 1513 when Ferdinand, in response to complaints by Balboa's
enemies in the colony, appointed Pedrarías Dávila as governor of what now

---

[16] Different versions of the Laws of Burgos and the instructions of Valladolid are reproduced in
Rafael Altamira, "El texto de las Leyes de Burgos de 1512," *Revista de Historia de América* 4
(1938); Casas, *Historia de las Indias*, 1775–835; Ronald D. Hussey, "Text of the Laws of Burgos
(1512–1513) Concerning the Treatment of the Indians," *Hispanic American Historical Review*
12, no. 3 (1932); Lesley Byrd Simpson, ed. *The Laws of Burgos of 1512–1513: Royal Ordinances
for the Good Government and Treatment of the Indians* (San Francisco: John Howell, 1960).
On the *juntas*, the ensuing legislation, and the *Requerimiento*, see Medina, *Una comunidad*;
Hanke, *Spanish Struggle*, 31–36; Moya Pons, *Después de Colón*, 70–98; James Muldoon, "John
Wyclif and the Rights of the Infidels: The Requerimiento Re-Examined," *The Americas* 36, no. 3
(1980); Pagden, *Fall of Natural Man*, 47–56; Ramos, "Hecho de la Conquista," 36–46; "El P.
Córdoba y Las Casas en el plan de conquista pacífica de Tierra Firme," *Boletín Americanista*
1, no. 3 (1959). The consultative institution of the *junta* is discussed by Pagden, *Fall of Natural
Man*, 27–28.
[17] Moya Pons, *Después de Colón*, 89–94.

was envisioned as an enlarged province of Castilla d'Oro. Temporarily delayed while the *junta* was deliberating in Burgos, Dávila took up his new position in America in 1514. His rule replaced Balboa's peaceful cohabitation with ruthless raiding, plundering, and enslavement of indigenous communities farther and farther inland.[18]

Despite these setbacks, the Dominicans continued to work after 1513 for changes in imperial policies on two fronts: a reform of existing exploitative institutions in Hispaniola and an attempt to prevent their spread on the American mainland that increasingly became the target of Spanish conquest. Montesino and Pedro de Córdoba returned to Hispaniola in 1513, the latter with a royal license authorizing preaching in Tierra Firme on the Venezuelan coast.

Perhaps the most significant development in these years was their success in recruiting into their ranks an *encomendero* who not only joined the humanitarian enterprise, but became the most radical and active agent for reform of Spanish imperialism in the coming decades: Bartolomé de Las Casas (1484–1566).[19] Las Casas had been exposed to the new world of Spanish overseas possessions ever since his childhood in Seville. His impoverished merchant father sought to improve his fortunes by enrolling in Columbus's second expedition. For his next overseas voyage, this time with the ships carrying the newly appointed governor Nicolás de Ovando to Hispaniola in 1502, the father was joined by the young Bartolomé, by now a priest. On the island, Las Casas established himself as *encomendero*. In 1513, he was enlisted as chaplain in the campaign for "pacification" of Cuba where the massacre of indigenous people by his fellow "pacifier" Pánfilo de Narváez was perhaps his first exposure to the atrocities of conquest. Las Casas withdrew from the campaign and, again, settled as *encomendero*, this time in Cuba.

In these years, Las Casas did not ponder much the injustice of the exploitation of indigenous labor. The first seeds of doubt seem to have been planted in him by encounters with Dominicans who, in Hispaniola and Cuba, questioned his conduct and once denied him the absolution of sins on the account of his exploitation of indigenous labor. Only in 1514 did Las Casas's view transform radically. As he reported the events more than a decade later in his *History of the Indies*, he began contemplating the suffering of the conquered and the Dominican policy to refuse confession and absolution to owners of Indians while studying, in preparation for a sermon, the passage from *Ecclesiasticus* (or *The Book of Sirach*, verse 34) on God's displeasure with offerings acquired through illicit means. After several days of meditation and reading, he was overwhelmed by a strong conviction that the "Indians were being treated unjustly and tyrannically all over the Indies." Adopting the Dominicans'

---

[18] Sauer, *Early Spanish Main*, 219–75.
[19] On Las Casas's date of birth, see Helen Rand Parish and Harold E. Weidman, "The Correct Birthdate of Bartolomé De Las Casas," *Hispanic American Historical Review* 56, no. 3 (1976).

radical position, Las Casas denounced the injustice and abuses committed by the Spaniards in his sermon for Assumption, proclaimed that no one owning and exploiting Indians could win salvation and, to prove his point, publicly announced that he relinquished his own charges.

Las Casas thus joined the team of humanitarian Dominicans and de Córdoba and Montesino couched him in the arts of political intervention. From that point on, critique of the Spanish treatment of indigenous people and reform of Spanish imperialism remained the main preoccupations of Las Casas's life. Along with Montesino, he returned to Spain in 1515 to seek again the intervention of authorities against the expropriation of the lands of indigenous people and their enslavement. Armed with letters of recommendation from de Córdoba, Las Casas was able to speak to the king, presenting him with a dire picture of the exploitation and the extinction of the Indians and urging measures against the *encomenderos* and their abuses. After another attempt to see the King failed, he had to present his petition to Archbishop Fonseca, the de facto minister of colonies, who scolded him as a fool in front of his servants. Las Casas's lobbying earned him the enduring animosity of both Fonseca and the powerful Royal Secretary Lope Conchillos who, *encomenderos* themselves, represented the interests of the settlers in the court.[20]

REFORM

The political situation at the court, however, became much more promising after Ferdinand's death in 1516. Adrian of Utrecht and Cardinal Francisco Jiménez de Cisneros were appointed regents during the minority of the new monarch, Charles V. Both were sympathetic to the Dominicans. Las Casas presented them with three memorials, describing the abuses against indigenous labor, the measures needed to be taken to prevent these abuses, and the corrupt character of the officials appointed by Ferdinand.

There was no doubt that the economy in Hispaniola was in a deep crisis and reforms were needed urgently to supplement the moribund gold production with other activities. Cisneros, in particular, was determined to reform the colonial administration. Fonseca and his clique who had run the affairs of the Indies up to this point found themselves in disgrace and were excluded from the administration.

Cisneros responded to Las Casas's memorials for reform in the overseas territories with yet another *junta* and investigation of the government of Hispaniola. Las Casas and Montesino presented an elaborate plan for reform that tried to reconcile two contradictory goals: the freeing of indigenous people

---

[20] See Casas, *History of the Indies*, 210–11; Casas, *Historia de las Indias*, 2080–85; and Giménez Fernández, "Fray Bartolomé de Las Casas: A Biographical Sketch," in *Bartolomé de las Casas in History: Toward an Understanding of the Man and His Work*, eds. Juan Friede and Benjamin Keen (DeKalb: Northern Illinois University Press, 1971); Medina, *Una comunidad*.

from forced labor while improving the economy and the welfare of Spanish settlers. In addition to the abolition of *encomiendas*, the plan recommended the emigration to Tierra Firme of Spanish laborers and farmers as alternative labor force.

After studying the plan, the royal bureaucrats adopted most of it. Cisneros appointed three members of the monastic order of Hieronymites to conduct the envisioned reforms in Hispaniola. They were given full authority over royal officers on the island, including the power to dismiss them. The goal was to eradicate abuses by establishing a paternalistic tutelary government over indigenous people resettled in villages free from the authority of Spanish settlers. In addition, a new judge, Alonso de Zuazo, was placed under the authority of the Hieronymites to examine and reform the administration on this island.

The Hieronymites (Luis de Figueroa, Alonso de Santo Domingo, and Bernardino de Manzanedo) arrived in Hispaniola in 1517 and, as a first step, tried to gain knowledge of the situation by interviewing fourteen officials and friars. Although the majority of the interviews were in favor of the continuation of the *encomienda* system, the Hieronymites moved toward dismantling the *encomiendas* and establishing free villages.

Yet they were forced to proceed more cautiously than they intended. The reform plans conceived by the Dominicans were simply too radical to be realistically implemented. With the gold deposits on the island exhausted, the Spanish community was in a demoralized critical condition. Diseases imported from Europe, malnutrition, and armed conflicts took their toll among Europeans and Taínos, the mortality among the latter significantly increased by the exploitation to which they were subjected by their Spanish overlords. Some of the Europeans moved to exploit the American mainland, while those remaining on the island feared that the Crown would abandon Hispaniola and deprive them of much-needed protection.

In this unsettled atmosphere, the Hieronymites were careful not to provoke an open rebellion by immediately dismantling all the *encomiendas*. Instead, they moved to free villages only the Indios assigned in *encomiendas* to absentee courtiers. Only in 1518 did they proceed toward creating villages for the rest of the indigenous population with the goal to abolish the entire *encomienda* system. Judge Zuazo, on his part, held court, heard accusations against judges and royal officials, and suspended the judges of the royal *audiencia*.

These actions provoked the resolute opposition of settlers and royal officials who sabotaged the reforms and sent a representative to the royal court to denounce the damage these plans were causing to the island society. Ironically, the Hispaniola Dominicans were equally unhappy with what they considered to be half-hearted measures against the exploitation and abuses and voiced their complaints to the Crown, too.

Meanwhile, they continued with their efforts to prevent the infiltration of the American mainland and hitherto unconquered islands by Spanish settlers and forestall the abuses to which they subjected indigenous people there. In cooperation with a group of observant Franciscans originating most probably from Picardy, they attempted to initiate peaceful and fair trading with the inhabitants of Tierra Firme, while excluding settlers from their territory. Yet despite the official ban, settlers continued to trade in pearls and capture slaves. Dominicans and Franciscans denounced the abuses in sermons and, in a letter addressed to the Hieronymites, they made the strong claim that it is far better to not Christianize the "Indians" than to expose them to the inhumane treatment allotted to them by the Spanish. Under increasing hostility of the settlers, Las Casas, who had returned shortly after the Hieronymites' arrival, had to seek refuge in the Dominican monastery.[21]

THE END OF THE FIRST WAVE OF PROTESTS AND REFORMS

In June 1517, Las Casas and another friar, Pedro de San Martín, were dispatched again to Castile to plead the reformist cause. There Las Casas delivered letters signed by the Dominicans and Franciscans to the regents and Charles's favorite, de Xevres, as well as a strongly worded letter to the king himself, in which Pedro de Córdoba warned that the salvation of the monarch's soul depended on urgent action to prevent the depopulation of his overseas territories.

In the interim, the situation in the court had changed for the worse. The reform-minded Cisneros died in 1517 exactly as Charles V, intent on taking possession of his Spanish dominions, was informing him in a letter that his services as regent would not be needed anymore. Lope Conchillos and others from the pro-settler clique in Ferdinand's administration who had been in disgrace during Cisneros's regency hastened to Flanders where they offered their services to Charles and were duly reappointed. Settlers in Hispaniola whose interests were harmed by the reforms of the Hieronymites and Zuazo sensed that the court might be more favorable to their grievances. In the elections for *procurador* in Spain, they were able to elect one Lope de Bardecí whose remonstrances against the reformers were lent a sympathetic ear by Fonseca and his clique, now reappointed by Charles. At the same time, Las Casas cultivated successfully contacts with the king's new Flemish courtiers around the chancellor Jean Le Sauvage who were opposed to Ferdinand's old hands around Fonseca.

Le Sauvage died in June 1518 and the administration of the Indies was entrusted once again to Fonseca. Empowered thus, he suspended the authority granted to the Hieronymites and Zuazo. After having prosecuted the abusers, now Zuazo himself was put on trial in Hispaniola by the judge who replaced him, Rodrigo de Figueroa. Charles V, responding to Las Casas and his Flemish

---

[21] Moya Pons, *Después de Colón*, 131–39; Medina, *Una comunidad*; Esteban Mira Caballos, "La primera utopía americana: Las reducciones de indios de los jéronimos en la Española (1517–1519)," *Jahrbuch für Geschichte Lateinamerikas* 39 (2002); Giménez Fernández, "Fray Bartolomé de Las Casas," 74–75.

allies in the court, did in fact instruct Rodrigo to implement strictly the Laws of Burgos. Yet it was too late. The Hieronymites had been able to set up seventeen nominally free villages for a population that now was being decimated by a smallpox epidemic. The villages failed to live up to their promise as the Spaniards appointed to supervise them continued the usual pattern of abuse and exploitation. The experiment failed and at the end, the few people remaining in the depopulated villages were again assigned as forced labor to Spanish overlords. Abetted by colluding Castilian nobles who would not let their vassals emigrate, Fonseca sabotaged the other part of Las Casas's project, the proposed settlement of Spanish laborers and farmers in Tierra Firme.

The demographic decline of the indigenous population of Hispaniola under the onslaught of European diseases and exploitation was irreversible. The Dominicans on the island turned their attention to the prevention of the trade in slaves that now increasingly provided the work force in the island. Pedro de Córdoba, however, was unsuccessful in his continuing attempt to impose ecclesiastical control over contacts with inhabitants of Tierra Firme. In 1519, in the face of the vigorous opposition of the Fonseca faction, Las Casas was able to obtain from the royal court authorization for a project of peaceful colonization and evangelization of Tierra Firme. Only royal officials and religious committed to peaceful evangelization were allowed in the territory allotted on the Venezuelan coast.

The project proved fraught with problems from the very beginning. The continuing entries of Spanish settlers from the islands in search of slaves and goods provoked the hostility of indigenous communities who killed the Observant Franciscan missionaries living among them in 1520. In Spain, Las Casas was not able to raise sufficient funds needed for the enterprise. After his arrival in Cumaná on Tierra Firme, the Spanish there openly contested his authority and continued their slaving raids among the indigenous people Las Casas had set out to evangelize peacefully. Unable to stop the slaving, he was forced to turn to the authorities in Cubagua and Hispaniola. In his absence, his second in command on the small settlement, Francisco de Soto, himself led the settlers on a slaving expedition. The remaining settlers were attacked by Indians. Las Casas's first experiment of peaceful colonization and evangelization was a complete failure.[22]

****

Two intertwined yet contradictory developments took shape in the first imperial outpost of Hispaniola: the consolidation of a predatory political and moral

---

[22] On these developments, see Cook, "Sickness, Starvation, and Death"; Elliott, "Spanish Conquest," 168–69; Giménez Fernández, "Fray Bartolomé de Las Casas," 77–82; Lewis Hanke, *The First Social Experiments in America: A Study in the Development of Spanish Indian Policy in the Sixteenth Century* (Cambridge: Harvard University Press, 1935); Lewis Hanke *Spanish Struggle*; Medina, *Una comunidad*; Mira Caballos, "Primera utopía"; Moya Pons, *Después de Colón*, 141–71; Ramos, "El P. Córdoba."

regime and the accompanying emergence of a religiously inspired confrontation with the dual morality of empire. By the 1520s, a network of Dominicans had mobilized political activities against the exploitation of indigenous labor in Hispaniola and the surrounding Caribbean Islands. By then, this network had also suffered its first defeat.

The sequence of events unleashed with Antón Montesino's sermon 1511 is exemplary of a persistent pattern of interactions that occurred repeatedly both before the beginnings of Spanish expansion overseas and in several imperial contexts afterward. The Dominican confrontation with political expansion was, as we saw, not different from what numerous religious specialists had already done and said in the context of expansionism into the European borderlands in Eastern Europe and the Canary Islands. And, as we will see, the same pattern of interactions will repeat itself at several junctures of European imperial history and will eventually take a life of its own as a taken for granted institutional model of long-distance advocacy. In this sense, Hispaniola, the first outpost of Spanish overseas expansion, was a microcosm in which we can clearly discern the outlines of the larger logic of European imperialism and, more importantly for the argument of this book, of the institutional genesis of a humanitarian counterpoint against this logic. The Dominicans' protests of the 1510s were the first systematic condemnation of the fundamental structures of an emerging predatory overseas imperialism. They also heralded a period of continuous religious assault on the ethics of Iberian conquest of America that forms the subject of Chapter 2.

2

Pro-Indigenist Advocacy in the Iberian Atlantic

After Hispaniola, Spanish expansion proceeded in the same exploitative and violent way. Restless adventurers sought to make their fortunes in the neighboring islands and the American mainland. Since 1514, the pattern established initially on the island repeated itself on the continent. Spanish authority in the Americas was spreading geographically and becoming more permanent with the establishment of government structures in new territories. At the same time, the Crown increasingly sought a tighter bureaucratic grip over American political and economic matters, creating in 1524 the Royal Council of the Indies as the supreme office overseeing colonial affairs.[1]

The exploitative arrangements "pioneered" in Hispaniola were reproduced elsewhere in the American main. After imposing his authority on the valley of Mexico, Hernán Cortés replaced the existing system of tribute with the *encomienda* that had been tried out already in Hispaniola with disastrous results. When a royal order prohibited *encomiendas* in 1523, Cortés disobeyed. Like Columbus earlier, he argued he had no choice but give in to his soldiers' demands for riches. The situation of the conquered Indians under *encomiendas*, especially in the first post-conquest years, was virtually undistinguishable from enslavement. Abuses were again rampant as indigenous communities were exploited to provide the required tribute and taxes. In addition, adjacent "unpacified" territories were raided for slaves who were then put to work for the Spaniards. Francisco Pizarro's conquest of Peru in the 1530s unleashed a similar sequence of events. Local populations, "liberated" from Inca dependency,

---

[1] Elliott, "Spanish Conquest," 290; John E. Kicza, "Patterns in Early Spanish Overseas Expansion," *The William and Mary Quarterly* 49, no. 2 (1992); Antonio Muro Orejón, "El Real y Supremo Consejo de las Indias," *Anuario de Estudios Americanos* 27 (1970).

were plundered, assessed tributes, assigned in *encomiendas*, and appointed as personal retainers to Spaniards.[2]

In each newly conquered territory, disease, demoralization, and exploitation assaulted the indigenous populations. To replenish dwindling labor supplies, the Spanish raided and enslaved people from neighboring territories who were nominally not yet the Crown's protected subjects. The exploitation of indigenous labor was institutionalized in a variety of local forms, many of them adopted from preexisting customs. Enslaved labor, often transported throughout the continent, consisted of both *esclavos de guerra* – captured Indians who presumably resisted Spanish authority unlawfully – and *esclavos de rescate* who were "legitimately" purchased and "rescued" from indigenous owners. There were other arrangements for communal and individual forced labor, such as the *naborías* or debt peons and the *tamemes* who served as burden bearers.[3]

THE RESUMPTION OF ADVOCACY IN AN EXPANDING EMPIRE

Even as military conquest gained momentum in the 1520s, the Dominican project initiated a decade earlier was a spent force. Shaken by the disastrous failure of his experiment in pacific colonization in Cumaná in 1522, Las Casas retreated from political involvement and prepared himself for admission into the Dominican order. The years around his profession of obedience to the order in 1524, he spent most of his time in seclusion, studying theological questions. He also began working on a series of books documenting the injustices of Spanish rule and outlining proposals for reform. Only occasionally did he emerge in public to address abuses, as when he denounced the flourishing trade in enslaved indigenous people in 1523. At the same time, a serious split

---

[2] See James Lockhart, *Of Things of the Indies: Essays Old and New in Early Latin American History* (Stanford: Stanford University Press, 1999), 1–26; Dan Stanislawski, *The Transformation of Nicaragua, 1519–1548* (Berkeley: University of California Press, 1983); Steve J. Stern, *Peru's Indian Peoples and the Challenge of Spanish Conquest: Huamanga to 1640* (Madison: University of Wisconsin Press, 1982); Kristine L. Jones, "Warfare, Reorganization, and Readaptation at the Margins of Spanish Rule: The Southern Margin (1573–1882)," in *The Cambridge History of the Native Peoples of the Americas*, Vol. III: *South America*, Part 2, eds. Frank Salomon and Stuart B. Schwartz (Cambridge: Cambridge University Press, 1999); Charles Gibson, *The Aztecs under Spanish Rule: A History of the Indians of the Valley of Mexico, 1519–1810* (Stanford: Stanford University Press, 1964); Luis J. Ramos Gómez and María Concepción Blasco, "En torno al origen del tributo indigena en la Nueva España y su evolución en la primera mitad del siglo XVI," in *Estudios sobre política indigenista española en América*, v. II (Valladolid: Seminario de Historia de América, Universidad de Valladolid, 1975); Karen Spalding, "The Crises and Transformations of Invaded Societies: Andean Area (1500–1580)," in *The Cambridge History of the Native Peoples of the Americas South America*, Vol. III: *South America*, Part 1, eds. Frank Salomon and Stuart B. Schwartz (Cambridge: Cambridge University Press, 1999).

[3] See O. Nigel Bolland, "Colonization and Slavery in Central America," *Slavery & Abolition* 15, no. 2 (1994): 12–18; Noble David Cook, *Born to Die: Disease and New World Conquest, 1492–1650* (Cambridge: Cambridge University Press, 1998); William L. Sherman, *Forced Native Labor in Sixteenth-Century Central America* (Lincoln: University of Nebraska Press, 1979).

developed within the Hispaniola Dominican community. Reacting, most likely, to the slaying of Dominican missionaries in Chiribichí on the American main, some friars retreated from the indigenist position and gradually developed a starkly negative view of indigenous people.

In 1526, Las Casas emerged again from his seclusion to protest the continuing slave trade with the *audiencia* in Santo Domingo. Almost immediately, however, his Dominican superiors ordered him to go and found a new friary in Puerto de Plata in the northern part of the island. There, too, he appealed to local authorities and to the Council of the Indies, denouncing violent conquest, the exploitation in *encomiendas*, and the flourishing trade in enslaved indigenous people.[4]

Meanwhile another mendicant, the Franciscan Juan de Zumárraga, found himself and his subordinates embroiled in a contentious confrontation with secular authorities in Mexico. In 1527, Zumárraga was appointed missionary bishop in the newly conquered territory. Ever since Las Casas received the official title of "Protector of Indians" in 1516, newly appointed bishops were granted the same title and the corresponding jurisdiction.[5] Zumárraga took this office seriously and referred indigenous complaints against Spaniards to the *audiencia*, the group of officials appointed to oversee the administration of the province as representatives of the monarch. Yet the *audiencia* rebuffed him, claiming that he did not have jurisdiction over such matters. When Zumárraga persisted, the *oidores* threatened him with legal sanctions and exile, while threatening to hang those Aztecs who should discuss their complaints with the bishop. The scare tactics worked and Zumárraga found himself increasingly isolated socially. Undaunted, he denounced the *oidores'* behavior in sermons and threatened to take the issue to "... the king (who by then was also the reigning emperor of the Holy Roman Empire as Charles V)". In secret, he was also contacted by the indigenous inhabitants of Huejotzingo who complained over the illegal tributes various Spanish functionaries imposed on them. Again, Zumárraga demanded an explanation from the *oidores*. They, in turn, not only threatened to hang him for treason, but also arrested the petitioners who, warned by the bishop, had taken refuge in a Franciscan convent.

As the conflict escalated with this violation of ecclesiastical refuge, the besieged Franciscans dispatched a friar, Antonio Ortíz, to denounce the abuses in a sermon in Mexico City. The sermon during mass on Pentecost produced a skirmish as partisans of the *oidores* assaulted Ortíz who, in response, barred them from attending mass and proclaimed them excommunicated the following

---

[4] Giménez Fernández, "Fray Bartolomé de Las Casas," 82–84; Carlos Sempat Assadourian, "Hacia la *Sublimis Deus*: Las discordias entre los dominicos indianos y el enfrentamiento del franciscano padre Tastera con el padre Betanzos," *Historia Mexicana* 47, no. 3 (1998); Helen Rand Parish and Harold E. Weidman, *Las Casas en México: Historia y obras desconocidas* (Mexico City, Mexico: Fondo de Cultura Económica, 1992), 90–91.

[5] Enrique Dussel, *Les évêques hispano-américains: Défenseurs et évangélisateurs de l'Indien, 1504–1620* (Wiesbaden: Franz Steiner, 1970).

day. The *audiencia* in turn proclaimed Ortíz exiled and cut off the food supply from the church where he took refuge. Bishop Zumárraga returned to Mexico City and eventually forced the *oidores* to do penance for their actions.[6]

In marked contrast with Zumárraga and the other Franciscans, the twelve Dominicans who had entered Mexico in 1526 did not bring along their earlier opposition to conquest. Their leaders, Tomás Ortíz and, later, Domingo de Betanzos, came from the faction that had become increasingly hostile to indigenous people in the aftermath of the massacre of missionaries in 1521. In fact, their memorials to the Council of the Indies lent support to a decree that legalized the enslavement of the inhabitants of Cumaná and, as we will see, Betanzos's statements were to produce a big controversy in the early 1530s.[7]

The indigenist Dominicans in Hispaniola, however, resumed their activities toward the end of the decade. In 1529, they dispatched to Spain a memorial against the enslavement of indigenous people. In the *junta* convened to discuss the issue, their representatives, most probably Antón de Montesino and Tomás de Berlanga, debated the representatives of the settlers. Around the same time, a denunciatory letter from Bishop Zumárraga in Mexico resulted in the deposition of the exploitative *audiencia*. The instructions for the new (second) *audiencia* in Mexico in 1530 explicitly prohibited enslavement and this prohibition was further strengthened by a more general law against slavery in the colonies.[8]

In Peru, another Dominican, Bernardino de Minaya, found himself embroiled in conflict with secular authorities. When indigenous people were enslaved there for sale in Panamá, Minaya went to remind Francisco Pizarro of the royal ban on enslavement. Apparently, Pizarro grudgingly made the law public, but in retaliation cut off the food supply for the Dominican and his companions. Minaya approached Pizarro again with request for assistance for a peaceful mission to the last remaining sovereign Inca ruler, Atahualpa. In Minaya's own words, he wanted to "explain to the Indians the reason for our coming: to make God known to them and not to rob them or despoil them of their lands." Pizarro bluntly refused, pointing out that he himself had come to Peru for no such reason, but to get the Indian gold. At the end, Minaya and his companions saw themselves forced to leave Peru for Mexico. Pizarro was courteous enough to offer Minaya his share of despoiled gold, which Minaya

---

[6] The tug of war between the Franciscans and the *audiencia* in Mexico continued for years afterward. See Robert Ricard, *The Spiritual Conquest of Mexico: An Essay on the Apostolate and the Evangelizing Methods of the Mendicant Orders in New Spain, 1523–1572* (Berkeley: University of California Press, 1966), 255–59; Jorge E. Traslosheros, "En derecho y en justicia: Fray Juan de Zumárraga, la administración de la justicia y el proyecto de iglesia de los primeros obispos de la Nueva España," in *Religión, poder y autoridad en la Nueva España*, eds. Alicia Mayer and Ernesto de la Torre Villar (Mexico City, Mexico: Universidad Nacional Autónoma de México, 2004).

[7] Assadourian, "Hacia la *Sublimis Deus*," 502–04.

[8] Parish and Weidman, *Las Casas en México*, 30.

refused, not wishing, in his words, "to lend approval by my presence to such robberies."[9]

By 1533, Las Casas, too, was in trouble with the secular authorities. As prior of the friary in Puerto de Plata, he had condemned abuses in sermons and had even persuaded a dying *encomendero* to free the indigenous laborers assigned to him and leave them his goods as reparation for their exploitation. Upset, the *audiencia* banned him from preaching for two years and forced him into the seclusion of a monastery in Santo Domingo.[10]

Advocacy Intensified

In 1532–33, the Royal Council of the Indies again solicited opinions from men on the spot on the American Indians' capacity for self-governance and Christianity. The majority of clergymen, including the first ecclesiastical *junta* of Mexico under bishop Zumárraga, reported back in terms favorable to indigenous people. Surprisingly, the Dominican Domingo de Betanzos, the Hispaniola vicar who earlier had persuaded Las Casas to enter the Dominican order, questioned, in his testimony, the ability of Indians to truly understand the Christian faith and "prophesied" the inevitable destruction of the heathen under God's dispensation as punishment for their sins. Correspondingly, Betanzos argued for perpetual *encomienda*, as well for repeal of several laws that protected indigenous rights. While in Rome, lobbying for the creation of a Dominican province in the newly conquered territory of New Spain (Mexico), Betanzos made similar statements on the inferiority of indigenous people in an audience with Pope Clement VII, supporting his negative views with a display of Aztec knives used in human sacrifices.

Betanzos's views provoked a strong reaction from Mexico where members of the new *audiencia*, Dominicans, and Franciscans sent to the royal court eight memorials of protest in 1533. This they did against the objections of local settlers who preferred that their "Indians" be subhuman and enslaveable. The memorials argued that those who proclaimed the Indians to be less than fully human and incapable of receiving the faith were in fact engaging in a conspiracy to make it easier to enslave and exploit indigenous people with impunity. In response, Betanzos reaffirmed his position in yet another memorial to the Council of the Indies in 1534. He also found a strong ally in the new president of the Council of the Indies, the Dominican bishop García de Loaysa who in 1534 revoked the anti-enslavement law of 1530.

These negative developments unleashed another wave of protest from Mexico. Slavery was again discussed and condemned by ecclesiastics in 1536 when the news reached Mexico of the harsh treatment meted out on local people by the

[9] Lewis Hanke, "Pope Paul III and the American Indians," *Harvard Theological Review* 30, no. 2 (1937): 20–21.

[10] Giménez Fernández, "Fray Bartolomé de Las Casas," 84–85; Parish and Weidman, *Las Casas en México*, 30.

former *oidor* Nuño de Guzmán in the territory he conquered to the north of the Mexico Valley, the province of Nueva Galicia. Bishops and representatives of the mendicant orders had gathered to resolve a contentious issue that divided them: the proper procedure of Indian baptism. The news of the atrocities in Nueva Galicia, however, prompted the viceroy Antonio de Mendoza to solicit the opinion of the ecclesiastical *junta* on the legality of slavery in both its legal forms: slaves of "war" captured in military conflict and "rescued" slaves – those already enslaved within indigenous communities. The *junta*, in response, condemned as illegal all varieties of slavery as well as the exploitative extraction of tribute from conquered communities. Mendoza then ordered that all slaves captured in Nueva Galicia be freed and launched an investigation on Nuño de Guzmán, who was imprisoned.[11] Meanwhile, Las Casas, freed from his detainment, continued to protest enslavement and abuses in memorials to the Council in the Indies and local authorities in Hispaniola. After a shipwreck during a trip to Peru confined him and his Dominican companions to the coast of Nicaragua in 1535, he denounced the Spanish abuses he witnessed there in yet another memorial to the emperor Charles V, while efforts to prevent a slaving expedition earned his group an expulsion from Nicaragua.[12]

Further intellectual support for the indigenist position at that time came from the faculty of the universities of Salamanca and Alcalá. In Salamanca, the Dominican professor of theology, Francisco de Vitoria, turned his attention to the problems of imperial governance after 1534. Having learned of the atrocities committed in the course of the Spanish conquest, and asked by the emperor to provide an authoritative scholarly answer to questions on the legitimacy of conquest raised by Las Casas and Bishop Zumárraga, Vitoria submitted Spanish activities in America to critical scrutiny in his lecture course and writings. Starting from the premise that all people are equal under natural law, he and his disciples made the argument that indigenous communities were autonomous and sovereign. The implication was that the imposition of Spanish control was only legitimate when based on the consent of these communities and when necessitated by the need to protect their rights. Vitoria's various disciples, mostly Dominicans trained or working at Salamanca, accepted and elaborated these views. While stopping short from a radical call for full withdrawal from America, the legal and theological critique of imperialism by this "school of Salamanca" strongly asserted the rights of American people and condemned what by then had become the typical procedure of Spanish conquest: violent warfare, appropriation of indigenous property, and forced Christianization.[13]

---

[11] *Las Casas en México*, 24–28. On the baptism controversy, see Ricard, *Spiritual Conquest*, 91–94.

[12] Giménez Fernández, "Fray Bartolomé de Las Casas," 86–88; Enrique Otte, "Un episodio desconocido de la vida de los cronistas de Indias, Bartolomé de Las Casas y Gonzalo Fernandez de Oviedo," *Ibero-Amerikanisches Archiv* 3, no. 2 (1977).

[13] See Pagden, *Fall of Natural Man*, 57–110; Luciano Pereña, "La Escuela de Salamanca y la duda Indiana," *Corpus Hispanorum de Pace* 25 (1984).

Thus, in the 1530s, despite the defection of figures like Betanzos, the indigenist network was expanding as more Dominicans and Franciscans adopted a core set of ideas: the need to reform the consolidating imperial order and prevent enslavement and abuses against the new imperial "others" who, fundamentally, shared a single human nature. Not only did these ideas spread, but the incidence and ambitions of political advocacy increased as more individuals engaged in an increasingly coordinated network. This advocacy was able to obtain two sets of official documents: one from the Papacy and one from the imperial court of Charles V. In the end, neither effected the thorough transformation of the imperial order that the friars had envisioned, yet the very production of these official statements reveals the increasing sophistication of a coordinated effort to advocate an ethical cause and influence the heads of both Church and Empire.

Sublimis Deus and the New Laws

The friar who, as a representative of the indigenist networks, was able to secure an important papal pronouncement on the rights of indigenous people was Bernardino de Minaya, whom we last saw leaving Peru after his confrontation with Pizarro. He arrived in Mexico precisely at the time the new pro-slavery ordinance of 1534 was promulgated. Armed with the written opinions of several indigenist ecclesiastics in America, he returned to Spain. Traveling from Seville to Valladolid on foot and begging, he appealed personally to Loaysa, the president of the Council of the Indies, who remained unmoved by arguments of the Indians' ability to become good Christians. Failing to persuade the council, Minaya was now determined to take his case to the Pope in Rome and a friendly council member arranged for a letter of introduction from the empress. In June 1537, he was able to secure a private audience with Paul III who was favorably disposed and appointed a committee of cardinals and theologians to study the issue. At the end, Minaya was given three official documents prepared by the committee and endorsed by the Pope.

Two of those documents were direct interventions in the debate on the humanity and rights of Indians. A brief (*Pastorale officium*) directed to Cardinal Juan Tavera, archbishop of Toledo and primate of Spain, declared that anyone who enslaved or despoiled indigenous Americans would be automatically excommunicated. The encyclical *Sublimis Deus* was addressed to all Christians and gave the papal imprimatur on virtually all the ideas that the indigenists had embraced. It stated that the Christian plan of salvation applied to the entirety of the human race and that the Indians were fully rational human beings capable of receiving the faith. In no uncertain terms, *Sublimis Deus* claimed that all Indians known so far – as well as yet to be "discovered" nations – had rights to freedom and private property, even if they were still heathen. It condemned (like the accompanying brief) those who oppressed the Indians on the pretext they were brutes and emphasized that their conversion to Christianity had to happen only through good example and preaching.[14]

Minaya's achievement was a victory for the indigenist network. Yet the endorsement by the Holy See was rendered ineffective by Charles V, intent on preserving his sovereignty in America from papal interference. The royal court was furious that Minaya had bypassed the standard royal channels of communication with Rome. In 1538, the Council of the Indies ordered Minaya sequestered in a convent and banned him from returning to America, while confiscating the originals of the papal decrees. The emperor and the empress instructed their ambassador in Rome to make sure no one received any decrees on the Indies without prior consent from the Council of the Indies. Pope Paul III himself was forced to issue a brief (*Non indecent videtur*) that annulled all his previous pronouncements on the Indies. Emperor Charles promulgated in 1539 the so-called *pase regio* ordinance, which ensured that all future papal communications in America had to be approved by the Council of the Indies for distribution. He also ordered viceroy Mendoza of New Spain to collect and destroy all copies of the decrees obtained by Minaya. Another order directed the prior of the Dominican Colegio San Esteban in Salamanca to stop any public discussions and lectures on the Indies and confiscate any books on the subject.[15]

That Charles had to explicitly ban public discussions of the New World problems in Spain was, in itself, an indication of the growing influence of the indigenist project and its power to disseminate information on abuses in the metropole. The Cortes of Castile, the meeting of the estates that otherwise had no say in overseas affairs, was moved in 1542 to petition the monarch to "remedy the cruelties inflicted upon the Indians," which would only serve God and preserve the Indies from impending depopulation.[16] Much of that was the work of Las Casas and his associates; in 1539, he and the Franciscan Jacobo de Tastera had returned to Spain as appointed procurators for American missions. They used this opportunity to bring their case directly to Charles, seeking him out in Flanders where he was at that time. Subsequently, they were joined in

---

[14] The third papal document granted to Minaya, the bull *Altitudo divino consilii* was an intervention in the controversy on baptism, directing missionaries to observe all prescribed ceremonies. See Assadourian, "Hacia la *Sublimis Deus*"; Bruna Bocchini Camaiani, "Il papato e il nuovo mondo: A proposito di una edizione di fonti," *Cristianesimo nella Storia* 16, no. 3 (1995); Lewis Hanke, *All Mankind is One: A Study of the Disputation Between Bartolomé de Las Casas and Juan Ginés de Sepúlveda in 1550 on the Intellectual and Religious Capacity of the American Indians* (DeKalb: Northern Illinois University Press, 1974), 12–21; Parish and Weidman, *Las Casas en México*, 15–20, 27; Hanke, "Pope Paul III."

[15] "Pope Paul III," 85–86; Parish and Weidman, *Las Casas en México*, 48–51; Pereña, "La Escuela de Salamanca y la duda Indiana," 297–98.

[16] Manuel Colmeiro, ed. *Cortes de los antiguos reinos de León y de Castilla*, Vol. 5 (Madrid: Rivadeneyra, 1903), 255.

their reformist efforts by other Dominicans like Juan de Torre and Pedro de Angulo.

Presented with documented evidence of abuses accumulated by indigenist clerics, Charles then initiated an official investigation of the bodies governing imperial policies and trade: the Council of the Indies and the Casa de Contratación. Even more consequential was the extraordinary *junta* convoked by the emperor that proceeded to propose the so-called New Laws of 1542. These laws, promulgated in November, again prohibited enslavement and personal service, placed Indios under the direct administration of the Crown, and proposed stricter rules for expeditions of "discovery."[17]

CONTENTIOUS INDIGENISM IN A CONTENTIOUS IMPERIAL STATE

Undoubtedly, the new comprehensive legislation lent new powers to the indigenist project. The provisions of the New Laws aimed at reducing the power of the *encomendero* oligarchy while empowering the religious networks of empire by entrusting them with the implementation and supervision of the new legislation. The reaction from America, however, was swift and unequivocal. The *encomenderos* resented the new limitations on their power and immediately set out to protest them. Throughout Mexico, the royal officials had to suspend most of the provisions of the Laws. In Peru, the Laws did not even get a chance to be introduced as the Viceroy Blasco Núñez Vela was captured and murdered in 1546 in the midst of an uprising led by Gonzalo Pizarro. At the end, instead of fulfilling its original intent of a thorough reconfiguration of the imperial order, the most durable effect of the new legislation was to intensify further the ongoing conflict between religious and secular networks of empire.

Las Casas emerged again as a central figure in these developments. While in Spain, he accepted an offer for a bishopric in Chiapas as an opportunity to put in practice the legislation he and his allies had worked on. After recruiting forty-five Dominicans, he sailed back to his new see. En route to Chiapas, the Dominicans experienced firsthand the animosity against Las Casas and his project. While waiting in Hispaniola for their passage to Mexico in 1544, they were exposed to the opprobrium and hostility of Spaniards who refused to provide the friars with food and shunned their sermons. Similar hostility awaited them in Chiapas, where Las Casas and his companions set out to work on the implementation of the New Laws after their arrival in 1545.[18]

---

[17] Parish and Weidman, *Las Casas en México*, 43–44; Juan Pérez de Tudela Bueso, "La gran reforma carolina de las Indias en 1542," *Revista de Indias* 18 (1958). See also Assadourian, "Hacia la *Sublimis Deus*," 517–19; Hanke, "Pope Paul III"; *Spanish Struggle*, 83–105; Isacio Pérez Fernández, "Análisis extrauniversitario de la Conquista de América en los años 1534-1549," *Corpus Hispanorum de Pace* 25 (1984).

[18] Giménez Fernández, "Fray Bartolomé de Las Casas," 98–103.

Spiritual Sanctions and Political Alliances
At this point, their project was built around to two related strategies. First, Las Casas used church discipline and the priest's power to withhold absolution from the unrepentant sinner in order to force *encomenderos* and slave owners into restitution for the evils they had committed. Second, a more politically ambitious strategy involved the formation of alliances with indigenous leaders to undermine the power of the *encomendero* oligarchy.

Canon law had traditionally defined the sacraments of confession, penance, and absolution as a juridical procedure where the confessing penitent acts as the defendant and the priest pronounces a verdict that includes the actions needed by the contrite sinner to expiate for the sins committed. The denial of absolution was thus a potentially important weapon in the priest's armory. Indeed, Las Casas had a firsthand experience with this procedure as *encomendero* in the Caribbean when an unnamed Dominican had denied the absolution of his sins. By the time he assumed the Chiapas bishopric, Las Casas the cleric had already used the same weapon several times to coerce settlers into reforming. Now, his newly found power in the church hierarchy provided an opportunity to use this strategy more systematically and authoritatively. In a pastoral letter to his new parishioners, he gave sinners nine days to repent and make amends for the abuses they had committed against indigenous people. Later he systematized this policy in *Twelve Rules for Confessors* that required priests to withhold absolution of sins from guilty settlers unless the latter provided restitution for the goods and labor they had unlawfully extracted. In 1546, two ecclesiastical *juntas* in New Spain (Mexico) reaffirmed this position, condemning also the imposition of tithes on Indians and the oppressive use of Indians as personal servants to Spaniards.[19] Similar documents in other parts of the empire, as well the documented practice of coaxing restitution from *encomenderos* before their death, testify to the popularity of this policy among religious specialists in the next two decades (1950s–1960s).[20]

Even more ambitiously, Las Casas's pastoral letter in Chiapas announced another guiding principle behind the actions of his group at that time: the Church as the defender of indigenous people and the poor of the community

[19] Parish and Weidman, *Las Casas en México*, 57–62, 71–2; Jesús Antonio de la Torre Rangel, "Confesionarios: Uso del derecho canónico a favor de los Indios," in *Memoria del X congreso del Instituto Internacional de Historia del Derecho Indiano*, vol. 2 (Mexico City, Mexico: Escuela Libre de Derecho, Universidad Nacional Autónoma de México, 1995).

[20] Guillermo Lohmann Villena, "La restitución por conquistadores y encomenderos: Un aspecto de la incidencia lascasiana en el Perú," *Anuario de Estudios Americanos* 23 (1966); Pedro Borges, "Posturas de los misioneros ante la duda indiana," *Corpus Hispanorum de Pace* 25 (1984); Antonine Tibesar, "Instructions for the Confessors of Conquistadores Issued by the Archbishop of Lima in 1560," *The Americas* 3, no. 4 (1947). In Peru, the Jesuit Diego de Avendaña recommended the negation of absolution to Spaniards who exploited indigenous people as late as the first half of the seventeenth century, although it is not clear to what effect. See Ángel Losada, "Diego de Avendaño S. I. moralista y jurista, defensor de la dignidad humana de indios y negros en América," *Missionalia Hispanica* 39, no. 115 (1982).

against exploitation. In doing so, he was using the traditional notion that it was the Church's duty to protect the disadvantaged, the *miserabiles personae* of medieval cannon law. A petition to the Audiencia de los Confines (in what is today Guatemala) presented in 1545 by Las Casas, Francisco Marroquín, bishop of Guatemala, and Antonio de Valdivieso, bishop-elect of Nicaragua, reproduced almost verbatim the cannon-law definition: "nature itself moves people to feel compassion" for such "miserable persons" who cannot "defend their cause and demand justice" because of "poverty, pusillanimity, fear, or lack of skills or experience."[21]

The idea of representing and defending the rights of indigenous people who, unlike the Spanish settlers with their municipalities (*cabildos*) and elected representatives to the court (*procuradores*), did not have effective representation found expression in an additional aspect of the indigenist project in the 1540s: a political alliance with the leaders of indigenous communities and a struggle for legislation that would give these leaders more power in the imperial polity.

The Spanish conquest did not, at least in theory, abolish the existing power structures in subjugated communities. In Mexico and Peru, the Spanish in a sense replaced Aztecs and Incas as the imperial overlord to whom various subordinate groups paid tribute. Inevitably, however, the new imperial power affected deeply the distribution of power within these communities. Indigenous leaders, *caciques* and *curacas*, were responsible for collecting the tribute in goods or labor. It was in the interest of the emerging *encomendero* oligarchy to intervene and depose chiefs who did not do their bidding, replacing them with more obedient local elites willing to help the Spaniards accumulate their wealth.[22]

It was against this background that Las Casas and his allies attempted to forge an alliance with the more independent old generation of hereditary *caciques*. Already in 1543, a petition by Las Casas and Rodrigo de Andrada not only insisted that the recently enacted New Laws be supplemented with more reforms and a complete suspension of expeditions of conquest, but also urged Charles V to preserve the power of the *señores naturales*, the indigenous leaders,

---

[21] Carlos Sempat Assadourian, "Fray Bartolomé de Las Casas obispo: La naturaleza miserable de las naciones Indianas y el derecho de la iglesia. Un escrito de 1545," *Historia Mexicana* 40, no. 3 (1991): 430–31. See also Francisca Cantù, "Potere vescovile, ministero pastoral ed immunità ecclesisastica in B. de Las Casas: Note per una storia dei rapporti tra stato e chiesa nel Cinquecento," *Annuario dell'Istituto Storico Italiano per l'Età Moderna e Contemporanea* 29 (1978). On Las Casas's use of canon law, see Kenneth J. Pennington, Jr., "Bartolomé de Las Casas and the Tradition of Medieval Law," *Church History* 39, no. 2 (1970).

[22] Amos Megged, "Accommodation and Resistance of Elites in Transition: The Case of Chiapa in Early Colonial Mesoamerica," *The Hispanic American Historical Review* 71, no. 3 (1991); Susan E. Ramirez, "The 'Dueño de Indios': Thoughts on the Consequences of the Shifting Bases of Power of the 'Curaca de los Viejos Antiguos' under the Spanish in Sixteenth-Century Peru," *The Hispanic American Historical Review* 67, no. 4 (1987).

and appoint a representative (*procurador*) for their communities.[23] After the Dominicans arrived in Chiapas in 1545, they embarked on a project to free the indigenous community now residing in the city of Chiapa de Indios from the grip of the *encomendero* oligarchy. They allied themselves with the local lord Pedro Nuti, reinstated him after he was forcibly deposed and exiled by the *encomenderos* in 1546, and initiated negotiations to install him as a leader of an alliance of indigenous communities. The following year, they led a delegation of 200 to the Spanish municipality in Ciudad Real to announce their project. The *encomenderos* responded with a military expedition that again deposed Nuti and replaced him with a more docile *cacique*.[24]

Nuti was again reinstated at the end of 1547 by an inspection of representatives of the Crown, members of the Audiencia de los Confines. Their assistance, however, came after another confrontation. In 1545, Las Casas and the Dominican Antonio de Valdivieso had turned to the *audiencia* to plead for enforcement of the New Laws and for support against the recalcitrant settlers who increasingly resented the Dominicans' interference in local affairs. The *audiencia*, however, was dismissive and its secretary went as far as to verbally assault the old Las Casas – a behavior in line with the general contempt for the Dominicans as eccentric troublemakers. Las Casas proclaimed the president of the *audiencia*, Alonso de Maldonado, automatically excommunicated by his actions, and more memorials to the royal court followed.[25]

THEOLOGICAL DEBATES AND POLITICAL PROJECTS

The pattern of confrontation between religious and secular networks was repeating itself. This time, the stakes were heavily stacked against the indigenist project. The opposition to the New Laws and the Dominicans was universal and violent. Unlike Las Casas and his cohort, the official representatives of the mendicant orders were in favor of a compromise and preservation of the *encomienda* system, a position they made clear to the royal court. Alarmed at the prospect of losing his overseas possession, the monarch, too, was ready to compromise with his rebellious subjects. In 1545–46, Charles V revoked the core provisions of the New Laws that had made them a weapon in the indigenist armory: the prohibition against new *encomienda* grants, the return of existing *encomiendas* to the Crown after the holder's death, and the expropriation of *encomiendas* from those who had participated in the Peru rebellion or

[23] Hanke, *All Mankind*, 61; Pérez de Tudela Bueso, "La gran reforma carolina," 487, 498.
[24] Megged, "Accommodation and Resistance," 485–86.
[25] A third petitioner, the bishop of Guatemala Francisco Marroquín who resented Las Casas's missionary intrusions into his diocese, withdrew his signature from the petition to the *audiencia* on the day following its presentation. Apparently, he also helpfully offered to absolve the sins of those refused absolution by Las Casas. See Assadourian, "Fray Bartolomé de Las Casas obispo," 97–105; Giménez Fernández, "Fray Bartolomé de Las Casas," 99–103; Parish and Weidman, *Las Casas en México*, 333–35.

had mistreated their Indians. Ceding to complaints against the strict rules of confession and absolution, a royal ordinance in 1548 ordered the confiscation of all manuscript copies of the *Twelve Rules for Confessors,* through which Las Casas had attempted to create a universal ecclesiastical procedure for the disciplining of greedy settlers.[26]

The *encomendero* party had also found an able apologist in the scholar Juan Ginés de Sepúlveda who at least since 1535 had propounded arguments against pacifism. Sepúlveda took advantage of the controversies over the legitimacy of imperial conquest and governance to assault his scholarly rivals, the natural rights theologians in the universities of Salamanca and Alcalá aligned with the indigenist position of Las Casas and his associates. In his treatise *Democrates alter,* he argued that all wars in America were just wars necessary for the Christianization and civilization of the Indians. In stark contrast to Vittoria's view, Sepúlveda described these Indians as less than fully capable humans and citizens. The only way toward the salvation of their souls was military conquest and subjection to the culturally superior Europeans.[27]

In an attempt to counteract these unfavorable developments, Las Casas returned to Spain for one last time in 1547. He and his companion Rodrigo de Andrada had been legally authorized by indigenous communities in Oaxaca and Chiapas to represent their interests in court. A symbolic victory was the retraction by Domingo de Betanzos of his negative views on the American Indian. One year after his return to Spain in 1548, Betanzos lay on his deathbed in the monastery of San Pablo in Valladolid. There, with other Dominicans as witnesses, he formally retracted his earlier opinion and the retraction was presented to the Council of the Indies. More support came from the universities in Salamanca and Alcalá where professors, after examining Ginés de Sepúlveda's *Democrates alter,* criticized his view of Indians as natural slaves and counseled against the publication of the book. Las Casas and his allies raised once more the general question of the legitimacy of conquest and the authorities were paying attention. Expeditions of conquest were again suspended and in July 1549, the Council of the Indies recommended that the emperor order another *junta* of lawyers, theologians and officials to determine the way in which American conquests could be made "in justice and without burdening the conscience."[28]

The *junta* was duly convoked in Valladolid a year later. During its sessions in 1550–51, Ginés de Sepúlveda and Las Casas presented their opposing

---

[26] Lino Gómez Canedo, "Aspectos caracteristicos de la acción Franciscana en America," *Archivo Ibero-Americano* 48, nos. 189–92 (1988): 462–72; Hanke, *Spanish Struggle,* 95–105.

[27] The full title is *Democrates secundus sive de justis causis belli apud Indos.* See Pagden, *Fall of Natural Man,* 109–18. On the context of the confrontation between theologians and "humanists" like Ginés de Sepúlveda, see Melquiades Andrés Martín, "Evangelismo, humanismo, reforma y observancias en España (1450–1525)," *Missionalia hispanica* 23 (1966).

[28] Cited in Jaime González Rodríguez, "La Junta de Valladolid convocada por el Emperador," *Corpus Hispanorum de Pace* 25 (1984): 215. See also Giménez Fernández, "Fray Bartolomé de Las Casas," 107–10; Hanke, *All Mankind,* 28–32; *Spanish Struggle,* 111–32.

arguments on the justification of Spanish conquest. The answer to the overriding question whether war was a proper way to spread Christianity in the "New World" depended on whether – as Ginés de Sepúlveda argued – its inhabitants were so inferior in their humanity and capacity that only violent conquest could lift them from this state of inferiority and barbarity. Ultimately, the result of the *junta* in Valladolid was inconclusive. It did not produce unambiguous policy guidelines and in the subsequent years the Crown continued its inconsistent and contradictory policies in America. Official documents largely banned further conquests. Yet there was no official sanction against the ongoing conquest of Chile, even though in 1554 the Council of Indies referred the King to the decisions of the *junta* of Valladolid, according to which the "grave sins" committed in such conquests endanger the royal conscience. In other instructions to royal representatives between 1555 and 1563, the Crown made sure to emphasize that war was only allowed when there were no other "means."[29]

The Struggle over Perpetuity

Although it was the Sepúlveda debate that mainly captured the imagination of posterity and the interest of intellectual historians, an even more intense battle raged at the same time over the institution of *encomienda* between networks of settlers and the religious. Emboldened by their success in repealing some of the provisions, *encomenderos* continued to press for the full revocation of the 1542 New Laws. Not only that, their memorials and deputations to the court increasingly insisted on fundamental change in the institution of *encomienda* that, at least on paper, was supposed to create a temporary and mutually beneficial relationship between the Spanish lord and the Indians "commended" to him. Now *encomenderos* demanded the legalization of hereditary ownership of *encomiendas* in perpetuity coupled with complete legal jurisdiction over Indians. The new imperial oligarchy attempted, in essence, to recreate itself as a hereditary aristocracy.

This, of course, went against the policy of the Crown that continued to install a growing number of royal officials to govern the overseas territories and collect the tribute of indigenous communities directly bypassing the *encomenderos*. This revenue was desperately needed by a royal treasury that, by the 1550s, was bankrupt in result of the expensive military conflicts Charles V and – after his abdication in 1556 – Philip II undertook against Protestants and the Ottomans.

In 1549, the *encomenderos* in Peru attempted to use this situation to their advantage by instructing their agents to offer Charles a huge monetary donation in exchange for the perpetuity of *encomiendas*. The emperor was not adverse to the suggestion and instructed the president of the Council of the Indies to convoke yet another *junta* and discuss the issue. When the experts

[29] González Rodríguez, "Junta"; Hanke, *All Mankind*.

met in 1550 in Valladolid, the majority of them were in favor of perpetuity. A final decision to that effect was prevented only by the last-minute intervention of Las Casas and his allies who proposed postponement until the absent emperor's return to Spain.

In 1552, the Royal Council of the Treasury (Hacienda) proposed again that *encomiendas* be sold in perpetuity against much needed revenue, not unlike the offices that the Crown began selling in 1556. Another *junta* convoked by Charles in London 1554 came with a recommendation confirming the legality of such sale. Two years later, however, when Philip instructed the Council of the Indies to initiate the procedure, the Council defied the order and responded with a detailed critique of the proposal that clearly reproduced the language of the indigenist project of alliance with indigenous rulers. The Council's letter pointed out that indigenous chiefs were the natural holders of civil and criminal jurisdiction and that the fate of the *encomienda* system had to be decided by convocations of the inhabitants of towns in Peru. Not ready to drop the issue, in 1559, Philip appointed three commissioners to investigate the propriety of granting perpetual *encomiendas*. The instructions they received also discreetly suggested the possibility of obtaining monetary donations from Indians, should the *encomenderos'* demand not be granted.

Already in 1552, the Franciscans in New Spain had sent their representative (and reformed *encomendero*) José Angulo not only to denounce the abuses against indigenous people, but also to make a counteroffer to the Crown: local lords were ready to pay an amount exceeding what the *encomenderos* offered in exchange for abolition of the *encomienda*. By 1559 in Peru, too, *curakas*, the local chiefs of Indian communities, began to mobilize against the *encomendero* project, delegating authority to Las Casas and another Dominican, Domingo de Santo Tomás, as their representatives.

Santo Tomás had memorialized Charles in 1550 from Peru, describing the Spaniards' abuses and decrying forced labor in the newly developed silver mines which he described as "the mouth of hell." Since his return to Europe in 1555, he had accompanied the peregrinations of the royal court lobbying for imperial reform. A memorial to Philip II in 1560 written jointly with Las Casas made a strong case against the perpetuity of *encomienda* inheritance which, the two Dominicans argued, would increase the exploitation of Indians and thus prevent the monarch from discharging his duty to protect and evangelize them. They asked that a representative assembly like the Spanish regional Cortes be convoked among the indigenous communities to discuss such an important question. Through Las Casas and Santo Tomás, the *curakas* in Peru offered the Crown 100,000 ducats more than what the *encomenderos* would bid in exchange of royal guarantees for the rights and liberties of their communities. The following year, Santo Tomás returned to Peru and along with other Dominicans and Franciscans, began a series of conferences with hundreds of *curakas*, continuing thus the indigenist mobilization against perpetuity. When the heads of the three mendicant orders in New Spain returned to Spain in

1562, the Dominican provincial Pedro de la Peña had the authorization from Mexican *caciques* to negotiate a pact with the Crown.[30]

THE CONSOLIDATION OF PROTEST AND THE CONSOLIDATION OF THE STATE

Despite the urgency displayed by competing indigenists and *encomenderos*, the Crown was biding its time. In fact, as we will see, when a more conclusive royal policy was articulated in the 1570s, it adopted neither of the two alternatives. In the meantime, while the struggle against hereditary *encomiendas* formed an important focus for advocacy by the indigenist party, its members continued to attack other imperial abuses.

In Seville, Las Casas was able to publish a series of treatises in 1552 and 1553, including his rules for confessors that had been confiscated earlier. The printing of these gave additional publicity to the indigenenist platform, this time even outside of Spain.[31] By that time, the indigenist members of the mendicant orders had developed an ambitious and systematic project of political advocacy. The two main targets of this advocacy were identified by Las Casas in his 1552 pamphlet, *A Most Brief Account of the Destruction of the Indies*, as two varieties of Spanish "infernal tyranny." First, "unjust, cruel, bloody, and tyrannical warfare" deprive indigenous societies of those who would represent them effectively, creating, second – "the hardest, harshest, and most heinous bondage to which men or beasts might ever be bound into."[32]

Although Las Casas himself passed away in 1566, the 1560s were years of particularly intense advocacy by a network of mendicants that had matured since the 1520s. Dominicans and Franciscans continued to assault military conquest and the economic exploitation of indigenous people in memorials and appeals to political authority. In fact, the language of these appeals became increasingly uncompromising, describing the intolerable burdens these abuses put on the monarch's conscience. The Franciscan Gerónimo de Mendieta from

---

[30] Carlos Sempat Assadourian, *Transiciones hacia el Sistema Colonial Andino* (Lima: Instituto de Estudios Peruanos, 1994); "Fray Alonso de Maldonado: La política indiana, el estado de damnación del Rey Católico y la Inquisición," *Historia Mexicana* 38, no. 4 (1989); Peter Bakewell, "La maduración del gobierno del Perú en la década de 1560," *Historia Mexicana* 39, no. 1 (1989); Giménez Fernández, "Fray Bartolomé de Las Casas," 112–14; Marvin Goldwert, "La lucha por la perpetuidad de las encomiendas en el Perú virreinal, 1550–1600," *Revista Histórica* 22 (1955–56); Gómez Canedo, "Aspectos caracteristicos," 471–72 (on Angulo); John V. Murra, "'Nos Hazen Mucha Ventaja': The Early European Perception of Andean Achievement," in *Transatlantic Encounters: Europeans and Andeans in the Sixteenth Century*, eds. Kenneth J. Andrien and Rolena Adorno (Berkeley: University of California Press, 1991); José María Vargas, *Fr. Domingo de Santo Tomás, defensor y apóstol de los indios del Perú: Su vida y sus escritos* (Quito, Ecuador: Editorial Santo Domingo, 1937).

[31] Hanke, *All Mankind*, 115; Giménez Fernández, "Fray Bartolomé de Las Casas," 112.

[32] Bartolomé de las Casas, *An Account, Much Abbreviated, of the Destruction of the Indies, with Related Texts* (Indianapolis: Hackett Publishing, 2003), 7.

Mexico insisted the monarch was "obligated" to preserve the power of indigenous leaders in a memorial that reminded Philip of the possible perdition of his soul should exploitation in his overseas realm continue. Francisco de Morales, another Franciscan in Peru, condemned a situation where "poor and wretched" Indians were paying not only for the vanity of the settlers, but also for royal ministers and wars in Flanders.[33]

The Growth of State Power and the Stifling of Religious Dissent

The monarch and the Council of the Indies were not insensitive to these pleas. Yet the rules of the political game were changing and the indigenist mendicants' influence was on the wane. With most of the vast American territories in Mexico, Central America, and Peru now firmly under Spanish authority, the Crown embarked on an ambitious and ultimately successful project to consolidate imperial governance and concentrate it in royal hands. Even as the Flemish revolt and the Morisco rebellion in Granada were putting additional pressures on an already depleted royal treasury, Philip II was able to exploit the American revenue to its fullest through a strengthening administration. In the process, the vexing question of the perpetuity of *encomienda* that formed such important focus of the indigenist protest was becoming simply irrelevant. With the steady growth of a tribute-collecting royal administration and successful restrictions and regulations of *encomiendas*, a numerically strong aristocracy of powerful *encomenderos* simply failed to materialize. At the same time, religious pleas for institutions that would represent indigenous interests and for more power to indigenous chiefs fell on deaf ears. The indigenous vassals to the Crown were now little more than a source of labor and revenue and their leaders were increasingly incorporated into the administrative machine, demoted in the process to collectors of royal tributes.[34]

The foundations of more assertive and consciously interventionist state policies were laid at an important *junta* convened by Philip II in 1568. Six years later, another royal decree, the *Ordinanza del Patronazgo*, claimed stronger royal jurisdiction over distinctively religious matters and greatly reduced the mendicants' power and influence. Since the very beginnings of Spanish overseas expansion, the religious orders had provided the eager personnel entrusted

---

[33] Mendieta in Carlos Sempat Assadourian, "Memoriales de Fray Gerónimo de Mendieta," *Historia Mexicana* 37, no. 3 (1988): 359. Morales's memorial is reproduced in his "Las rentas reales, el buen gobierno y la hacienda de Dios: El parecer de 1568 de Fray Francisco de Morales sobre la reformación de las Indias temporal y espiritual," *Historica* 9, no. 1 (1985): 113. See also his "Fray Alonso de Maldonado."

[34] "The Colonial Economy: The Transfer of the European System of Production to New Spain and Peru," *Journal of Latin American Studies* 24 Supplement (1992); *Transiciones hacia el Sistema Colonial Andino*; J. H. Elliott, *Imperial Spain, 1469–1716* (New York: Penguin Books, 1963); Horst Pietschmann, *Staat und staatliche Entwicklung am Beginn der spanischen Kolonisation Amerikas* (Münster: Aschendorff, 1980); Ramirez, "'Dueño de Indios'"; Bakewell, "Maduración del gobierno"; Gibson, *Aztecs under Spanish Rule*.

with the creation of religious structures in America. Gradually, with the consolidation of Spanish settlement, religious officeholders were recruited increasingly from the ranks of the secular clergy, religious who owed their allegiance
not to the inherently transnational religious orders, but to the national church
hierarchy and its chief patron, the king.

A conflict over religious jurisdiction between seculars (the parish clergy and
bishops) and regulars (the mendicants) did not fail to develop. In important
ways, this new conflict fueled even further indigenist energies. Thus, in the
1550s, in the aftermath of a proscribed lecture course by the Augustinian ex-
Salamanca professor Alonso de la Cruz, the orders in Mexico protested vigor-
ously the imposition of tithes financing the regular church as an infringment
on the rights of indigenous people already overburdend by tributes and forced
labor. From the state's point of view, however, the implications of this conflict
were that now the Crown could exploit it for its own purposes by increasingly
vesting authority in loyal seculars. Thus, by the 1570s in the consolidating
imperial territories in America, the royal network of governance was able to
subdue its imperial rivals: the network of wealth-seeking settlers and the indigenist network of earnest evangelists.[35]

In Peru, where the unusually energetic and loyal viceroy Francisco de Toledo
governed since 1569 following the instructions provided by the 1568 *junta*, this
increasing power of the imperial state led to an outright assault on the indigenist
program and its representatives. Initiating a multiyear personal inspection of
the viceroyalty, Toledo embarked on an ambitious program of reforming the
political and economic structures there. He defeated the last bastion of Inca
resistance in Vilcabamba, organized a massive census of indigenous populations, resettled them on mass scale to rationalize taxation and the collection of
tributes, and boosted the production of silver in the mines of Potosí by reviving
and systematizing *mita*, the Incaic institution of rotating compulsory migratory
labor. Simultaneously, Toledo initiated an ideological project of codifying a
history that served the royal claim to power. According to this official historiography certified in 1572 by a gathering of Inca descendants, the Inca who had
ruled Andean communities had been usurpers and tyrants, not "natural" rulers
of the realm. It had been, in fact, the Spaniards' glorious accomplishment to
have liberated these communities from Inca tyranny.[36]

[35] Robert Charles Padden, "The Ordenanza del Patronazgo, 1574: An Interpretative Essay," *The
Americas* 12, no. 4 (1956); Demetrio Ramos, "Las crisis indiana y la Junta Magna de 1568,"
Jahrbuch für Geschichte von Staat, Wirtschaft und Gesellschaft Lateinamerikas 23 (1986);
Pietschmann, *Staat und staatliche Entwicklung*. On the tithes controversy in Mexico, see Ernest
J. Burrus, "Alonso de la Vera Cruz (†1584), Pioneer Defender of the American Indians," *Catholic
Historical Review* 70, no. 4 (1984); Georges Baudot, "L'institution de la dîme pour les Indiens
du Mexique. Remarques et documents," *Mélanges de la Casa de Velázquez* 1 (1965); Magnus
Lundberg, *Unification and Conflict: The Church Politics of Alonso de Montúfar OP, Archbishop
of Mexico, 1554–1572* (Uppsala: Swedish Institute of Missionary Research, 2002), 152–71;
Ricard, *Spiritual Conquest*, 252–54.
[36] Hanke, *Spanish Struggle*, 162–72; Manfredi Merluzzi, *Politica e governo nel Nuovo Mondo:*

This was, of course, a ringing endorsement of the harsh views represented earlier by Ginés de Sepúlveda and the exact negation of what Toledo, referring to Las Casas's former episcopal seat, disdainfully called "the doctrine of Chiapa." At the core of indigenist propaganda was a depiction of Spaniards as violent conquerors and abusers. Its proponents argued for a strengthened power of indigenous rulers and even questioned the legitimacy of conquest and royal rule over America. Now the imperial state, armed with a newly codified historiography and ideology, was able to expose the dangerous errors of the indigenists that undermined the God-given power of the Castilian Crown.

The conflict was not just a matter of historiography and ideology. A more assertive royal administration began to suppress more systematically the expressions of religious indigenist dissent. Alonso de Maldonado, a Franciscan who had returned to Spain after witnessing the harsh treatment of Chichimec prisoners of war in 1561 presented several memorials sounding the typical indigenist themes: the cruelty of Spanish oppression and the need for restitution. By 1566, he was under investigation by the Inquisition and committed to a monastery on suspicions that in his sermons he had claimed that His Majesty and the members of the Council of the Indies had their souls condemned to perdition by committing the mortal sin of oppressing the Indians. After his release in 1568, Maldonado traveled to the Vatican to bring his advocacy directly to the Pope. In Peru, viceroy Toledo similarly took advantage of the newly established tribunal of the Inquisition to intimidate his indigenist foes and went as far as to confiscate copies of Las Casas's polemical writings, apparently a popular reading material for friars in the viceroyalty. Dominicans, Augustinians, and Jesuits, in turn, waged a campaign against Toledo's new regime of forced labor in the silver mines that exposed workers to long hours, abuses, and diseases. The viceroy continued retaliating against the meddlesome friars and priests whom he thought undermined royal power in the viceroyalty.[37]

The Persistence of Conflict and Indigenism

This standoff in Peru is indicative of a highly dynamic and contentious state of affairs. Despite the strengthening of state power and its successful efforts to silence humanitarian troublemakers, the indigenist confrontations with rival networks of empire persisted. This was all the more so in the new unsettled frontiers of continuing imperial expansion where less-developed political structures were underequipped to control and stifle religious dissent. Thus, the Dominican Juan del Valle's effort to implement the New Laws in his bishopric

---

Francisco de Toledo viceré del Perù (1569–1581) (Rome: Carocci, 2003); Carlos Sempat Assadourian, "Acerca del cambio en la naturaleza del dominio sobre las Indias: La mit'a minera del virrey Toledo, documentos de 1568–1571," *Anuario de Estudios Americanos* 46 (1989); Stern, *Peru's Indian Peoples.*

[37] Assadourian, "Fray Alonso de Maldonado"; Assadourian, "Acerca del cambio"; Pedro Borges, "Un reformador de Indias y de la Orden Franciscana bajo Felipe II: Alonso Maldonado de Buendía, O.F.M.," *Archivo Ibero-Americano* 20–21, nos. 79, 80, 81 (1960/61).

in Popayán (in today's Colombia) locked him in conflict with refractory settlers. Franciscans and Jesuits protested the warfare against the unconquered agriculturalists and nomads around the silver mining center of Zacatecas in the New Spain viceroyalty, as well the exploitation of their labor. Similar protests were waged by Dominicans and Jesuits for decades in the frontiers of Chile where the independent Mapuche, by checking the southernmost flank of imperial advance, provoked the violent appetites of land- and labor-hungry settlers. From the 1570s until at least the end of the century, Augustinians and Dominicans were engaged in political struggles in the last far-flung outpost of the Mexico arm of conquest in the Philippines. Nor did the same conflictual dynamics fail to reappear in the new territories of Portuguese conquest of Brazil where the protagonists were Franciscans and Jesuits.[38]

Thus, in the second half of the sixteenth century, the members of one more – and newer – Catholic organization, the Society of Jesus, were increasingly identified with indigenist protests. In several of these instances of continuing political struggles, its actors were able to develop further the indigenist program that had crystallized earlier in the century. The Jesuits in Chile, for instance, initiated a series of peace conferences with Mapuche

---

[38] See Dauril Alden, "Black Robes Versus White Settlers: The Struggle for 'Freedom of the Indians' in Colonial Brazil," in *Attitudes of Colonial Powers toward the American Indian*, eds. Howard Peckham and Charles Gibson (Salt Lake City: University of Utah Press, 1969); Juan Friede, *Vida y luchas de don Juan del Valle, primer obispo de Popayán y protector de indios* (Popayán, Colombia: Editorial Universidad, 1961); John E. Groh, "Antonio Ruíz De Montoya and the Early Reductions in the Jesuit Province of Paraguay," *Catholic Historical Review* 56, no. 3 (1970); Lucio Gutiérrez, *Domingo de Salazar, O.P.: First Bishop of the Philippines, 1512–1594: A Study of His Life and Work* (Manila, Philippines: University of Santo Tomas, 2001); Patricio Hidalgo Nuchera, "¿Esclavitud o liberación? El fracaso de las actitudes esclavistas de los conquistadores de Filipinas," *Revista Complutense de historia de América* 20 (1994); *Las Polémicas Iglesia-Estado en las Filipinas: La posición de la Iglesia ante la Cobranza de los Tributos en las Encomiendas sin Doctrina y las Restituciones a Fines del s. XVI* (Córdoba, Spain: Universidad de Córdoba, 1993); Maxime Haubert, *L'Église et la défense des "Sauvages": Le Père Antoine Vieira au Brésil* (Brussels: Académie Royale des Sciences d'Outre-Mer, 1964); Mathias C. Kiemen, *The Indian Policy of Portugal in the Amazon Region, 1614–1693* (Washington, DC: Catholic University of America Press, 1954); Eugene H. Korth, *Spanish Policy in Colonial Chile: The Struggle for Social Justice, 1535–1700* (Stanford, CA: Stanford University Press, 1968); Miguel Ángel Medina, "La primera comunidad de dominicos en Filipinas y la defensa de los derechos de los naturales (1587–1605)," *Ciencia Tomista* 80 (1989); Ralph H. Vigil, "Bartolomé de las Casas, Judge Alonso de Zorita, and the Franciscans: A Collaborative Effort for the Spiritual Conquest of the Borderlands," *The Americas* 38, no. 1 (1981); Alida C. Metcalf, *Go-Betweens and the Colonization of Brazil, 1500–1600* (Austin: University of Texas Press, 2005); Stafford Poole, "The Last Years of Archbishop Pedro Moya de Contreras, 1586–1591," *Americas* 47, no. 1 (1990); Maria Beatriz Nizza da Silva, "Vieira e os conflitos com os Colonos do Pará e Maranhão," *Luso-Brazilian Review* 40, no. 1 (2003); Mauricio Beuchot, "Fray Juan Ramírez, O.P., y sus escritos en contra de la esclavitud de los Indios (1595)," in *Dominicos en Mesoamérica: 500 años* (Mexico City, Mexico: Provincia Santiago de México, 1992); Stafford Poole, *Pedro Moya de Contreras: Catholic Reform and Royal Power in New Spain, 1571–1591* (Berkeley: University of California Press, 1987).

leaders. The Dominicans Domingo de Salazar and Miguel de Benavides from the Philippines engaged in a remarkable attempt to give voice to otherwise voiceless imperial subjects when they wrestled from Philip II an important concession: that the legitimacy of Spanish authority be discussed in a series of public meetings of indigenous communities in 1599. The underlying pattern remained the same, however. In all these cases, the struggle was centered on attacking the intertwined issues that Las Casas had identified earlier: morally unjustified violence against non-Europeans and exploitative economic and political institutions. In all of them, religious actors were locked in a conflict with rival imperial networks. And in all of them, indigenist actors engaged in heavy political advocacy taking on the Spanish and Portuguese courts, as well as the Papal Curia in Rome.

THE INSTITUTIONALIZATION OF A POLITICAL PRACTICE

The century following Columbus's first "discoveries" witnessed the deepening of the moral divide between a Europe of increasing liberties and American colonies based on the exploitation of non-Europeans. A variety of exploitative institutions were imposed in the territories violently conquered by the Spanish Crown. These institutions created a deep inequality between European settlers and indigenous people and exposed the new imperial subjects to endless series of abuses. At the same time, the old religious counterpoint to violent conquest continued to reassert itself in the activities of various religious specialists who opposed in different ways imperial policies. Initially, this work was carried out by the network that had already taken shape with the protests and lobbying of Hispaniola Dominicans. This network grew and recruited new adherents while also provoking violent opposition and creating enemies. Simultaneously and often unconnected with this core group of activists dominated now by Bartolomé de las Casas, new groups appeared and embarked on the same collision course with exploitative secular networks of empire.

The resumption of indigenist advocacy after the initial setbacks to the Dominican project was able to produce important and consequential official legislation that, although not reaching the goals of spiritual and economic equality and justice, changed the field and rules of the imperial game. The principles enshrined in the New Laws of 1542 provided a new environment in which indigenist religious actors could take advantage of the ideological support of the imperial state. At the same time, however, their activities in this period increasingly collided with the growing strength of the state that, while in principle supportive of indigenist initiatives, grew increasingly concerned with asserting and protecting its jurisdictional powers. Yet this did not check fully the assertion of indigenist critique and reformism, which continued to flare up especially on the expanding frontiers of empire: the outposts of Spanish expansion and the new settlements under Portuguese authority.

Transpiring, as they were, at different points of time and at different parts of an enlarging imperial world, these episodes add up to a complex and unruly set of events, often deeply connected with the particulars of local circumstances and the idiosyncrasies of individual and collective mindsets. Yet we can also discern remarkably uniform patterns behind the surface of historical contingency. These developments are suggestive of two interlocking causal processes that produced them. There was the persistent and recurrent activation of the same antagonistic interactions between religious networks and their rival secular networks of empire that first emerged with such clarity within the imperial microcosm of Hispaniola. Superimposed on this cyclical pattern was another cumulative trajectory in which previous struggles leave their sediment, influencing subsequent contentious episodes and – in the process – institutionalizing standard and reproducible scripts of behavior and habits of thought.

Ideologically, there crystallized a heterogeneous yet relatively stable cultural idiom of indigenism and critique of imperialism. Las Casas's "doctrine of Chiapa" was the most consistent statement of this ideology. At one extreme, this ideology escalated into a wholesale denial of the legitimacy of Spanish conquest. The more moderate version attacked the unjust institutions of Spanish power or, even more mildly, the abuses of these institutions by unscrupulous settlers.

Concurrently, there consolidated a relatively standardized script of action – the institutional core of long-distance advocacy in its first historical version. This script involved a set of repeatedly employed activities: appeals to secular and ecclesiastical authorities in the colonies, in the royal court, and in the papal curia; the forging of political alliances with indigenous leaders; written and oral propaganda even in a restrictive environment where the publishing of books required a formal authorization; and – after Las Casas's codification of the rules of confession – the standard use of the disciplinary power of the church to influence behavior.

Note the deep historical contingency inherent in these developments. The script of long-distance advocacy was assembled in its typical configuration – and connected with a cultural idiom of indigenism – in the course of repeated and cumulative conflictual interactions.[39] The end result of this assemblage was not predetermined by the intentions of the actors involved. The friars did not set out to Spain's new imperial possessions in order to defend and represent the interests of indigenous people. Nor were all friars consistently and consciously involved in such practices. The fundamental intention behind their activities

---

[39] The analytical imagery of assemblage and creativity in collective action employed here draws on Elisabeth S. Clemens, "Organizational Form as Frame: Collective Identity and Political Strategy in the American Labor Movement, 1880–1920," in *Comparative Perspectives on Social Movements: Political Opportunities, Mobilizing Structures and Cultural Framings*, eds. Doug McAdam, John D. McCarthy, and Mayer N. Zald (Cambridge: Cambridge University Press, 1996).

was the fulfillment of the apostolic commandment to evangelize the world. Only in the course of their conflicts with opposing imperial networks of settlers and governance did they consolidate and institutionalize the distinct political practice of long-distance advocacy.

Religious Orders and Reforming Activism

Why conflicts occurred repeatedly and persistently in the overseas imperial environment was to an important extent determined by the characteristics of the specific religious actors participating in and often initiating these conflicts: the mendicant orders of Dominicans, Franciscans, and Augustinians; and later, the Jesuits – an order of clerks regular, priests who vow to lead a monastic life. That it was predominantly these organizations – and not alternative religious actors, such as the secular clergy – that were active in the administering of religion and the conversion of indigenous people in the course of Iberian imperial expansion was in a sense the natural outcome of the fact of their existence as the specialized evangelizing organs of the Catholic Church. For both the monarchy and the Papacy, the "New World" presented itself as an enticing field for evangelical activities, especially as a compensation for the lands and souls lost to the Protestant Reformation.[40] It was almost inevitable that mendicant orders would serve the self-proclaimed "Catholic" monarchs in spreading the Gospel to territories with no established regular ecclesiastical structures.

Although this choice may seem, in hindsight, inevitable and predetermined, the very fact that the first authorized purveyors of Christian grace in the Americas were members of religious orders had far-reaching implications for the trajectory of conflictual interactions. Orders were not simply the agents of evangelization, but also the repositories of a distinctive reformist and activist organizational culture. When they first emerged as a distinct organizational form in the thirteenth century, the mendicant orders were the end product of a long organizational evolution of Christian monasticism throughout the Middle Ages. The *vita apostolica* of monasticism was an enduring manifestation of the reformist impulse in Christianity toward high standards of religious observance.[41] Especially after the establishment of the influential Cistercian

---

[40] On evangelization overseas as a compensation for souls "lost" to the Reformation, see Klaus Koschorke, "Konfessionelle Spaltung und weltweite Ausbreitung des Christentums im Zeitalter der Reformation," *Zeitschrift für Theologie und Kirche* 91, no. 10–24 (1994): 15; R. Po-chia Hsia, "Mission und Konfessionalisierung in Übersee," in *Die katholische Konfessionalisierung : Wissenschaftliches Symposion der Gesellschaft zur Herausgabe des Corpus Catholicorum und des Vereins für Reformationsgeschichte, 1993*, eds. Wolfgang Reinhard and Heinz Schilling (Münster: Aschendorff, 1995), 185; Frieder Ludwig, "Zur 'Verteidigung und Verbreitung des Glaubens': Das Wirken der Jesuiten in Übersee und seine Rezeption in den konfessionellen Auseinandersetzungen Europas," *Zeitschrift fur Kirchengeschichte* 112, no. 1 (2001).

[41] See Gerhart B. Ladner, *The Idea of Reform: Its Impact on Christian Thought and Action in the Age of the Fathers* (Cambridge, MA: Harvard University Press, 1959); Ernest W. McDonnell, "The *Vita Apostolica*: Diversity or Dissent," *Church History* 24, no. 1 (1955); Koschorke, "Gnosis, Montanismus."

order in the twelfth century, the early, small, and disconnected local communities of monks grew into institutionally and financially sophisticated organizations with complex administrative structures spread throughout the territory of Latin Christendom. In the process, the initial emphasis on monastic claustration was increasingly replaced by a monastic lifestyle of mendicancy and engagement with the world.[42]

This disposition of activist intervention in worldly affairs was only strengthened by the incessant reformist strivings of reformist groups that constantly emerged within the religious orders. By the time Franciscans started the evangelization of America, for example, the institutional culture of their order was shaped by the victorious reforming movement of the Observant Franciscans that only reinforced the activist disposition of its members. The Observantine faction within the Franciscan order emerged in the fifteenth century and fought – against the opposition of the Conventuals – for a thorough reform of *vita apostolica* and return to the precepts of poverty, humility, and renunciation of worldly goods in St. Francis's original rule of the order from 1223. In this, they were the heirs of a series of reformers and "extremists" that had operated within the order at least since the thirteenth century: Spiritual Franciscans, Beguines, Fraticelli, and Brothers of Penitence. By the end of the fifteenth century, the Observants had taken over the friars' houses in Spain and their reform was consolidated by the rise in prominence of Francisco Ximenes de Cisneros, the Observantine provincial of the order for Castile, as archbishop of Toledo and chancellor of Spain (whom we met previously as an early ally of the Hispaniola Dominicans). One implication of this Franciscan "Reformation" was that the friars understood their order as the true apostolic organization in contrast to the inadequate "church of the clerics." Although ultimately under papal jurisdiction, they represented an oppositional and activist organizational and spiritual culture within the Catholic Church. The Society of Jesus was the end result of a similar reformist impulse in the sixteenth century – a "society of reformed and apostolic priests."[43]

---

[42] See Bartlett, *Making of Europe*, 255–60; Alexander Hamilton Thompson, "The Monastic Orders," in *The Cambridge Medieval History*, Vol. V, eds. J. R. Tanner, C. W. Previté-Orton, and Z. N. Brooke (Cambridge: Cambridge University Press, 1926); C. H. Lawrence, *The Friars: The Impact of the Early Mendicant Movement on Western Society* (London: Longman, 1994).

[43] H. Outram Evennett, *The Spirit of the Counter-Reformation* (Cambridge: Cambridge University Press, 1968), 44. On the reformist movements within the Catholic Church, the orders, and their activities in America, see also E. Randolph Daniel, *The Franciscan Concept of Mission in the High Middle Ages* (Lexington: University Press of Kentucky, 1975); Lawrence, *The Friars*; Ernst Benz, *Ecclesia spiritualis: Kirchenidee und Geschichtstheologie der franziskanischen Reformation* (Stuttgart: W. Kohlhammer, 1934); Mullett, *The Catholic Reformation*; Robert Bireley, *The Refashioning of Catholicism, 1450–1700: A Reassessment of the Counter Reformation* (Washington, DC: Catholic University of America Press, 1999); R. Po-chia Hsia, *The World of Catholic Renewal, 1540–1770*, 2nd ed. (Cambridge: Cambridge University Press, 2005), 25–33; Kenneth Scott Latourette, *A History of the Expansion of Christianity*, Vol. III: *Three Centuries of Advance, A.D. 1500–A.D. 1800* (New York: Harper & Brothers, 1937),

In short, the orders active in the evangelization of America were the organizational end result of a long evolution of Christian monasticism. This long-term history had imprinted some distinctive features onto the organizational and cultural environment out of which came the first practitioners of principled long-distance advocacy. An activist disposition was inscribed into the specific organizations that provided the first religious personnel to work in the newly conquered American territories. The cultural idiom of religious reformism enshrined in the culture of these organization provided incentives for activist engagement and concerted transformation of earthly realities. For this activist disposition, the evangelization of the Americas was an opportunity not only to follow the apostolic commandment to spread the Gospel, but also to build a truly pure and apostolic church free of the errors and deviations of the European religious life. Furthermore, this reformist impulse was conceived within the framework of a millennialist biblical vision of human history. The suffering of the Indians – the "most salvable" people "in the world" – was like the bondage of God's chosen people in Egypt – and their liberation obviously imminent, as the Old Testament model predicted. The hope of the immediate reformation and renovation of the church and the world imparted urgency to combatting the profoundly irreligious practices of secular Spanish exploiters. A fervent reformism was thus connected with an incipient, if unintended and limited, ideology of emancipation and justice.[44]

Ideologies of Nonviolence

The orders active in the evangelization of America embodied also a historically new ideology of a peaceful mission of conversion articulated first by Dominicans and Franciscans in the thirteenth century. Consider, for example, the contrast between the principles of mendicant practice in the Iberian empires with an earlier organizational form of monasticism deeply connected with territorial expansion and conquest: the military orders. If the twelfth-century military orders were the institutional carriers of a religious ideology of violent conquest of nonbelievers, the Catholic orders most active in the evangelization of Iberian America represented the opposing principle of peaceful evangelization.

18–23. It is not by accident that, as Evennett points out (p. 71), friars were overrepresented among the early proponents of the Protestant Reformation.

[44] "Más salvable que hay en le mundo," according to Franciscan Gerónimo de Mendieta in a letter addressed to the order superior in Mexico, quoted in Assadourian, "Memoriales," 378–79. See also John Leddy Phelan, *The Millennial Kingdom of the Franciscans in the New World*, 2nd ed. (Berkeley: University of California Press, 1970); Delno C. West, "Medieval Ideas of Apocalyptic Mission and the Early Franciscans in Mexico," *Americas* 45, no. 3 (1989). On the idea of the restoration of *ecclesia primitiva* (the primitive church) as the source of religious perfectionism and reformism, see Glenn Olsen, "The Idea of the *Ecclesia Primitiva* in the Writings of the Twelfth-Century Canonists," *Traditio* 25 (1969).

The peculiar institutional model of the military order, combining the contradictory principles of military violence and monastic devotion, was established by the Templars founded in 1118. The several orders that copied this model in the twelfth century were to become some of the most politically and financially powerful organizations of Western European Christendom. They were active participants in the Crusades, again a curious combination of religious pilgrimage and military conquest, where, as the apologist of the Templars Bernard of Clairvaux put it, "the Christian glories in a pagan's death, because Christ is glorified." Similarly, they were important players in the Reconquista of the Iberian Peninsula from Muslims. Perhaps the clearest contrast with the later activities of religious orders in the evangelization of America is provided by the Swordbrothers and, later, the Teutonic Knights who were the spearheads of the territorial expansion of Christendom into Eastern Europe and the Baltic. It was their violent treatment of the conquered populations that provoked the first documented contestations of religious violence against non-Christians.[45]

In the thirteenth century, peaceful evangelists like the Dominicans and the Franciscans replaced the warrior monks after the demise of the military orders and the Crusades' repeated failure to accomplish their professed aim to expand Christendom. Dominic's Order of Friars Preachers was the preeminent representative of this tradition of pacific "philosophical" mission. The emphasis on preaching in Dominican evangelism was coupled with the assumption that the "heathen" were rational thinkers who could be persuaded through logical argument. For their preaching missions, the friars were trained in variety of disciplines, including "heathen" languages and Islamic and Judaic theology. The Franciscans similarly adopted the principle of peaceful missions through their reformist wing, the Spirituals, who appropriated the prophetic tradition originating from Joachim of Fiore. Critical of the futility of the Crusades and emphasizing the leading role of "spiritual men" in the future triumph of the Catholic Church, Joachimitism reinforced Franciscan commitment to peaceful conversion through mendicancy. In important ways, this specifically religious interest in the peaceful conversion of the "heathen" motivated the humanitarian concern of friars, especially as they opposed the exploitative practices of other Europeans in the process of overseas expansion.[46]

The humanitarian disposition of religious orders was further reinforced by a tradition in theology and canon law which was ready to admit the legitimate

---

[45] See Chapter 1. On the military orders and the crusades, see Bartlett Bartlett, *Making of Europe*, 261–68; Maschke, *Deutsche Orden*; Roger Bigelow Merriman, *The Rise of the Spanish Empire in the Old World and in the New* (New York: Macmillan, 1918), v. 1, 177–78.

[46] See Benz, *Ecclesia spiritualis*; E. Randolph Daniel, "Apocalyptic Conversion: The Joachite Alternative to the Crusades," *Traditio* 25 (1969); E. Randolph Daniel, *Franciscan Concept*. By the mid-fifteenth century, when the first religious attempts to protect the dignity of Canary Islanders occurred, the Papacy, too, increasingly adopted this stance of peaceful evangelization and, in contrast to its earlier sponsorship of Crusading wars, began to provide indulgencies and other incentives for peaceful missions. See Rumeu de Armas, "Problemas derivados."

character of non-Christian political arrangements and, by extension, the rationality of non-Christians. Affirmed by the Council of Constance in the early fifteenth century, this canonical tradition of acknowledging, in however circumscribed fashion, the legitimacy of the infidels' dominion over their territories goes back again to the thirteenth century when Pope Innocent IV articulated it in opposition to an earlier view equating the legitimacy of political power with the ruler's state of grace. Another important doctrinal influence on the humanitarian activities of Catholic orders was the revival by Dominicans (and later Jesuits) of the natural-law theology of Thomas Aquinas in the sixteenth century. Thomism argued that natural law, although subordinated to the eternal law by which God acts and to the divine law that God reveals in the scripture, is directly accessible to all humans who have the innate capacity to grasp its principles. This, in turn, led to acknowledgment of the inherent humanity of the indigenous populations religious specialists encountered in America.

The ascendance and diffusion of such ideas, as well as their availability as cultural resources for the humanitarian activities of religious specialists in the New World was a development rooted deeply in the religious controversies of the time. The emphasis on natural law and the recognition of the political legitimacy of non-Christian polities was partly mobilized by Catholics in defense of the institutional power of the Church against reformers from Wycliff to Luther who insisted that the only legitimate political organization was the one ordained by God. Such theocratic views anchored the legitimacy of political forms in the salvational status of the ruler. Taken to their logical conclusions, they threatened the monopolistic position of the Catholic Church as an institutional dispenser of grace with their suggestion that grace was a property of the individual, not imparted by the corporate institutions of Roman Catholicism. Cultural idioms that emphasized the rationality of distant strangers crystallized, in this sense, in the course of Catholic defense against anti-institutionalist reformist ideas. An unintended implication of these cultural idioms, however, was that they provided a cultural resource for the humanitarian activities of religious orders.[47]

This is not to say, of course, that all friars were pacifists. Indeed, some religious in America did advocate violent conquest if only as a precondition for successful evangelization, whereas others were complicit with the exploitation of indigenous labor. Nor were all friars driven by reformist impulses to defend the welfare of indigenous people or treat their charges with respect. After all, they were the members of organizations created, among other things,

---

[47] On these developments in canon law and theology, see Bireley, *Refashioning of Catholicism*, 78–81; Bernice Hamilton, *Political Thought in Sixteenth-Century Spain* (Oxford: Clarendon Press, 1963); Muldoon, "Wyclif and the Rights"; Pennington, "Las Casas and the Tradition"; Höffner, *Kolonialismus und Evangelium*, 264–304; Quentin Skinner, *The Foundations of Modern Political Thought*, Volume Two: *The Age of Reformation* (Cambridge: Cambridge University Press, 1978).

to extirpate heresy and "idolatry."[48] Yet a significant number of members of the religious orders did embark on a conflictual trajectory of radicalization in opposition to competing networks of empire. Although the position they advocated is hardly identical with the norms of human rights and anti-imperialism as we know them today, their activities coalesced into an impressive program aiming to affirm the humanity and dignity of distant others and to give them voice and representations. The religious orders did not uniformly create humanitarians. Yet their organizational culture was an important factor for the radicalization of religious actors in the imperial context. And it is in this process of radicalization that long-distance advocacy was configured as a distinctive political practice.

---

[48] A few examples not mentioned so far: some Franciscans were supporters of Sepúlveda; the Jesuit Alonso Sánchez advocated a military conquest of China that otherwise remained closed to Christian missionary effort and was able to recruit for a period the Dominican bishop of the Philippines, Domingo de Salazar; the Franciscan Juan de Zumárraga persecuted indigenous idolatry as head of the Inquisition in Mexico. See Mariano Delgado, "Alonso Sánchez SJ und José de Acosta SJ in der Kontroverse über die Conquista und Evangelisation Chinas am Ende des 16. Jahrhunderts," *Zeitschrift für Missionswissenschaft und Religionswissenschaft* 90, nos. 3–4 (2006); Richard E. Greenleaf, *Zumárraga and the Mexican Inquisition, 1536–1543* (Washington, DC: Academy of American Franciscan History, 1961); Jaime González Rodríguez, "Los amigos franciscanos de Sepúlveda," *Archivo Ibero-Americano* 48, nos. 189–92 (1988). On the role of mendicants in the extirpation of heresy, see Lawrence, *The Friars*, 181–94. Yet reports of friars exploiting and punishing indigenous people, often produced by secular settlers, should be put in the context of the conflict between the two parties.

3

Religious Radicalization and Early Antislavery

Deeply embedded in the dynamics of European overseas expansion, the indigenist advocacy discussed in the previous chapters can be also seen as an ongoing albeit discontinuous project to change the course of this imperial expansion by reforming, humanizing, and even repudiating it. Even more generally, the pro-indigenist counterpoint to expansion was a confrontation with the inherent moral duality of imperialism: a moral regime in which different sets of behavioral norms were customarily applied in the European core and the expanding imperial periphery overseas respectively.

As important and, occasionally, successful as this project of moral "homogenization" of space was, the divided moral regime of imperialism persisted. In fact, its inherent moral discontinuity was only reinforced in the seventeenth century as new European powers – England, France, and the Netherlands – entered the imperial game previously dominated by the two Iberian states. Yet, although the indigenist project had largely failed to achieve its objective by that time, the same interactional pattern of religious radicalization over the treatment of imperial "others" continued to assert itself and confront the moral duality of empire. This time, however, it was taking place in a more fragmented and complex field demarcated by the religious divisions and hostilities of Western Christianity. And the focus of this conflict increasingly became colonial slavery and the Atlantic trade in enslaved Africans – two mutually reinforcing pillars of the new imperial moral regime.

THE NEW ATLANTIC SLAVERY AND THE HARDENING MORAL
DUALITY OF IMPERIALISM

Several factors contributed to the persistence and deepening of this dual moral regime in the new post-Iberian imperial world, but the basic structural conditions were provided by the political and military rivalries between the new set of European powers in overseas territories. The various military conflicts and religious struggles that had dominated the European landscape in the sixteenth century were largely settled by the end of the century. Castile, the dominant imperial power after the assumption of the Portuguese Crown by Philip II in 1580, concluded a series of peace treaties with its rivals: England, France, and the Netherlands. Yet these treaties applied only to European territories. Despite continuing efforts, no comparable agreements were reached or enforced in the overseas world across the Atlantic that remained largely exempt from the emergent legal framework regulating interstate relations on the continent. There hostilities between older and newer entrants into the imperial game continued at least until the 1690s, creating a lawless colonial world of continuous plunder and warfare.[1]

Particularly striking was one feature of this lawless world: the enduring institutionalization of racialized slavery in the colonies in an important discontinuity with the customary moral order in the European heartland. The colonial institution of slavery arose at the interstices of two developments: the spread of large plantations growing cash crops – most notably sugar – and the rise of a transatlantic traffic in enslaved Africans. The Portuguese were the pioneers of both. They brought the sugar plantation from the Mediterranean first to the islands off the African coasts and then to Brazil. Even earlier, around the mid-fifteenth century, Portuguese merchants and adventurers had connected with African trading networks that offered the traditional "commodity" of people captured in wars and slaving raids. By the mid-sixteenth century, sugar plantations were firmly established in Brazil. By the end of the century, the labor force in them consisted predominantly of enslaved Africans who had replaced indigenous people. Finally, by the middle of the following century, English, French, and Dutch colonists in the Caribbean and North America had adopted the Portuguese innovation of cash crop plantations exploiting the labor of enslaved Africans and their merchants inserted themselves into an ever-thriving slave trade.[2]

---

[1] Philip D. Curtin, *The Rise and Fall of the Plantation Complex: Essays in Atlantic History* (Cambridge: Cambridge University Press, 1990), 87–89; Richard S. Dunn, *Sugar and Slaves: The Rise of the Planter Class in the English West Indies, 1624–1713* (Chapel Hill: University of North Carolina Press, 1972), 11–12; A. Pearce Higgins, "International Law and the Outer World," in *The Cambridge History of the British Empire*, Vol. I: *The Old Empire from the Beginnings to 1783*, eds. J. Holland Rose, A. P. Newton, and E. A. Benians (Cambridge: Cambridge University Press, 1929).

[2] The exception was the Spanish Empire, where the number of enslaved Africans remained limited compared to their numbers in other colonial possessions. See Curtin, *Plantation Complex*; Jack P. Greene, "Early Modern Southeastern North America and the Broader Atlantic and American Worlds," *Journal of Southern History* 73, no. 3 (2007); Paul E. Lovejoy, *Transformations in Slavery: A History of Slavery in Africa*, 3rd ed., (New York: Cambridge University Press, 2012); David Eltis, *The Rise of African Slavery in the Americas* (Cambridge: Cambridge University Press, 2000); Robin Blackburn, *The Making of New World Slavery: From the Baroque to the Modern, 1492–1800* (London: Verso, 1997); Emilia Viotti da Costa, "The Portuguese-African

The practice of enslaving human beings and treating them like property had a long history by that time; Atlantic slavery crystallized along several coexisting and occasionally overlapping circuits of traffic and employment of enslaved humans in other parts of the world. What was new, however, was that now enslaved labor was put to use in a highly intensive, harsh, complex, and capitalist agricultural production system – a contrast with traditional systems where slaves provided mostly domestic services to their owners. Equally striking was another feature of this new system of enslavement: its strict geographical "containment" in European overseas possessions and exclusion from the "old" world.[3]

The long decline of slavery had been in progress at least since the eighth century in Northwestern Europe. Since the High Middle Ages, labor there was increasingly recruited not through force or enserfment, but through fiscal incentives and legal privileges granted to "free" towns intended to attract new settlers. Rigorous penal practices – such as forced labor, indenture, and impressment of vagrants – persisted or were introduced anew in Europe and in the overseas colonies. Yet, although such practices could often be as harsh as slavery, they differed from enslavement in two important aspects: they were the punishment for a specific crime and they were not hereditary, but confined to a specified amount of time.[4]

Slave Trade: A Lesson in Colonialism," *Latin American Perspectives* 12, no. 1 (1985); James A. Rawley, *The Transatlantic Slave Trade: A History*, rev. ed. (Lincoln: University of Nebraska Press, 2005); David Brion Davis, *Inhuman Bondage: The Rise and Fall of Slavery in the New World* (New York: Oxford University Press, 2006); Stuart B. Schwartz, *Sugar Plantations in the Formation of Brazilian Society: Bahia, 1550–1835* (Cambridge: Cambridge University Press, 1985); José Capela, *Escravatura: A empresa de saque, o abolicionismo (1810–1875)* (Porto, Portugal: Afrontamento, 1974); Anne Pérotin-Dumon, "French, English and Dutch in the Lesser Antilles: From Privateering to Planting, c. 1550–c. 1650," in *General History of the Caribbean*, Vol. II, *New Societies: The Caribbean in the Long Sixteen Century*, ed. Pieter C. Emmer (London: Macmillan, 1997); Russell R. Menard, *Sweet Negotiations: Sugar, Slavery, and Plantation Agriculture in Early Barbados* (Charlottesville: University of Virginia Press, 2006); Michael Craton, *Empire, Enslavement, and Freedom in the Caribbean* (Kingston, Jamaica: Ian Randle, 1997); Robert William Fogel, *Without Consent or Contract: The Rise and Fall of American Slavery* (New York: Norton, 1989).

[3] On other circuits of slavery and slave trade in the period, see Seymour Drescher, *Abolition: A History of Slavery and Antislavery* (Cambridge: Cambridge University Press, 2009); Lovejoy, *Transformations in Slavery*; Ronald Segal, *Islam's Black Slaves: The Other Black Diaspora* (New York: Farrar, Straus and Giroux, 2001); Markus Vink, "'The World's Oldest Trade': Dutch Slavery and Slave Trade in the Indian Ocean in the Seventeenth Century," *Journal of World History* 14, no. 2 (2003).

[4] Eltis, *Rise of African Slavery*, 71–73. See also Bartlett, *Making of Europe*, 119–20, 72–73; Michael Guasco, "Settling with Slavery: Human Bondage in the Early Anglo-American World," in *Envisioning an English Empire: Jamestown and the Making of the North Atlantic World*, eds. Robert Appelbaum and John Wood Sweet (Philadelphia: University of Pennsylvania Press, 2005), 241–43; Nicholas Rogers, "Vagrancy, Impressment and the Regulation of Labour in Eighteenth-Century Britain," *Slavery & Abolition* 15, no. 2 (1994); Merriman, *Rise of the Spanish Empire*, vol. 1, 185–86.

By the seventeenth century – even as the new colonial slavery consolidated – slavery in Europe was virtually extinct. The last to delegalize slavery on their territories were the Iberian states. Portuguese legislation to abolish slavery was passed in 1773, and Spain abolished slavery in the adjacent islands and its African territories only in 1837. It was indeed the persisting Iberian tradition that was transposed in the colonies and, adopted by the new English, French, and Dutch plantation owners, produced the new Atlantic slavery. Nevertheless, it is significant that the growth of overseas slavery did nothing to strengthen existing slavery in Portugal or Spain. There the numbers of slaves remained relatively low, especially when considered against the background of expanding colonial slave trade and slaveholding.[5]

With the extinction of slavery in Europe, the status of slaves as property of their owners upon entering the territory of European imperial metropoles became increasingly anomalous. In several documented instances, African slaves were freed upon arrival in European ports on the ground that local laws did not recognize slavery. Slaves brought by the Spanish to the Flemish city of Middleburg were declared free in 1691 and, even earlier, the Parliament of Bordeaux ordered the release of imported slaves in 1571. Only the intense lobbying of French colonial interests in 1716 and 1738 led to the passing of legislation allowing colonists to bring a limited number of slaves to France. The Parliament of Paris, however, refused to officially register the laws, making them unenforceable and hundreds of enslaved Africans were able to win their freedom in courts that upheld the principle of "free soil."

English courts failed to produce a similar unambiguous decision and conflicting rulings in the seventeenth and eighteenth centuries created an inconsistent record of common-law decisions on whether the presence of an African slave on English territory was legal or not. Yet by the 1730s at the latest, it was generally taken for granted that there was no need for a formal ceremonial manumission of slaves in order for them to be free once they were on the territory of the metropole. Even in Iberian states where slavery was abolished relatively late, legislation declared slaves free upon entering the territory of Portugal (since 1761) and of Spain (since 1680).[6]

[5] Robin Blackburn, *The Overthrow of Colonial Slavery, 1776–1848* (London: Verso, 1988), 38–39; José Capela, "Abolicion y abolicionismo en Portugal y sus colonias," in *Esclavitud y derechos humanos: La lucha por la libertad del negro en el siglo XIX*, eds. Francisco de Solano and Agustín Guimerá Ravina (Madrid: Consejo Superior de Investigaciones Científicas, 1990), 578–79; Eltis, *Rise of African Slavery*, 6–8; Francisco C. Falcon and Fernando A. Novais, "A extinção de escravatura africana em Portugal no quadro da política económica Pombalina," in *Anais do VI Simposio nacional dos professores universitarios de historia* (São Paulo: s.n. 1973); A. J. R. Russell-Wood, "Iberian Expansion and the Issue of Black Slavery: Changing Portuguese Attitudes, 1440–1770," *The American Historical Review* 83, no. 1, Supplement (1978); Enriqueta Vila Vilar and Luisa Vila Vilar, eds., *Los abolicionistas españoles: Siglo XIX* (Madrid: Ediciones de Cultura Hispánica, 1996), 108–09.
[6] See Capela, "Abolición," 578; William B. Cohen, *The French Encounter with Africans: White Response to Blacks, 1530–1880* (Bloomington: Indiana University Press, 1980), 45–46; Shelby

In other words, the institutionalization of the new Atlantic slavery in the seventeenth century was part and parcel of the hardening of the moral duality of the imperial world that was now based on a strong, if implicit, dichotomous normative structure. Geographically, slavery was inadmissible on European territories, while accepted as normal in distant colonial possessions "beyond the line." Symbolically, a strong norm against the enslavement of fellow Christian Europeans coexisted with the normality of enslaving Africans. Thus, as Thomas Brady writes, slavery completed a "gradient of contempt," which, "boundless in its expansibility, began at home and spread its shadow from nearby hearts of darkness to those far over the sea."⁷

Two factors combined to buttress the acceptance and centrality of the new Atlantic slave trade within the moral regime of empire: the geographical disconnection of the imperial world from the circumscribed world of European "freedom" and enduring legal and philosophical traditions that justified enslavement, albeit only in specific circumstances. Slavery was normalized as long as it applied to a specific kind of human. Thus, the enslaved African was codified as a distinct category – apart not only from unenslaveable Europeans, but also from other non-European individuals. Although the enslavement of Africans became largely a taken-for-granted practice in European colonies, the subjection of American and Caribbean indigenous people to forced labor never reached a similar degree of acceptance. Clearly, American Indians in all colonies were increasingly "racialized" as distinct from "white" Europeans.

T. McCloy, *The Negro in France* (Lexington: University of Kentucky Press, 1961), 11–62; Sue Peabody, *"There Are No Slaves in France": The Political Culture of Race and Slavery in the Ancien Regime* (New York: Oxford University Press, 1996), 137; Capela, *Escravatura*, 146; Arthur F. Corwin, *Spain and the Abolition of Slavery in Cuba, 1817–1886* (Austin: University of Texas Press, 1967), 167–68; Robert Louis Stein, *The French Slave Trade in the Eighteenth Century: An Old Regime Business* (Madison: University of Wisconsin Press, 1979), 194–95; James Walvin, *England, Slaves, and Freedom: 1776–1838* (Jackson: University Press of Mississippi, 1986), 32–42; George Van Cleve, *"Somerset's Case* and Its Antecedents in Imperial Perspective," *Law & History Review* 24, no. 3 (2006); Seymour Drescher, "Manumission in a Society without Slave Law: Eighteenth Century England," *Slavery and Abolition* 10, no. 3 (1989); J. M. Pérez-Prendes y Muñoz de Arraco, "La revista 'El abolicionista' (1865–1876) en la genesis de la abolición de la esclavitud en las Antillas españolas," *Anuario de Estudios Americanos* 43 (1986): 10–11; Markus Vink, "Freedom and Slavery: The Dutch Republic, the VOC World, and the Debate over the 'World's Oldest Trade'," *South African Historical Journal* 60, no. 1 (2008): 29.

⁷ Brady, "Merchant Empires," 156. See also David Brion Davis, *The Problem of Slavery in Western Culture* (Ithaca, NY: Cornell University Press, 1966), 58–70; Susan Dwyer Amussen, *Caribbean Exchanges: Slavery and the Transformation of English Society, 1640–1700* (Chapel Hill: University of North Carolina Press, 2007); Seymour Drescher, *Capitalism and Antislavery: British Mobilization in Comparative Perspective* (New York: Oxford University Press, 1987), 12–24; *Abolition*, 1–87; Christopher Leslie Brown, *Moral Capital: Foundations of British Abolitionism* (Chapel Hill: University of North Carolina Press, 2006), 44–55; Seymour Drescher, *From Slavery to Freedom: Comparative Studies in the Rise and Fall of Atlantic Slavery* (Houndmills, UK: Macmlllan, 1999), 19–24; Eltis, *Rise of African Slavery*.

Furthermore, enslavement-like practices did persist in Iberian and British America; preexisting traditional slavery within indigenous communities was tolerated and attempts were made – with some regularity – to legislate the legitimate enslavement of specific indigenous groups (the Caribbean islanders, the Chichimecs, the Mapuche, and some Brazilian tribes) as long as they could be represented as actively hostile to the spread of the Gospel and of "civilization." Yet the very fact that Brazilian settlers defined the indigenous people they enslaved – illegally – as *negros da terra* (blacks of the land) is indicative of an emerging conceptual framework that distinguished enslaveable Africans from all other non-enslaveable categories of humans, even if this distinction was often blurred in practice.[8]

The crystallization of this dichotomous lay anthropology itself was the result of several interlocking developments. In the 1490s, in the immediate aftermath of the first explorations, Columbus himself and other Genoese and Spanish traders initiated a trade in enslaved Caribbeans that could have developed into a counterpart to the Portuguese-led Atlantic slave trade, consolidating in turn a different conceptual framework of human enslaveability. After a lengthy consultation with theologians, however, Isabel and Ferdinand imposed a ban on such trade, arguing that the Indian subjects of Castile were inherently free. The shrinking of indigenous populations under violence, exploitation, and diseases provided further incentives for the acceptance of enslaved labor imported from Africa. And finally, the very indigenist advocacy discussed in the previous chapters disseminated a norm against the enslavement of Amerindians.[9]

The emerging conceptual framework of human enslaveability normalized a practice otherwise unusual in Europe and problematic for the European mind by reserving its ambit to a specific kind of human beings and sequestering it in distant territories. Thus, the combination of a geographically partitioned morality and an ingrained vision of human diversity – one that distinguished sharply between inherently free and inherently enslaveable individuals – provided the general cultural and political background against which ideas and

---

[8] See John Manuel Monteiro, "From Indian to Slave: Forced Native Labour and Colonial Society in São Paulo during the Seventeenth Century," *Slavery & Abolition* 9, no. 2 (1988): 114. On changing and overlapping understandings of black slaves and indigenous people, see Michael Guasco, "To 'Doe Some Good upon Their Countrymen': The Paradox of Indian Slavery in Early Anglo-America," *Journal of Social History* 41, no. 2 (2007); Alden T. Vaughan, *The Roots of American Racism: Essays on the Colonial Experience* (New York: Oxford University Press, 1995); John A. Sainsbury, "Indian Labor in Early Rhode Island," *New England Quarterly* 48, no. 3 (1975). On ideological justifications of slavery, see Davis, *Slavery in Western Culture*; *Slavery and Human Progress* (New York: Oxford University Press, 1984). On "human kinds": Ian Hacking, *The Social Construction of What?* (Cambridge, MA: Harvard University Press, 1999).

[9] Nader, "Desperate Men," 417–18. See also Chapter 1. On depopulation as incentive for the Atlantic slave trade, see Davis, *Inhuman Bondage*, 99.

activities directed toward the eradication of slavery emerged. This was a normative climate that was strongly biased against such ideas and activities. Entrenched conventions and cultural understanding militated against the possibility of articulating anything approaching our current moral disgust with slavery.

This persistent moral insulation between a European world of increasing freedoms and rights and a colonial world of human bondage has important implications for the development of long-distance advocacy targeting the institution of colonial slavery. For one, the remarkable strength of the moral divide casts doubts on an understanding of the eventual assault and extinction of slavery as the inevitable extension of European norms to the outside world. From today's vantage point, it is tempting to think of principled opposition to slavery as something that was inevitably bound to appear. Yet for long centuries, a powerful combination of economic, political, and cultural factors entrenched the co-existence of two incompatible and contradictory sets of moral norms and prevented the "export" and application of European discourses of liberty and rights to the colonies – including an intellectual tradition going all the way back to the Stoics in Antiquity that problematized the contradiction inherent in the treatment of humans as inanimate possessions.[10]

To understand how, in the long run, the balance eventually shifted toward a fairly institutionalized global norm against slavery, it is useful to see how this normal state of affairs began to not only be persistently questioned but also – moving from the level of ideas and norms to the level of practices – how certain individuals and groups began to engage in a concerted political attack on slavery. Until the emergence of an international antislavery network in the late eighteenth century – the subject of Chapter 4 – such critics of slavery remained a minority unable to effect the social and political change it envisioned. Still, a closer look at their ideas and activities is instructive in that it reveals important continuities and similarities with the pattern of religious radicalization identified in the preceding chapters. On the Catholic side, early political interventions against colonial slavery developed out of the culture of indigenist activism. In Protestant territories, there was no preexisting tradition of activism on behalf of imperial "others." Nevertheless, the first Protestant initiatives against slavery followed the logic of the religious mobilization of earlier Iberian indigenism – they arose among adherents of reform movements in their conflict with competing imperial networks. And finally, despite a cultural pressure to separate the rights of enslaved Africans from the issue of the rights of indigenous Americans, in the political practices of both Catholic and Protestant early antislavery activists, the two issues remained intertwined and indeed, feed into each other.

[10] *Slavery in Western Culture*; Edward Derbyshire Seeber, *Anti-Slavery Opinion in France during the Second Half of the Eighteenth Century* (Baltimore, MD: Johns Hopkins Press, 1937).

CATHOLIC CONFRONTATIONS WITH SLAVERY

In 1454, Pope Nicholas V indirectly legitimized the flourishing of the slave trade in his bull *Pontifex romanus* that authorized the Portuguese monarch "to invade, conquer, combat, subjugate, and submit and reduce to servitude ... all Saracens and pagans and other enemies of Christ." In 1462, his successor, Pius II, exhorted a missionary bishop departing for Guinea to use all means to prevent the enslavement of newly converted Africans.[11] These two documents reveal, *in nuce*, the extremes of ecclesiastical attitudes toward slavery in the first period of Iberian imperial expansion. At the one end of the continuum, the Church provided ideological legitimation for the new racialized slavery; in the other extreme, a concern for converts – or, indeed, potential converts – to Christianity, provoked moral objections against enslavement of Africans.

As the previous chapters have shown, the first imperial agents of the Catholic Church – the mendicant orders – while providing the personnel of the first principles long-distant advocacy networks, displayed a variety of attitudes toward indigenous populations. The spread of attitudes was perhaps even broader and more incongruous in regard to African slavery. Whereas some mendicants and other religious encouraged slavery and lent ideological and practical support to its endurance, it was from the ranks of the same orders that the first serious attempts to question or even annihilate slavery came.

Perhaps the most jaded reaction was the pragmatic acceptance of the inevitability of a slavery already entrenched deeply in the customary economic order. The Jesuit mission in Angola in 1580, for example, was faced with rather hard choices for its maintenance: survival on alms, the incurring of debts, or economic self-sufficiency that included the acceptance of slaves as a form of payment. In the end, the instruction by the general of the Society and the Portuguese provincial congregation that banned the ownership of slaves were disobeyed. The leadership eventually accepted the fact and Jesuit colleges became large-scale slaveholders, while only marginally involved in the slave trade.

A series of Jesuit theologians in the sixteenth and seventeenth centuries produced several treatises that sought to provide a normative framework for the legality of slavery, especially in the context of what we today would call "business ethics." While largely conceding the troubling moral implications of slavery, the main purpose of these works seemed to be a certain calibration of moral responsibility in proportion to the distance from the initial act of enslavement. Thus, perhaps the most influential treatise, Luis de Molina's *De iustitia et de iure* of 1593, accepted that most slaves had been acquired

[11] José Andrés Gallego and Jesús María García Añoveros, *La Iglesia y la esclavitud de los Negros* (Pamplona: Ediciones Universidad de Navarra, 2002), 19–21; Enriqueta Vila Vilar, "La postura de la iglesia frente a la esclavitud. Siglos XVI y XVII," in *Esclavitud y derechos humanos: La lucha por la libertad del negro en el siglo XIX*, eds. Francisco de Solano and Agustín Guimerá Ravina (Madrid: Consejo Superior de Investigaciones Científicas, 1990).

illegitimately, yet advised the freeing of slaves only when this illegitimacy had been clearly established.[12]

Other ideas provided a stronger religious justification for the perpetuation of slavery, while also indicating the insidious normalization of this imperial institution. There was the widely held belief that slavery, with all the moral problems it entailed, provided at least the opportunity to do some good: convert and evangelize individuals who otherwise would remain outside the reach of the "true Gospel." In addition, the exploitation of enslaved Africans was considered a humanitarian alternative to the exploitation of indigenous people. In fact, in 1517 Bartolomé de las Casas used his influence in the court to arrange for the royal consent to the importation of enslaved Africans into Spanish possessions as a replacement of indigenous labor. Soon thereafter, he realized that "black slavery was as unjust as Indian slavery." In Brazil, the pro-indigenist Jesuit António Vieira never reached such a realization and consistently urged, instead, the introduction of Black slaves as alternative to forced indigenous labor.[13]

A More Critical Position

Alongside this direct or indirect acceptance of slavery, there emerged – in response to the various moral tensions that slavery invariably produced – also a religious project that began to question and problematize the nature of slavery. Although not an outright rejection of the very institution, these were repeated attempts – in various locations – to regulate and soften the exploitative and dehumanizing practices involved. Many members of religious orders were genuinely engaged in bettering the conditions of enslaved Africans, whether on principle or for narrow evangelistic purposes. Conversion and evangelization was impossible without at least some free time and personal autonomy, which many settlers refused to grant their enslaved laborers – not only because they wanted to exploit them to the fullest, but also because of fears that exposure to religious teachings would foster insubordination.

The conflict between these two views was very similar to the oppositions that gave rise to the jurisdictional conflict between religious and secular

---

[12] Dauril Alden, *The Making of an Enterprise: The Society of Jesus in Portugal, Its Empire, and Beyond, 1540–1750* (Stanford, CA: Stanford University Press, 1996), 506–46; Andrés Gallego and García Añoveros, *Iglesia y la esclavitud*. See also Manuel Lobo Cabrera, "El clero y la trata en los siglos XVI y XVII: El ejempio de Canarias," in *De la traite à l'esclavage: Actes du colloque international sur la traite des Noirs, Nantex 1985*, Vol. 1, ed. Serge Daget (Nantes, France: Centre de Recherche sur l'histoire du monde atlantique, 1988); Vila Vilar, "Postura de la iglesia."; David G. Sweet, "Black Robes and 'Black Destiny': Jesuit Views of African Slavery in 17th-Century Latin America," *Revista de historia de América* 86 (1978). For a similar contemporaneous intellectual tradition in Africa of both Muslim and non-Muslim origins that tried to set the legitimate limits of enslavement and correct abuses, see Lovejoy, *Transformations in Slavery*, 85–87.

[13] Casas, *History of the Indies*, 257; *Historia de las Indias*, 2323–24; Haubert, *L'Église et la défense des "Sauvages": Le Père Antoine Vieira au Brésil*.

networks out of which the wave of long-distance advocacy emerged in the six-teenth century. In fact, the very first radical critiques of slavery as institution arose exactly from the indigenist tradition. An early source for this critique was the Dominican ideology of peaceful and voluntary evangelization that under-mined an important argument in favor of enslavement: that despite its inher-ent evils, slavery at least exposed benighted Africans to the spiritual riches of Christianity.

As early as 1552, Las Casas countered this argument in his *Most Brief Account of the Destruction of the Indies*. In 1560, the Dominican bishop of Mexico, Alonso de Montúfar, informed Philip II of an ongoing discussion among many "learned and conscientious" people in the viceroyalty of the para-dox of African slavery coexisting with the postulated freedom of Amerindians. The letter contained a refutation of the various arguments usually given in defense of the spiritual advantages of enslavement, and appealed for an effec-tive ending of slavery and the slave trade. Nine years later, another Dominican, Tomás de Mercado, published in Seville a treatise on contracts in which he sounded another Lascasian theme: that the buying and selling of slaves is a mortal sin.[14]

In the 1580s, two Jesuits in Brazil – Miguel Garcia and Gonçalo Leite con-demned slavery publicly. For these activities, they were disciplined and sent back to the Iberian Peninsula, which, incidentally, exercised a chilling effect on potential Jesuit critics of slavery. Later, similar confrontations with the harsh reality of slavery emerged in the Caribbean possessions of France, the only Catholic state among the new imperial powers.[15]

A Radical Catholic Network

The most focused attack on slavery and the slave trade was the work of two new actors in the Catholic religious world: the order of Capuchins, a reform-ist offshoot of Observant Franciscans, and the Propaganda Fide, the papal Congregation for the Propagation of the Faith. Founded in 1622, the Propaganda was an organizational attempt to strengthen and extend Catholic missions, especially in the context of rising Protestantism, while also reappropriating

[14] Andrés Gallego and García Añoveros, *Iglesia y la esclavitud*.
[15] See Alden, *Making of an Enterprise*, 508–09; Charles Frostin, "Méthodologie missionnaire et sentiment religieux en Amérique française aux 17e et 18e siècles: Le cas de Saint-Domingue," *Cahiers d'Histoire* 24, no. 1 (1979); Metcalf, *Go-Betweens and the Colonization of Brazil, 1500–1600*, 316; George Breathett, "Religious Protectionism and the Slave in Haiti," *The Catholic Historical Review* 55, no. 1 (1969); Laënnec Hurbon, "The Church and Slavery in Eighteenth-Century Saint-Domingue," in *The Abolitions of Slavery: From Léger Félicité Sonthonax to Victor Schoelcher, 1793, 1794, 1848*, ed. Marcel Dorigny (New York: Berghahn Books, 2003); Joseph Janin, *La religion aux colonies françaises sous l'Ancien Régime (de 1626 à la Révolution)* (Paris: D'Auteuil, 1942), 128–30; Sue Peabody, "'A Dangerous Zeal' : Catholic Missions to Slaves in The French Antilles, 1635–1800," *French Historical Studies* 25, no. 1 (2002).

for the Church at least some of the executive control over missions and ecclesiastical matters ceded to Iberian monarchs. As early as 1630, the cardinals of Propaganda reacted to an almost incidental report of the enslavement and harsh treatment of Angolans by condemning the slave trade as "scandalous" and resolving to plead with the king in Madrid for more humane treatment of slaves.

The Propaganda was pushed into an even stronger antislavery position in subsequent years by appeals from Capuchins, who since the 1640s were deployed in Africa, South America, and the Caribbean as part of the new strategy of strengthening Catholic missions. The strongest tension was produced by their encounter with slavery in Kongo, where several of the problematic aspects of the new colonial slave trade were particularly visible: the persistence of traditional African slavery in one of the very few Christian kingdoms in Africa, the sale of enslaved indigenous Christians to non-Catholic Dutch and English traders, the involvement of fellow religious like the Jesuits in the slave trade, and even the intractable problem of how to deal with slaves donated to the mission. Two Italian Capuchins, upon their return from Kongo, addressed the Propaganda with critical reports on the assorted evils of slavery and the slave trade. In response, the prefect of Propaganda Fide sent letters to Capuchin missionaries and to the people of Kongo publicizing the organization's resolve to stop the enslavement of black Christians.[16]

As appeals over the evils of enslavement and the treatment of American Indians continued from Capuchins in South America and Africa to the Propaganda and the Council of Indies, a uniquely strong condemnation of colonial slavery emerged from the actions of two friars, Francisco José de Jaca and Épiphane (Epifanio) de Moirans, who became slavery's most consistently radical critics so far. Not only do their activities parallel the trajectories of clerical radicalization in the century before, but their confrontation with slavery arose in close connection with their concern for the treatment of indigenous people in America.

After a brief stay in the Capuchin mission near Caracas, Jaca was ordered to return to Spain, possibly because of the problems he created with his opposition to slavery and to the exploitation of indigenous people, a matter he had addressed in a letter to the king in 1678. Three years later and en route to

---

[16] Richard Gray, "Ingoli, the Collector of Portugal, the 'Gran Gusto' of Urban VIII and the Atlantic Slave trade," in *Ecclesiae memoria: Miscellanea in onore del R. P. Josef Metzler O.M.I., prefetto dell'Archivio segreto vaticano*, ed. Willi Henkel (Rome: Herder, 1991); Mukuna Mutanda, "L'attitude de la Sacrée Congregation de la Propagation de la Foi et des missionnaires Capucins vis-à-vis de la traite negriere au Kongo et an Angola (1645–1835)," *Revue Africaine de Théologie* 15, no. 31 (1992); Miguel Anxo Pena González, *Francisco José de Jaca: La primera propuesta abolicionista de la esclavitud en el pensamiento hispano* (Salamanca, Spain: Publicaciones Universidad Pontificia de Salamanca, 2003), 356–57; Graziano Saccardo, "La schiavitù e i Cappuccini," *L'Italia Francescana* 53 (1978).

Spain, another letter from the major slave-trading port of Cartagena de Indias besought His Majesty to grant freedom to all slaves lest their souls be lost.

During another stopover in Havana, Jaca provoked the local settlers' hostility by preaching against slavery and attempting to make them liberate their slaves with the standard indigenist disciplinary instrument: refusal of absolution of sins. In Cuba, Jaca found an ally in another Capuchin awaiting transportation to Europe: Épiphane de Moirans who, as a French subject hailing from Franche-Comté, had been expelled from the mission in Cumaná. When, after repeated warnings, Jaca refused to tone down his preaching, he was forced to leave the Franciscan convent where he was quartered. He moved into a cemetery chapel with Moirans and the duo began antislavery preaching sorties to sugar plantations and farms. This time they provoked the hostility of the vicar of the bishop of Cuba who excommunicated them and had them moved to a different location. In response, Jaca and Moirans fought back by notifying the vicar through a notary that, in fact, he had excommunicated himself by depriving two ecclesiastics from outside of his jurisdiction of their privileges: as missionaries, they were under direct papal authority and not accountable to local hierarchies.

After this series of mutual excommunications, claims, and counterclaims – as well as imprisonment and a trial – the two friars were shipped to Spain with the convoy of July 1682. Thus, they were handed over to the royal Council of the Indies a year after Jaca's arrival to Cuba. In the process, the two Capuchins' radical antislavery stance led to a contest over ecclesiastical jurisdiction and some diplomatic intrigue. As the Spanish state tried to muzzle the subversive ideas that jeopardized the legitimacy of a prosperous and lucrative slave trade, Rome tried to assert its control over the fate of two papal employees. In the meantime, while shuttled between various convents in Spain, Jaca and Moirans were able to present their written arguments against slavery in writing to Tomás Carbonell, bishop of Sigüenza and confessor of Charles II, through a friendly Dominican in court, José de San Juan. The royal confessor's support clearly mattered, because the king referred the matter to the State Council and issued, in 1683, a decree and a circular to royal officials in America urging the human treatment of slaves and indigenous people.

Yet this was the end of any effective antislavery influence on Spanish policies. Two years later, in what was the last serious discussion of the legitimacy of slavery and the slave trade, Charles requested from the Council of the Indies yet another learned opinion. The Council obliged by producing a collection of arguments confirming the legality of slavery and neglecting any dissent. In fact, Jaca's and Moirans's persecution by authorities was presented as a dire warning of the unrest that would follow any legislation outlawing slavery and the slave trade.

Rome, on the other hand, was more sympathetic to antislavery opinion. In 1684, while the two Capuchins' case was still pending before the very same Council of the Indies, Propaganda Fide considered a memorial against the enslavement of Christians by Lourenço de Silva de Mendouça, an Afro-Brazilian acting as procurator for the 'Mulattoes' of Brazil, Portugal, and Castile. The cardinals sent a letter to missionaries in Kongo reminding them of the evils and cruelty of the slave trade. Another circular was dispatched to papal nuncios in Spain and Portugal, urging them to seek a ban of enslavement from the monarchs. By March the following year, after the conclusion of the Spanish investigation of their case, Jaca and Moirans were in Rome and this is when the Capuchin order presented to the Propaganda a petition with a comprehensive indictment of the evils of slavery, regardless of whether its victims were Christian or not. Another petition considered at the same time and authored by Moirans drew attention to the situation of American Indians. In 1686, the Propaganda discussed yet another petition, this time from enslaved blacks in Brazil and London. Later that year, the Holy Office expressed its full agreement with the Capuchin condemnation of the slave trade and sent these resolutions to bishops and nuncios in Spain and Portugal. That Capuchin protests against slavery and the slave trade, although less radical, continued until the eighteenth century is proof of the inefficacy of these measures, even if the Papacy had made the strong and unprecedented gesture of condemning the slave trade.[17]

ANOTHER CARIBBEAN BEGINNING

Approximately a decade before Jaca and Moirans began excommunicating slave owners in Cuba, another Caribbean island – Barbados – was the site of the first serious contention over slavery in the relatively new British colonial empire. By that time, Barbados had become the principal hub of British colonization. Through immigration and conversions, the Society of the Friends of the Truth – a new religious organization that had emerged in the north of England during the unsettled times of the Civil War – developed a sizable community on the island.

Unlike the Puritan English colonies in the American Northeast, Barbados offered Friends a relatively hospitable and tolerant environment. Increasingly, however, they became the target of attacks by colonial authorities and the contentious issue of the treatment of enslaved Africans became an important

---

[17] See also John M. Lenhart, "Capuchin Champions of Negro Emancipation in Cuba (1681–1685)," *Franciscan Studies* 6, no. 2 (1946); Richard Gray, *Black Christians and White Missionaries* (New Haven, CT: Yale University Press, 1990); Richard Gray "The Papacy and Africa in the Seventeenth Century," in *Il Cristianesimo nel mondo atlantico nel secolo XVII* (Vatican City: Libreria editrice vaticana, 1997); Losada, "Diego de Avendaño," 10–11; Miguel Anxo Pena González, ed. *Resolución sobre la libertad de los negros y sus originarios, en estado de paganos y después ya cristianos: La primera condena de la esclavitud en el pensamiento hispano* (Madrid: Consejo Superior de Investigaciones Científicas, 2002); José Tomás López García, *Dos defensores de los esclavos negros en el siglo XVII (Francisco José de Jaca y Epifanio de Moirans)* (Maracaibo, Venezuela: Biblioteca Corpozulia, 1982).

strand in this developing conflict. By the 1640s, after experimentation with various crops, the colonists on the island had settled on the large-scale production of sugar – and on slave labor. Like in other colonial settlements, these developments and the increasing slave population resulted in a harsh regime of forced labor with repressive legal measures. The establishment of a militia in 1652 meant, among other things, to prevent slave uprisings was one such measure that created tensions with the Quakers on the island.

Around that time, and partly in a strategic move to appease fears that its members were intent on subverting the existing political order, the Society of Friends developed and codified a set of principles known as the "peace testimony" that repudiated violence and banned members from using weapons or engaging in fighting. Although the enforcement of these principles was often piecemeal and unsystematic, they presented an ethical dilemma for conscientious Quakers in Barbados who were called on to participate in the island militia. Their reluctance to do so provoked the hostility of the non-Quaker elites. By 1660, and in the context of an increasing persecution of unorthodox religion ushered in by the Restoration in England, the island authorities responded with the first of a series of laws that targeted Quakers and their unorthodox practices.[18]

It was on this intensifying conflict between civil authorities and Quakers that the issue of slavery superimposed itself. One of the practices that provided organizational cohesion to the growing Quaker movement was the circulation of letters under the Apostolic designation "epistles" and one of the first of these dispatched by the Society's founder, George Fox, in 1657 to Friends in the colonies urged slaveholding members to simply recognize the slaves' common humanity and treat them "mercifully." In 1671, when Fox along with other leading Quakers visited Barbados on a tour of the colonies, he reiterated this message and asked masters to provide religious instruction for their slaves. The religious meetings for slaves – and the accompanying criticism of Church of England ministers who did little to Christianize enslaved Africans – stirred a controversy. In the aftermath of his visit, six Anglican ministers petitioned the Barbados legislature to ban Quakers for their hostility to the established

---

[18] Dunn, *Sugar and Slaves*, 238–41; Larry Dale Gragg, *The Quaker Community on Barbados: Challenging the Culture of the Planter Class* (Columbia: University of Missouri Press, 2009); Katharine Gerbner, "The Ultimate Sin: Christianising Slaves in Barbados in the Seventeenth Century," *Slavery & Abolition* 31, no. 1 (2010). On the genesis and early period of Quakerism, see H. Larry Ingle, *First Among Friends: George Fox and the Creation of Quakerism* (New York: Oxford University Press, 1994); Rosemary Moore, *The Light in Their Consciences: Early Quakers in Britain, 1646–1666* (University Park: Pennsylvania State University Press, 2000); William C. Braithwaite, *The Beginnings of Quakerism*, 2d ed. (Cambridge: Cambridge University Press, 1955 [1912]); Barry Reay, *The Quakers and the English Revolution* (New York: St. Martin's, 1985). On Quaker "peace testimony," see Meredith Baldwin Weddle, *Walking in the Way of Peace: Quaker Pacifism in the Seventeenth Century* (Oxford: Oxford University Press, 2001).

church. In his turn, Fox addressed the legislature with denials of the allegation that the Quakers' religious outreach to slaves fomented rebellion. Although the colonial Assembly at that time seemed to have been unwilling to go as far as the petitioning Anglicans wanted it, the discovery and brutal repression of a slave conspiracy in 1675 made political authorities strengthen the oppressive slave regime and introduce further measures against Quakers. The fact that another visiting Quaker leader, William Edmundson, organized religious meetings for slaves in the same year did not help stifle the intensifying conflict. When forced to answer accusations of instilling insubordination and rebellion before the Governor and Council of Barbados, he responded that it was the current situation of keeping slaves "in Ignorance and under Oppression" that was more likely to produce social unrest.

In the aftermath of the unsuccessful slave conspiracy, the series of repressive measures introduced by the island legislature included laws designed specifically to prevent Quakers from holding religious meetings for slaves or providing any instruction to them; the punishment included, among other things, awarding half of the slaves discovered in such meetings to the person reporting them to the authorities. Quakers nevertheless continued to hold such meetings and paid their fines. Fox and Edmundson, while never articulating a principled critique of the institution of slavery as such, continued to produce epistles to their brethren in Barbados in which they emphasized the humanity of slaves and criticized the harshness of the slavery regime.

Yet theirs was a losing battle. The authorities were unyielding in their persecution, going so far as banning Quaker meetings altogether in 1680. Meanwhile, by the 1690s, the initially strong Quaker community on the island was decimated by epidemics and emigration, especially after a 1681 grant to Friend William Penn authorized the foundation of a religious tolerant colony in what was to become Pennsylvania.[19]

The Echoes of the Barbados Conflict

It was this atmosphere of increasingly oppressive slavery that the obstreperous Francisco José de Jaca must have witnessed in 1681 when he made a trip on a slaving ship from Cuba to Barbados.[20] Although we can only speculate in the

---

[19] Brycchan Carey, "'The Power that Giveth Liberty and Freedom': The Barbadian Origins of Quaker Antislavery Rhetoric, 1657–76," *ARIEL* 38, no. 1 (2007); Dunn, *Sugar and Slaves*, 103–06; William Edmundson, *A Journal of the Life, Travels, Sufferings and Labour of Love in the Work of the Ministry of that Worthy Elder and Faithful Servant of Jesus Christ, William Edmundson*, 2nd ed. (London: Mary Hinde, 1774), 81–85; Gerbner, "Ultimate Sin"; Gragg, *Quaker Community*; Amussen, *Caribbean Exchanges*; Kenneth L. Carroll, "George Fox and Slavery," *Quaker History* 86, no. 2 (1997). The Quakers' inclusion of slaves in worship provoked a similar hostility in seventeenth-century Virginia. See David S. Lovejoy, *Religious Enthusiasm in the New World: Heresy to Revolution* (Cambridge, MA: Harvard University Press, 1985), 198.

[20] Pena González, *Primera Propuesta*, 159.

absence of any direct evidence, it is not unlikely that what he saw there only reaffirmed his commitment to attack the practice of slaveholding, an activity that at the end led to the concerted Catholic protests against the slave trade later in the decade. It was a rare moment when the trajectories of two developments separated by strong confessional boundaries overlapped momentarily and most likely without any direct contact: on the one hand, the Capuchin attack on slavery, perhaps the last significant manifestation of the indigenist tradition initiated by the Dominicans of the early sixteenth century; on the other, the rather unpromising beginnings of what was to become a strong (and mostly Protestant) antislavery movement of international dimensions.

While hardly subversive of the principle of slaveholding itself, the Friends' insistence on holding religious meetings for their slaves threatened the consolidating moral order of colonial slavery that legitimized the enslavement of Africans by relegating them to a category apart from Christian Europeans. If Christians were, by definition, unenslaveable, the conversion of slaves to Christianity disrupted this dichotomy at the foundations of institutionalized colonial slavery. In this sense, the conflict that emerged in Barbados was not different from the conflictual pattern that had, by that time, occurred repeatedly in Iberian imperial possessions. The jurisdiction over non-European imperial subjects became a source of controversy between religious and nonreligious actors.

Yet inherent in this strictly jurisdictional conflict, was the deeper ethical question of the moral regime of empire and relations between Europeans and non-Europeans. The fight over the admittance of enslaved Africans to Christian worship in seventeenth-century Barbados reproduced ideological divisions and moral debates from an earlier imperial period. Like the Dominican "doctrine of Chiapa," Quaker concern to involve slaves in worship was based on the fundamental assumption of the equality of human beings regardless of their social status. When, on the other hand, the legislature of Barbados stated in 1681 that "slaves could not become Christian because of their 'savage brutishness,'"[21] it reproduced the logic of the *encomendero* argument of unbridgeable differences between Europeans and non-Europeans as it was articulated by Sepúlveda in the 1550s.

A similar cleavage emerged around the mid-seventeenth century in Dutch Calvinist circles regarding slavery within the possessions of the Dutch East India Company. Followers of the reformist wing within the Reformed Church around Gisbertus Voetius and of the movement known as the "Further Reformation" (*Nadere Reformatie*) criticized slavery as an infringement of the biblically postulated equality of all humans.[22]

---

[21] Amussen, *Caribbean Exchanges*, 115.
[22] Vink, "Freedom and Slavery." On the Voetian movement, see also Martin H. Prozesky, "The Emergence of Dutch Pietism," *Journal of Ecclesiastical History* 28, no. 1 (1977).

Nevertheless, throughout the period the opposing view eclipsed such considerations in the Protestant imperial world. Perhaps the most persistent legacy of the conflict over the Christianization of slaves in Barbados was the codification of a stringent and repressive legislation governing slavery that not only denied enslaved Africans' and American Indians' access to Christianity, but placed them outside of the legal regime that guaranteed Europeans their rights.

The Barbados Slave Code of 1688 on which similar statutes in the English Caribbean and the American South were based did not mince its words. It started from the observation that slaves "are of such barbarous, wild and savage nature, and such as renders them wholly unqualified to be governed by the Laws, Customs, and Practices of our nation."[23] Correspondingly, even such a minimal potential threat to the slave order as the religious specialists' access to slaves remained, as we will see, a highly charged and contentious issue in British colonies.

The promoters of the new Protestant empires had from the very beginning defined their enterprise as a more humane alternative to the Catholic conquest of America. Ironically, the Dutch and English translations of Las Casas's denunciations of Spanish cruelties were employed in this imperial propaganda war ever since the late sixteenth century when opponents of the Habsburgs in the Netherlands used his atrocity stories as an indictment of Spanish authority, drawing a direct parallel between the unjust treatment of American Indians and Dutch Protestants.[24] Yet by the late seventeenth century, the dominant discourse on human diversity in Protestant overseas empires was, paradoxically, one that fit best with the views of Las Casas's enemies for whom non-European imperial subjects were less than fully human.

This does not mean that the more humanitarian position represented by Quakers in Barbados vanished fully. Although the conflict on the island had no direct impact on legislation and policies, the ideas aired there continued to influence. No grouping within Quakerism comparable to the Lascasian factions in Catholic orders emerged to represent these ideas, yet they were disseminated in the 1680s in England by two figures influenced by Friends. One was the Church of England minister Morgan Godwyn who took seriously the Quaker harangues against the Anglican neglect of pastoral care for slaves. In fact, the pamphlet he published in 1680 under the title *The Negro's & Indians Advocate, Suing for Their Admission into the Church* was a direct response to an accusatory letter by George Fox asking Anglicans "who made them ministers of the Gospel to White People only, and not to the Tawneys and Blacks also." In this and other pamphlets, Godwyn sounded the typical theme of the inherent common humanity of the slave and condemned the brutality of the

---

[23] Quoted in Amussen, *Caribbean Exchanges*, 139.
[24] Vink, "Freedom and Slavery," 23; Philippe Rosenberg, "Thomas Tryon and the Seventeenth-Century Dimensions of Antislavery," *The William and Mary Quarterly* 61, no. 4 (2004): 637.

slave system.[25] Two more tracts that articulated a similar religious critique of slavery and were published and distributed by Quaker printers in 1684 were penned by Thomas Tryon who had lived in Barbados in the 1660s. Although invested in the system of colonial slavery through his position as agent of West Indian planters in England, Tryon was also influenced by the then fashionable mysticism of Jacob Böhme and his critique of slavery was part of a more general concern for moral improvement and reform of slave-based colonial economies.[26]

Similar ideas continued to circulate within the international (and transatlantic) networks of reform-minded Protestantism around the turn of the eighteenth century. In Massachusetts in 1700, Samuel Sewall, the only judge on the Salem witch trials to publicly repent for what he described as "judicial murder," a man deeply involved in various schemes for religious improvement, and – like Quakers – an advocate for friendly relations with Indians, published his pamphlet *The Selling of Joseph*, a strong condemnation of slavery. For years afterward, he distributed it among public officials and correspondents internationally.[27]

Goodwyn's *Negro's and Indians Advocate* was familiar to – and approved by – some of the founding members of the Anglican missionary organization that emerged from this international environment of religious reformism, the Society for the Propagation of the Gospel. The missionaries it appointed in American colonies began engaging with African slaves and American Indians. One of these, the Huguenot Francis Le Jau, who had experienced galley slavery personally as a member of a persecuted minority in France, encountered the typical opposition of planters and slave owners in Carolina. By 1709 he began complaining to the Society and the Bishop of London regarding the obstacles created by Europeans: they thwarted his outreach to American Indians that they thought would prevent lucrative slaving raids and there was a general dissatisfaction with his religious classes for slaves. Le Jau also condemned the

---

[25] Morgan Godwyn, *The Negro's & Indians Advocate, Suing for Their Admission into the Church* (London: J. D., 1680), 4–7. It is possible that Godwyn, like the Quakers, experienced the settlers' opposition to his plans to Christianize slaves in Virginia before his move to Barbados. See Travis Glasson, *Mastering Christianity: Missionary Anglicanism and Slavery in the Atlantic World* (New York: Oxford University Press, 2012), 47–50; Brown, *Moral Capital*, 69–71; Vaughan, *Roots of American*.

[26] Amussen, *Caribbean Exchanges*, 180–84; Rosenberg, "Thomas Tryon"; Daniel Carey, "Sugar, Colonialism and the Critique of Slavery: Thomas Tryon in Barbados," in *Interpreting Colonialism*, eds. Bryon R. Wells and Philip Steward (Oxford: Voltaire Foundation, 2004); Vaughan, *Roots of American*, 75–76. As early as 1673, the prominent Presbyterian divine Richard Baxter had also reminded masters to treat slaves humanely and give them opportunity to accept the Christian faith in his *Christian Directory*. See Amussen, *Caribbean Exchanges*, 180; Vaughan, *Roots of American*, 74.

[27] Mark A. Peterson, "The Selling of Joseph: Bostonians, Antislavery, and the Protestant International, 1689–1733," *Massachusetts Historical Review* 4 (2004); Lawrence W. Towner, "The Sewall-Saffin Dialogue on Slavery," *The William and Mary Quarterly* 21, no. 1 (1964).

cruelty of the punishments meted out on slaves. Another former Huguenot missionary, Elias Neau in New York, encountered the same hostility by slave owners against his teaching of slaves, especially after a slave revolt.[28]

Three decades later, a similar conflict erupted in South Carolina where Le Jau had worked until his death, but this time the context and the leading motives were provided by another wave of pan-Protestant reformism that swept the American colonies under the name of the Great Awakening. During his visit to the colony in 1740 George Whitefield, one of the most successful and visible religious entrepreneurs of the Awakening, published an open letter to planters accusing them, among other things, of "abuse and cruelty to the poor Negroes." Deeply troubled by what he saw as an alarming decline of religion in his environment, the wealthy planter Henry Bryan, one of Whitefield's converts in South Carolina's backcountry, began holding religious meetings for slaves. Although Bryan never gave up slaveholding, the South Carolina House of Commons was alarmed enough to appoint in 1742 a committee to investigate these potentially subversive "frequent and great Assemblies of Negroes." The committee recommended that existing laws against such meetings should be enforced and the planter elites and the Anglican establishment – both of which Bryan had offended with his attacks on rampant irrelegiosity – closed ranks, forcing him to recant publicly.[29]

CONCLUSION

At least since the seventeenth century, the dual moral regime of European imperialism was strengthened by the pervasive exploitation of enslaved Africans in overseas colonies. At the same time, a principled political practice of opposition to colonial slavery began to take shape. There were two distinct starting points of this practice. First, an attack on slavery emerged from within the ranks of Catholic religious actors as an extension of Iberian indigenism. As the previous chapters in this study have shown, this wave of advocacy was mainly concerned with the morality of attitudes towards indigenous people. By the seventeenth century, however, members of Catholic religious orders steeped in the indigenist tradition began increasingly to problematize the exploitation of

---

[28] Faith Vibert, "The Society for the Propagation of the Gospel in Foreign Parts: Its Work for the Negroes in North America before 1783," *The Journal of Negro History* 18, no. 2 (1933); Glasson, *Mastering Christianity*; Brown, *Moral Capital*, 55–91; Edgar Legare Pennington, "The Reverend Francis Le Jau's Work Among Indians and Negro Slaves," *The Journal of Southern History* 1, no. 4 (1935); Michael Anesko, "So Discreet a Zeal: Slavery and the Anglican Church in Virginia, 1680–1730," *Virginia Magazine of History & Biography* 93, no. 3 (1985): 273.

[29] Glasson, *Mastering Christianity*, 125–26; Harvey H. Jackson, "Hugh Bryan and the Evangelical Movement in Colonial South Carolina," *William & Mary Quarterly* 43, no. 4 (1986); Lovejoy, *Religious Enthusiasm*, 200–01; Leigh Eric Schmidt, "'The Grand Prophet,' Hugh Bryan: Early Evangelicalism's Challenge to the Establishment and Slavery in the Colonial South," *The South Carolina Historical Magazine* 87, no. 4 (1986).

enslaved Africans. Around the same time, another wave of opposition to slavery took off within the Protestant imperial environment.

There was no interaction between these two traditions of emerging antislavery thought and practice. Their practitioners were separated both by the political borders of competing empires and by the doctrinal differences and hostilities that had hardened with the division between the Catholic Church and the new Protestant churches during the Reformation. Furthermore, the trajectories of these two traditions were quite different. In an intense sequence of events, from Francisco José de Jaca's confrontation with white settlers near Caracas to the Holy Office's solemn pronouncement against slavery, the indigenist legacy fueled a strong, if short-lived, outburst of Capuchin mobilization. Urging that all slaves be freed immediately, the two friars at the origin of this mobilization, Jaca and Moirans, were precocious radicals who espoused an uncompromising position that the future Anglo-American antislavery movement would not accept officially until the 1830s.[30] Perhaps not surprisingly, their radical message was diluted when the Capuchin order and Papal institutions adopted it. Nevertheless, the two Capuchins became the catalysts for an instance of unprecedented concerted action and political mobilization coordinated by the order.

By contrast, Protestant initiatives in this early period did not produce a continuous political mobilization and their critique of slavery was relatively mild. Even as Jaca and Moirans were preaching immediate manumission to Cuban slaveholders, Quakers in Barbados were persecuted for demanding nothing more than humane treatment and Christianization of slaves – a position virtually identical with the mainstream Catholic doctrine of ameliorating slavery that had taken shape with Luis de Molina's work toward the end of the sixteenth century. And for a very long time, this remained the most radical extreme of Protestant attacks on slavery. From today's point of view, more than two centuries after the first emergence of an international and predominantly Protestant antislavery network in the late eighteenth century, the Capuchin campaign of the 1680s appears almost as an aberration: a doomed and precocious flare-up of antislavery sentiment before the time was right. Yet were we to reflect on the Catholic-Protestant contrast during the 1750s, the unimpressive modesty of the Protestant effort would be a more apt conclusion.

Despite these differences in outcomes, however, in both the Catholic and Protestant cases, the same interactional pattern reasserted itself. Religious actors turned toward an activist stance against slavery while on the path of radicalization against competing imperial networks. Like their Catholic predecessors and contemporaries, Quakers and other early critics of slavery in

---

[30] On this transition from gradual to immediate emancipation as the main ideology of antislavery, see David Brion Davis, *From Homicide to Slavery: Studies in American Culture* (New York: Oxford University Press, 1986), 238–72; Duncan MacLeod, "From Gradualism to Immediatism: Another Look," *Slavery & Abolition* 3, no. 2 (1982).

English colonies began to question the legitimacy of slavery in the course of their jurisdictional conflicts over the Christianization of enslaved Africans. And all these contentious episodes were characterized by the reappearance and re-articulation of the same pair of mutually antagonistic ideologies of human difference: one which defined enslaved Africans as intrinsically different and "inconvertible," and another set of ideas that posited the fundamental unity of humankind. Like the Lascasian ideology of common humanity, this latter position, once advocated by Quakers in Barbados, continued to inform religious actors in various parts of the consolidating British-American Empire, while adherence to it led religious actors on a collision course with imperial segments interested in maintaining and strengthening the institution of colonial slavery.

The parallel trajectories of incipient Catholic and Protestant antislavery were rooted in the structural similarities of religious actors in both religious environments. One invariant characteristic of the episodes of early Protestant engagement with the ethics of slavery, from Quakers' outreach to slaves in Barbados in the 1670s to Bryan's religious meetings in the 1740s, is that they, like previous Catholic confrontations, were motivated by various waves of movements for religious reform. Despite doctrinal hostilities and antagonistic self-representations, the two varieties of Christianity in equal measure inherited and nurtured within their spheres the long-standing reformist impulse. Indeed, the Protestant Reformation itself – along with the various attempts to further reform already "reformed churches," such as English Puritanism or the Dutch *nadere reformatie* – had deep continuities with and run parallel to ongoing projects to reform the Catholic Church from within.[31]

In English and Dutch colonies, the first principled critics of slavery came from a complex ecclesiological landscape that, almost in a hall-of-mirror fashion, consistently reproduced in various configurations these oppositions between reformism and the orthodoxy that this reformism opposed. Invariably, these critics occupied the reformist end of the complex doctrinal spectrum. Thus, the Quakers belonged to the ranks of Dissent, the churches that for princi-pled reasons worshiped outside the insufficiently reformed Church of England, while someone like Morgan Godwyn came from the reformist wing of the very same established state church. On the Catholic side, the Society of Jesus and the Capuchin order whose members were particularly active in the emerging critique of colonial slavery were the product of similar reformist impulses in the sixteenth century. Like the various "puritans" who wanted to reform what

---

[31] On Protestant movements of "further reform," see Martin Brecht, ed. *Der Pietismus vom sie-bzehnten bis zum frühen achtezehnten Jahrhundert* (Göttingen: Vandenhoeck & Ruprecht, 1993); Patrick Collinson, *The Elizabethan Puritan Movement* (London: Methuen, 1967); Fulbrook, *Piety and Politics: Religion and the Rise of Absolutism in England, Württemberg and Prussia*; S. van der Linde, "Der Reformierte 'Pietismus' in den Niederlanden," in *Pietismus und Reveil*, ed. J. van den Berg and J. P. van Dooren (Leiden, the Netherlands: E. J. Brill, 1978). On the Catholic Reformation, see Mullett, *The Catholic Reformation*; Hsia, *Catholic Renewal*; Bireley, *Refashioning of Catholicism*.

they thought was an insufficiently reformed Protestant church, the Capuchins started as a movement to reform the Italian Observants, the carriers of the Franciscan "Reformation" of a century earlier.[32]

On both sides of the theological divide, critics of slavery emerged out of reformist religious organizations or reformist religious subcultures driven by the perceived need to institute stricter and more adequate patterns of religious observance. Like Catholic orders, their Protestant reformist counterparts understood their activities as an effort to return to the pristine origins of unadulterated "primitive" Christianity, while their members understood themselves as direct heirs to the first apostles. In both cases, the combination of a reformist disposition with evangelistic conviction motivated engagement with the fate of culturally and geographically distant strangers. For this type of activist religion, whether Catholic or Protestant, there was little difference between converting members of rival Christian confession, exhorting 'nominal' Christians of one's church to conform to higher standards of religious behavior, or the evangelization of the "heathen" who have not been exposed to Christian doctrine. The main difference between individuals, from this point of view, was their relationship to God, not their cultural attributes, racial characteristics, or social status.[33]

Seen in this context, these incipient antislavery initiatives did not arise, as they have been characterized recently, simply "from the particular personalities and needs of individual critics" and "isolated moralists."[34] It is true that none of these outbursts produced an organizationally enduring practice comparable to the two phenomena bookending this period: an earlier Iberian indigenism and a later international antislavery movement. Yet at the same time the activities of early antislavery critics were deeply embedded in the organizational field of religion whose structure provided the conditions for the articulation of an ethical and political stance opposed to the colonial status quo. Religious reformism was an important source for these critical engagements, leading religious actors into a conflict with other imperial networks. And, in important ways, previous religious struggles had long-lasting effects on subsequent developments. Thus, the practice and doctrines of Lascasian indigenism influenced the first Catholic

[32] On English Dissent and Quakers within the tradition of radical reformation, see Davis, *Slavery in Western Culture*, 291–332; Michael R. Watts, *The Dissenters: From the Reformation to the French Revolution* (Oxford: Clarendon Press, 1978). On Catholic religious orders, see Bireley, *Refashioning of Catholicism*; Hsia, *Catholic Renewal*, 25–33; H. Outram Evennett, "The New Orders," in *The New Cambridge Modern History*, Vol. 2: *The Reformation, 1520–1559*, ed. G. R. Elton (Cambridge: Cambridge University Press, 1990).

[33] Ward, *Christianity under the Ancien Régime, 1648–1789*. The similarities between Catholic orders and reforming Protestantism are noted by Koschorke, "Konfessionelle Spaltung," 17–18. See also Hartmann Tyrell, "Weltgesellschaft, Weltmission und religiöse Organisationen: Einleitung," in *Weltmission und religiöse Organisationen: Protestantische Missionsgesellschaften im 19. und 20. Jahrhundert*, eds. Artur Bogner, Bernd Holtwick, and Hartmann Tyrell (Würzburg: Ergon, 2004), 23–28.

[34] Brown, *Moral Capital*, 39–41.

critics of slavery. Similarly, the controversy in Barbados influenced subsequent antislavery engagements in the British imperial world.

Thus, the underlying processes were largely analogous to the processes that had driven the rise of Iberian indigenism earlier. Yet these first attacks on slavery occurred in a political and cultural context that had evolved significantly since the first Dominican appeals to the royal court at the dawn of Spanish colonization of the Caribbean. The very issues raised by the trans-Atlantic slave trade were of a different – and politically more intractable – nature than the issues arising from the incorporation of indigenous Americans in the political and labor structure of Iberian imperialism. The Atlantic slave trade had evolved rapidly into a profitable commercial enterprise to which all imperial states in the period were deeply committed.[35] Royals and state administrators were correspondingly unwilling to tinker with a well-functioning source of income, as well as change the conditions in the colonies that provided the ready demand for the slave traders' cargo.

Other conjunctural factors presented additional obstacles impeding the emergence of a coherent movement in this early period. Catholic antislavery protests emerged at the tail end of the wave of indigenist mobilization, in a context where, as we saw in Chapter 2, the imperial state had been able to subdue imperial religious networks and thus derail the religious reformers' initiatives. In many ways, the constellation of forces in the British Empire, the most powerful Protestant empire of the period, remained strikingly different from its Iberian counterpart. Yet, although for different reasons, this context was equally unpropitious for the development of an extensive and continuous mobilization.

In Iberian possessions, the very ideological framework of a unified Catholic realm to which new overseas territories were being annexed took it for granted that new imperial subjects were Christians-to-be. The basic idea of the "convertibility" of new imperial subjects was, at least in theory, adopted as official policy and served as the natural focus for the activity of highly organized and specialized religious organizations like the mendicant orders and the Society of Jesus who enjoyed state support, even if it was often given begrudgingly and with various limitations. The situation was different in the newer English colonies. Not only was political authority there much more fragmented than in the relatively centralized Iberian possessions. England's colonies also lacked a unified ecclesiastical hierarchy or even an overarching church policy in ethnically and religiously heterogeneous settlements – a diversity fueled in part by the inherently fissiparous tendencies of Protestantism, otherwise the dominant religious brand in the empire. In this context, religious organizations were in an inherently weaker political position and had more incentives to compromise with prevailing norms.

Furthermore, an even stricter slavery regime emerged in the context of greater local autonomy that distinguished English colonies from Iberian counterparts.

---

[35] Rawley, *Slave Trade.*

In the aftermath of the early conflicts around the evangelization of slaves in Barbados, a harsh disciplinary treatment of enslaved Africans was enshrined in statutes, especially in the Caribbean and the American South. Even more ominously, the very issue of granting slaves access to religion became highly charged and sensitive for local slave-holding elites. In their eyes, even something as basic as the Christianization of slaves would be a subversive proposition for decades to come. This widespread distrust made the conflict between the two views on human diversity represented by slaveholders and religious reformers respectively more intractable and even hopeless in comparison with Iberian empires. It is hardly surprising, for example, that in an environment where the access to potential slave converts was tightly policed by edgy local elites, the Anglican Society for the Propagation of the Gospel chose by the 1740s to accommodate the slaveholding society's values and accept the legitimacy of slavery to the extent of actively supporting legislation that reassured nervous slave owners that conversion to Christianity did not change the legal status of human chattel.[36] In the end, representatives of a humanitarian position critical of slavery remained in a structurally weak position in the British colonies of the period.

Thus, the interaction between the political context of empires and continuing religious reformism continued to inform developments in this period. By the mid-eighteenth century, however, for a variety of mutually reinforcing reasons, the political conditions of consolidating overseas empires committed to enslaved labor both strengthened even further the moral divide between Europe and the colonies. These conditions also made the consistent advocacy on behalf of enslaved Africans costly, if not impossible. Yet, whereas the Capuchin protest of the 1680s failed to ignite an enduring movement, a century later the foundations of a long-lasting antislavery were securely laid with the beginnings of several initiatives and organizations in the British imperial world. What changed to make it possible that a predominantly Protestant antislavery network develop out of some rather unpromising beginnings? Chapter 4 focuses on the developments that led American Quakerism to create the initial foundations for an influential and long-lasting advocacy network.

---

[36] Glasson, *Mastering Christianity*; "'Baptism doth not bestow Freedom': Missionary Anglicanism, Slavery, and the Yorke-Talbot Opinion, 1701–30," *William & Mary Quarterly* 67, no. 2 (2010). For the continuing opposition to incorporating slaves into religious practices, see also Sandra Rennie, "Virginia's Baptist Persecution, 1765–1778," *Journal of Religious History* 12, no. 1 (1982). On the general context of religion in British colonies in the period, see Charles L. Cohen, "The Colonization of British North America as an Episode in the History of Christianity," *Church History* 72, no. 3 (2003); Carla Gardina Pestana, *Protestant Empire: Religion and the Making of the British Atlantic World* (Philadelphia: University of Pennsylvania Press, 2009). Pestana suggests also that the relatively doctrinal rigidity and high criteria for membership in Protestant churches (in contrast to the Catholic Church's universal claims) could have been a disincentive for Europeans to accept colonial "others" as co-religionists (p. 71).

4

Quaker Reformers and the Politicization of Antislavery

Although the Quakers' initial confrontation with slavery in Barbados did not produce an enduring movement comparable to Iberian indigenism, a century later they formed the backbone of a politically and organizationally coherent network acting against the source of colonial slavery, the Atlantic trade in enslaved Africans. The foundations of a long-lasting international antislavery movement were laid with several initiatives and organizations: the formation of a London Committee for the Abolition of the Slave Trade and the revival of an earlier American organization as the Pennsylvanian Abolition Society in 1787; the formation of the *Société des Amis des Noirs* in Paris the following year; the first petition drives against the slave trade organized by Quakers, Methodists, and the new abolitionist organizations; as well as the increasing institutional commitment by the Society of Friends both in America and Britain to the cause of slave trade abolition.[1] For the first time now, the general uneasiness and concern that had characterized the episodic confrontations in the previous century was supplanted by a concrete political program for the abolition of the slave trade through activities targeting various sites of imperial political power in London and Paris and the colonies. Intermittent

---

[1] Marcel Dorigny and Bernard Gainot, *La Société des Amis des Noirs, 1788–1799: Contribution a l'histoire de l'abolition de l'esclavage* (Paris: Éditions UNESCO, 1998); Frederick William Pfister, "In the Cause of Freedom: American Abolition Societies, 1775–1808" (Ph.D. Dissertation, Miami University, 1980); Richard K. MacMaster, "Liberty or Property? The Methodist Petition for Emancipation in Virginia, 1785," *Methodist History* 10, no. 1 (1971); Wayne J. Eberly, "The Pennsylvania Abolition Society, 1775–1830" (Ph.D. Dissertation, Pennsylvania State University, 1973); Judi Jennings, *The Business of Abolishing the British Slave Trade, 1783–1807* (London: F. Cass, 1997); J. R. Oldfield, *Popular Politics and British Anti-Slavery: The Mobilisation of Public Opinion against the Slave Trade, 1787–1807* (Manchester: Manchester University Press, 1995); Albert Mathews, "Notes on the Proposed Abolition of Slavery in Virginia in 1785," *Publications of the Colonial Society of Massachusetts* 6 (1904).

and disjointed conflicts over the morality of slavery were transformed into a coherent political movement.

This transformation was a complex and multi-faceted process, yet throughout it was driven by the same basic dynamics that had been in play in the preceding wave of Catholic pro-indigenist advocacy: it arose from the conflictual radicalization of religious actors in the imperial context. This time the activist group that initiated the process of politicization of Protestant antislavery was a small nucleus of Quaker reformers around Anthony Benezet, a humble Philadelphia schoolmaster of Huguenot origins. Benezet compiled and distributed widely the first systematic corpus of antislavery propaganda: a series of pamphlets and books documenting the atrocities of the slave trade. He was the author and tireless promoter of the first comprehensive political project against colonial slavery. And, perhaps most importantly, he created a network of allies in America and – first in 1763 and then in 1771 – launched a broad and eventually successful search for potential allies in Britain with the ultimate aim of affecting a legislative abolition of the trade.[2] Thus, whereas earlier attacks on slavery in the British imperial context had been relatively short-lived and local affairs, with Benezet's intervention, a relatively coherent political program for a comprehensive attack on the commercial foundations of slavery emerged. What is more – as we will see in Chapter 5 – his initial blueprint for political action had important implications for the creation of a wider antislavery network of international dimensions.

The role of the group of reformers around Benezet – and the religious radicalization at the origins of their antislavery project – deserve a closer look, if only because it has been obscured, if not overlooked, by what has emerged as the "standard" historiographic account of the origins of the abolitionist movement. The general template for this account was laid out by David Brion Davis's influential *Problem of Slavery in the Age of Revolutions*. Davis credited Quaker networks in the British Empire as the originators of antislavery, yet, drawing on Sydney James's earlier treatment, he explained their contribution to abolitionism as an apolitical charity project that arose from the alliance of two segments within the Society of Friends: reformers (for whom withdrawal from slavery was a strategy of moral regeneration) and successful capitalists (for whom giving up slavery was a "compromise of limited sacrifice" between economic success and adherence to strict religious precepts). Thus, according to Davis, having lost their political power in the Pennsylvania Assembly (and having chosen the wrong, pro-British loyalist side during the Revolution), Friends

---

[2] Maurice Jackson, *Let This Voice Be Heard: Anthony Benezet, Father of Atlantic Abolitionism* (Philadelphia: University of Pennsylvania Press, 2009); Jonathan D. Sassi, "With a Little Help from the Friends: The Quaker and Tactical Contexts of Anthony Benezet's Abolitionist Publishing," *Pennsylvania Magazine of History & Biography* 135 (2011); Kirsten Sword, "Remembering Dinah Nevil: Strategic Deceptions in Eighteenth-Century Antislavery," *The Journal of American History* 97, no. 2 (2010).

turned from a political to a "social" leadership that proved to serve multiple useful functions. By carrying visibly the virtuous antislavery badge, they were able to restore their reputation tarnished by accusations of loyalism and treason during the Revolution, to create prestigious connections with capitalists and urban elites of other denominations in middle-class civic associations, and – ultimately – to normalize an ideology of nominally free yet disciplined labor with a "highly selective response to labor exploitation."[3]

If the Quaker origins of antislavery were so inherently consensual, calculative, and apolitical, how did abolitionism acquire its remarkably political and contentious character in the late eighteenth century, especially as it manifested itself in the wide popular mobilization against the slave trade in Britain? Historians have sought to untangle this seeming paradox by seeking those additional factors from outside of the field of religion that transformed an idiosyncratic and politically nonthreatening "sectarian" concern with the morality of slavery into a bona fide political movement. Thus, Seymour Drescher identified the manufacturers and artisans of industrialized Northern England as the agents whose political attitudes, sensitivities, and skills transformed a "low-key lobby" with a "self-limiting ... agitational style" into "the prototype of the modern social reform movement." Whereas in this interpretation the ultimate source for the politicization of antislavery sentiment is the particulars of British capitalism, more recently Christopher Brown has shifted the lens toward the larger imperial context. He argues that slavery became a truly political issue only in the ideological conflict around the American Revolution when colonial claims for universal liberty and accusations of British tyranny revealed indirectly their own inconsistency with the persisting toleration of human bondage in America. While this did not make proto-revolutionary and revolutionary Americans abolitionists, it opened up a political debate over the morality of empire and made it possible for critics of slavery to claim safely a higher moral ground, especially in the context of British self-scrutiny following the loss of North American colonies. In a nod to Davis's account, Brown explains the conversion of British Quakers to abolitionism by this changing moral calculus. Induced in this context to display their relatively cheap antislavery virtuousness, they provided the "infrastructure" for a social movement that, however, only took shape when two outsiders, Thomas Clarkson and William Wilberforce, imparted on it "a grandeur it had lacked" in its pre-political Quaker origins.[4]

---

[3] David Brion Davis, *The Problem of Slavery in the Age of Revolution, 1770–1823* (New York: Oxford University Press, [1975] 1999), 251. See also his *Slavery in Western Culture*; and Sydney V. James, *A People among Peoples: Quaker Benevolence in Eighteenth-Century America* (Cambridge, MA: Harvard University Press, 1963). Jack Marietta has identified some important inconsistencies in the James-Davis interpretation. See Jack D. Marietta, *The Reformation of American Quakerism, 1748–1783* (Philadelphia: University of Pennsylvania Press, 1984), 124–25, 273.

[4] See Drescher, *Capitalism and Antislavery*, especially 61–72; Brown, *Moral Capital*. Between these two books, Robin Blackburn's treatment both repeated and amplified Drescher's statement

Thus, with the tone set by Davis's influential book, the general trend has been to minimize the role of Quakers as political actors while still crediting them as early adopters of antislavery norms. In the resulting aggregate historiographical picture, only a combination of structural factors and external allies transformed their pre-political abhorrence of slavery into a genuine social movement. More generally, this explanation rests on a basic dichotomy of two successive variants of abolitionism: a charity-oriented early Quaker version and a truly political post-Quaker movement.

Yet there are good reasons to question the validity of this distinction. In fact, when Quaker reformers engaged the issue of slavery in the mid-eighteenth century, they initiated a deeply political project. This was a project that arose out of their confrontations with imperial authorities around a different issue: the question of peaceful and just relations with Native Americans. The reformers' distinctly political program that crystallized out of this conflict amounted to a crucial transformation in the pattern of moral engagement with slavery in the Protestant imperial context. It was also a decisive step toward the organizational concentration of antislavery energies toward the end of the century that produced the first popular movement for the abolition of the slave trade. The rest of this chapter focuses on this formative moment in Protestant antislavery by examining the processes through which a group of Quaker reformers revived, intensified, and ultimately politicized an earlier Quaker tradition of opposition to slavery.

QUAKER REFORM AND DIVESTMENT FROM SLAVERY

Although the Quaker community on Barbados, where the first conflicts over the Christianization of enslaved Africans flared up, proved short-lived, Friends succeeded in establishing themselves in the English colonies on the American main. Sizable Quaker populations were present in Rhode Island, New York, and Carolina and a royal grant for a colony to a Quaker proprietor, William Penn, made Pennsylvania the natural stronghold of American Quakerism. In all these territories of Quaker settlement, slavery and the slave trade were practiced and everywhere Friends established themselves as slave owners and participants in the trade. At the same time, the ethics of slavery continued to provoke doubts as groups and individuals, at least since 1688, voiced their discomfort with the ownership of human beings.

The production of these and subsequent critiques of slavery occurred within the specific organizational and cultural environment of the Society of Friends, where, in the absence of a written confessional or disciplinary constitution, official policies and binding rules of behavior were arrived at by representative bodies in consensual decisions. These representative bodies, in turn, were structured

on the importance of Manchester and prefigured Brown's emphasis on the American Revolution. See Blackburn, *Overthrow of Colonial Slavery*.

in a pyramidal hierarchy of monthly, quarterly, and yearly meetings. By the 1710s, an increasing number of Monthly Meetings in Pennsylvania, New York, and Rhode Island were introducing the issue of slavery in the organizational decision-making process by addressing their superiors with requests to rule on the ethics of slaveholding and participation in the slave trade. In response, the Philadelphia Yearly Meeting, perhaps the most influential American Quaker body, turned to the Quaker "headquarters," the Yearly Meeting in London with official requests for clarification on policies on slavery.

Perhaps not surprisingly, Yearly Meetings, dominated as they were by increasingly wealthy and prosperous "weighty" Friends, while not dismissing the critics' concerns, were unwilling to adopt a radical antislavery stance. More insistent and committed critics found themselves disciplined and "disowned" or expelled from membership, partly because in order to publicize their views, such early Quaker abolitionists resorted to publishing their arguments without the consent of the official hierarchy, which, at this point, was not able or willing to articulate a unified and unequivocal position against slavery.[5]

All this was to change under the impact of a strengthening movement for reform within transatlantic Quakerism. The first stirrings came in the 1730s in England when concerns were expressed about the relaxation of religious discipline within the Society of Friends compared to the heroic age of the founders in the seventeenth century. By the 1750s, a critical mass of Friends actively engaged in a reformist project that had emerged on both sides of the Atlantic. The crucial channel for the spread of this project was the Quaker institution of "traveling ministry." Although there was no separate class of ministers among Quakers, local meetings granted a special informal authority to individual men and women who could prove a calling to lead in matters spiritual. Even more formally, such spiritual leaders were certified to travel and

---

[5] On these early confrontations with the ethic of slavery within the Society of Friends, see Herbert Aptheker, "The Quakers and Negro Slavery," *The Journal of Negro History* 25, no. 3 (1940), e.g., 399; Ira V. Brown, "Pennsylvania's Antislavery Pioneers: 1688–1776," *Pennsylvania History* 55, no. 2 (1988); Brycchan Carey, "Inventing a Culture of Anti-Slavery: Pennsylvanian Quakers and the Germantown Protest of 1688," in *Imagining Transatlantic Slavery*, eds. Cora Kaplan and John Oldfield (Basingstoke, UK: Palgrave Macmillan, 2010); Kenneth L. Carroll, "William Southeby, Early Quaker Antislavery Writer," *Pennsylvania Magazine of History and Biography* 89, no. 4 (1965); J. Herbert Fretz, "The Germantown Anti-Slavery Petition of 1688," *Mennonite Quarterly Review* 33, no. 1 (1959); Katharine Gerbner, "Antislavery in Print," *Early American Studies* 9, no. 3 (2011); Rufus Matthew Jones, *The Quakers in the American Colonies* (London: Macmillan, 1911); Andreas Mielke, "'What's Here to Do?' An Inquiry Concerning Sarah and Benjamin Lay, Abolitionists," *Quaker History* 86, no. 1 (1997); Alan M. Rees, "English Friends and the Abolition of the British Slave Trade," *Bulletin of Friends Historical Association* 44, no. 2 (1955); Jean R. Soderlund, *Quakers & Slavery: A Divided Spirit* (Princeton, NJ: Princeton University Press, 1985); Roberts Vaux, *Memoirs of the Lives of Benjamin Lay and Ralph Sandiford; Two of the Earliest Public Advocates for the Emancipation of the Enslaved Africans* (London: W. Phillips, 1816); Arthur J. Worrall, *Quakers in the Colonial Northeast* (Hanover, NH: University Press of New England, 1980).

address coreligionists' meetings in other locations. By mid-century, British and American traveling ministers crossing the Atlantic formed a mobile spiritual elite within Quakerism that pushed the reform program locally in the course of their itinerancy.

What is more, in the 1750s, representatives of this nucleus of reformers was able to occupy formal positions of authority within the administrative structures of Pennsylvania Quakerism. This was partly a result of generational change: an older cohort that had grown to be wealthy, comfortable with things of the world, and relaxed in its adherence to Quaker ethical principles was gradually being replaced by a younger generation of leaders devoted to the moral regeneration of the Society.

Theirs were the religious reformer's standard preoccupations to improve morality and combat decay by enforcing stricter adherence to the foundational rules and conventions. Thus, reformers attacked all the manifestations of what they considered violations of the Quaker moral code: sexual relations and marriage to nonmembers, alcohol consumption and Sabbath-breaking, as well as the abandonment of traditional "plainness" in dress, speech, and behavior. Intertwined with these preoccupations, however, was another complex of issues related to the ethic of Quaker relations with the "outside" world: the moral implications of wealth and the adherence to what had become the traditional precept of nonviolence. These issues, in turn, pushed the reformers toward a renewed scrutiny of the institution of slavery and of European's relations with American Indians.[6]

The ascendance of reformers within the leadership structures of Quakerism in the 1750s led finally and for the first time to an unequivocal official condemnation of slavery and to a comprehensive disciplinary program to disengage members from slaveholding and participation in the slave trade. Central to these developments were two reformers of the new generation: the schoolmaster Anthony Benezet of Philadelphia and the tailor John Woolman of Mount Holy, New Jersey. By 1754, the Pennsylvania Yearly Meeting approved the publication under Quaker official imprimatur of a pamphlet entitled *An Epistle of Caution and Advice, Concerning the Buying and Keeping of Slaves*. The publication of what was to be the first in an influential series of antislavery printed materials produced by Benezet signaled for the first time an official condemnation not only of participation in the slave trade, but of slaveholding itself. An even more consequential measure was a 1758 decision of the Philadelphia Yearly Meeting to introduce concrete disciplinary sanctions against participation in the slave

---

[6] Kenneth L. Carroll, "A Look at the 'Quaker Revival of 1756'," *Quaker History* 65, no. 2 (1976); Rebecca Larson, *Daughters of Light: Quaker Women Preaching and Prophesying in the Colonies and Abroad, 1700–1775* (New York: Knopf, 1999); Marietta, *Reformation of Quakerism*; Peter Silver, *Our Savage Neighbors: How Indian War Transformed Early America* (New York: W. W. Norton, 2008), 28–30; Soderlund, *Quakers & Slavery*, 32–47; Worrall, *Quakers in the Colonial*, 81–95.

trade and against slave ownership. Local meetings were empowered to remove slave owners from administrative positions and were encouraged to form "visiting committees" to persuade members to abandon any involvement with slavery. At the same time, the Yearly Meeting in London similarly gave in, finally, to the reformers' pressure. In 1757, a subcommittee on Quaker participation in the slave trade was appointed and the following year, the Yearly Meeting, while not adopting any concrete disciplinary measures, made for the first time a strong official pronouncement against slavery by advising members everywhere to not participate in the slave trade. Finally, in 1761, London decreed the disownment of any British Friend still engaged in the trade.

From Pennsylvania, both the official strictures against slavery and the institution of visiting committees radiated to Quaker settlements throughout the American colonies. Although the enactment of these policies varied locally, they also became increasingly restrictive as more and more meetings in the 1770s adopted a rule against the ownership of slaves among their members who now faced "disownment" if they refused to disentangle themselves from any commercial interactions involving enslaved individuals. By the 1780s, Quakers had virtually divested from slave-holding.[7]

The Meaning of Divestment

In American colonies, the slaves' upkeep was the responsibility of their owners, whereas – under the poor laws of the time and in the absence of any modern social security – slaves transitioning into freedom became automatically the local tax payers' responsibility. This provided a strong incentive for legislation that, at least at face value, aimed to prevent masters from "abandoning" their charges and transferring the burden of their upkeep to the local community. The statutes of the Southern colonies made manumission particularly costly and hard which, in turn, raised significantly the costs for the Quaker divesting project in these communities. And whereas, for example, the Virginia legislature, under Quaker pressure, modified laws to make manumission easier in 1782, North Carolina legislators went in the opposite direction in 1777.

[7] Roger Anstey, *The Atlantic Slave Trade and British Abolition, 1760–1810* (London: Macmillan, 1975), 204–20; Michael J. Crawford, *The Having of Negroes is Become a Burden: The Quaker Struggle to Free Slaves in Revolutionary North Carolina* (Gainesville: University Press of Florida, 2010); James, *People among Peoples*, 217–21; Judi Jennings, "Mid-Eighteenth Century British Quakerism and the Response to the Problem of Slavery," *Quaker History* 66, no. 1 (1977): 23–25; Jones, *Quakers in American Colonies*; Marietta, *Reformation of Quakerism*; *A Narrative of Some of the Proceedings of North Carolina Yearly Meeting on the Subject of Slavery within Its Limits* (Greensboro, NC: Swain and Sherwood, 1848); Rees, "English Friends"; Thomas P. Slaughter, *The Beautiful Soul of John Woolman, Apostle of Abolition* (New York: Hill and Wang, 2008); Soderlund, *Quakers & Slavery*; Mack Thompson, *Moses Brown, Reluctant Reformer* (Chapel Hill: University of North Carolina Press, 1962), 93–94; Darold D. Wax, "Reform and Revolution: The Movement against Slavery and the Slave Trade in Revolutionary Pennsylvania," *Western Pennsylvania Historical Magazine* 57, no. 4 (1974); Worrall, *Quakers in the Colonial*, 161–63.

Alarmed at the prospect of Quaker manumissions, they made it even harder for owners to free their slaves and even enacted the re-enslavement of those manumitted so far. This, of course, directly thwarted compliance with what were now general disciplinary rules of the Society of Friends. North Carolina Quakers challenged the laws in court and petitioned repeatedly the legislature to modify them yet, for decades, none of these challenges was successful. As it was virtually impossible to free slaves legally, they had to use the only option available: transfer of ownership away from individual Quakers to the local organizational structures of the Society.[8]

Seen in this light, the purge of slavery from within Quaker ranks, however slow, halting, incomplete and – in certain cases – impossible, was a remarkable achievement. There had been, simply, no other organization or group in history that had not only explicitly prohibited its members from owning enslaved humans, but had also successfully enforced this injunction. Judged by today's moral standards, there is nothing extraordinary about the principled refusal not to own other humans as property. The majority of our contemporaries not only does not have to face the choice whether or not to be a slave owner, but also has a very clear moral intuition of what the right thing to do is. In its social and cultural context, however, the Quaker divestment from slavery was a radical innovation and a challenge to prevailing norms.[9]

The consequences of the Quaker reformation movement of the mid-eighteenth century reached even further – and its full significance lies in something else. Above and beyond reshaping the culture of their organization, the reformers increasingly experimented with new ways to influence the larger political process. At the same time, they articulated in these new political activities an even stronger commitment to principles: including a rejection of violence and an embrace of fairness and justice in relations with non-Europeans. Thus, the divestment from slavery within the Society of Friends is best seen as one part of a set of related projects arising out of the push for reform. And the dynamics of these projects within their political context provide important indications on how the disciplinary concern with slavery by an otherwise peculiar religious organization grew to form the focus of a broader movement.

---

[8] Crawford, *Having of Negroes*; *Narrative of Some of the Proceedings*; Benjamin Joseph Klebaner, "American Manumission Laws and the Responsibility for Supporting Slaves," *The Virginia Magazine of History and Biography* 63, no. 4 (1955); Richard K. MacMaster, "Arthur Lee's 'Address on Slavery': An Aspect of Virginia's Struggle to End the Slave Trade, 1765–1774," *The Virginia Magazine of History and Biography* 80, no. 2 (1972); Patrick Sowle, "The North Carolina Manumission Society, 1816–1834," *North Carolina Historical Review* 42, no. 1 (1965).

[9] Quaker divestment of slaves was highly unusual even in the context of Pennsylvania where the practice spread among only very few non-Quakers. In fact, Irish and Scotch Presbyterians in the west of the colony became slave owners exactly at the same time in the 1770s. See Gary B. Nash and Jean R. Soderlund, *Freedom by Degrees: Emancipation in Pennsylvania and Its Aftermath* (New York: Oxford University Press, 1991), 73–98, 151.

IMPERIAL CONFLICTS

Three features distinguished the proprietary colony of Pennsylvania from other English settlements ever since its establishment in the 1680s, all three intrinsically connected with the ethical principles of Quakerism: friendly and consensual relationships with the Indians from whom the founder and initial proprietor William Penn and his agents purchased the land, tolerance of religious diversity, and a relatively open and democratic form of government. Yet soon, lured by the prospect of profitable land speculation, wealthy Pennsylvanians began violating Penn's precepts of equitable dealing with Indian nations and increasingly sought to take over land by any seemingly legal means. By the 1730s, the original policies were honored mostly in the breach.

When Penn died debt-ridden in England in 1718, his inheritance became a matter of dispute between the sons from his two marriages and his creditors. The main concern of the sons of his second wife, who eventually became the proprietors, was to extract as much revenue from their patrimony. For this purpose, they initiated a series of land purchases of dubious legality and tried to collect as much profit from the land sold and rented out to European farmers. Perhaps the most blatant violation of the tradition of good relations was the infamous "Walking Purchase" of 1737 when, on the basis of a possibly forged treaty, three specially prepared men were used to walk the perimeter of a territory far exceeding the dimensions stipulated in the original map. In addition, European squatters increasingly occupied Indian land – first in the uncertain atmosphere immediately after Penn's death while his ownership was being disputed, and later in an attempt to avoid paying the increasing quitrents on proprietary land imposed by his impoverished sons.

All these pressures resulted in a gradual souring of relations with neighboring Delawares who were now exposed to the escalating pressure of land-hungry proprietary agents and settlers. Another conflict brew within the province where now the proprietor Thomas Penn, the lieutenant governor he appointed, and a clique of supporters were consistently opposed in the colonial assembly by what became to be known as the "Quaker Party." Thomas Penn and the men in his faction were mainly interested in deriving the maximum profit possible from the land in the colony. On the other hand, the Assembly was dominated by a group of elected officials who sought to rein in proprietary appetites and took pains to cultivate a close relationship with local settlers and represent their interests and rights. Although not exclusively Quaker in membership, this "Quaker Party" subscribed to the general Quaker values of nonviolence and egalitarianism. A chronic conflict thus crystallized between the two interests, centered on the relative power of the representatives in the Assembly over financial and other policies.[10]

---

[10] Steven Craig Harper, *Promised Land: Penn's Holy Experiment, the Walking Purchase, and the Dispossession of Delawares, 1600–1763* (Bethlehem, PA: Lehigh University Press, 2006); James H. Hutson, *Pennsylvania Politics, 1746–1770: The Movement for Royal Government*

These tensions and cleavages only intensified with the eruption of large-scale war in the 1750s. The direct stake in what emerged as the North American theater of the Seven Years' War was a British-French struggle over the frontier between their respective empires in the Ohio Valley. British defeats in the early months of hostilities, however, unleashed the simmering discontent of Pennsylvania's immediate neighbors. The various Indian groups in and around the colony were officially under the jurisdiction of the Iroquois Six Nations Federation and, up to that point, the Pennsylvania proprietors had preferred to negotiate land sales directly with the Iroquois, disregarding the interests of local Indians. Now that the military conflict exposed British weaknesses, Delawares and Shawnees of Pennsylvania seized the opportunity to assert their independence from Iroquois overlords and prevent further incursions on their land by staging horrifying raids on European frontier settlements occupied by mostly Ulster Presbyterian and German immigrants.[11]

A NEW QUAKER ACTIVISM

Thus, between the 1730s and 1750s, the strengthening movement for reform within transatlantic Quakerism coincided with the degeneration of Pennsylvania, the Friends' "holy experiment," into a site of intense and many-sided conflict. From the collision of these two developments, a new mode of Quaker political activism emerged that provided the foundation of an antislavery movement.

The Quakers' Pennsylvania was exceptional among American colonies: for seventy years since its foundation, it not only managed to maintain pacific relations with neighboring Indians, but also avoided direct participation in the warfare that periodically erupted between other English colonies and their Indian and French neighbors. All this was consistent with the Quaker "peace

and its Consequences (Princeton, NJ: Princeton University Press, 1972); Francis Jennings, "The Scandalous Indian Policy of William Penn's Sons: Deeds and Documents of the Walking Purchase," *Pennsylvania History* 37, no. 1 (1970); *The Ambiguous Iroquois Empire: The Covenant Chain Confederation of Indian Tribes with English Colonies from Its Beginnings to the Lancaster Treaty of 1744* (New York: Norton, 1984); Kevin Kenny, *Peaceable Kingdom Lost: The Paxton Boys and the Destruction of William Penn's Holy Experiment* (New York: Oxford University Press, 2009); David L. Preston, *The Texture of Contact: European and Indian Settler Communities on the Frontiers of Iroquoia, 1667–1783* (Lincoln: University of Nebraska Press, 2009), 121–24; Theodore Thayer, *Pennsylvania Politics and the Growth of Democracy, 1740–1776* (Harrisburg: Pennsylvania Historical and Museum Commission, 1953); Alan Tully, *Forming American Politics: Ideals, Interests, and Institutions in Colonial New York and Pennsylvania* (Baltimore: Johns Hopkins University Press, 1994).

[11] Fred Anderson, *The Crucible of War: The Seven Years' War and the Fate of Empire in British North America, 1754–1766* (New York: Alfred A. Knopf, 2000); Krista Camenzind, "From the Holy Experiment to the Paxton Boys: Violence, Manhood, and Race in Pennsylvania during the Seven Years' War" (Ph.D. Dissertation, University of California San Diego, 2003); Kenny, *Peaceable Kingdom*; Preston, *Texture of Contact*; Silver, *Savage Neighbors*; Matthew C. Ward, *Breaking the Backcountry: The Seven Years' War in Virginia and Pennsylvania, 1754–1765* (Pittsburgh, PA: University of Pittsburgh Press, 2003).

testimony" that abhorred violence. Remarkably, there was no standing defense force in the colony and the Quaker-dominated Assembly responded to pressure from London to contribute to imperial wars with a series of compromises: instead of directly financing military activities, it gave the monarch a monetary "gift." Yet the Indian raids on frontier settlements in the 1750s fatally disrupted this precarious equilibrium. Now legislators had to directly tackle the issue of defense and respond to intensifying demands for military assistance from within the province.[12]

While constrained by religious scruples against violence, the Quaker Party legislators in the Assembly were far from being unreasonable pacifists. What made a coherent defense policy next to impossible, however, were the consistent attempts by the absentee proprietor Thomas Penn to keep his own contribution toward defense funds – as in any other area – at the bare minimum. His lieutenant governors had strict instructions to veto any legislation that might infringe on his economic interests. Thus, the question of defense was also an issue of economic fairness, setting the rights of the Assembly representing the inhabitants of Pennsylvania against the privileges of the absent proprietor and his clique to derive profit from the colony.

With the frontier conflicts of the 1750s, the standoff between the Assembly and the Proprietary Party over defense funds and policies intensified. Meanwhile, inhabitants of the frontier settlements peopled mostly by Irish Presbyterians and Germans began to take matters in their hands, organizing their own military groups, while also appealing to the Assembly for assistance with defense against Indian raids. In November 1755, hundreds of German settlers marched on Philadelphia to request help and made their point by displaying publicly the scalped bodies of raid victims. These sentiments were seized by men associated with the Proprietary Party who similarly applied increasing pressure on the Assembly to adopt a defense bill, while blaming Quakers for betraying the frontier and willfully neglecting the security of the colony.

When the Assembly, under all this pressure, passed a defense-funding bill earlier that month, it became the target of another set of protestors: the reform-minded Quakers. In their conflict with the proprietor, the Assemblymen were increasingly keen to pass measures that would give them at least the power to control defense spending. Yet in the reformers' eyes, this clearly violated Quaker principles of nonviolence as now even the fiction of a gift for the "King's use" was dispensed with. Not only were Pennsylvanians to be taxed

[12] This account of the complex developments in Pennsylvania during the Seven Years' War is based on the rich historiography that has examined them. See Anderson, *Crucible of War*; Camenzind, "Holy Experiment"; Harper, *Promised Land*; Kenny, *Peaceable Kingdom*; Marietta, *Reformation of Quakerism*; Samuel L. Parrish, *Some Chapters in the History of the Friendly Association for Regaining and Preserving Peace with the Indians by Pacific Measures* (Philadelphia: Friends's Historical Association of Philadelphia, 1877); Silver, *Savage Neighbors*; Theodore Thayer, *Israel Pemberton, King of the Quakers* (Philadelphia: Historical Society of Pennsylvania, 1943); Ward, *Breaking the Backcountry*.

for the purposes of war, but the use of the funds collected was to be decided by Quakers in the Assembly. The very foundations of the Pennsylvania project as a pacific settlement of religious and ethnic tolerance were threatened.

While increasingly concerned with improving discipline and eradicating slaveholding, the reformers in the Philadelphia Yearly Meeting had begun already to discuss the ethics of paying taxes explicitly designed to support war efforts. After the November defense bill passed, a group of reformers was alarmed enough to first address Quaker legislators in private and then present to the Assembly a formal protest against the bill. They accused the Assemblymen of violating the charter of the province and pledged not to pay the new war tax. Instead of adopting an aggressive policy, they argued, the Assembly should investigate the reasons that led Indians to attack and then work for peaceful negotiations to end the hostilities.

Thus, by late 1755, the Pennsylvania Assembly was besieged on two flanks. On the one side, back-country settlers and the Proprietary Party accused it of indifference to the suffering of frontier raid victims and demanded a stronger military defense. On the other, pacifist reformers urged a return to traditional nonviolence. Even though Quaker legislators were not particularly happy to endure their zealous coreligionists' strictures, the Assembly was at least open to the idea of a proper investigation of the causes underlying the Indians' discontent and working to discontinue injustice and abuses against them. Yet Lieutenant Governor Robert Morris, who earlier had deliberately withheld alarming reports from the frontier to give an even more negative spin on the Assemblymen's inaction on defense matters, was now enraged that the Assembly should spend time on appeasing Indians instead of addressing the white settlers' suffering.

Things came to a head in April 1756 when the legislators entrusted with spending the defense funds, including two Quakers, requested that Morris declare war on the Delaware Indians and post a bounty on Indian scalps. The two offending Quakers were duly disowned by the Society and alarmed reformers approached the Lieutenant Governor first privately and then with a "humble address" that later appeared in the *Pennsylvania Gazette*. Their last-ditch effort failed, however, and on April 14, Morris issued a formal war declaration on the Delawares that promised the rewards for Indian scalps that frontier settlers had clamored for. For the first time in its history, Pennsylvania was now fully engaged in a war.

Having failed in their attempt to prevent the provincial authorities from taking this momentous step, Quaker reformers immediately regrouped and tried a different route. The group, centered around the wealthy merchant Israel Pemberton, Jr., appealed to the Lieutenant Governor's Provincial Council for permission to reach out to the Delawares, hear their grievances, and negotiate a peaceful settlement of the conflict. At the same time, they contacted Sir William Johnson, an influential power broker with connections to the powerful Iroquois Confederacy to whom the Pennsylvania Delawares were subjected. The Crown had recently given Johnson the royal appointment of Superintendent for Indian Affairs in New York in an effort to wrestle control over relations with Indian nations from competing colonies and consolidate royal jurisdiction over colonial affairs.[13] Pemberton's reformers thus secured the cooperation of both the local colonial government and London's representative. Although the upper chamber of the Pennsylvania legislature, the Council, was wary of any potential interference in official Indian policy, it reluctantly granted its permission to the Quakers who had volunteered to cover all the costs of the peace overtures. Johnson also gave his approval, sensing an opportunity to counteract the damage to his own standing with Indian allies caused by the Pennsylvania Governor's unilateral decision to declare war without consulting him.

The Quaker group hastily appointed a board of trustees and collected the funds needed for the diplomatic effort that, according to Indian traditions, involved the exchange of wampum belts and the presentation of gifts. A series of meetings over dinner were held in Pemberton's Philadelphia house with representatives of the Iroquois Federation of Six Nations. At the end, an agreement was reached to convey to the Delawares an invitation for peace talks and messengers were paid and dispatched to broadcast this proposal.

The Friendly Association and Peace Conferences
This preliminary agreement opened up the possibility for the beginning of a series of peace conferences that ultimately did achieve the goal of brokering peace. At the same time, however, the conflict between pacifist-reforming Quakers and other imperial actors invested in relations with American Indians only intensified. While Pemberton's Quakers were able to forge an alliance with the Delawares and win important concessions in the peace talks, in the end the hostility of competing imperial interests undermined their efforts to restore a nonviolent Pennsylvania.

The first conference with the Delawares at which a preliminary peace agreement was reached opened in the town of Easton in July 1756 amid the hostility of the local population. In preparation, the Quakers involved in the peace effort organized a meeting at which 2,000 pounds were subscribed toward gifts presented to the Indians. At the conference, Teedyuscung – the Wyoming Valley Delawares' leader – immediately sought close contact with the Friends whom he seemed to trust as potential allies, provoking a displeased Lieutenant Governor Morris to order the Quaker delegation not to meddle in official business.

By the time of the following conference in November, the Quakers had raised the impressive sum of 5,000 pounds for gifts and had organized themselves formally as the Friendly Association for Regaining and Preserving Peace with the Indians by Pacific Measures. The representatives of the Association

[13] John R. Alden, "The Albany Congress and the Creation of the Indian Superintendencies," *The Mississippi Valley Historical Review* 27, no. 2 (1940); Jennings, *Iroquois Empire*, 369–74.

at the conference, along with some of the Assemblymen present, insisted that this time the deep reasons for Indian grievances be discussed. They were able to make this happen against the vociferous opposition of Proprietary interest supporters who tried to avoid any questioning of land purchase treaties that might threaten their possessions and who clung instead to the convenient fiction that the Indians were simply incited to hostility by the cunning French. Teedyuscung, in an alliance with his Quaker supporters, enumerated publicly the various complaints of his people: fraudulent purchases of land, encroachment by European settlers on traditional hunting grounds, and the unethical practices of European traders. As a result, the Provincial Council was finally forced to give in to the Quaker reformers' initial demand and appoint a committee investigating the Delawares' claims of illegal land purchases. What is more, in January 1757 a committee of the Friendly Association began its own investigation by requesting from the unwilling Council secretary copies of all records related to Indian affairs.

The next conference in May of 1757, however, was a temporary setback for the peace project. The representatives of the Friendly Association were there despite warnings by Sir William Johnson and British Commander-in-Chief Lord Loudoun to stop meddling in official Indian diplomacy. European settlers were also there, protesting the conference with the display of mutilated corpses of four victims of Indian attacks. Yet perhaps the most important person, Teedyuscung, was missing. Most probably, he tried to avoid a direct showdown with the Iroquois representatives who were now present. While sympathetic to his claims of fraud and abuses, the Iroquois insisted that because of their sovereignty over the Delawares, they were the only party authorized to negotiate with the colony of Pennsylvania.

For the next peace conference in the months of July and August, the Friendly Association representatives were forced do a preliminary round of diplomacy on their own. This time the Proprietors and the current Lieutenant Governor William Denny were absolutely unwilling to admit them to the proceedings. In fact, at Thomas Penn's suggestion, Denny went to great lengths to rebuke the Quakers for infringing on royal jurisdiction in negotiations with the Indians, supporting his attack with a stern letter by Lord Halifax, the president of the Board of the Trade in London. Loath to lose the gifts Quaker wealth provided for Indian diplomacy, however, at the end he reluctantly agreed to allow their presence at the conference, strictly as private individuals. During the negotiations, Denny made another concession to the Indian demands supported by the Quakers by agreeing on a discussion of the original deeds by which Indian lands were sold to the colony. Teedyuscung obtained not only this reluctant recognition of his grievances, but also an official promise of land and houses for his people in the Wyoming Valley. The Friendly Association readily committed to raising the funds for the construction of the eastern Delawares' new town. As his part of the bargain, however, Teedyuscung agreed to Denny's offer that the land grievances be examined by Sir William Johnson who would then refer his conclusions on the legality of land transfer to the British Crown for a conclusive ruling.

Despite these concessions, the Proprietary Party's dogged determination not to give in to Indian claims was revealed again in November when the committee appointed by the governor issued its report on land purchases with its two Quaker members dissenting. Relying on legal sophistry, it reaffirmed the lawfulness of all land transfers now in proprietary hands and again hinted at the "true" source for the Delawares' discontent and hostility: French and Quaker intrigue. A couple of months later, however, the Friendly Association's position was strengthened with the arrival of the new British Commander-in-Chief, John Forbes, who recognized the tactical utility of the Quakers' contacts for a potential peace settlement and alliance with hostile Indians and encouraged their involvement in negotiations. Simultaneously, Israel Pemberton, the brain of the Friendly Association, contacted politically connected Quakers in London. He asked them to persuade the government to remove relations with Pennsylvania Indians from the jurisdiction of an increasingly hostile Sir William Johnson and to appoint a commission entrusted with the establishment of definitive peace boundaries between British settlements and Indian territories.[14]

The result of these activities was another big peace conference in Easton in October 1758 with more than 500 Indians from 13 nations present. Despite Forbes' support, however, the Quakers were kept at bay during the proceedings and at the end, their ally Teedyuscung was stripped of all the advantages he had been able to accrue in earlier negotiations. The proprietary faction redeployed its tactics of playing different Indian nations against each other by giving up some land, but returning it to the Iroquois who claimed to be the Delawares' sovereign. While this appeased the Iroquois well enough to break their alliance with the French, it also meant that the Delawares' claims against the illegal purchase were silently dismissed with their superiors' connivance.

For several years after that, the conflict over Indian policies was played out largely in London where it had become a part of the ongoing struggle between the Pennsylvania proprietary faction and the Assembly Quaker Party to sway imperial authorities to their side. A fresh round of the contest opened when the Provincial Council forwarded its strongly anti-Quaker official report on the legality of Indian land purchases to the Board of Trade. In 1759, the Philadelphia Yearly Meeting protested in an address to Lieutenant Governor Denny the report's claim that Quakers wanted "to injure the reputation of the Proprietories by unduly influencing the Indians to complain of frauds" and collected documents that proved the true nature of their activities to London authorities. Meanwhile, Benjamin Franklin, the Assembly's agent in London engaged in various projects designed to undermine the Proprietors' position, was entrusted to present a petition with the Delawares' grievances directly to

---

[14] Harper, *Promised Land*, 112–14; Thayer, *Israel Pemberton*, 152–53; Ward, *Breaking the Backcountry*, 178.

the Board of Trade. When the Board spoke in June, it acknowledged the existence of "Frauds & Abuses" as the reason of Indian discontent, yet stopped
short of assigning any concrete responsibility for these problems. At the
same time, its members expressed their displeasure with "the irregular and
unwarrantable Interferings ... of particular Persons" who encouraged the
eastern Delawares to make their grievances heard. Finally, they approved
the deal made at the 1757 conference that Sir William Johnson investigate the
grievances.[15]

Despite his initial openness to the Quaker peace project, by this point
Sir William had become increasingly unhappy with their "unwarrantable
Interferings." In addition, British military success against the French along with
a growing Indian defection to the British side – an outcome made possible, ironically, by the peace conferences – decreased the perceived tactical utility of the
Quaker project to seek remedies for the grievances of the Delawares, a nation
whose political significance had now been eclipsed by the treaties with the
Iroquois and Ohio Indians. Finally, the Delawares' position was further eroded
by continued encroachment on their territory by European settlers. In a more
peaceful environment, the pressure from land-hungry Pennsylvanians resumed
while, to make things even worse, settlers organized by the Susquehanna
Company of Connecticut began occupying land in the Delawares' Wyoming
Valley.

By the time another conference met to offer a final settlement of the land dispute in 1762, Johnson was clearly on the Proprietary Party's side and lost his
patience. The conflict grew out of hand when the Quakers present supported
Teedyuscung's demand that he be given a proper translation of the official
documents of the Board of Trade case. Johnson responded with a verbal assault
so vitriolic that the proceedings had to be suspended. At the end, he barred
Quakers from the conference and using some heavy-handed tactics, forced
Teedyscung to admit publicly that his allegation of land fraud were in error.

This effectively spelled the end – and the ultimate failure – of the Quaker
reformers' project to restore Pennsylvania to its past pacific glory and, in the
process, strengthen the position of their allies, the Delawares. By initiating
the negotiations that led to the end of the war, they were successful in steer-
ing the course of provincial politics away from militarism, particularly in the
period between 1756 and 1758. At the end, imperial authorities in London also
adopted the Quaker idea of a formal boundary between European and Indian
territories. Yet, when established by a royal proclamation in 1763, this boundary remained largely unenforceable and failed to prevent settler encroachment
on Indian land. A weakened Teedyuscung continued to appeal to no avail to his
Iroquois overlords and the Pennsylvania government for support against the
influx of Connecticut settlers to his lands. In 1763, he died in a suspicious fire

[15] Parrish, *History of the Friendly Association*, 106–08; Ward, *Breaking the Backcountry*, 194.

that destroyed the Wyoming Valley settlement built with Quaker money and conveniently cleared the territory for white settlers from Connecticut.

Almost simultaneously, Native American leaders around the Ottawa Chief Pontiac initiated another war against the British, and the years that followed brought to Pennsylvania not peace, but escalating hostilities and violence. While Thomas Penn's lieutenant governor continued to veto defense bills unless they exempted proprietary lands from taxes, frontier settlers felt abandoned by the government in Philadelphia and blamed Quakers for protecting "savage" Indians instead of helping white victims of Indian raids. They increasingly took matters into their own hands and organized local militias for counterraids. The senseless violence culminated in the horrific massacre of the pacific Conestoga Indians by a gang from the mostly Irish Presbyterian township of Paxton. Local authorities were less than willing to bring the perpetrators to justice and the "Paxton Boys" put Philadelphians on the defensive when they embarked on a march toward the city in February 1764. At the end, they did not make it to the city and their next intended victims, a group of Christian Indians from a Moravian community who had sought from the Pennsylvania government shelter from settler violence. Yet the fact that despite the Assembly's efforts the Paxton boys were never prosecuted and that their march initiated a vitriolic pamphlet war between defenders and opponents of their actions is indicative of how far away the colony had drifted from its pacific past. Now pacifist Quakers and their Indian policies were denounced and ridiculed by an emerging coalition of frontier settlers, Presbyterian leaders, and proprietary men.

THE REFORMERS' EVOLVING POLITICS

How much things had changed by that time in an empire that had advertised itself as the benign alternative to Spanish oppression is indicated by the correspondence between Colonel Henry Bouquet and the commander of British forces, Sir Jeffrey Amherst, in July 1763. As they considered the infamous plan of spreading smallpox among Indians with infected blankets, they approvingly referred to the "Spaniard's Method" of using dogs to remove "the Vermine." The same month, Anthony Benezet addressed to Amherst a long letter explaining the legitimate grievances leading Indians to be hostile to Europeans and entreating him "for our blessed Redeemer's sake" to "condescend and use all moderate measures" to prevent a full-blown war.[16]

The commanding officers' invocation of the Spanish precedent is an unwitting commentary on the essential similarity between the dynamics of the Friendly Association episode and the standard pattern of colonial conflict that had erupted multiple times in Iberian empires earlier. Perhaps the Spanish frontiers with the Chichimecs in Mexico or with the Mapuche in the south of

---

[16] Kenny, *Peaceable Kingdom*, 121–22; George S. Brookes, *Friend Anthony Benezet* (Philadelphia: University of Pennsylvania Press, 1937), 248–53.

Chile briefly discussed in Chapter 2 offer the closest parallel. There, like in Pennsylvania, European settlers imposed themselves as troublesome neighbors on independent and unconquerable indigenous people. In all these settings, the conflict between Europeans and the communities they found there escalated with increasing violence on both sides. Invariably, the settlers called for even more violence against their unruly neighbors. Thus, Spaniards in Mexico and Chile called for total war against the Chichimecs and the Mapuche and for an official authorization of their enslavement. Finally, in all these cases, a religious faction emerged that urged reconciliation and peace, initiated negotiations, and called for investigation and rectification of the Europeans' unjust practices.[17]

In Pennsylvania, the crucial stimuli for the activation of the standard conflict pattern were provided by the 1756 declaration of war and the unwillingness of the Pennsylvania Assembly to conduct an investigation of the sources of Indian hostility. It was against these troubling developments that reforming Quakers embarked on a new strategy of political intervention in defense of a humanitarian disposition toward non-Europeans. Their activities emerged out of their opposition to rival visions of politics represented by other imperial networks: the Pennsylvania Proprietary interest, white back-country settlers, and agents of imperial governance. Like Dominicans and other mendicants in Mexico, Peru, Chile, and the Philippines earlier, they created an alliance with indigenous leaders and tried to influence imperial policies. And, in the course of their political intervention, the conflict with opposing imperial networks grew only stronger.

Politicized antislavery did not emerge directly out of this conflict. Compared to the issue of relations with Indians, the institution of slavery, although clearly a major concern for Quaker reformers at that point, was a less contentious matter, especially in Pennsylvania. Because of the relatively low numbers of slaves there, in the other "middle colonies," and in New England, the question of abolition was less incendiary than in the South where, as we saw, even mild attempts to reach out to enslaved Africans provoked a disproportionate and almost paranoid hostility by slaveholding interests.[18] Still, the conflict over Indian policies and the concomitant confrontation of rival imperial networks had important ramifications for the Quaker creation of a politically engaged antislavery movement that was distinct from the project of internal divestment from slavery. This was so because the two issues were intrinsically connected

---

[17] In addition to the references listed in Chapter 2, see also Charlotte M. Gradie, "Discovering the Chichimecas," *The Americas* 51, no. 1 (1994); Robert Charles Padden, "Cultural Change and Military Resistance in Araucanian Chile, 1550–1730," *Southwestern Journal of Anthropology* 13, no. 1 (1957); Philip Wayne Powell, *Soldiers, Indians & Silver: The Northward Advance of New Spain, 1550–1600* (Berkeley: University of California Press, 1952).

[18] This does not mean, of course, that the issue was settled even in Pennsylvania. For opposition by various groups to the 1780 Pennsylvania abolition act, see Owen S. Ireland, "Germans against Abolition: A Minority's View of Slavery in Revolutionary Pennsylvania," *Journal of Interdisciplinary History* 3, no. 4 (1973); Nash and Soderlund, *Freedom by Degrees*, 104.

in the program of reforming Quakerism and because the experience of the Friendly Association shaped, in the long run, the tactics of the emerging anti-slavery coalition.

The Sin of Slavery

Although the enslavement of Africans and relations with Indians were two substantively separate issues, the Quaker reformers' expanding attack on slavery was simultaneously a critique of Pennsylvania's new bellicose Indian policies. One way in which the settlers from the frontiers sought to rouse the public and the officials to provide security against Indian raids was to display the dead and scalped bodies of victims of Indian attacks – as they did when they carted corpses in a silent protest against the appeasement of Indians at the peace conference of 1757. John Churchman, one of the Quaker reformers, witnessed an earlier instance of such a grisly display in the spring of 1756 in Philadelphia, even as the lieutenant governor and the Assembly were preparing to declare the war that prompted the formation of the Friendly Association. The attempt not only to win public sympathy for the victims, but also to instill an anti-Indian militancy was obviously working. The crowd, as Churchman remembers, "was cursing the Indians, [and] also the Quakers, because they would not join in war for destruction of the Indians." His first reaction was to read in this disturbing sight the unmistakable signs of God's displeasure punishing Pennsylvanians for the standard list of sins that would trouble any devout monotheist: "pride, profane swearing, drunkenness, with other wickedness." Yet as Churchman continued to ponder how this could happen exactly in Pennsylvania, "a land of peace, and as yet not much concerned in war," his "eyes turned to the case of the poor enslaved negroes [sic]." It then "appeared plain" to him that it was those who purchased, sold or owned slaves who were the "partakers in iniquity, encouragers of war, and shedding of innocent blood."[19]

The same theme of the close connection between the sins of slavery and current hostilities in Pennsylvania was further developed by another reformer, Anthony Benezet, when he published in 1759 his antislavery pamphlet *Observations on the Inslaving, Importing and Purchasing of Negroes*. The first antislavery publication directed to a general, non-Quaker audience to gain the official approval of the Philadelphia Yearly Meeting's Overseers of the Press, the pamphlet was also the first salvo of what would become Benezet's campaign to build a wider antislavery movement. He wrote it in the same year he was engaged, as a representative of the Yearly Meeting, in defending the increasingly embattled antiwar position of reforming Quakers. He was one of the two members entrusted with the preparation of documentary evidence

---

[19] John Churchman, *An Account of the Gospel Labours, and Christian Experiences of a Faithful Minister of Christ, John Churchman, Late of Nottingham, in Pennsylvania, Deceased* (London: James Phillips, 1781), 239–40. On the public display of scalped corpses, see Silver, *Savage Neighbors*.

disproving the accusations hurled against Friends by the biased official report on land purchases in which they were described as meddlesome busybodies creating Indian grievances where there were none.[20]

In his *Observations*, Benezet made an explicit connection with another aspect of Indian "savagery" that was used by pro-war Europeans to justify retaliation: the practice of taking white captives. As many as 2,000 Europeans were captured in Pennsylvania in the 1750s and 1760s. In 1756, the printed account of the Fleming family's abduction by the Delawares became a bestseller in Pennsylvania with several editions in English and German. William Smith, the spokesman for the Proprietary interest, listed the capture of European women among the "Shocking Inhumanities committed by the Incursions of the *Indians*" in an anonymously published pamphlet that sought popular support by explicitly depicting Quakers as abettors of Indian atrocities. In his words, captivity among "Savages, whose tender mercies may be accounted more cruel than Cruelty itself" was "perhaps, a worse Fate than ... Death in all its horrid Shapes."[21]

Whereas for Smith captivity was a compelling reason for a stronger military response to Indian raids, Benezet drew an uncomfortable parallel between the experience of European captives and enslaved Africans in his antislavery pamphlet. Relying on eyewitness accounts, he described the violence involved in the capture of men and women for the slave markets in Africa. The sympathetic response to European suffering under Indian captivity, he argued, should be extended to include the African victims of enslavement. And like Churchman before, Benezet asked rhetorically if slavery was "not one Cause for the Calamities we at present suffer," calamities that were the expression of God's justified anger with Pennsylvanians. His conclusion was that "the Captivity of our People" should "teach us to feel for others" and "induce us to discourage a Trade, by which many Thousands are Yearly captivated." Although Indian violence was not explicitly mentioned in Benezet's next pamphlet in 1762, the words he chose clearly links his antislavery argument with the symbolic struggles over violence and war in Pennsylvania at the time. Praying that "the Almighty preserve the inhabitants of Pennsylvania from being further defiled" by the slave trade, he asked this time: "May not this Trade be truly said to be the most iniquitous and cruelest Act of Violence and Rapine ... that to our Knowledge is perpetrated in any Part of the World."[22]

---

[20] Parrish, *History of the Friendly Association*, 108; Sassi, "With a Little Help," 42–44.

[21] William Smith, *A Brief View of the Conduct of Pennsylvania, for the Year 1755* (London: R. Griffiths, 1756), 46–47; Silver, *Savage Neighbors*, 196. On the numbers of captives, see Ward, *Breaking the Backcountry*.

[22] Anthony Benezet, *Observations on the Inslaving, Importing and Purchasing of Negroes*, 2nd ed. (Germantown, PA: Christopher Sower, 1760), 3–4; *A Short Account of That Part of Africa, Inhabited by the Negroes* (Philadelphia: W. Dunlap, 1762), 6, 30. For, as he argued, "what Distress can we conceive equal to the Alarms, the Anxiety and Wrath, which must succeed one another in the Breasts of the tender Parents, or affectionate Children, in continual Danger of being torn one from another, and dragged into a State of cruel Bondage." Ibid., 29.

Thus, the reforming Quakers' call for action against slavery was closely connected with the intensifying political conflicts of mid-eighteenth century Pennsylvania. Among other things, it formed an integral part of the religious reformers' project to restore the province to its pacific and harmonious past by redressing the wrongs committed against enslaved Africans. Confronting the unsettled political situation and the horrific consequences of military conflict, they interpreted them through the lens of the traditional prophetic understanding conveyed by the Bible of suffering as divine punishment for one's sins and, particularly, for the sin of oppressing others. This prophetic framing of the situation called for a distinct course of action. The answer to Indian "savagery" was not, as the increasingly militant Proprietary interest and European settlers claimed, a counter-escalation of hostility but a careful examination and rectification of the continuing injustices against non-Europeans, whether they be the fraudulent appropriation of Indian lands or the enslavement of Africans.[23]

One manifestation of this intensifying concern with slavery that resulted from – and coincided with – the direct Quaker involvement with Indian policy was the extension of the divestment project into a pressure to get the London Yearly Meeting involved. It is not incidental that the Meeting responded to the American reformers' demands in 1757, directing a specially formed subcommittee of the Meeting for Sufferings to distribute to all members in Britain and the colonies the disciplinary rules against participation in the slave trade. Two years later, the Philadelphia Yearly Meeting produced another letter asking London to again counsel Friends against engaging in the trade even as the Philadelphia Meeting for Sufferings was preparing documentary evidence to respond to the accusations against Quakers in the Pennsylvania Provincial Council's report.[24]

Organizational Advances

Apart from contributing toward the intensification and expansion of the anti-slavery platform, the reformers' engagement with Pennsylvania and imperial Indian policies was a formative experience affecting the course of subsequent Quaker political actions. The formation and activities of the Friendly Association was a significant organizational development that was to leave its

---

[23] For the connection between sin and suffering in the Bible, see Bart D. Ehrman, *God's Problem: How the Bible Fails to Answer Our Most Important Question – Why We Suffer* (New York: HarperCollins, 2009). A similar reaction to the Seven Years' War, emphasizing the need for social reformation, was articulated by the "New Divinity" ministers in New England who were to get involved in the antislavery network. See Mark Valeri, "The New Divinity and the American Revolution," *The William and Mary Quarterly* 46, no. 4 (1989).

[24] Parrish, *History of the Friendly Association*, 108; Jennings, "Mid-Eighteenth Century Quakerism," 23; Betty Fladeland, *Men and Brothers: Anglo-American Antislavery Cooperation* (Urbana: University of Illinois Press, 1972), 14; Rees, "English Friends," 75.

imprint on the emerging antislavery campaign. Most generally, the Association was an important innovation in the social context of its time. Pennsylvania was the home of a population remarkably diverse in ethnic and religious terms. By the 1740s, the various segments of the population had started building their own associations. Englishmen, Germans, and Irishmen, Anglicans and Presbyterians had their own societies, usually intended to provide mutual aid to co-ethnics and co-religionists. While using the same standard vocabulary of associational action, the Friendly Association represented diametrically opposed ethics. Instead of promoting ethnic or religious cohesion, as other associations did, it was driven by a more abstract ideal to restore justice in relations with colonial "others." In this sense, the Association – like emerging antislavery – was strongly influenced by the reforming Quakers' conviction about the equality of all humans as children of God.[25]

But apart from this innovative substantive orientation of the Association, it presented also an important organizational departure within Quaker circles. The Society of Friends had several specialized bodies within its structure, some of which had a specifically political function. Starting in the 1660s, these bodies and the accompanying political practices made the Society the best organized and the most influential among the various religious groups to try to exert influence on authorities in London. Since 1675 the London Meeting for Sufferings collected detailed information on cases of persecution against Quakers both in Britain and the colonies, interceded with authorities, and disseminated information for effective legal defense among members. A committee of the Meeting for Sufferings monitored parliamentary proceedings and lobbied with members of parliament since 1685.[26] Yet the Friendly Association was the first Quaker political organization that was both outside of the official structures of the Society and addressed an issue that was not focused directly related to the rights or interests of members.

The core of the Association consisted of a relatively small number of Philadelphia reformers and its activities were dominated by Israel Pemberton's strong personality. There were no significant efforts to attract outside support or membership, although in 1756 a financial contribution by the German Pietist group of Schwenckfelders was accepted and a short-lived local association was

---

[25] On ethnic and religious associations in Pennsylvania, see Silver, *Savage Neighbors*, 100–01. On the Quaker reformers' commitment to equality, see Churchman, *Gospel Labours*; Jackson, *Let This Voice*; Slaughter, *Beautiful Soul*.

[26] On early Quaker political activities, see Kenneth L. Carroll, "American Quakers and Their London Lobby," *Quaker History* 70, no. 1 (1981); Craig W. Horle, *The Quakers and the English Legal System, 1660–1688* (Philadelphia: University of Pennsylvania Press, 1988); N. C. Hunt, *Two Early Political Associations: The Quakers and The Dissenting Deputies in the Age of Sir Robert Walpole* (Oxford: Clarendon Press, 1961); Ethyn Williams Kirby, "The Quakers' Efforts to Secure Civil and Religious Liberty, 1660–96," *The Journal of Modern History* 7, no. 4 (1935); Alison Gilbert Olson, *Making the Empire Work: London and American Interest Groups, 1690–1790* (Cambridge, MA: Harvard University Press, 1992).

founded in New Jersey by antislavery reformer John Woolman the following year.[27] Yet it is precisely the exclusively Quaker membership that is important here for this was the first time that Friends established a voluntary associational body that was not a part of the church hierarchy and did not have the Society's official approval.

This was perhaps the truly innovative move that the Friendly Association presented. In themselves, its activities were not different from what Quakers had done in their Society for decades: using the tools of a voluntary religious organization to influence authorities and policies. Even the fund-raising for the gifts needed for Indian diplomacy was nothing new as Friends' meetings had traditionally collected money for their own purpose and the "National Stock," the central fund kept in London, financed the lobbying by the Meeting for Sufferings.[28] Yet now – and later, in the antislavery campaign – the typical tools and "know-how" of Quaker organizing were being applied for an issue that was both larger than and distinct from the standard and narrower concern to protect the members' rights and alleviate their persecution. The same logic of applying standard practices to a larger issue drove the emergence of a wider movement against slavery. When in 1772 Anthony Benezet urged fellow Friends in England to petition parliament for the abolition of the slave trade, he reminded them of the past uses of this practice while arguing that the suffering of the enslaved surpassed Quaker problems. "We as a people," he wrote "have not been backward in applying to Parliament, in cases where our sufferings have been by no means comparable to the present case."[29]

Imperial Contests
A final implication of the Friendly Association episode for the crystallization of a politicized antislavery network came from the failure of the Quaker reformers' effort in the conflict over Indian policies in Pennsylvania. This failure clearly demonstrated the increasing importance of imperial authorities in London who, not incidentally, were to become the main target of antislavery organizing. Thus, in important ways, the future course of antislavery was shaped by the interaction and even collision of the Friends' political project with British imperial state-making.

In the early days of its attempts to shape Pennsylvanian politics, the Friendly Association found a tactical opening in its alliance with the royal representative for Indian affairs, Sir William Johnson, against the bellicose policies of a lieutenant governor and an Assembly succumbing to pressure from settlers on the frontier. At a later date, it enjoyed the support of the new Commander-in-Chief, John Forbes. Yet at the end, Quaker efforts to obtain redress for the

---

[27] Parrish, *History of the Friendly Association*, 52–54, 63; Marietta, *Reformation of Quakerism*, 188.
[28] Carroll, "American Quakers."
[29] Brookes, *Friend Benezet*, 286, 95.

Delawares' grievances provoked the hostility of imperial authorities and the stern rebuke of the Board of Trade.

This strong imperial reaction was not incidental. Since 1748, a reinvigorated Board of Trade – the sole official body in London overseeing the colonies – had embarked on a program of tightening its control on colonial governance under its energetic president, the second Earl of Halifax. Alarmed both by possible inroads of French or Spanish rivals and the increasing independence of colonial legislatures, the Board abandoned what Edmund Burke would call the imperial policy of "salutary neglect" of the previous decades and began to intervene more forcefully in colonial affairs. Relations with Indian nations were an important part of the imperial affairs that the Board worked to centralize under its power and it clearly drew a line when the Quaker initiative threatened its jurisdiction. In addition, Halifax seemed to have been not particularly sympathetic to Quakers and new Board members appointed in the mid-1750s were in general less open to colonial demands than their predecessors.

The Board of Trade was at its apex in the years when the Friendly Association was active and its influence in colonial affairs was eclipsed soon by an increasingly interventionist parliament. Yet, while the specific center changed, power itself was clearly gravitating toward London. The Board's displeasure with Quaker Indian initiatives was just an integral part of an emerging trend of efforts to consolidate metropolitan power over the colonies. In the process, established patterns and networks of lobbying were changing. The Board's censure of Quaker peace efforts was an early signal of both changing political conditions and the limitations of standard channels of influence over metropolitan policies.[30]

If the Board's bid to take over the conduct of Indian affairs showed a newfound assertiveness, the metropolitan grip on slavery – the other issue that preoccupied Quaker reformers – was both long-standing and much more firmly established. Ever since its introduction to Caribbean settlements, the institution of colonial slavery itself was regulated by local statutes and there was no central imperial legislation. The Atlantic slave trade, however, was solidly under the control and protection of London authorities. Partly responding to pressure by London, Bristol, and Liverpool merchants who dominated the trade, the Board of Trade consistently fenced off any measures prejudicial to its profitability, such as increases in import duties.[31] In other words, any attempt to interfere with the commercial source of slavery – the mercantilistically

---

[30] See Alden, "Albany Congress"; Jack P. Greene, *Peripheries and Center: Constitutional Development in the Extended Polities of the British Empire and the United States, 1607–1788* (Athens: University of Georgia Press, 1986); Jennings, *Iroquois Empire*; P. J. Marshall, *The Making and Unmaking of Empires: Britain, India, and America, c.1750–1783* (Oxford: Oxford University Press, 2005); Jack P. Greene, "'A Posture of Hostility': A Reconsideration of Some Aspects of the Origins of the American Revolution," *Proceedings of the American Antiquarian Society* 87, no. 1 (1977); Olson, *Making the Empire*.

[31] Brown, *Moral Capital*, 144–45, 241–42; Rawley, *Slave Trade*; David Richardson, "The British Empire and the Atlantic Slave Trade, 1660–1807," in *The Oxford History of the British Empire*,

protected imperial slave trade – presented a challenge of even greater order than the shaping of Indian policies, a challenge magnified ever further at this point by an increasing metropolitan assertiveness and control.

The Friendly Association had engaged imperial authorities in the tried and tested ways: trying to forge an alliance with local representatives of the imperial government and appealing to the established and historically responsive target of colonial lobbying, the Board of Trade. Yet when Anthony Benezet, an active participant in the Friendly Association, made his first attempt at antislavery organizing in 1763, there were important differences in strategy. Sending his latest antislavery pamphlet, *A Short Account of that Part of Africa, Inhabited by the Negroes*, Benezet wrote to London Quaker coal merchant Joseph Phipps that "proper Check" to the slave trade "must come from amongst you." He requested that the pamphlet be reprinted and "dispersed amongst those in whose power it is to put a restraint upon the Trade": the king, his counselors, and all members of both Houses of Parliament.[32] Not only was London now the preeminent target, but the attempt to influence legislation was directed toward a broader set of power-holders. It also began with an important preparatory work: creating a general climate of opinion critical of slavery with targeted information about the grisly realities of the profitable trade. Coming at the heels of the Friendly Association episode and authored by Benezet who had been involved in appeals to the Board of Trade, this multi-pronged and information-oriented approach was motivated, at least partially, by the need to locate potential alternatives to the Board that had effectively thwarted the Pennsylvania Quaker intervention in Indian affairs, as well as by a desire to prepare the ground more carefully by changing the "official mind" in a direction favorable to antislavery policies.

A NEW RADICALISM IN THE IMPERIAL CONTEXT

Despite the substantively different issues around which they were organized, the two Quaker campaigns on Indian issues and on slavery were firmly rooted in the context of colonial Pennsylvania. More specifically, both were in important ways the outcome of an intensifying conflict between opposing imperial networks. The initial efforts of Benezet and his fellow reformers to build a transatlantic

Vol. 2: The Eighteenth Century, ed. P. J. Marshall (Oxford: Oxford University Press, 1998); Darold D. Wax, "Negro Import Duties in Colonial Virginia: A Study of British Commercial Policy and Local Public Policy," *The Virginia Magazine of History and Biography* 79, no. 1 (1971). On colonial slavery legislation, see Jonathan A. Bush, "Free to Enslave: The Foundations of Colonial American Slave Law," *Yale Journal of Law & the Humanities* 5 (1993); Craton, *Empire, Enslavement*, 94–97; Dunn, *Sugar and Slaves*, 238–41; William M. Wiecek, "The Statutory Law of Slavery and Race in the Thirteen Mainland Colonies of British America," *The William and Mary Quarterly* 34, no. 2 (1977).

[32] Anstey, *Atlantic Slave Trade*, 221–22; Roger Bruns, *Am I Not a Man and a Brother: The Antislavery Crusade of Revolutionary America, 1688–1788* (New York: Chelsea House, 1976), 97; Sassi, "With a Little Help," 45–46.

antislavery project emerged out of a reformist disposition to intervene in an ongoing symbolic struggle over the future of the pacific Quaker project in Pennsylvania against the growing hostility of the Proprietary Party and frontier settlers. In this sense, the very beginnings of modern antislavery were the product of the recurrent conflict between religious actors developing an interest in political activities on behalf of colonial "others" and their rival imperial networks.

At the same time, the Friendly Association and subsequent incipient politicized antislavery are illustrative of an emerging trend among reforming Friends to experiment with new organizational modalities for their political activities. Above and beyond the consistent project of divestment from slavery within the Friends' American community, this movement for organizational innovation would eventually result in the crystallization of a politicized antislavery network outside the official structures of the Society of Friends.

In this sense, the expansion and intensification of Protestant antislavery paralleled closely the development of the earlier Catholic indigenist networks. In both cases, a network of activists grew out of the initial radicalization of a small group of religious reformers. In Pennsylvania, this process of religious radicalization began with Quaker reformers reacting against military policy and anti-Indian sentiment in the context of the Seven Years' War. And the importance of radicalization is crucial even if exact parallels with Catholic militancy are difficult to perceive at first sight.

With their fiery rhetoric, excommunication of sinners, and oftentimes involvement in direct physical confrontations, the friars conform much better to our idea of radicalism than the "meek" Quakers. And indeed, after an initial period of militant nonconformity, Friends had developed by that time a remarkably subdued modality of expressing political opposition. The early confrontational spirit had been reduced to a sediment of routine behaviors with oppositional overtones: plain dress and speech, the refusal to remove hats or use anything but "thou" when addressing social superiors, and abstention from oaths. In addition, the codification within the Society of Friends of the "peace testimony" meant in practice the principled avoidance of any violent and disruptive behavior. Yet the fact that antislavery reformers used nonviolent means does not mean that the substance of their program was not radical. Nor should this obscure the ambitiously transformative and deeply political thrust of the Quaker antislavery network from its very inception, even if it did not produce any easily visible spectacles of public contention.

As I pointed out, the Quakers' voluntary divestment from slave ownership was a historically unprecedented act which, especially in the American South, was a subversive affront to the established social order. Even more radical was the demand around which the first political antislavery project coalesced: the full cessation of the trade in slaves, a long-standing institution buttressed by all imperial centers of the time. These radical political claims were, furthermore, the focus of an inherently political project engaged closely, from the very beginning, with the power structures of the Atlantic imperial world.

This radical political core of early Quaker antislavery is quite at variance with the idea of a "charity"-oriented calculative project in Davis's influential and subtly functionalist interpretation according to which Friends embraced abolitionism, among other things, in order to restore their reputation after their ill-fated reluctance to embrace the revolutionary project of American independence. Like any explanation from function, Davis's account extrapolates causes and motives from consequences and in the process attributes to early antislavery a complacent Victorian respectability that it lacked. It would have been hard for abolitionist Quakers to score popularity points with their new co-nationals simply because the majority of the Americans, to put it mildly, did not share the reformers' concerns. As we will see in Chapter 5, the idea of a widespread popular revulsion to slavery in America was a strategic fiction cultivated by Benezet and his allies. Nor is it clear how a group that had been accused of caring more for the "savage" Indians than for white Americans would have redeemed itself by displaying interest in the lot of another group of non-whites.[33] More perniciously, perhaps, the view of antislavery as charity and a weapon of social control overemphasizes its consensual component and thus obscures the inherently contentious political dimensions of its emergence.

Politicized antislavery emerged from – and developed further – a project to regulate and humanize relations with American Indians. Arising from a principled opposition against strengthening anti-Indian policies and sentiments, the activities of the Friendly Association were an intervention in the political struggles both within the colony of Pennsylvania and in the larger imperial context. Starting in 1756, Quaker members of the Pennsylvania Colonial Assembly did start to resign voluntarily for two reasons: a political deal struck in London to avoid the worse fate of a permanent ban of Quakers in the Assembly that the Proprietary Party had been able to engineer with imperial authorities and a principled opposition, reinforced by the reforming wing of the Philadelphia Yearly Meeting, to the increasing militarization of provincial policies. Yet this did not spell the end of Quaker influence in the assembly. As Allan Tully has shown, the "Quaker party" in Pennsylvania politics was designated as such not because it consisted of Quakers, but because it had gathered a wide constituency under the banner of a "civil Quakerism." A remarkably early specimen of a distinctively ideological and representative political party, the Quaker Party in Pennsylvania persisted until the late 1770s when it disintegrated under the pressure of revolutionary developments. What changed in the 1750s was that the Quaker party lost its near-absolute hegemony in the Assembly which,

---

[33] See Marietta, *Reformation of Quakerism*, 124–25, 273. For a more nuanced interpretation of the complex nature of early U.S. abolitionism as both radically transcending racial prejudice and reinforcing existing social distinctions, see Paul J. Polgar, "'To Raise Them to an Equal Participation': Early National Abolitionism, Gradual Emancipation, and the Promise of African American Citizenship," *Journal of the Early Republic* 31, no. 2 (2011).

combined with the opposition of the Proprietary Party, made it more difficult for reformers to achieve their radical objectives through legislation.[34]

Increasing Indian hostility in the context of the war with France and the need to develop a working defense against raids; the intractable conflict with the Proprietary Party and its successful lobbying in London: all these developments led to a transformation of Pennsylvania politics that prevented reformers from gaining an easy access to the legislative agenda if they wanted to implement their radical program of non-violence. The Friendly association was created thus with the purpose to surmount these obstacles and influence Indian and war policies on the provincial and imperial level from outside the legislature. The abolition of the slave trade, the next step in the reformers' political program, had to confront even harder political obstacles. Even if they had been able to sway the Pennsylvania legislature to fully ban the importation of slaves, this ban would have been easily overturned by the Board of Trade and Privy Council in London. This is why, in an effort to secure this imperial front, Benezet began to search for potential antislavery allies in England in 1763.

In this sense, the development of antislavery was not a retreat from politics into charity, but rather the intensification of the Quaker alternative project of political influence that had started with the forays into the Indian policies of the colony and of the imperial center in the 1750s. If anything, the antislavery project as it developed was even more "imperial" and far-reaching in its political ambitions. From his first overtures to potential allies in England, Benezet insisted on exercising pressure on authorities in London who, as the unsuccessful struggles over Indian rights had shown, were at this point the ultimate arbiters of colonial affairs and policies. Seen in its wider imperial context, the antislavery project was from its very beginning a self-consciously political enterprise for social change in so far as it focused explicitly on exerting targeted pressure on political authorities. It was not the manifestation of a Quaker exit from politics, but rather the elaboration of alternative modes of political engagement. And this elaboration occurred at the intersection of the principled imperatives of religious reform and a changing political configuration in Pennsylvania.

Thus, like earlier indigenist networks, incipient political antislavery was deeply engaged with the dynamic, multi-tiered and tension-filled political field of empire. Similarly, the initial crystallization of a Protestant antislavery network was the end product of the radicalization of religious reformers. In the Quaker case, the source of this radicalization was emphatically not the need to access souls for potential conversion. The Society of Friends, unlike friars, were not in the business of converting non-Europeans. Yet, like their Catholic predecessors, Quaker reformers were moved by a similarly prophetic vision of unethical treatment of non-Europeans, be they American Indians or enslaved Africans, as an affront to God.

---

[34] Marietta, *Reformation of Quakerism*, 159–61; Owen S. Ireland, "The Crux of Politics: Religion and Party in Pennsylvania, 1778–1789," *William & Mary Quarterly* 42, no. 4 (1985); Wayne L. Bockelman and Owen S. Ireland, "The Internal Revolution in Pennsylvania: An Ethnic-Religious Interpretation," *Pennsylvania History* 41, no. 2 (1974); Tully, *Forming American Politics*.

5

Forging an Abolitionist Network

That British power-holders should be asked to stop the venerable Atlantic slave trade was, in 1763, the idea of a single schoolmaster in Philadelphia. Between February 1 and May 9, 1788, the same request was made by thousands in more than 100 petitions to the British House of Commons.[1] This is just one indication of how much – and how effectively – the Pennsylvania antislavery project had grown within less than three decades. By 1788, schoolmaster Anthony Benezet's antislavery concerns engaged in practical activities individuals in Britain, France, and North America. In Britain only, thousands of men and women had developed an at least rudimentary understanding of the wrongs of previously distant colonial slavery.

Envisioning a political plan of action is one thing; putting it into practice, obviously, is something quite different. This second aspect, the transformation of the initial antislavery vision born in the unsettled context of mid-eighteenth-century Pennsylvania into an influential advocacy network is the focus of this chapter. This was a protracted and complex process that involved the search for political allies and adequate political strategy in a complex and changing imperial environment. Indeed, in many ways the course of these developments was significantly different from the dynamics of earlier pro-indigenist networks in the Iberian empires. Yet the underlying pattern and logic were the same: a small group of Quaker religious reformers initiated an advocacy network that grew gradually yet steadily between the 1760s and 1780s.

THE INITIAL GROWTH

By the 1760s, a small community of Quaker reformers in America had developed an incipient and inchoate program for political intervention against colonial

---

[1] Oldfield, *Popular Politics*, 49.

slavery. This program was intertwined with the reformers' project of transforming their religious organization and restoring its early glory by instilling
a stricter discipline that included, among other things, a principled divestment
from slaveholding. It was also intricately connected with a more ambitious
project of reshaping the larger political and social framework of empire – a
project that gained prominence with the reformers' increasing involvement
in a political mobilization for peaceful relations with Native Americans. In
their urgent prophetic vision, the sinfulness of slavery – like violence against
Indians – tainted the entire social fabric of an empire in which Quakers were
deeply implicated despite their separate religious and corporate identity.

Substantively, the attack on slavery formed an important focus of the reformers' activity both within the Society of Friends and in colonial (and imperial)
society at large. Yet there were important asymmetries in the practical implementation of these two related visions. The divestment from slaveholding
within Quaker ranks was a relatively straightforward disciplinary process for
which the abolitionist groups could take advantage of the organizational structures of the Society in the colonies, especially after they took over the stronghold of the influential Philadelphia Yearly Meeting. Confronting slavery on the
outside, however, was a much more complex task. There was simply no legal
or institutional precedent of voluntary abolition of slavery or voluntary withdrawal from the Atlantic slave trade. Both institutions were supported by the
strong and entrenched economic interests of slave owners and participants in
the trade. Southern colonial authorities made even voluntary manumissions
next to impossible, whereas authorities in London resisted any attempts to
limit or regulate the slave trade. More generally, colonial slavery was governed
by a complex system of multitiered imperial power: individual colonial assemblies had authority over the local regulation of slavery while London ruled
over the slave trade. Finally, the American reformers' position was politically
precarious even after they took over Quaker meetings in Philadelphia and elsewhere. They could not rely on the unqualified support of their coreligionists in
Britain and especially in London where an established Quaker pressure group
could have advanced their claims with imperial authorities. At this point, the
London Yearly Meeting was still dominated by moderate and "comfortable"
men who, unlike the early generations of Quakers, had achieved wealth and
social respectability. They were rather troubled by the American reformers' rig-
orist initiatives, such as the principled nonpayment of war-promoting taxes in
Pennsylvania, and were thus loath to use their political capital for controversial
purposes like tampering with the well-oiled machine of colonial slavery.[2]

The first Quaker attempt to abolish slavery outside of the Society predated,
in fact, the organizational ascendance of Philadelphia reformers. It was initiated in 1712 by William Southeby, one of the early committed antislavery

---

[2] On the tensions between Philadelphia and London Quakers, see Marietta, *Reformation of Quakerism*; Larson, *Daughters of Light*, 228–29.

reformers, who petitioned the Pennsylvania Assembly to free all the enslaved Africans in the province. Another petition, signed by "many of the inhabitants of the Province" and "praying for the prohibition of Negroes" (that is, the cessation of the importation of slaves) was presented concurrently. While the Assembly rejected Southeby's radical proposal, considering it "neither just nor convenient" to emancipate slaves, it increased ten times the existing import duty to the highly prohibitive twenty pounds.[3]

Southeby was an early antislavery radical and precursor of the later genera-tion of Quaker reformers. He shared with his successors a general concern with religious precepts and the ethics of relations with Native Americans. Unlike the later generation, however, he was forced to work outside the formal structures of the Society of Friends as the Philadelphia Yearly Meeting tried quietly to silence his radicalism. He incited in Philadelphia Quaker elders of his time the same uneasiness later reformers would produce among established elders in London.

Despite this official rejection, his actions had consequences. It is not entirely clear how involved Southeby himself was in the accompanying less-radical petition for a ban on slave imports, but the fact that the two petitions were pre-sented concomitantly in the Quaker colony was hardly coincidental. And this second petition resulted in an important precedent. Although the prohibitive duty that the Assembly introduced in response to this petition was annulled by the Privy Council in London, this was the first time that a colonial legis-lature acted to limit the slave trade with economic sanctions – a practice that would acquire a new salience in the context of intensifying economic struggles between colonies and imperial administration in the 1760s.

In that decade, Quaker reformers, acting from a much stronger organiza-tional platform, reemployed the petitioning tactics in two colonies where their coreligionists had a substantial presence in the legislature. During a ministry trip to New England in 1760, John Woolman, one of the principal antislav-ery reformers, was struck by the prominence of slavery around Newport, the major American hub of the Atlantic slave trade. Convinced that "this trade was a great evil" that "tended to multiply troubles and bring distresses on the people in those parts," he prepared a petition asking the legislature to ban slave imports that he offered to politically connected members of the Rhode Island Yearly Meeting. They approved but suggested that the petition be signed "out of meeting": adding, that is, signatures from non-Quakers and presenting the petition as an expression of a wider popular opposition to the slave trade.[4]

[3] Carroll, "William Southeby, Early Quaker Antislavery Writer," 423–24; Darold D. Wax, "Negro Import Duties in Colonial Pennsylvania," *Pennsylvania Magazine of History & Biography* 97, no. 1 (1973): 35–37.

[4] Phillips P. Moulton, ed. *The Journal and Major Essays of John Woolman* (New York: Oxford University Press, 1971), 109–12.

Most likely, this first petition outside of Pennsylvania was never presented to the Rhode Island Assembly. Woolman's actions, however, indicate how a political project to confront slavery and the slave trade was emerging out of the Quaker reformers' engagement both with their religious organizations and the wider imperial world. The primary goal of his trip to New England was, after all, the strengthening of Quaker discipline, and he was as much concerned with slavery as with, for example, ensuring that his brethren abstain from lotteries and their "spirit of selfishness."[5] His petitioning project coincided, also, with the ongoing work of the Friendly Association to shape peaceful relations with Native Americans and avoid war. In this context, the next successful petition "for a Law to prevent or discourage" slave imports was presented to the Pennsylvania Assembly in 1761. Again, it was framed not as a Quaker initiative but as a "Remonstrance from a great Number of Inhabitants of the City of Philadelphia." Yet the signs of Quaker design were unmistakably imprinted. After the Assembly ignored a counterpetition by merchants and passed, in response to the petition, a law increasing again the import duty to ten pounds, the Philadelphia Meeting for Sufferings contacted London Friends asking them to persuade the Board of Trade not to repeal the new law.[6]

It is in the aftermath of these first petitioning attempts that Anthony Benezet, acting on the realization that the only way to effectively stop the slave trade was to change opinion in the imperial center, tried to recruit allies in Britain in 1763. He asked his contact, Joseph Phipps, to help with the reprinting and distribution of his latest antislavery pamphlet and thus enlighten powerholders in Britain. Yet nothing came out of Benezet's first attempt to extend the campaign into Britain. It is not entirely clear why Phipps did not follow up or indeed how he responded to Benezet's requests. One possible obstacle was perhaps the fact that the *Short Account*, the pamphlet Benezet had enclosed, was published without the official consent of the Overseers of the Press, the Philadelphia Quaker body that licensed publications. This unofficial status prevented the publication from being distributed within the Society of Friends' networks.

Three years later, however, Benezet produced another pamphlet, *A Caution and Warning to Great Britain and Her Colonies*. For the first time now, he appealed explicitly not only to fellow Friends or Pennsylvanians, but to the larger imperial audience of the "British nation" as well. This time the publication was granted official approval and the Philadelphia Meeting for Sufferings not only ordered 2,000 copies to be distributed in the American colonies, but financed a London reprint. The following year, the London Meeting for Sufferings delivered copies to members in parliament, while Benezet continued

[5] Ibid., 110; Worrall, *Quakers in the Colonial*, 160–61.
[6] Jennings, "Mid-Eighteenth Century Quakerism," 25; Pennsylvania General Assembly, *Votes and Proceedings of the House of Representatives* (Philadelphia: Franklin, 1761), 21; Wax, "Import Duties in Pennsylvania," 35–37.

to circulate the pamphlet privately to officials and Friends in America and England.[7]

Again, Benezet's initiative produced no tangible results. Toward the end of 1771, however, he began another letter-writing campaign addressing potential allies in England. This time his vision of a concerted appeal to the king and parliament was supplemented by his latest book, *Some Historical Account of Guinea*: his most extensive compendium of antislavery arguments and information. He sent the book to several influential Quakers in England and Ireland, suggesting that they place excerpts from it in newspapers. He also explicitly urged them to organize petitions asking for a ban of the slave trade and invoked religiously charged precedents to convey his sense of urgency. "Is it not the duty of every one," he asked "to do all in their power, in imitation of the good Bishop of Chapia [*sic*] ... to bring this matter before King and Parliament?" Then he compared the current situation of the Society of Friends to the predicament of the biblical Esther who had the courage to brave the death penalty and appear before the king in order to save the Jews from extermination. Maybe Quakers were "intended for such a service as this"? More pragmatically, Benezet cited current Quaker-led petitioning efforts for the ban of slave imports in Maryland and Virginia. Thus, he argued, Friends should take the lead and he assured his correspondents that the petitions would have "the unity of many upright people of other religious persuasions."[8]

An Imperial Political Strategy

The Virginia petition Benezet referenced did not materialize, but Maryland Quakers obliged and in November 1771 presented to the colonial assembly a petition against the slave trade. The legislature rejected it yet increased, in a separate measure, the import duty on slaves by five pounds.[9] Thus, as Benezet was searching for transatlantic allies, antislavery ideas and practices were spreading along Quaker networks in the colonies.

In Britain, in addition to fellow Quakers, Benezet had tried to connect with British allies of "other persuasions" since 1763. Among his targets were the Society for the Propagation of the Gospel, John Wesley, the head of the growing Methodist movement, and Benjamin Franklin – who in 1764 had moved to

[7] Anthony Benezet, *A Caution and Warning to Great Britain and Her Colonies, in a Short Representation of the Calamitous State of the Enslaved Negroes in the British Dominions* (Philadelphia: Henry Miller, 1766); Jackson, *Let This Voice*, 62–66; Rees, "English Friends," 76; Sassi, "With a Little Help." Benezet was a member of the Overseers and in fact had helped usher into publication various antislavery materials, including his 1759 tract. It is not clear why he failed to do this with the *Short Account*.

[8] Brookes, *Friend Benezet*, 283–87; Sassi, "With a Little Help," 54; Sword, "Remembering Dinah Nevil," 325–26.

[9] Raphael Semmes, ed. *Proceedings and Acts of the General Assembly of Maryland, 1771 to June-July, 1773* (Baltimore: Maryland Historical Society, 1946), 20, 127; MacMaster, "Lee's Address," 149–50.

London as the agent of the Pennsylvania Assembly. The Society was noncommittal, to say the least. Wesley and Franklin proved much more valuable allies who wrote their own antislavery publications.[10] But perhaps the most important connection was the one Benezet was able to establish in 1772 with a clerk in the Ordnance Office named Granville Sharp.

In London, Sharp had been providing legal services since 1765 to slaves who contested their enslavement after he met Jonathan Strong, a slave severely mistreated by his master. Simultaneously, he developed a strong interest in contesting the legality of slavery. In 1767, he incidentally found on a bookstall a copy of Benezet's *Short Account* and had it reprinted in London. Two years later he published his own antislavery work, *A Representation of the Injustice and Dangerous Tendency of Tolerating Slavery*, an abridged version of which Benezet reprinted in Philadelphia in 1772. Although borrowing from and reprinting each other's work, the two had not been formally introduced. Benezet's first letter reached Sharp in 1772 even as he won a decisive and influential legal battle with Judge Mansfield's decision in the case of James Somerset whose owner wanted to send him back forcibly to the West Indies. Hardly a sweeping condemnation of slavery, the decision still affirmed the illegality of slavery on English soil and provoked wide public interest, both in Britain and in America.[11]

An important implication of this incipient cooperation between Benezet and Sharp was that for the first time the Philadelphian's program of attacking slavery with appeals to the highest imperial authorities was translated into a concrete, if not necessarily viable, political strategy. In his first letter, Benezet repeated his urgent call for an appeal to the king and parliament and apart from the current petitioning project in America, referred to the recent parliamentary investigation of the conduct of the East Indian Company as a potentially useful precedent. Writing back, Sharp agreed and offered specific suggestions on

[10] Frank Baker, "The Origins, Character, and Influence of John Wesley's Thoughts Upon Slavery," *Methodist History* 22, no. 2 (1984). On Franklin's cautious adoption of the Quaker reformers' antislavery principles, see Gary B. Nash, "Franklin and Slavery," *Proceedings of the American Philosophical Society* 150, no. 4 (2006); David Waldstreicher, "The Origins of Antislavery in Pennsylvania: Early Abolitionists and Benjamin Franklin's Road Not Taken," in *Antislavery and Abolition in Philadelphia: Emancipation and the Long Struggle for Racial Justice in the City of Brotherly Love*, eds. Richard Newman and James Mueller (Baton Rouge: Louisiana State University Press, 2011).

[11] On Sharp, see Brown, *Moral Capital*, 155–206; Gretchen Gerzina, *Black London: Life before Emancipation* (New Brunswick, NJ: Rutgers University Press, 1995); Prince Hoare, *Memoirs of Granville Sharp, Esq* (London: Henry Colburn, 1828); F. O. Shyllon, *Black Slaves in Britain* (London: Oxford University Press, 1974). On the Somerset trial and Mansfield decision, see Jerome Nadelhaft, "The Somersett Case and Slavery: Myth, Reality, and Repercussions," *The Journal of Negro History* 51, no. 3 (1966); William M. Wiecek, "Somerset: Lord Mansfield and the Legitimacy of Slavery in the Anglo-American World," *The University of Chicago Law Review* 42, no. 1 (1974); Steven M. Wise, *Though the Heavens May Fall: The Landmark Trial that Led to the End of Human Slavery* (Cambridge, MA: Da Capo Press, 2005).

how to organize the petitions. In addition to naming potential allies in government and parliament who could be entrusted with presenting the petitions, he outlined a three-pronged approach: petitions targeting the abolition of colonial slavery directed to the king, another set of petitions praying for the abolition of the slave trade directed to parliament, and petitions for the ban of slave imports directed to colonial legislatures.[12]

So far, Benezet had not been able to see his vision of antislavery appeals to metropolitan authority put in practice. Nor had the distribution of his pamphlets to power-holders in London produced any tangible results. Sharp now provided a concrete plan for an expanded coordinated action. On his part, Sharp had mostly devoted his energy to efforts to elicit a definitive pronouncement on the illegality of slavery in Britain through legal precedent. Yet he had also appealed to various individuals, including Prime Minister Lord North, in an attempt to weaken the colonial entrenchment of slavery. Now Benezet's insistence on concerted pressure on the king and parliament, as well as his promise of imminent copiously petitions from the colonies, encouraged Sharp to conceive of a more ambitious and better organized political campaign.

At the end, what emerged out of this exchange was a project to expand to a wider imperial frame an already existing tradition of Quaker-led interventions against slavery and the slave trade. In Benezet's and Sharp's new strategy, this practice was now to be applied in the wider world of empire, not only in the individual colonies. When Benezet received Sharp's encouraging response in October 1772, he immediately set out to organize and circulate the petitions his correspondent had recommended by using his contacts in the American colonies. By the end of November, the Pennsylvania petition to the king and parliament was ready. Yet, Benezet and James Pemberton decided to, literally, miss the next boat leaving from Virginia and "wait for a future opportunity" to send it to London. As Benezet explained later to Sharp, he – along with "some thoughtful people" – had concluded that colonial assemblies, "the Voice of the people they represent," had to be addressed first. As we will see, at that point the American abolitionist group and Sharp were becoming increasingly sensitive to a spreading sentiment of colonial autonomy against the interventionist imperial government.

In January the following year, the petition to the Pennsylvania Assembly was presented. As Benezet had promised his British correspondents, it had among its 200 signatures the names of Anglicans, Baptists, and Presbyterians. In accordance with the strategy outlined by Sharp, the petitioners asked the Assembly to make, through its London agent, a "Representation to the King and Parliament" for the cessation of the slave trade to the province. As it had done in the past, the Assembly responded favorably to the idea of discouraging slave imports by imposing the old prohibitive duty of twenty pounds. Yet, according to Benezet, the Assemblymen preferred to wait and see if the

[12] The letters are reprinted in Hoare, *Memoirs of Sharp*, 146–54.

Privy Council would approve the law before considering the "representation" to London authorities the petitioners had prayed for.[13]

The only coordinated transatlantic activity emerged, somewhat circuitously, around an address from the Virginia legislature to the king in the spring of 1772 that referenced the "inhumanity" of the slave trade and the dangerous consequences of its official support in London, implying that by preventing the immigration of free labor these pro-trade policies endangered the security of the royal dominions in America. The address accompanied a bill in which the House of Burgesses imposed a ten-percent levy on slave imports from Africa and an even higher duty of five pounds on human cargo imported from other colonies. The House had already tried to increase duties to twenty percent in 1769, but that law was repealed by the Privy Council in response, partly, to the opposition expressed in petitions by Liverpool and Lancaster merchants to the Board of Trade. The Virginia legislators, thus, took the rather unusual step to supplement a law awaiting the needed royal assent with a direct appeal to the king in an effort to neutralize preemptively the influence of British merchants. However valid and moving the humanitarian and security arguments in the address, they were subordinated to this more prosaic goal. The true motives behind the legislation were rather less altruistic: the need to raise revenue, preserve and enhance the value of large landowners' existing slaves, prevent potential slave insurrections, and, perhaps most importantly, close a loophole that allowed slave owners to practically smuggle slaves through the neighboring colonies under a statute that exempted slaves "for personal use" from taxes.[14]

Seen from a different angle, however, the Virginia Address was a testament of the effectiveness of Benezetian antislavery propaganda. By presenting themselves as the noble-minded authors of a law designed primarily to "check" the "pernicious commerce," the Burgesses were using the rhetorical potential of antislavery ideology to which they must have been exposed at least since 1769, when Virginia Quakers began lobbying legislators for a law allowing manumission in the colony and distributed among them Benezet's pamphlets. Although the Virginia Burgesses did not legalize manumission until 1782, with their address they had given the abolitionist network an unexpected gift. Even if it only parroted antislavery "talking points," it served admirably the purposes of the new Benezet-Sharp axis. Benezet could reuse it in his propaganda as yet another proof of an allegedly wildly spreading antislavery sentiment in the colonies. Although adopted before the new plan of action coordinated with Sharp, it also fit perfectly with Sharp's sub-strategy of having colonial

[13] Brookes, *Friend Benezet*, 297, 422–23; Bruns, *Am I Not*, 266; Pennsylvania General Assembly, *Votes of the House of Representatives* (Philadelphia: Henry Miller, 1773), 8, 23, 28; Sassi, "With a Little Help," 57; Wax, "Import Duties in Pennsylvania," 37–38.

[14] John Pendleton Kennedy, ed. *Journals of the House of Burgesses of Virginia, 1770–1772* (Richmond: Colonial Press, 1906), 293–94; MacMaster, "Lee's Address"; Wax, "Duties in Virginia."

legislatures petition the Crown to stop the slave trade. And, coming with the imprimatur of an impeccably respectable source, it could be used to twist the arms of politically connected London Quaker grandees.

In July 1772, the London Yearly Meeting received a request from Virginia Quakers to do something for a favorable reception of the address, as well as for help with easing manumission in the colony. In August, the Standing Committee of North Carolina Friends forwarded the same request, while reporting of an effort to produce a similar address in the local provincial assembly. Both actions bore the mark of Benezet's influence if not his direct guidance. The London Meeting duly appointed a committee and wrote, in turn, to the Friends' Meetings in Maryland and New Jersey, encouraging them to follow the Virginia example. In early spring the following year, the London committee approached the Board of Trade.

At that time Granville Sharp had high hopes about the newly appointed colonial secretary of state, Lord Dartmouth, a pious evangelical. As First Lord of the Trade in the Board, he concurred with the Quaker sentiment favoring abolition of the trade, yet discouraged any further appeals.[15] As late as early 1774, Sharp still continued to urge his Philadelphia correspondents to produce well-subscribed petitions that he would present to the king through Dartmouth who continued to give Sharp false assurances. It was clear, however, that the three-pronged strategy was not working. After Benezet and his associates decided to focus on pressuring colonial legislatures, no petitions from colonials materialized either to the king for the regulation and abolition of slavery or to parliament for the abolition of the slave trade. What worked – and only to a limited extend – was the third part of the strategy: appeals to assemblies to stop slave "cargoes" from entering the colonies. While the Pennsylvania campaign produced only an increase in import duties, Rhode Island Quakers were able to get a somewhat watered-down version of their project for a complete ban of slave imports approved by the Assembly.[16]

PREREVOLUTIONARY SYNERGIES AND TENSIONS

The record, then, of this first decade of politicized antislavery effort was decidedly mixed. Benezet's first articulation of a vision to suppress the source of slavery – the British slave trade – by appeals to metropolitan authorities had evolved significantly. His network of correspondents and associates in the colonies and in Britain had grown. In the process, information on the cruelty of

[15] Anstey, *Atlantic Slave Trade*, 224; Fladeland, *Men and Brothers*, 22; Olson, *Making the Empire*, 143; MacMaster, "Lee's Address"; *Narrative of Some of the Proceedings*, 7–9; Rees, "English Friends," 76–77. On Dartmouth and Sharp, see Brown, *Moral Capital*, 176.
[16] Bruns, *Am I Not*, 303–04; Thompson, *Moses Brown*, 97–98; John A. Woods, "The Correspondence of Benjamin Rush and Granville Sharp, 1773–1809," *Journal of American Studies* 1, no. 1 (1967).

slavery and the slave trade had reached wider audiences and the political project of antislavery had become much more concrete, producing some real if less than fully satisfying effects on policy makers. In fact, as a historian has noted recently, Benezet's outreach effort "modeled tactics that would characterize the antislavery movement for generations."[17] At the same time, this was also a decade of false starts. In particular, the ambitious petitioning strategy suggested by Sharp failed to materialize. At the end, the only approach that worked – at least to some extent – was to apply pressure on colonial assemblies to prevent or inhibit the importation of slaves.

So far, I have presented the admittedly modest yields of this first decade of transatlantic antislavery efforts with no reference to the simultaneous developments whose momentous consequences have captured the historians' imagination much more securely than the somewhat quixotic efforts of Benezet, Sharp, and their associates: the gathering storm of North American opposition to British imperial authority. This, of course, is deceptive. The choices and intentions of actors like Benezet and Sharp are impossible to understand outside of the meaningful context of intensifying imperial confrontations. And indeed, influential works insist on the importance of the prerevolutionary political struggles and the subsequent revolution as perhaps the most important catalyst for the emergence of an antislavery movement.[18]

Following its course of strengthening imperial governance in the aftermath of the Seven Years' War, London governments used parliament to impose a series of mercantilist measures, most notably the Stamp Act of 1765, the Townshend Act of 1767, and the Coercive Acts of 1774. Each of these measures further deepened the simmering tensions between colonial legislatures and royally appointed (or proprietary) governors. A faction of white colonials, enraged at the new taxes decreed by a distant London, increasingly mobilized to express its opposition to what it perceived as an infringement of the rights of British colonial subjects. Assemblies protested, mobs attacked, merchants signed non-importation agreements, and consumers pledged nonconsumption of British goods in an effort to hurt the mercantilist imperial state. In three successive waves of mobilization, these oppositional networks expanded, coordinated action across the colonies, and began establishing alternative institutions of political power. They also increasingly radicalized and escalated their claims of rights and freedom against what they began to consider as an unjust, tyrannical, and distant imperial regime.[19]

[17] Sword, "Remembering Dinah Nevil," 325.

[18] Blackburn, *Overthrow of Colonial Slavery*; Brown, *Moral Capital*; Davis, *Age of Revolution*, 231.

[19] Anderson, *Crucible of War*, 557–728; T. H. Breen, *The Marketplace of Revolution: How Consumer Politics Shaped American Independence* (Oxford: Oxford University Press, 2004); Marshall, *Making and Unmaking*.

Historians of antislavery have typically identified the new language of liberty and natural rights espoused by North American proto-revolutionaries as the most decisive positive influence on antislavery thought and action. Once committed to defending their opposition in the idiom of rights and oppression – and complaining of being treated like slaves by the king and parliament – "patriots" were forced, often unintentionally, to start questioning the much more real enslavement of human being in their midst.[20]

Even before the prerevolutionary crisis, the metaphor of slavery had been a standard rhetorical move against illegitimate and sprawling authority, as exemplified by the Pennsylvania Assembly's complaints against its governor lieutenant. It is not clear, however, if the proliferation of this trope in the 1760s made those who used it more aware of the plight of enslaved Africans. In an early statement defending the rights of the colonies, for example, the Massachusetts lawyer James Otis made the radical claim that both whites and blacks in the colonies were born free. While highly critical of the slavery system and its pernicious effects on freedom, this claim of equality, however, was subordinated to Otis's real argument: that British legislation brought liberty-loving white colonials into a situation dangerously close to the enslavement of Africans. In other words, he was afraid of the potential enslavement, real or metaphorical, of whites, and not necessarily interested in securing freedom for Africans. Another early influential promoter of the discourse of colonial liberties, Patrick Henry, responded to an antislavery pamphlet forwarded to him by Benezet's Virginia associate Robert Pleasants with a rambling statement of agreement, hedged with the admission that he still owned slaves because of "the general inconvenience of living without them." At the end, what the newly popular discourse of liberty and oppression did was open up a rhetorical possibility for those so inclined to point out the inconsistency involved in complaining against figurative "enslavement" by taxation while neglecting the moral evil of real-life slavery. Benezet himself was perhaps one of the first to invoke this inconsistency in his *Caution to Great Britain* published in the aftermath of the Stamp Act crisis.[21]

A more pronounced synergy between the political project of colonial assertiveness and Benezet's antislavery project emerged on the more specific issue of the discontinuation of the Atlantic slave trade. The trade was regulated and

---

[20] See, e.g, Ira Berlin, *Many Thousands Gone: The First Two Centuries of Slavery in North America* (Cambridge, MA: Belknap Press, 1998), 229; Blackburn, *Overthrow of Colonial Slavery*, 89–90; Brown, *Moral Capital*, 105–14; Douglas R. Egerton, *Death or Liberty: African Americans and Revolutionary America* (Oxford: Oxford University Press, 2009), 44; Gordon S. Wood, *The Radicalism of the American Revolution* (New York: A. A. Knopf, 1992), 186–87.

[21] Bruns, *Am I Not*, 221–22; Jack P. Greene, *Imperatives, Behaviors, and Identities: Essays in Early American Cultural History* (Charlottesville: University Press of Virginia, 1992), 236–89; Nash and Soderlund, *Freedom by Degrees*, 73–98; Egerton, *Death or Liberty*, 45; Hutson, *Pennsylvania Politics*; James Otis, *The Rights of the British Colonies Asserted and Proved* (Boston: Edes and Gill, 1764); Benezet, *Caution and Warning*, 3.

protected by London authorities and its main beneficiaries were English merchants. Conceptually, the question of the slave trade was then relatively easily
added to the colonials' list of economic grievances that fueled their claims for
larger political autonomy. Opposition to the importation of human cargoes
was also easily assimilated into the new protest practices of economic disaf-
filiation: the commitment to nonimportation and nonconsumption of goods
that brought profits to the metropole. It is in this context that earlier efforts
to impose higher duties on "imported" slaves were revived and intensified by
colonial legislatures in an effort to tax or fully ban the slave trade out of existence. Although there was often genuine antislavery sentiment behind these
initiatives, especially in the Northern and middle colonies, in the South with
its self-reproducing population of enslaved labor, the imposition of higher
duties and the discontinuation of imports was simply a matter of economic
rationality.[22]

Another way in which the prerevolutionary crisis did help focus the attention on the problem of slavery was rooted in clerical reaction to the unprecedented and intensifying conflict with authorities in London. In the aftermath
of parliament's 1774 unyielding legislation trying to decisively squash colonial
opposition, the conflict was reaching new proportions. At that time, a new
framing of the current situation emerged as ministers in the North began to
invoke the persistent sin of slaveholding as one reason for the deep crisis in
which the colonies had found themselves. As John Churchman had done a
decade ago in Pennsylvania, now clerical voices explained the deeply unsettled
situation as the result of divine punishment for the hypocritical oppression of
Africans by allegedly freedom-loving colonials and urged repentance, reformation, and the emancipation of slaves. Even Thomas Paine, the soon-to-be
main propagandist of American independence (and chastiser of Quaker hypoc-
risy), argued in his first anonymous antislavery newspaper article that "the
punishment with which Providence threatens us" was "suitable" to the crime
of slaveholding, a sin "than which no other vice ... has brought so much guilt
to on the land." This clerical discourse clearly facilitated the spread of antislavery ideas and some of its important carriers, the "New Divinity" men in New
England became important antislavery allies. Yet, in contrast to the Quaker
reformers' persistent engagement with slavery, in New Divinity sermons the
intensification of conflict coincided with a gradual shift of emphasis as "warnings against American sins" were overshadowed by invocations of the "virtue
of the patriot cause."[23]

[22] James J. Allegro, "'Increasing and Strengthening the Country': Law, Politics, and the Antislavery
Movement in Early-Eighteenth-Century Massachusetts Bay," *New England Quarterly* 75, no. 1
(2002); W. E. B. Du Bois, *The Suppression of the African Slave-trade to the United States of
America, 1638–1870* (New York: Longmans, Green and Company, 1904), 7–52; MacMaster,
"Lee's Address"; Rawley, *Slave Trade*, 268–76; Wax, "Import Duties in Pennsylvania"; Wax,
"Duties in Virginia."

[23] Valeri, "New Divinity," 766. Paine's pamphlet is reproduced in Bruns, *Am I Not*, 378. For

Clearly the newly ascendant rhetoric of liberty in the 1760s, as well the newly assertive mood of economic opposition to metropolitan mercantilism, provided opportunity for the spread and amplification of antislavery ideas. Yet the argument that colonial contention and the new language of freedom from oppression was the primary catalyst for antislavery is somewhat one-sided. It is more appropriate to understand these developments as the inter-action between two frequently intersecting yet ultimately separate political projects: a steadily growing project of increasing mobilization against London economic policies perceived as unjust and oppressive, and a less spectacu-larly successful project, largely Benezet's initiative, to eradicate slavery and the Atlantic slave trade. If the new assertions of colonial autonomy provided an opening for the diffusion of the antislavery arguments, the preparatory work of Benezet and his growing number of allies pushed prerevolutionary protest into an antislavery direction. It is remarkable, for example, that virtually all published antislavery statements in the period relied not only on the rhetoric of liberty and oppression, but also on the extensive information about the atrocities and abuses of the slave trade compiled authoritatively for the first time by Benezet in his pamphlets. Similarly, the activation of the argument of the inconsistency between claims of political oppression by London and the ongoing oppression of enslaved Africans often derived from exposure to the principled stance against slavery disseminated by Benezet and his correspon-dents and associates.

The Ideological Constraints of Prerevolution

Besides these synergies, there was an important tension between the two political projects. By 1763, Benezet had reached a firm realization that the only way to undermine effectively the colonial system of slavery was through pressure on imperial authorities in London. The ultimate goal of the several escalating waves of protest against imperial policies that began the follow-ing year with the mobilization against the Stamp Act were similarly directed toward these same authorities. Yet the continuing colonial protests and the invocations of the principles of colonial autonomy, equality, and rights also effected an important change in the ideological balance of power among imperial institutions. Although American proto-revolutionaries did not resort to claims of independence and an overthrow of royal authority until 1775, the very commitment to the principles of colonial rights increased the rele-vance of colonial assemblies as alternative sites of power whose prerogatives needed to be taken into account much more seriously. The political landscape of empire was undergoing a shift and the antislavery project had to navigate what were increasingly uncharted waters between rival sources of political authority.

sermons that reproduce the same framing the sin of slaveholding as the reason for the escalating crisis and call for repentance, see ibid., 316–37, 59–65.

The effect of these changes can be seen in the decisions Benezet and Sharp made when elaborating a strategy of political antislavery. Sharp was highly sensitive to the proper authority of colonial legislatures. His convictions would lead him to resign from his position in the Ordnance Office in 1777 in protest against British military action against the colonies and to develop a strong interest in projects for equitable parliamentary representation and political reform. When he argued that petitions for the regulation and abolition of slavery should be directed to the king, and not to parliament, his reasoning was both a reflection of existing political arrangements and a principled attempt to honor emerging colonial claims for legislative independence. As he had explained in a letter to Prime Minister Lord North, it *"rests entirely with the King and his Privy Council,* to recommend to the several Assemblies a formal repeal" of the "unjust laws" of slavery, "for no … Parliament can have a just right to enact laws for places which it does not *represent."* When in late 1772 Benezet and his associates in Philadelphia decided against sending the prepared petitions to the king and parliament, they were similarly constrained by the consideration that colonial assemblies should not be bypassed as they were "the Voice of the people they represent."[24]

By acknowledging the ideals of proper political representation, these were principled and even prudent choices in the context of intensifying contention between London and colonial assemblies. Yet these choices also minimized the opportunity for the issue of slavery to gain the political visibility and salience that would have come from its introduction into parliament's agenda. At least for the time being, it was a political fact that colonial policies were being increasingly parliamentarized in the period, even as this process provoked the increasing discontent of politically astute colonials and their British sympathizers like Sharp. The Commons had intervened directly in colonial matters as early as 1757 when they censured the Jamaica Assembly for its resistance to instructions from London. By the time Benezet and Sharp were devising a coordinated political strategy, there were at least two cases of parliamentary intervention in colonial affairs with a humanitarian twist. First, there was the parliamentary inquiry in the practices of the East Indian Company that had brought famine and various abuses in Bengal, and second, the discussion of the military expedition against free blacks in the newly conquered island of St. Vincent. In fact, Benezet referenced the India inquiry in his first letter to Sharp as an encouraging precedent, and Sharp contacted Colonial Secretary Dartmouth on the St. Vincent issue.[25]

---

[24] *Am I Not,* 266; Hoare, *Memoirs of Sharp,* 117–20. On Sharp's resignation and involvement with political reform, see Brown, *Moral Capital,* 188–89; Hoare, *Memoirs of Sharp,* 188–89, 261–63.

[25] Greene, "Posture of Hostility," 62–63; Hoare, *Memoirs of Sharp,* 159–66. On the two parliamentary inquiries in the 1760s see H. V. Bowen, *Revenue and Reform: The Indian Problem in British Politics, 1757–1773* (New York: Cambridge University Press, 1991); Paul Thomas, "The

It is far-fetched to suppose that a parliamentary intervention at that time would have led to a ban of the Atlantic slave trade. The air of certainty exuding from the tripartite division of labor Sharp proposed to Benezet was misleading. It was highly unlikely that either the king or parliament would respond to direct appeals from colonials as such appeals were simply not part of the established conventions of political lobbying. Traditionally, colonial interests had been represented and mediated in London by local brokers of influence who had access to officials and members of parliament. Yet Sharp himself admitted that one such class of brokers, the London agents of colonial legislatures, was out of the question because, apart from Pennsylvania's Franklin, they were supporters of the slave trade. As parliament increasingly took over imperial policies, colonial groups and assemblies began doing exactly what Sharp suggested: petitioning directly both Houses and the king. In the end, however, none of the eight petitions submitted between 1764 and 1774 met a favorable response, partly because colonial interests did not have a critical mass of committed members of parliament to make a difference in debates.[26]

Because of the MPs' more direct connection to their domestic constituencies, a petitioning drive from within England and Britain would have been perhaps more effective in potentially drawing the Commons' attention to colonial slavery. And indeed, that was Benezet's hope when he contacted British Quakers in 1772 urging them to organize petitions. At the end, however, Sharp's deference to colonial rights ruled out this strategy. His own efforts to confirm authoritatively the illegality of slavery on English soil – and his firm personal belief that this was a fact already guaranteed by the constitution – almost automatically made slavery a colonial problem whose solution, in the atmosphere of increased contention between the imperial center and the colonial legislatures, he was careful to assign to the efforts of colonials.

In other words, the pursuit of the fundamental aim of the antislavery project, change of the British legislation providing the institutional foundation of the slave trade and slavery, was thwarted, among other things, by the project's main instigators' deference to the ascendant ideals of colonial legislative autonomy. These developments indicate the complex and often contradictory ways in which the proto-revolutionary project of North American autonomy and the antislavery project interacted. While in certain aspects the two projects were mutually reinforcing, the ideology of colonial autonomy was also in deep tension with the pan-imperial reach of the emerging antislavery movement that targeted in a comprehensive fashion the legislative foundations of colonial enslavement.

Caribs of St. Vincent: A Study in Imperial Maladministration, 1763–73," *Journal of Caribbean History* 18, no. 2 (1983); Paul Thomas, "Changing Attitudes in an Expanding Empire: The Anti-Slavery Movement, 1760–1783," *Slavery & Abolition* 5, no. 1 (1984): 64–65.

[26] Olson, *Making the Empire*, especially 158–64; Bruns, *Am I Not*, 199.

IMPERIAL RUPTURES

This tension also highlights the relatively autonomous logic of the antislavery project that was not simply an outgrowth of the anti-London mobilization in the colonies. Seen in this light, the first decade of the antislavery effort spearheaded by Benezet in 1763 was a period of substantial growth and coordination as important allies joined his project to target imperial authorities in London. At the same time, this was also a period of a somewhat disjointed and frustrating search for viable and often untried ways to exert pressure on the various centers of power in the British Empire's rapidly changing political environment.

For the political environment of empire was changing rapidly and irreversibly. The escalation of the conflict with the American colonies led to the establishment of the first institution of alternative political authority, the Continental Congress of 1774. After that came the military conflict and the Declaration of Independence, resulting, by the end of hostilities in 1783, in the emergence of a new federated state. These developments brought changes favorable to some of the goals of the antislavery movement. Thus, the Continental Congress declared, and two years later reaffirmed, a unilateral withdrawal from the Atlantic slave trade – a culmination of sorts of the long-standing politics of resisting imperial authority by avoiding its protected commercial goods. And several of the new states, especially in the North, banned slavery or the slave trade.

Yet in many ways, the victorious oppositional movement that was now firmly transformed into a political project of independent state-building remained firmly closed to antislavery aspirations. Partly that was a side effect of changing political proportions. Now, as George Van Cleve has written, slaveholding states became "far larger stakeholders in a much smaller country." In the context of the new weak federalism, it was even easier for pro-slavery interests in the South to deflect attempts at regulation of slavery than in the older imperial setting. Thus, while some Northern states were banning slavery, the North Carolina legislature passed an "Act to Prevent Domestic Insurrections" that made the manumission of slaves next to impossible and re-enslaved the blacks whom the Quakers had already freed.[27]

In addition, the standard accusation that imperial Britain was the evil perpetrator of the slave trade lost its edge. Thus the final version of the Declaration of Independence disposed of any references to universal rights or slavery in earlier drafts. Instead, it accused the king of "exciting" the very same "domestic insurrections" that North Carolinian slaveholders tried to prevent, a thinly

---

[27] George Van Cleve, *A Slaveholders' Union: Slavery, Politics, and the Constitution in the Early American Republic* (Chicago: University of Chicago Press, 2010), 41. See also Don E. Fehrenbacher, *The Slaveholding Republic: An Account of the United States Government's Relations to Slavery* (Oxford: Oxford University Press, 2001). On the anti-manumission legislation in North Carolina, see Crawford, *Having of Negroes*, 111–13; Sowle, "North Carolina Manumission Society."

veiled reference to policies of offering freedom to slaves enlisting in the British Army. The sentence continued with a complaint against royal efforts "to bring on the inhabitants of our frontiers the merciless Indian savages." Blacks and Indians were now branded, to use a current epithet, un-American – as were the Quakers, the main carriers of antislavery practices and ideas. The Society of Friends' avoidance of violence and refusal to enthusiastically adopt the project of independence were grating to the suspicious patriotic mind. In 1777, a committee of the Continental Congress investigated several prominent Pennsylvania Quakers for their "disaffection" and, on the strength of a forged letter proving "a Disposition highly inimical to the American cause," ordered their arrest. Last but not least, the war completely disrupted the established pattern of Quaker traveling ministry between Britain and the colonies that had been an important vector of the transmission of antislavery ideas and information.[28]

Under the circumstances, the transatlantic connection of the incipient imperial antislavery project initiated by Benezet and Sharp inevitably disintegrated. Instead, activities were now sharply bound by the two new separate political units. In 1775, a group of Philadelphia Quakers around the English-born tailor Thomas Harrison formed a Society for the Relief of Free Negroes Held in Bondage that tried to replicate Sharp's legal strategy of emancipating slaves in court. Hard as they tried, they were unable to produce a positive and binding judicial ruling comparable to the Mansfield judgment in England. Much more encouraging was the passage in 1780 of a bill for the gradual abolition of slavery in Pennsylvania – a first, if flawed, example of emancipation through legislative action that Benezet and his associates tried to reproduce in neighboring states.[29]

[28] Robert F. Oaks, "Philadelphians in Exile: The Problem of Loyalty during the American Revolution," *Pennsylvania Magazine of History & Biography* 96, no. 3 (1972); Owen S. Ireland, "The Ethnic-Religious Dimension of Pennsylvania Politics, 1778–1779," *William & Mary Quarterly* 30, no. 3 (1973): 429–30; Larson, *Daughters of Light*, 108, 293–95; Robert G. Parkinson, "'Manifest Signs of Passion': The First Federal Congress, Antislavery, and Legacies of the Revolutionary War," in *Contesting Slavery: The Politics of Bondage and Freedom in the New American Nation*, eds. John Craig Hammond and Matthew Mason (Charlottesville: University of Virginia Press, 2011). On the negative effect of the Revolutionary War on legislation abolishing slavery, see also Art Budros, "Explaining the First Emancipation: Social Movements and Abolition in the U.S. North, 1776–1804," *Mobilization* 16, no. 4 (2011).

[29] Egerton, *Death or Liberty*, 106–10; Gary B. Nash, *Forging Freedom: The Formation of Philadelphia's Black Community, 1720–1840* (Cambridge, MA: Harvard University Press, 1988), 61–63; Nash and Soderlund, *Freedom by Degrees*, 99–136; Sword, "Remembering Dinah Nevil"; Arthur Zilversmit, *The First Emancipation: The Abolition of Slavery in the North* (Chicago: University of Chicago Press, 1967), 126–32. In Massachusetts, slavery was largely abolished in 1783 by a judicial interpretation of the state constitution comparable to the Mansfield ruling in England. See also John D. Cushing, "The Cushing Court and the Abolition of Slavery in Massachusetts: More Notes on the 'Quock Walker Case'," *The American Journal of Legal History* 5, no. 2 (1961); Emily Blanck, "Seventeen Eighty-Three: The Turning Point in the Law of Slavery and Freedom in Massachusetts," *The New England Quarterly* 75, no. 1 (2002).

These efforts to enact an abolition law in New Jersey, New York, Connecticut, and Rhode Island are indicative of the maintenance and even growth of the networks initiated by Benezet – despite the challenges and uncertainties of the near-chaotic reordering of political space. In Philadelphia, Benezet had been able to recruit the prominent physician Benjamin Rush who wrote an antislavery pamphlet to accompany the petition to the Assembly in 1773. In New England, several Congregational ministers expressed their opposition to slavery in print and in sermons. Samuel Hopkins, a student of the leading "New Divinity" figure Jonathan Edwards, converted to antislavery after 1769 when he became exposed to the working of the institution in his ministry in Newport, the center of the Rhode Island slave trade. Another Rhode Islander – and recent convert to Quakerism – Moses Brown led the antislavery movement in the state and provided a connection with New England Congregationalists.[30]

Apart from the new state legislatures, the Continental Congress was an obvious target for antislavery lobbying. At least since 1769 when it discouraged its members from participation in nonimportation initiatives, the Society of Friends had officially distanced itself from the growing Patriot movement and the Continental Congress. Even so, Benezet and his associates did not miss the opportunity to press antislavery measures on the delegates convening in Philadelphia. Similarly, in 1776, Samuel Hopkins sent to each member of Congress a copy of his *Dialogue Concerning Slavery*. Benezet was equally opportunistic in his effort later, during the British occupation of Philadelphia, when he approached Commander-in-Chief William Howe with his concerns about slavery.[31]

The severing of the colonial link seemed to doom the chances of a comparable antislavery activity in Britain. And this was certainly the case before the resumption of coordinated action after the peace of 1783. Rather unexpectedly, in 1775 parliament did what Benezet had been hoping to accomplish since 1763: the issue of slavery was for the first time introduced in a debate, if only tangentially. David Hartley – the MP whose Hull seat five years later would, ironically, be taken over by William Wilberforce, the future parliamentary voice of antislavery – introduced a motion for reconciliation with the rebellious colonies. To break the standoff between the warring parties, he

---

[30] Charles Rappleye, *Sons of Providence: The Brown Brothers, the Slave Trade, and the American Revolution* (New York: Simon and Schuster, 2006); David E. Swift, "Samuel Hopkins: Calvinist Social Concern in Eighteenth Century New England," *Journal of Presbyterian History* 47, no. 1 (1969); Jonathan D. Sassi, "'This whole country have their hands full of Blood this day': Transcription and Introduction of an Antislavery Sermon Manuscript Attributed to the Reverend Samuel Hopkins," *Proceedings of the American Antiquarian Society* 112, no. 1 (2002); John Saillant, "'Some Thoughts on the Subject of Freeing the Negro Slaves in the Colony of Connecticut ...' by Levi Hart; With a Response from Samuel Hopkins," *New England Quarterly* 75, no. 1 (2002); Thompson, *Moses Brown*; Sassi, "With a Little Help," 57.
[31] Olson, *Making the Empire*, 168; Bruns, *Am I Not*, 129–30; 321–23; 30–31, 48–50; Marietta, *Reformation of Quakerism*.

suggested that parliament pass a law granting slaves the constitutional right of trial by jury. Colonial legislatures would then willingly assent to the law, thus reaffirming their submission to parliamentary authority. The implicit calculation was that if North Americans and parliament could not agree on the extent of parliamentary privilege and colonials' rights, they could certainly agree on a piece of legislation extending rights and liberties, albeit to a reduced extent, to a severely underprivileged population. Yet the measure was defeated handily and no serious consideration of the issue of slavery emerged in the debate.[32]

Hartley's motion was an instance where petitions would have potentially amplified the issue, if only in parliamentary debates. Yet throughout the 1770s there was in England no activity outside of parliament comparable to what American abolitionists were trying to do at the same time. After the break-down of the petitioning project he had envisioned with Benezet, Sharp devoted his antislavery energies to contacting the bishops of the Church of England, hoping that swayed by his lobbying they would intervene in an impending parliamentary inquiry on the African trade to voice antislavery concerns. Similarly, the British Quakers who Benezet hoped would take a lead in petitioning, remained unmoved. Despite periodic yearly reminders from the Philadelphia Yearly Meeting, the London Meeting failed to mobilize its members.[33] All this changed only in 1783, when Benezet launched another letter-writing offensive and a re-energized group of London Quakers began the preparatory work for a public campaign that not only restored transatlantic coordination and cooperation, but was also to change crucially the balance in Britain's favor.

MOBILIZATION CROSSES THE ATLANTIC

Sometime in late 1782 or early 1783, Benezet made yet another and final attempt to mobilize various correspondents in North America and Britain for political action. For the first time, the London Yearly Meeting responded positively to Philadelphia's call for action and instead of the typical complacent expression of support, decided to take concrete steps for the appeal to parliament that Benezet had urged for twenty years. Although there is no record of the deliberations of the 1783 Yearly Meeting, all indications suggest that like the Philadelphia Quakers' move to decisively purge themselves from slaveholding in 1750, this change in attitude was the result of a generational revolt within the Yearly Meeting. The year before, a new group of reform-minded younger

---

[32] Brown, *Moral Capital*, 146–49; John Pollock, *Wilberforce* (New York: St. Martin's Press, 1978), 12–15; *The Parliamentary History of England, From the Earliest Period to the Year 1803*, vol. XVIII (London: T. C. Hansard, etc., 1813), 1042–56. On the context of British parliamentary and extra-parliamentary activities for reconciliation with the colonials in 1775, see Marshall, *Making and Unmaking*, 342–52.

[33] Anstey, *Atlantic Slave Trade*, 225–26, 46; Brown, *Moral Capital*, 193–94, 412–13; Hoare, *Memoirs of Sharp*, 276–77; Rees, "English Friends," 77.

Quakers who would play a prominent part in the antislavery movement had carried the consensus of the Meeting against the risk-averse established elders. They were also helped by the presence of American reformers committed to concerted action against slavery.[34]

Thus, later that year, Benezet's vision materialized and the first British Quaker petition for abolition of the slave trade was presented to the Commons as they discussed regulations of the African trade. Subsequently, Philadelphia Friends presented a petition to the Continental Congress requesting that the suspended Atlantic slave trade not be renewed.[35] While these petitions produced no immediate result, they were the first indications of a strengthening drive toward a coordinated action. Less visible yet more important was the increased commitment among Quakers and their allies to consistent antislavery activities on both sides of the Atlantic.

In Philadelphia, the Society for the Relief of Free Negroes was revived in 1784 and began providing legal assistance to blacks seeking freedom. The following year, Methodist preachers in Virginia made the very first Southern attempt to pressure a state legislature to ban slavery. As early as 1778, Francis Asbury, one of the British-born emissaries of the rapidly growing American Methodist movement had decided that Methodists had to follow the Quaker example and work for the freeing of slaves or risk God's wrath. The commitment persisted even in the increasingly hostile Southern environment and resulted in a successful petition drive for emancipation.[36]

In London, the Yearly Meeting was now firmly committed to the Benezetian model of action. An official committee on the slave trade was appointed while at the same time an informal group began to operate outside of official structures. Both groups targeted elected officials and influential individuals, as well as the general public. They placed antislavery materials in newspapers, published and distributed pamphlets, and gradually established a network of potential allies in the provinces.[37]

---

[34] Anstey, *Atlantic Slave Trade*, 227–29; Brown, *Moral Capital*, 414–20; Bruns, *Am I Not*, 486–88; Sassi, "With a Little Help," 64–68; Brookes, *Friend Benezet*, 372–75.

[35] Anstey, *Atlantic Slave Trade*, 229–30; Thomas E. Drake, *Quakers and Slavery in America* (New Haven, CT: Yale University Press, 1950), 93–94; Sassi, "With a Little Help," 70; Brown, *Moral Capital*, 422–25; Jennings, *Business of Abolishing*, 41; Rees, "English Friends," 78.

[36] Eberly, "Pennsylvania Abolition Society," 24–27; Donald G. Mathews, *Slavery and Methodism: A Chapter in American Morality, 1780–1845* (Princeton, NJ: Princeton University Press, 1965), 6–7; MacMaster, "Liberty or Property"; Mathews, "Proposed Abolition"; Sword, "Remembering Dinah Nevil," 334.

[37] Jennings, *Business of Abolishing*, 23–30; Peter Marshall, "The Anti-Slave Trade Movement in Bristol," in *Bristol in the Eighteenth Century*, ed. Patrick McGrath (Newton Abbot: David and Charles, 1972), 187–88; Rees, "English Friends," 79–82. See also "Minute Book of the Meeting for Sufferings Committee on the Slave Trade," Library of the Religious Society of Friends, London, Box F1/7, as well as the circular accompanying the distribution of *The Case of Our Fellow-Creatures* and the follow-up circular (Tract Volume G/22 and 24).

The New British Allies

Londoners now not only adopted one of Benezet's tactics, the recruitment of non-Quaker allies, but in fact outperformed the Pennsylvanians. For however committed Benezet's "external" recruits were, they never matched the devotion, persistence, and contribution of the new British allies of the 1780s. The first of them was Thomas Clarkson who was to become with Quaker support, if not the earliest, then the first successful full-time social movement organizer in history. In 1785, Clarkson was finishing his Master of Art degree at Cambridge and envisioning a comfortable career as a churchman when he decided to try and be the first student in the university's history to win a second essay prize after his win the year before. The topic that year was "Is it lawful to make slaves of others against their will?" Peter Packard, the Vice-Chancellor who chose it, had become increasingly critical of the slave trade, most likely after exposure to the ideas of Granville Sharp who in the course of his lobbying of the bishops had found a receptive audience among clergymen connected with Cambridge. Trying to remedy his ignorance on the subject, Clarkson chanced upon a newspaper advertisement for Benezet's *Some Historical Account*, a book where, as he later admitted, he "found everything" he needed. At the end, not only did he win the coveted prize, but also developed an almost obsessive concern with the horrors of slavery and with ways to change the status quo. Upon his graduation and return to London, he began collecting additional information and decided, as a first step, to translate his award-winning essay from the original Latin and publish it. A Quaker from his hometown of Wisbech, whom Clarkson saw by chance on the street, immediately asked him why the essay had not been published and introduced him to the group of abolitionist Friends who had been trying to get in touch with the essay's author.[38]

One consequence of this encounter was that Clarkson was given a public platform. Finding a publisher for an unprofitable "serious" manuscript like his prize essay was next to impossible, as Granville Sharp had complained in 1774 to Benjamin Rush when he failed to locate an English publisher for the American's antislavery tract.[39] Yet only a few months after Clarkson's chance encounter, his *Essay on the Slavery and Commerce of the Human Species* was published almost simultaneously in England and the United States by the Quaker printer and bookseller James Phillips, publisher of most of the antislavery propaganda at the time. The book was well received and established the author's credentials. In exchange, Clarkson offered his commitment to antislavery action and access to polite Anglican circles that were out of reach for his Quaker patrons.

---

[38] Thomas Clarkson, *History of the Rise, Progress, and Accomplishment of the Abolition of the African Slave Trade by the British Parliament* (London: J. W. Parker, 1839), vol. 1, 210–17; Brown, *Moral Capital*, 194–95; Ellen Gibson Wilson, *Thomas Clarkson: A Biography* (Basingstoke: Macmillan, 1989).

[39] Brookes, *Friend Benezet*, 446–47.

William Dillwyn, Benezet's former pupil who had settled in Walthamstow near London in the 1770s, told Clarkson of the work of Sharp and the Quaker committee and facilitated introductions. Perhaps the most consequential of these introductions was the one to the vicar of the village of Teston in Kent, James Ramsay – an acquaintance that served to cement the connection between the emerging British Quaker antislavery project and the strengthening evangelical faction within the Church of England.

Ramsay was one of the few Anglicans that had developed a strong critical attitude toward colonial slavery. Posted on the island of St. Kitts in 1762, he began inquiring about the conditions of the slaves who he thought should be offered salvation through conversion to Christianity. Soon he was appalled by their inhumane treatment and realized that the first step would be to secure them decent living conditions. His efforts, however, earned him the unrelenting hostility of the European planters that resulted in vicious character assassination attacks on Ramsay until his death in 1789. By 1777 he saw himself forced to leave St. Kitts and resume his earlier career of naval chaplain, and in 1781 he returned to England when offered the living of Teston. The Comptroller of the Navy, Sir Charles Middleton, under whom Ramsay had served, and his wife, Margaret, were his patrons there. Both belonged to the growing group of upper-class evangelicals and came to share Ramsay's concern about the Christianization of slaves in the colonies. In 1784, encouraged by Lady Middleton and one of Sharp's bishop converts, Beilby Porteus, bishop of Chester, Ramsay published his *Essay on the Treatment and Conversion of the African Slaves in the British Sugar Colonies*. When a reviewer suggested that the pamphlet implicitly condoned the slave trade, he immediately published another pamphlet arguing for its abolition.[40]

Ramsay had been on the Quaker committee's contact list at least since 1783 when he was sent a copy of one of the first London-produced antislavery tracts. Soon after Dillwyn provided a letter of introduction, Ramsay called on Clarkson in London and invited him to Teston. There the Middletons organized a small retreat on the issue of slavery and evangelization of slaves with other two invitees: Beilby Porteus and Benjamin La Trobe of the Moravian Brethren, perhaps the only Protestant church that had succeeded in establishing missions among slaves. At a dinner, Clarkson again reaffirmed his commitment to serve the cause of the "oppressed Africans." Even more important was a breakfast conversation, possibly after Clarkson's departure, in which Lady Middleton urged her husband to bring the issue of the abolition of slave trade to parliament and initiate an inquiry. The admiral, whose modest debate record consisted of two speeches on the subject of the Navy, suggested that another MP would handle the matter much better than him. Then someone

[40] Ian Bradley, "James Ramsay and the Slave Trade," *History Today* 22, no. 12 (1972); F. O. Shyllon, *James Ramsay: The Unknown Abolitionist* (Edinburgh: Canongate, 1977); Brown, *Moral Capital*, 333–89.

mentioned the name of the young MP William Wilberforce. A friend of one of the Middletons' son-in-laws, Wilberforce seems to have grown closer to the couple after his conversion to evangelicalism the year before. At Lady Margaret's request, Middleton wrote to Wilberforce who although far from eager to embrace the issue, promised to consider it.[41]

Meanwhile in London, Clarkson and his publisher's cousin, soon-to-be Quaker Richard Phillips, began to plot a concrete strategy for political action in the cause of the "oppressed Africans." Not surprisingly, in light of the direction the Quaker antislavery project had taken, they settled on two main goals: targeting "the members of the legislature" and collecting additional information on the slave trade in order to neutralize its defenders. Wilberforce, whom Clarkson educated in all the details of the slave trade, was one of his prime targets. And the Quaker antislavery group, for whom Clarkson effectively had become the middleman, monitored with attention the progress of his lobbying. Despite the pressure from Clarkson and the Middletons, however, Wilberforce, a life-long vacillator, was biding his time. It was only in May 1787, after a warning by his close friend, Prime Minister William Pitt, that with his inaction he was risking losing out to more enterprising parliamentary competitors, that Wilberforce signaled he was ready to introduce a motion for the abolition of the slave trade.[42]

Clarkson immediately reported to the Quaker group the news of Wilberforce's commitment and plans were drawn for a political campaign to support the projected motion for abolition of the trade. For this purpose, a public Society for the Abolition of the Slave Trade was constituted. A month earlier, the Relief Society in Philadelphia had expanded its mission. Reconstituting itself as the Pennsylvania Society for the Abolition of Slavery, now its ambitions went beyond simply facilitating the freeing of illegally enslaved individuals. In August, the London Committee considered a letter from an ambitious French hack writer, Jacques Pierre Brissot, who offered his services. The Society recommended that he establish an abolition committee in France. Early the following year, the French organization was founded under the name *Société des Amis des Noirs*.[43]

---

[41] Rees, "English Friends," 79–80; Christian Ignatius La Trobe, *Letters to My Children; Written at Sea during a Voyage to the Cape of Good Hope, in 1815* (London: Seeleys, 1851), 21–24; Pollock, *Wilberforce*, 52–53. La Trobe's is the only account of these events and because of his freely admitted animosity toward Clarkson, it is possible that he minimized the latter's role.

[42] *Wilberforce*, 54–57; Wilson, *Thomas Clarkson*, 22–23.

[43] Eberly, "Pennsylvania Abolition Society"; Jennings, *Business of Abolishing*; Nash, *Forging Freedom*, 105–06; Marcel Dorigny, "Mirabeau and the Société des Amis des Noirs: Which Way to Abolish Slavery?" in *The Abolitions of Slavery : From Léger Félicité Sonthonax to Victor Schoelcher, 1793, 1794, 1848*, ed. Marcel Dorigny (New York: Berghahn Books, 2003); Dorigny and Gainot, *Amis des Noirs*; Nash and Soderlund, *Freedom by Degrees*, 124–25; Daniel P. Resnick, "The Societé des Amis des Noirs and the Abolition of Slavery," *French Historical Studies* 7, no. 4 (1972); Clarkson, *History*, vol. 1, 243–58; Oldfield, *Popular Politics*.

Non-Quaker allies were now firmly embedded in the antislavery network. While British Friends remained heavily committed to the financing and managing of the incipient political campaign, three of the twelve members of the London Society were Anglicans. The reconstituted Pennsylvania Abolition Society similarly included now prominent notables of Philadelphia from outside the Society of Friends. To project a nonsectarian inclusiveness, both societies gave the chairmanship to well-known non-Quakers who otherwise did little of the work, Granville Sharp and Benjamin Franklin. In Paris, the *Amis des Noirs* was launched by a group of Anglophile reformers around the Count of Mirabeau, including members of the exiled set of Reformed Protestant bankers from Switzerland.

In addition to this intensified recruitment across denominational boundaries, an equally significant development was the geographical spread of the movement. By 1788, Philadelphia, London, and Paris became the hubs of a new antislavery network. While still addressing an inherently imperial problem – the problem of slavery and the slave trade – the dimensions of a network of this kind for the first time was not coextensive with an empire, but had what can be called an international dimension. Partly, this was because of the historical contingency of the antislavery project's persistence on both sides of the Atlantic after the American exit from the British imperial structure. Yet the French adoption of the model was a first instance of a diffusion pattern in which the British original would be transplanted to other imperial centers or nation states: from the Netherlands in the 1840s to Spain and Brazil in the 1880s.[44]

THE DYNAMICS OF NETWORK EXPANSION

In the 1760s, a small group of Quaker reformers developed an incipient political antislavery project and tried to organize, with no great success, pressure on two colonial legislatures for the regulation or ban of the slave trade. By the 1780s, organizations espousing even more ambitious political goals were established in London, Paris, and Philadelphia. Politicized antislavery had acquired an international dimension with societies that had an explicitly interdenominational leadership and were poised to engage seriously political authorities through lobbying and the organization of popular support for their abolitionist platform.

So remarkable is the difference of the organizational profile of abolitionism in the 1760s and 1780s that it is hard, at first sight, to locate a meaningful

---

[44] Christopher Schmidt-Nowara, *Empire and Antislavery: Spain, Cuba, and Puerto Rico, 1833–1874* (Pittsburgh: University of Pittsburgh Press, 1999); Robert Conrad, *The Destruction of Brazilian Slavery, 1850–1888* (Berkeley: University of California Press, 1972); J. M. van Winter, "Public Opinion in the Netherlands on the Abolition of Slavery," in *Dutch Authors on West Indian History: A Historiographical Selection*, ed. M. A. P. Meilink-Roelofsz (The Hague: M. Nijhoff, 1982).

connection or continuity between these two dates. It is not surprising perhaps that historians have been tempted to seek factors outside of the initial nucleus of Quaker reformers as the most important determinant for the abolitionist network's strengthening political muscle and radicalism: whether the American Revolution and its rhetoric of liberty or the acquisition of external allies like Clarkson and Wilberforce. Furthermore, because the resulting organizational structures of the 1780s were with a distinctive national orientation in their goals and self-presentation, they have been sequestered into separate historiographical boxes. Thus, for example, the Pennsylvania Abolition Society has been inscribed into the analytical narrative of a distinct U.S. antislavery, separate from the phenomena of British and French antislavery where the other two Societies are inscribed by the conventions of historiographical sub-specialties.

Yet seen in a wider imperial and international context, the three new abolitionist organizations of the 1780s are better understood as the end product of a single abolitionist network initiated by Pennsylvania Quakers that for twenty or so years grew, evolved, and – at the end – spawned a set of "national" offshoots. Throughout, the antislavery project preserved its large-scale connectedness. The resulting international dimension was thus the effect of progressive accretion: the initially small North American group, cultivated most notably by Benezet, expanded decisively into Britain when the London Yearly Meeting was recruited under the pressure of Quaker reformers, and then French admirers like Brissot transplanted the model across the Channel. And in many ways, the changing character of abolitionism, its increasing political assertiveness and effectiveness, arose organically out of this process of accretion as a spreading network interacted with the political givens of its new locales.

One important implication of this networked growth was that the initial core group of Quaker reformers – itself growing in the process – exerted a strong formative influence on the direction and nature of the growth. It was this group's dogged search for allies on both sides of the Atlantic that, in fits and starts, spurred the continuous enlargement of the network. In this sense, what emerged in the 1780s was not simply the mechanical agglomeration of the efforts of separate individuals whose respective contributions added up to the new composite of international abolitionism. Although non-Quaker latecomers clearly contributed their own added value, the Quaker core acted as an important "multiplier" by continuing to provide resources, shape the growth of the network, and orchestrate the political practices in which it engaged.

It is true that several key individuals, such as Sharp, Ramsay, Clarkson, or Wilberforce, developed their commitment against slavery independently or at least with no direct prompting from the small Pennsylvania group of Quaker reformers who, in the context of the Seven Years' War, decided to expand their Society's injunction against slaveholding into a more general political project. Yet the specific shape of the network that, by the 1780s, encompassed such originally unaffiliated individuals was actively constructed by the initial Quaker core. Most generally, the growing corpus of antislavery propaganda assiduously compiled and amplified by Benezet provided the basic ideological fodder for the network. Here was a compendium of facts and arguments that gave potential recruits a strong justification for commitment to antislavery – as it did for Clarkson who found in Benezet's pamphlet everything he needed to flesh out his thesis against enslavement. Even more consequential was the Quaker reformers' core group strategic action: their persistent search for individuals who would not only adopt and further disseminate the newly codified antislavery ideology, but would commit to practical activities toward the accomplishment of the abolitionist political agenda. And in addition to recruiting such individuals, the core group also encouraged them to interact directly among themselves, bypassing the Quaker "center" of operations – as when Benezet connected Benjamin Franklin and Granville Sharp or when Dillwyn connected Thomas Clarkson and James Ramsay, thus facilitating Clarkson's entry into the clique of Anglican evangelicals. These independent interactions, in turn, strengthened further the fabric of the emerging network as now antislavery ideas, commitments, and practices circulated even outside the initial nucleus. Simultaneously, because they were not mediated directly by Quakers, these exchanges served the reformers' goal even further: such interactions were a visible proof of their claim that antislavery ideas were not simply an idiosyncratic sectarian concern. Now they could point to public pronouncements and activities by non-Quakers as a clear sign of the independent existence of an antislavery "public opinion."

As Kirstin Sword has recently shown, non-Quakers were "strategically deceived" to join the abolitionist network. One can see the same strategy of deception being pressed on cautious British Quakers by Philadelphia reformers in their effort to create a self-fulfilling prophecy of an abolitionist landslide. Ambitious youngsters like Benjamin Rush, Thomas Clarkson, or William Wilberforce were gently coaxed into participation with praise overestimating their contribution to the movement. When Benezet made his overtures to Granville Sharp and Benjamin Franklin in 1772, he described the people in "the Northern Colonies," "New England," and "Virginia and Maryland" as equally ready to take action against the slave trade. He repeated the same claim in his letters to British Quakers. In both cases he embellished the truth in rather un-Quakerly ways: what he described as nearly spontaneous popular mobilization was something that he and other reformers were actively orchestrating through their local contacts.

Similarly, after persuading Rush to publish an antislavery tract to coincide with the petition to the Pennsylvania assembly, Benezet discreetly used the fact that now a non-Quaker was engaging in antislavery pamphleteering as proof of the spread of abolitionist feeling. Sending copies of the pamphlet for distribution in Virginia, he described it simply as "pamphlet published here by a respectable member of the Presbyterian Communion." American abolitionists'

British correspondents were routinely given an exaggerated picture of growing antislavery in America, while antislavery occurrences in Britain were similarly amplified to American audiences to suggest the independent growth of abolitionism across the ocean. In his first letter to Granville Sharp, Benjamin Rush claimed that "three-fourths" of Pennsylvania and the entire city of Philadelphia "cry out against ... Negro slavery." In February 1786, long before the start of the first British campaign, Moses Brown in Providence in his attempt to get New England Congregationalist clergy on board had reassured Samuel Hopkins in Newport that the British "dissenting clergy are joining to promote the utter abolition of slavery in the British dominion, and the slave trade."[45]

Imperial Complexity, Political Strategy, and Social Heterogeneity
A variety of factors and motivations drove Friends and non-Friends to support – or not – the reformers' project of politicized antislavery. Yet the crucial push for the creation of the international abolitionist network was given by the small nucleus of North American Quaker reformers – if not single-handedly by Anthony Benezet, the most committed and active member of this nucleus. In this sense, the expansion of antislavery paralleled closely the development of the earlier Catholic pro-indigenist networks. In both cases, a network of activists grew out of the initial radicalization of a small group of religious reformers – in the case of the new abolitionist network out of the Quaker reformers' reaction against military policy and anti-Indian sentiment in the context of the Seven Years' War.

Along these similarities, Iberian indigenism and Quaker-led abolitionism followed significantly divergent trajectories. Compared to what had occurred earlier in Iberian empires, the growth of British imperial antislavery was a much more complex and even protracted process. Indigenist practice and ideology began to coalesce within decades of the establishment of the first Spanish imperial outpost in the Caribbean. Protestant antislavery, however, crystallized much more slowly and haltingly. Whereas a tradition of religious and, more specifically, Quaker confrontation with the evils of colonial slavery took its initial shape in the early period of British colonization, a true political antislavery project only started with the American reform movement among Friends in the mid-eighteenth century.

Significantly different, too, were the respective activist networks that emerged as the result of these developments in the two cases. In Iberian empires, the Lascasian ideology and the political activities in defense of imperial "others" circulated mostly within the bounds of the religious orders, the supranational organizations of the Catholic Church – or within alliances of representatives of different orders. In contrast to the uniformity and narrow social spread of the

---

[45] Brookes, *Friend Benezet*, 287–93, 302; Bruns, *Am I Not*, 270; Edwards Amasa Park, *Memoir of the Life and Character of Samuel Hopkins, D. D.* (Boston: Doctrinal Tract and Book Society, 1854), 121; Sword, "Remembering Dinah Nevil."

earlier Catholic indigenist networks, the incipient abolitionist network became inherently heterogeneous, encompassing men (and, less visibly so, women) of different religious, political, and social backgrounds. And, as we will see, it was exactly this heterogeneity of the network that made possible by the 1780s the extensive mobilization of ordinary people around the issue of the slave trade of the British case – an extensive mobilization that set the institutional template of distinctively modern forms of long-distance advocacy.

Yet why the need for external allies? Why did not Benezet, aware of and inspired by Las Casas's political activities, follow exactly in his steps? The typical indigenist procedure had been to appoint representatives who would try to work on the pinnacles of political power in the Iberian imperial world: the monarch, his Council, or the Papal Curia in Rome. By contrast, while invoking the example of Las Casas's interventions in the royal court, Benezet never considered making the journey to the Court of St. James and pleading there for abolition of colonial slavery. Instead, from Benezet's very first attempt to mobilize support in the imperial center, the biggest share of antislavery work was in fact allotted to the mobilization of potential allies from within or outside the power structures. Although both antislavery Quakers and Lascasian indigenists sought support from potential influential allies in the corridors of power, Benezet and his cohort in addition strategically searched for "horizontal" allies: ordinary middle-class men who would commit to the antislavery platform and, at a minimum, would with their adherence signal a growing support for the antislavery cause.

In this sense, the analytically interesting question is not why or how the latecomers identified by the historians I discussed in Chapter 4 joined to give numerical strength and political muscle to the abolitionist movement. Rather, the question is why the initial political vision of the small number of Quaker reformers was centered, from its inception, on securing these "horizontal" alliances. When seen in this light, the development of the abolitionist project reveals its deep connection, from its very beginning, with the particulars of the imperial power constellation in which it operated. The engagement with this power constellation resulted in the strategic search for allies and, in turn, the more circuitous and protracted trajectory of the emerging network.

Britain's imperial world presented a more complex and more challenging political environment than the world of the Spanish Habsburgs. The British Empire was a much more tolerant, if not more democratic, space where settlers enjoyed more rights and privileges than their Iberian counterparts. At the same time, precisely because of the relative openness of the political system and because of various historically contingent factors, the costs of exerting effective pressure on the political center were much higher. In eighteenth-century Britain, there were simply more – and better established – imperial "interest groups" with their agents and representatives in London than in earlier Iberian empires – a fact reflecting the religious and ethnic diversity of the settlers. In itself, this denser population of colonial interests made the London power universe less accessible to any one of these interests. Unlike Iberian friars who were, after all, the king's employees, ordinary inhabitants of the British colonies had a more distant relationship with the imperial center.

Even more importantly, perhaps, the rise of parliament as center of political power and its increasing involvement with colonial affairs complicated this relationship even further. By the end of the seventeenth century, the political settlement in the aftermath of the Glorious Revolution had consolidated a new power position for the House of Commons. From a largely consultative auxiliary to royal power, it had become an increasingly equal partner of the Crown. What this meant for colonial affairs was that now in addition to the traditional imperial institutions of power – the monarch, his Privy Council, and the Board of Trade – parliament claimed an important stake in colonial jurisdiction. And the Commons increasingly claimed that stake after the 1740s.

While the parliamentarization of domestic affairs was an important step in the secular trend toward the democratization of politics, in the imperial context, the new parliamentary powers had the unintended consequence of making any colonial input into legislation and decision even more difficult. There were simply no elected representatives from the colonies to push their constituents' concerns into the legislature – nor was there a clear institutional model for their direct incorporation in the metropolitan parliament. At the same time, the involvement of parliament in imperial affairs did not necessarily mean the diminution of the power of the Crown or the ministers over the colonies. In fact, a more interventionist House of Commons was part and parcel of a general drive toward reforming and streamlining imperial governance in cooperation with the government and the monarch. In this context, the standard consensual and cooperative relationship between political authorities and colonial interests that had emerged after the Glorious Revolution began to disintegrate. The Board of Trade became less open to colonial lobbying, while parliament was increasingly interfering in imperial legislation without offering colonials the relatively open access the Board had given them earlier.[46]

In sum, when Quaker reformers in Pennsylvania embarked on their project against the slave trade, the costs of political access to London authorities had become exceedingly high on account of both the more complex landscape of imperial political authority and the increasing interventionist spirit of imperial governance. In fact, the limited responsiveness of London authorities had already been made clear in the course of the Friendly Association's appeals

---

[46] On these complex developments in the second half of the eighteenth century, see Greene, "Posture of Hostility"; *Peripheris and Center*; H. G. Koenigsberger, "Composite States, Representative Institutions and the American Revolution," *Historical Research* 62, no. 148 (1989); Marshall, *Making and Unmaking*; Olson, *Making the Empire*; "The Board of Trade and London-American Interest Groups in the Eighteenth Century," in *The British Atlantic Empire before the American Revolution*, eds. Peter Marshall and Glyndwr Williams (London: Cass, 1980); "Parliament, Empire, and Parliamentary Law, 1776," in *Three British Revolutions: 1641, 1688, 1776*, ed. J. G. A. Pocock (Princeton, NJ: Princeton University Press, 1980).

around the Indian issue during the Seven Years War. As the abolitionist network crystallized, it had thus to confront two challenges. First, as Benezet articulated it as early as 1763, the abolition of the slave trade could only be achieved through successful appeals to both Crown and parliament. And second, external allies were needed to make London authorities consider seriously the issue. This is why by 1772 Benezet was casting his web quite wide in an effort to recruit anyone in England among Quakers and non-Quakers alike who could be instrumental in successfully attracting the political authorities' attention.

Of course, this was not a prescient master plan, but rather a trial-and-error experiment in a time where older established procedures of political lobbying had lost their usefulness. Benezet was looking to locate anyone who would respond positively to his entreaties. In this sense, however, the social and confessional heterogeneity of the international abolitionist network as it took shape in the 1780s was, to an important degree, an unintended consequence of this initial wide search for allies who would be instrumental for achieving the ultimate goal of swaying imperial authorities to consider the issue of the Atlantic slave trade. And the initial impulse toward social inclusiveness was born from the tension between the ambitious political vision of the Quaker reform movement and the increasingly complex and costly political context of empire. This is why from its Philadelphian beginnings the abolitionist project was thrown into a trajectory different from the trajectory of earlier Iberian indigenism.

How much the institutional model of long-distance advocacy evolved in the process will become clear in Chapter 6, where we will see how a series of campaigns against the slave trade in Britain carried further this impulse toward social inclusivity and mobilized even more constituencies to attain an impressively wide social base for mobilization around a distant issue. The end result was a social movement that created the model of modern forms of long-distance advocacy. Despite its modernity, however, the origins of this pattern belong to the early modern world. Its deep source was the very same conflictual pattern of religious radicalization that produced the indigenist networks during the first century of Iberian imperial expansion. Now however, responding to a significantly different imperial constellation of power, religious activists created an advocacy network that since its inception was socially inclusive and heterogeneous. In the longer term, this consistent inclusiveness as a strategy to navigate a difficult political landscape created the conditions for long-distance advocacy movements of an impressive popular scale.

6

The Emergence of a New Model

The last two decades of the eighteenth century were a period of important transformation of the international abolitionist network initiated in the 1760s. There were several interlocking developments in this transformation. Not only did the network continue to grow, acquiring new personnel and spreading geographically, but in the process, its center of gravity shifted to London that now hosted the most active and successful branch of the network. If in 1787 London abolitionists were following the example of Philadelphia, by the 1830s American abolitionists looked for inspiration and organizational support from Britain, whose parliament had already abolished colonial slavery in the wake of a rather spectacular wave of popular mobilization. And, finally – and most importantly – the practice of long-distance advocacy acquired a new configuration and a new institutional model that has been with us ever since. The crucial events that heralded this transformation were two campaigns against the slave trade in Britain in 1787–88 and 1792.

THE NEW BRITISH ABOLITIONISM

By the 1780s, the initial nucleus of Quaker reformers had grown into a denominationally and socially mixed complex network of international dimensions. Within Britain, France, and the United States, abolitionists were guided by the same set of principles and engaged in constant exchanges. At the same time, the various branches of the network were embedded in their national and local contexts. They were oriented toward the political authorities of the British, French, and American central states, as well toward the local legislatures of the new federated "united" states in North America. In Britain, the almost self-propelling network was by then able to capture the kind of persons Benezet had tried to recruit in the older imperial context. The British Society of Friends was securely behind the abolitionist agenda. The number of important non-Quaker allies had grown. They included Thomas Clarkson as well as an increasing number of Church of England evangelicals. Prominent among them was William Wilberforce, the first committed abolitionist in parliament who persistently moved various measures for the abolition of the slave trade until he reached his goal in 1807.

Before that date, none of Wilberforce's motions produced definitive legislation, although the goal seemed tantalizingly close in 1792 when the Commons voted to end the trade by 1796 – a resolution subsequently killed by the Lords who insisted on their own investigation of the slave trade before voting.[1] Still, an important breakthrough occurred out of the expanding British abolitionist network In 1788 and again in 1792, two mass campaigns produced a stream of petitions for the abolition of the slave trade. A remarkable number of ordinary people gave their signatures and got involved in other politicized activities oriented toward the distant issue of the colonial slave trade. By May 1788, when Prime Minister William Pitt in the absence of an ailing Wilberforce moved that the Commons should investigate the slave trade, more than 100 petitions had been produced and submitted, constituting more than half of the total number of petitions in the parliamentary session. The next campaign, even more carefully prepared, supported Wilberforce's abolition motion in 1792. The 519 petitions delivered represented every single English county with the signatures of about thirteen percent of the adult male population according to John Oldfield's estimates.[2]

These numbers are indicative of the unprecedented breadth of these campaigns – both within the context of antislavery and within the larger history of popular mobilization.[3] For the first time in history, large numbers of ordinary people were engaging with a distant issue. There had been by then a long-standing pattern of political engagement with the welfare of distant imperial strangers. Yet with the British mobilization for the abolition of the slave trade this pattern acquired a qualitatively new scale.

The strong effect of this concerted display of "public opinion" in the 1780s and 1790s is beyond doubt, even if parliament agreed on abolition in 1807 without any significant public mobilization. The bill passed because of careful parliamentary maneuvers and the independent Wilberforce's strategic alliance with the Whigs. At that time, the Abolition Society decided to abstain from another petitioning effort. Instead, the network in the country prepared the ground by supporting pro-abolition candidates in the parliamentary elections the year before, most visibly in Wilberforce's contested election in Yorkshire. Members of the London Society then worked on MPs in the new parliament

---

[1] Dale H. Porter, *The Abolition of the Slave Trade in England, 1784–1807* (Hamden, CT: Archon Books, 1970).

[2] Drescher, *Capitalism and Antislavery*, 80; Oldfield, *Popular Politics*, 49–50, 61, 114.

[3] For the significance of these campaigns within the larger context of British popular politics, see Stamatov, "Religious Field."

to procure their votes.[4] And, of course, the earlier campaigns were closely connected with, if not subordinated to, parliamentary politics: they were orchestrated to support and amplify parliamentary motions. Yet by casting the mobilization net so wide, they were able to create for the first time in history an enduring popular constituency for a distant humanitarian issue. And in this sense, they had important consequences reaching far beyond the specific legislation they eventually helped.

The Genesis of the First Campaigns

The petitioning campaigns against the slave trade were a less than fully intended consequence of the practical problems the committee of the newly established London Abolition Society faced. Having secured a committed member of parliament to introduce the issue of abolition, they needed to collect evidence and identify witnesses for a parliamentary inquiry of the British slave trade, as well as generate petitions in an expression of popular support for Wilberforce's motions. Shortly after the formation of the Society in 1787, Thomas Clarkson volunteered to undertake an investigative journey to the British ports and collect firsthand testimony from sailors involved in the slave trade. In Bristol, his first stop, he found the Friends' local Men's Monthly Meeting already engaged in distributing antislavery materials and helped with the formation of a cross-denominational group to support the London initiative. From then on in his travels, he combined the collection of evidence with support for the establishment of local structures.[5]

Thus, in the four months of this first tour of the provinces, Clarkson assumed – somewhat unexpectedly – the novel role of organizer of local committees, a role he would take on repeatedly. Unlike his investigative work, where he often met with the hostility of people involved in the slave trade, in his organizing efforts he (and the London Committee) could most often rely on a positive attitude. Throughout the provinces, the often overlapping networks of Dissenters and men interested in political reform, embraced enthusiastically the idea of petitioning parliament for an abolition of the slave trade. Now the network of local supporters that abolitionist Quakers had cultivated since 1783 grew into a network of formally established committees.[6]

---

[4] Anstey, *Atlantic Slave Trade*, 360–98; Drescher, *Capitalism and Antislavery*, 89–90; Robin Furneaux, *William Wilberforce* (London: Hamilton, 1974), 246–55; Jennings, *Business of Abolishing*, 105–12; Pollock, *Wilberforce*, 200–14; Porter, *The Abolition of the Slave Trade in England, 1784–1807*, 133–37; E. A. Smith, "The Yorkshire Elections of 1806 and 1807: A Study in Electoral Management," *Northern History* 2 (1967).

[5] Oldfield, *Popular Politics*, 45–46; Wilson, *Thomas Clarkson*, 30–33.

[6] John H. Y. Briggs, "Baptists and the Campaign to Abolish the Slave Trade," *Baptist Quarterly* 42, no. 4 (2007); Madge Dresser, *Slavery Obscured: The Social History of the Slave Trade in an English Provincial Port* (London: Continuum, 2001), 139–42; G. M. Ditchfield, "Manchester College and Anti-Slavery," in *Truth, Liberty, Religion: Essays Celebrating Two Hundred Years of Manchester College*, ed. Barbara Smith (Oxford: Manchester College, 1986); E. M. Hunt, "The Anti-Slave Trade Agitation in Manchester," *Transactions of the Lancashire and Cheshire*

Hand in hand with the geographical spread of institutionalized structures went the development of new technologies for the mobilization of popular support that, at the end, "democratized" the practices of long-distance advocacy, making what had earlier been the preserve of small networks of religious specialists into a truly popular movement. The general contours of the campaigns against the slave trade were not particularly novel. Since at least the early eighteenth century, the established practice was for an interest group in London to first coordinate a legislative initiative in their favor with the government and then drum up support for its passing by lobbying MPs and petitioning the House.[7] The London Abolition Committee simply followed standard procedure by securing the commitment of Wilberforce and his prime-minister friend and then orchestrating the expression of extra-parliamentary support for the parliamentary measure. Remarkably different, however, were the novel production techniques that transformed the scale and meaning of this popular support.

Of crucial importance was, of course, Thomas Clarkson who, along with his contemporary Major John Cartwright, became the first professional reformer dedicated full time to the generation of popular commitment. Like Cartwright, Clarkson was a gentleman of strained yet independent means and while his activities were financed by the London Committee, he was not a paid employee. Yet with his remarkable success in coordinating activities in the provinces he was a forerunner of the salaried agent or organizer that was to become later a fixture of social-movement activities. For the second campaign in 1792, Clarkson's work in England was supplemented by the work of William Dickson, a representative for the London Committee in Scotland.[8]

With such representatives in the field, the London Committee was able to generate and coordinate popular commitment of unprecedented geographical and numerical scale. Equally significant was the employment of new techniques of mobilization and new forms of expression of popular support which, at the end, gave campaigns that were initially was just subsidiaries to a parliamentary motion, an independent life of their own. Partly, these techniques and forms were used in order to facilitate the generation of popular commitment. Partly,

Antiquarian Society 79 (1977); Marshall, "The Anti-Slave Trade Movement in Bristol"; Iain Whyte, *Scotland and the Abolition of Black Slavery, 1756–1838* (Edinburgh: Edinburgh University Press, 2006); Oldfield, *Popular Politics*; David Turley, *The Culture of English Antislavery, 1780–1860* (London: Routledge, 1991).

[7] Olson, *Making the Empire*, 119–20.

[8] Naomi C. Miller, "John Cartwright and Radical Parliamentary Reform, 1808–1819," *English Historical Review* 83, no. 329 (1968); Wilson, *Thomas Clarkson*. For the use of stipendiary agents in the later antislavery campaigns of the 1830s, see Ronald M. Gifford II, "George Thompson and Trans-Atlantic Antislavery, 1831–1865" (Ph.D. Dissertation, Indiana University, 2000); John Lytle Myers, "The Agency System of the Anti-Slavery Movement, 1832–1837, and Its Antecedents in Other Benevolent and Reform Societies" (Ph.D. Dissertation, University of Michigan, 1961).

they were deployed as an alternative to the parliamentary petitioning proce-dure, especially when the gap between the commitment thus generated and the responsiveness of parliament became clear after the first campaign of 1788 failed to achieve its legislative objectives.

Thus, local societies resorted to the relatively novel practice of pressur-ing directly their members of parliament to vote for abolition. When the Nottingham society was revived in December 1791, its meeting resolved to "instruct" local members on this matter. By threatening to withdraw their sup-port, the voters in Tewkesbury were able to force one of the candidates in the election to promise his support for abolition or lose the nomination.[9] Another practice that spread in the course of the second abolition campaign in 1791–92 was the abstention from the consumption of colonial goods produced with slave labor. A 1791 bestselling pamphlet by William Fox with 26 editions and 200,000 copies sold advised "the people of Great Britain ... on the propriety of abstaining from West Indian Sugar & Rum." A spate of similar publications preceded and followed Fox's, quite a sizable number of individuals engaged in the practice and grocers either discontinued the sale of Caribbean slave-produced sugar or replaced it with sugar from India. The London Society never officially endorsed abstention, yet Clarkson distributed Fox's pamphlet semi-officially and encouraged nonconsumption locally.[10]

In addition to this attempt at modifying consumer behavior, abolition entered the everyday lives of at least the respectable middle classes with distinctive representations in visual and other media. In 1787, the Unitarian pottery man-ufacturer Josiah Wedgewood presented to the London Abolition society the design of its seal representing a kneeling African under the words "Am I Not a Man and Brother?" He began mass producing the image on ceramic cameos with a large batch timed to coincide with the onset of the second campaign in 1791. At the end, the kneeling slave became the highly recognizable logo of the

---

[9] "Resolutions of Meeting of Inhabitants of Nottingham, December 21, 1791," Library of the Religious Society of Friends, London, Tract Volume H/178; *Diary, or Woodfal's Register*, April 2, 1792. Paul Kelly, "Constituents' Instructions to Members of Parliament in the Eighteenth Century," in *Party and Management in Parliament, 1660–1784*, ed. Clyve Jones (New York: St. Martin's Press, 1984).

[10] William Fox, *An Address to the People of Great Britain, on the Propriety of Abstaining from West India Sugar & Rum* (Birmingham: [s.n.] 1791). See also Briggs, "Baptists and the Campaign," 279; Clarkson, *History*, vol. 2, 347–50; Hunt, "Agitation in Manchester," 66–67; Jennings, *Business of Abolishing*, 68–69; Oldfield, *Popular Politics*, 57; Whyte, *Scotland and the Abolition*, 84; Wilson, *Thomas Clarkson*, 73–74. Other abstentionist pamphlets of the same time include Anonymous, *A Subject for Conversation and Reflection at the Table* (London: M. Gurney, 1788); Samuel Bradburn, *An Address to the People Called Methodists Concerning the Evil of Encouraging the Slave Trade*, 4th ed. (London: G. Paramore, 1792); Thomas Cooper, *Considerations on the Slave Trade, and the Consumption of West Indian Produce* (London: Darton and Harvey, 1791); *Considerations Addressed to Professors of Christianity of Every Denomination on the Impropriety of Consuming West-India Sugar & Rum, As Produced by the Oppressive Labour of Slaves*, (s.l.: s.n., 1792).

abolitionist "brand." According to Clarkson, gentlemen had the cameo inlaid in their snuff boxes and the ladies wore it in bracelets and hairpins.

Another powerful image was initially printed and distributed by the strongest local committee of the Southwest in Plymouth. With no reference to any real slave vessel, it showed how the legally allowed 482 bodies would be crammed in a ship's cargo area – depicting, as the Southern eloquence of an indignant U.S. congressman had it in 1790, "Negros packed togr. as Tobacco in a Hogshead." In the winter of 1788, Thomas Clarkson brought the image to London and it was adopted by the Society. Later three-dimensional models of the hypothetical slaving vessel were produced. These widely distributed images, along with a growing taste in oil paintings of sentimental scenes depicting the inhumanity of slavery, created a distinctive abolitionist visual culture. In addition, "The Negro's Complaint," a poem William Cowper had offered the London Society in 1788, was set to music and, again according to Clarkson's testimony, enjoyed popularity as a street ballad.[11]

Finally, for women antislavery mobilization meant more than just bracelets and hairpins. The possibility for them, defined inherently as dependent on their male parents and spouses, to engage in autonomous acts of political expression was practically nonexistent in British society at the time. Yet the early antislavery campaigns opened up a space for women's political engagement. That was partly the result of some abolitionist men's desire to further increase the numbers of supporters by appealing to the "fair sex" for assistance in the highly circumscribed ways contemporary social norms considered appropriate and inoffensive. And women eagerly seized this opportunity. The Abolition Society's 1788 list of subscribers includes 206 mostly middle-class women who made a significant financial contribution. Women seem to have been the local leaders in the abstention campaigns and suggestions circulated that they should join in petitioning, a traditionally male activity.[12]

The Campaigns as a Turning Point
Two intertwined developments occurred in the course of the British campaigns of 1787–88 and 1791–92: the social base of long-distance advocacy

[11] Congressman Jackson quoted in William C. DiGiacomantonio, "'For the Gratification of a Volunteering Society': Antislavery and Pressure Group Politics in the First Federal Congress," *Journal of the Early Republic* 15, no. 2 (1995): 190–91. See Clarkson, *History*, vol. 2, 187–92; L. A. Compton, "Josiah Wedgwood and the Slave Trade: A Wider View," *Northern Ceramic Society Newsletter* 100 (1995); Oldfield, *Popular Politics*, 99, 159, 65; Wilson, *Thomas Clarkson*, 49–50; Marcus Wood, "Packaging Liberty and Marketing the Gift of Freedom: 1807 and the Legacy of Clarkson's Chest," *Parliamentary History* 26 Supplement (2007). A copy of the printed score of the song under the title "Forc'd from Home and All It's [sic] Pleasures. For One or two Voices, the Words from Mr. Cowper's Negro's Complaint" can be seen in the Beinecke Rare Book and Manuscript Library at Yale University.
[12] Clare Midgley, *Women against Slavery: The British Campaigns, 1780–1870* (London: Routledge, 1992), 14–40; Jennings, *Business of Abolishing*, 43; Oldfield, *Popular Politics*, 141. Some women are reported to have signed a petition in Belford, Northumberland in 1792. See Midgley, *Women Against Slavery*, 24.

was extended to qualitatively new dimensions while a set of new technologies for popular mobilization was introduced. Immediately after that, the broad coalition of British abolitionists disintegrated in a context of an increased polarization between radicals and conservative defenders of the status quo, Burkean conservative paranoia, repressive government policies, and war with revolutionary France.[13] Yet the same set of political practices was reactivated after the end of the Napoleonic Wars. By then the British and American branches of the Atlantic slave trade had been abolished and the signing of the peace treaty with France offered the opportunity for further eradication of the trade, should a commitment to discontinuation of its French version be included in the treaty. Another petitioning campaign orchestrated by London abolitionists in 1814 resulted in 1,370 petitions asking parliament to intervene for the abolition of the French slave trade. This was even more impressive than the earlier efforts: the number of petitions was greater than the annual total number of parliamentary petitions on other subjects between 1811 and 1815 and perhaps as many as 1,375,000 individuals had signed – at least a fifth of all eligible males.[14] After that, the efforts were redirected toward propaganda aimed at rousing public opinion in France and direct lobbying with the dignitaries at the international congresses in Vienna and Paris. Although these international campaigns did not achieve their immediate goals, nine years later British antislavery was revived again with its by now typical organizational features. This time, however, it adopted a more ambitious and comprehensive program leading to the immediate abolition of slavery in British colonial possessions.[15]

Not only was, in the process, British foreign policy pushed toward a firm commitment to the abolition of the slave trade internationally. These reincarnations of British antislavery also reinforced, expanded, and institutionalized the typical set of mobilization technologies that had crystallized in the course of the first campaigns between 1787 and 1792. Yet it was this first wave of antislavery mobilization that produced a critical mass of activist commitment and organizational knowledge that were to influence the future course of

---

[13] On the polarized political context in Britain, see Albert Goodwin, *The Friends of Liberty: The English Democratic Movement in the Age of the French Revolution* (London: Hutchinson, 1979); Mark Philp, "Vulgar Conservatism, 1792–3," *English Historical Review* 110, no. 435 (1995); Clive Emsley, "Repression, 'Terror' and the Rule of Law in England during the Decade of the French Revolution," *English Historical Review* 100, no. 397 (1985); H. T. Dickinson, *The Politics of the People in Eighteenth-Century Britain* (London: Macmillan, 1995).

[14] Drescher, *Abolition*, 229–30.

[15] K. Charlton, "James Cropper and Liverpool's Contribution to the Anti-Slavery Movement," *Transactions of the Historic Society of Lancashire and Cheshire* 123 (1971); Howard Temperley, *British Antislavery 1833–1870* (London: Longman, 1972); Davis, *From Homicide to Slavery: Studies in American Culture*; Betty Fladeland, "Abolitionist Pressures on the Concert of Europe, 1814–1822," *Journal of Modern History* 38, no. 4 (1966); William Allen, *Life of William Allen, With Selections from His Correspondence* (Philadelphia: H. Longstreth, 1847); Jerome Reich, "The Slave Trade at the Congress of Vienna: A Study in English Public Opinion," *Journal of Negro History* 53, no. 2 (1968).

antislavery both in Britain and other locations of a continuously – if haltingly – expanding and changing network. In this sense, they represented an important turning point in the development both of antislavery and of the institutional model of long-distance advocacy.

In many ways, however, this turning point was a transformation arising out of persistent continuities. Its first precondition was the already existing accretion of the international abolitionist network, which by that time had gathered strength in Britain with the recruitment of the local Society of Friends and important non-Quaker allies. When the London Abolition Societies launched its first petitioning campaign in 1787, it continued this project of further recruitment by adding new constituencies who responded positively to the abolitionist message. In the process of this further growth, new activities and forms of mobilization were introduced. And as it had been the case throughout the development of the abolitionist network until then, these new activities and forms were the result of a pragmatic experimentation, of attempts to maximize chances of success within the constraints of the concrete political and social situation. In this sense, the first British campaigns against the slave trade, while producing a qualitatively new model of popular politics, were deeply conditioned by the political project that had been originated in the 1760s by Quaker reformers. They grew out of the reformers' ever-expanding network and continued to follow the logic of action that informed this network ever since its beginning. They were, when considered in the long term, the first true instantiation of the old Benezetian vision of pressure on authorities by petitioning.

If the first antislave-trade campaigns arose out of the preexisting abolitionist network, they – in turn – had important effects on the subsequent development of that network. They consolidated a specific organizational model that was reemployed and redeveloped in later iterations of the antislavery political project in Britain. They also cemented the position of Britain and London as the main center and repository of this new model of long-distance advocacy. And because the British branch was already part of the larger international abolitionist network, these developments affected the further trajectory of the network by providing incentives for its expansion in new locales, such as the Netherlands, Spain, and Brazil where the already consolidated London model of action could be "exported" – or, as in the case of the older hubs in the network in France and the United States – re-exported with various degrees of adaptation and success.

AMERICAN DECLINE

What then of these existing nodes in the network during that period? Until 1787, the Philadelphia-led North American branch of antislavery was the trailblazer. Yet in contrast to the expansion of the London network that year, United

States abolitionism began to lose speed. Abolition societies were formed in different states and various antislavery projects continued to generate support locally, especially in the North, for the legal protection of unlawfully enslaved individuals as well as petitions for statewide abolition of slavery or, as in North Carolina, for the relaxation of the stringent manumission laws. Particularly active was Moses Brown, who was able to mobilize public support for the abolition of the slave trade in its most important center in Rhode Island and then tried, with less success, to replicate the campaign in other New England states.

Yet no successful campaign comparable to the British ones emerged on a scale coextensive with the new federal political unit. In 1787, the revived Pennsylvania Abolition Society prepared an address asking the Constitutional Convention to include a ban on the importation of slaves in the new constitution. Benjamin Franklin, the Society's president, preferred not to stir the hostility of Southern delegates and never presented the address. At the end, instead of banning slave imports, the Convention agreed to ban any discussions of such ban until 1808 and the Constitution, more generally, provided political protection for the institution of slavery.[16]

With this opportunity missed, the first popular appeal to the new Federal Congress occurred in 1790 when three petitions were presented: two from the Philadelphia and the New York Yearly Meetings, and one from the Pennsylvania Abolition Society. The Quaker petitions asked for definitive cessation of the Atlantic slave trade, while the Society's address requested, more ambitiously, the freeing of slaves domestically according to the principles of the new constitution. The Senate declined outright to consider the petitions. The House of Representatives, in deference to Franklin's involvement with the Pennsylvania petition, appointed a committee to consider them. The Quaker delegation that had delivered the petitions continued to lobby politicians, hoping that the committee would produce a clear statement on the extent of federal power to regulate slavery. The largely sympathetic committee report produced an acrimonious debate in the course of which Southern representatives launched a passionate defense of slavery and did not miss the opportunity to taint Quakers with their non-revolutionary past as subversive anti-American elements. At the end, the House resolved to reassert its power over the regulation of the foreign slave trade while renouncing the prerogative to tax these "imports." More ominously, however, it decided not to interfere with the emancipation of slaves or the

---

[16] Fehrenbacher, *Slaveholding Republic*, 35; Richard S. Newman, *The Transformation of American Abolitionism: Fighting Slavery in the Early Republic* (Chapel Hill: University of North Carolina Press, 2002), 47; Rappleye, *Sons of Providence*; Thompson, *Moses Brown*; Van Cleve, *Slaveholders' Union*, 9; Paul Finkelman, *Slavery and the Founders: Race and Liberty in the Age of Jefferson*, 2nd ed. (Armonk, NY: M. E. Sharpe, 2001).

regulation of their treatment by masters, delegating these powers to individual states.[17]

After this first attempt, the Pennsylvania Society decided to launch another and better coordinated effort, asking the existing abolition societies in various states to prepare petitions for a congressional ban of the slave trade. These were presented to the Second Congress in 1792, yet this time the appointed committee simply refused to act and returned them to the senders. The following year another petition, this time just the individual initiative of Quaker Thomas Mifflin, was again rejected outright. Following the New York Manumission Society's suggestion that a meeting of representatives of the local societies might produce a more forceful public statement of the sentiments of abolitionists scattered through the states, the Pennsylvania Society organized and hosted the first meeting of an American Convention for Promoting the Abolition of Slavery in 1794. The delegates of the eight societies present adopted several addresses: to Congress, to slave-holding states asking them to stop the importation of enslaved Africans and provide for their eventual emancipation, and a general appeal to American citizens. For the first time, a coordinated abolitionist initiative met its legislative objective. In response to petitions from the New England Yearly Meeting, the Providence Abolition Society, and the Convention, a law prohibiting American residents from engaging in the slave trade to foreign countries was passed. Yet this was to remain the only true achievement in the history of the newly formed Convention – and of American abolitionism in the period. Although the Convention continued to meet in the following years, it was never able to produce a campaign of national proportions or again influence the legislature.[18]

FRENCH TURBULENCE

Similarly, no critical mass of popular support coalesced in France in the last decades of the century. In 1788, as we saw earlier, the *Société des Amis des Noirs* joined the Anglo-American network, relying on the expertise of – and actively cooperating with – London and Philadelphia. The announcement of

---

[17] During the same session, the U.S. Congress affirmed what was basically now a policy of expansion of slavery by agreeing not to legislate emancipation in the territory it accepted from North Carolina, the future state of Tennessee. See DiGiacomantonio, "For the Gratification"; Van Cleve, *Slaveholders' Union*, 202–03; Fehrenbacher, *Slaveholding Republic*, 138–39, 256; Parkinson, "Manifest Signs"; Howard A. Ohline, "Slavery, Economics, and Congressional Politics, 1790," *Journal of Southern History* 46, no. 3 (1980).

[18] DiGiacomantonio, "For the Gratification," 196–97; Richard S. Newman, "Prelude to the Gag Rule: Southern Reaction to Antislavery Petitions in the First Federal Congress," *Journal of the Early Republic* 16, no. 4 (1996); *Transformation of Abolitionism*, 49; Fehrenbacher, *Slaveholding Republic*, 140; Rappleye, *Sons of Providence*, 294–300; Robert Duane Sayre, "The Evolution of Early American abolitionism: The American Convention for Promoting the Abolition of Slavery and Improving the Condition of the African Race, 1794–1837" (Ph.D. Dissertation, Ohio State University, 1987).

the king's convocation of the long-suspended parliamentary institution of the *états généraux* offered a welcome opportunity for the Society to pursue its goals. The following year, like its British counterpart, it attempted to produce support in the provinces by circulating a letter to local assemblies that asked them to incorporate the issue of slavery in their *cahiers de doléances*, the list of grievances and proposed reforms that the king had asked the three estates of the realm to prepare for the first meeting of the parliament. Thus, when the *États* opened in May 1789, a total of forty-nine *cahiers* asked for the abolition of colonial slavery or the slave trade.[19]

By the end of the year, however, the momentum for a potentially popular mobilization was irretrievably lost. Both in the *États généraux* that soon proclaimed itself a National Constituent Assembly and in the provinces, the Paris society was outperformed by an emerging alliance of colonial planters organized in the so-called Club Massiac and commercial interests represented by lobbyists of the local chambers of commerce, the *Deputés extraordinaires des manufactures et du commerce*. Not even Thomas Clarkson's arrival on what was perhaps the first mission of transnational activist consultancy helped.

Sensing that the rapidly changing political conditions in France would make possible a speedy abolition of at least the French slave trade, the London committee dispatched Clarkson to Paris in June 1789. The following year, he returned to London feeling defeated and rather frustrated with the French abolitionist set. What made the two British campaigns at the time particularly effective was the coordination of Wilberforce's parliamentary motions with the mass-produced petitions supporting them. Yet such coordination failed to materialize in France. In a mirror image of the British developments, the petitions that began to arrive to the National Assembly toward the end of 1789 were mostly from slave trading ports, organized by the pro-slavery interests and asking for the preservation of the colonial status quo. The only petition in favor of gradual abolition from Bordeaux was withdrawn by the city's representative and Brissot, now a deputy, presented to the Assembly a defensive address denying that his Society wanted the immediate abolition of slavery. Clarkson painstakingly helped Mirabeau prepare a big well-argued speech on the slave trade that at the end the National Assembly never got the chance to hear or discuss. The speech produced "*vifs applaudissements*" when delivered to fellow members of the *Amis*, but failed to impress the Jacobin Club in the spring of 1790.[20]

[19] Dorigny and Gainot, *Amis des Noirs*; Charles O. Hardy, *The Negro Question in the French Revolution* (Menasha, WI: George Banta, 1919); Beatrice Fry Hyslop, *French Nationalism in 1789 according to the General Cahiers* (New York: Columbia University Press, 1934), 266–67.

[20] Dorigny and Gainot, *Amis des Noirs*; Florence Gauthier, *L'aristocratie de l'épiderme: Le combat de la Société des citoyens de couleur, 1789–1791* (Paris: CNRS, 2007), 63–65; Lucien Leclerc, "La politique et l'influence du Club de l'Hôtel Massiac," *Annales Historiques de la Révolution Française* (1937); Jean Tarrade, "Les colonies et les principes de 1789: Les assemblées revolutionnaire face au problème de l'esclavage," *Revue française d'histoire d'outre-mer*

Gradually, however, the Jacobin Club, the most influential among the prolif-
erating political societies of the time, became increasingly committed to ideas
of antislavery and racial equality. This was the result of several developments:
the gradual ascendance within the Parisian Club of the group around Brissot,
one of the founders of the *Amis*, an appeal for universal liberty originating
from the Jacobin Club in Angers, and the struggle for recognition of the group
designated as "free men of color" (*gens de couleur libres*) – typically wealthy
offspring of mixed marriages and often slaveholders themselves who suffered
various forms of discrimination in the colonies.

The resuscitation of a long-disused parliamentary tradition with the convocation of *États generaux* raised questions about the proper representation
of colonial inhabitants therein. Almost immediately, representatives of white
planters in the major slaveholding colony of Saint Domingue – by then the
French part of Columbus's Hispaniola – sought to be seated. They were admitted to the Third Estate despite opposition from members of the *Amis* who
objected to their support of slavery. The free men of color, who were excluded
from the Saint Domingue assembly, similarly organized a competing pressure
group in Paris. The Constituent Assembly, however, was more reluctant to
include them in its midst or legislate that non-whites be included in colonial
assemblies.

By November 1789, the committee of men of color had made contact with
the *Amis des Noirs* and now the issue of their civil rights increasingly dominated
the activities of the society. Despite their allied effort, however, the Assembly
and the Jacobin Club, both with a substantial presence of colonial interests,
remained closed to their demands. This began to change in March 1791 when
the local Jacobin affiliate in Angers, most likely at the initiative at the maver-
ick antislavery colonial planter Claud Michel Milscent, sent a circular to other
provincial clubs in support of universal liberty and rights for non-whites. As
many as seventeen clubs responded with addresses of support to the National
Assembly and requests for affiliation with the *Amis des Noirs*. In May, after
a heated debate, the Assembly finally granted suffrage rights to blacks born
of two free parents. The decree, however, provoked the reaction of colonial

76, nos. 282–83 (1989); Françoise Thésée, "Autour de la Société des Amis des Noirs: Clarkson,
Mirabeau et l'abolition de la traite (août 1789-mars 1790)," *Présence africaine* 125 (1983);
Valerie Quinney, "Decisions on Slavery, the Slave-Trade and Civil Rights for Negroes in the Early
French Revolution," *Journal of Negro History* 55, no. 2 (1970); Jean Tarrade, "Le groupe de
pression du commerce à la fin de l'Ancien régime et sous l'Assemblée Constituante," *Bulletin de
la Société d'histoire moderne* 69, no. 13 (1970); Gabriel Debien, *Les colons de Saint-Domingue
et la Révolution: Essai sur le club Massiac (août 1789-août 1792)* (Paris: Armand Colin, 1953);
"Le Club des Colons de La Rochelle (Septembre 1789-Octobre 1790)," *Revue d'Histoire des
Colonies* 43, nos. 3–4 (1956); Hardy, *Negro Question*; Lucie Maquerlot, "Rouen et Le Havre
face à la traite et à l'esclavage: Le mouvement de l'opinion (1783–1794)," in *Esclavage, résistances et abolitions*, ed. Marcel Dorigny (Paris: Éditions du CTHS, 1999); Wilson, *Thomas
Clarkson*, 53–58; Dorigny, "Mirabeau and the Société."

interests for whom this was the first step toward the abolition of slavery. After discussing their petitions, the National Assembly revoked the decree.[21]

Yet, public opinion was changing and white colonials were increasingly perceived as counterrevolutionary. The faction around Brissot was gaining power both in the new Legislative Convention and in the Jacobin Club that voted to oust members who had protested against the May decree. With antislavery Brissotins in ascendency in 1792, the Legislative voted to dissolve existing colonial assemblies and guarantee voting rights regardless of color, while also discussing ways to curb the slave trade.

Soon, however, the Brissotins lost their position under the onslaught of their political opponents in the Assembly allied with the Parisian sansculotte radicals and the founding generation of the *Amis des Noirs* was decimated in a purge in 1793. Still, the anti-Brissotin Montagnards who now dominated the Assembly and the Jacobin Club continued to hold on to antislavery principles. Even as the Brissotins were tried and executed, the men of color who had proven their revolutionary credentials by organizing an American Legion to support the war made a concerted appeal to the Jacobins and the Assembly for the full abolition of slavery. Meanwhile, the two commissaries that the Brissotin government had sent to Saint Domingue proclaimed the abolition of slavery on the island. When three of the new Saint Domingue representatives elected under the 1792 law – one white, one black, and one "mulatto" – arrived in Paris in 1794, they were seated in the Assembly that adopted a decree abolishing slavery in all the colonies. There was indeed a wide popular support for the cause of universal freedom at that time and revolutionary political societies staged numerous celebrations of the abolition throughout the country.[22]

[21] See also Gabriel Debien, "Gens de couleur libres et colons de Saint-Domingue devant la Constituante (1789–mars 1790)," *Revue d'histoire de l'Amérique française* 4, nos. 2, 3, 4 (1950–1951); David Geggus, "Racial Equality, Slavery, and Colonial Secession during the Constituent Assembly," *American Historical Review* 94, no. 5 (1989); Jean-Daniel Piquet, *L'émancipation des noirs dans la Révolution française (1789–1795)* (Paris: Karthala, 2002); Valerie Quinney, "The Problem of Civil Rights for Free Men of Color in the Early French Revolution," *French Historical Studies* 7, no. 4 (1972); Robert Stein, "The Free Men of Colour and the Revolution in Saint Domingue, 1789–1792," *Histoire Sociale: Social History* 14, no. 27 (1981); John D. Garrigus, "Opportunist or Patriot? Julien Raimond (1744–1801) and The Haitian Revolution," *Slavery & Abolition* 28, no. 1 (2007); J. Godechot, "De Joly et les gens de couleur libres," *Annales historiques de la Révolution Française* 23, no. 121 (1951).

[22] See also Claire Blondet, "Quand les 'terroristes' font le procès du colonialisme esclavagiste les thermidoriens organisent son oubli," in *Périssent les colonies plutôt qu'un principe! Contributions à l'histoire de l'abolition de l'esclavage, 1789–1804*, ed. Florence Gauthier (Paris: Société des études robespierristes, 2002); Jean-Claude Halpern, "The Revolutionary Festivals and the Abolition in Slavery in Year II," in *The Abolitions of Slavery : From Léger Félicité Sonthonax to Victor Schoelcher, 1793, 1794, 1848* (New York: Berghahn Books, 2003); Florence Gauthier, "The Role of the Saint-Domingue Deputation in the Abolition of Slavery," in *The Abolitions of Slavery: From Léger Félicité Sonthonax to Victor Schoelcher, 1793, 1794, 1848*, ed. Marcel Dorigny (New York: Berghahn Books, 2003); Robert Stein, "The Revolution of 1789 and the Abolition of Slavery," *Canadian Journal of History* 17 (1982); Gary Kates, *The Cercle social, the*

This was an unprecedented achievement. In the midst of the Reign of Terror, the French parliament passed the most radical abolition of colonial slavery to date. Unlike earlier laws, like the one in Pennsylvania that established a future date for emancipation and compensated owners, the French decree freed all enslaved people unconditionally and with no compensation for their owners. The incorporation of the cause of black freedom into revolutionary festivities also popularized the issue of racial equality among a wider audience. Yet for various reasons, the abolition legislation failed to achieve its goals. The planters' determined resistance undermined its implementation in the Mascarene Islands. And soon, in the context of the Thermidorian reaction, French colonial policies began to reverse toward the prerevolutionary status quo until Napoleon restored slavery in 1802 and passed several orders discriminating against blacks in France.[23]

Another consequence of the turbulent trajectory of antislavery in the French revolution was the failure to establish a viable network of activists. The proponents of antislavery in Parisian politics were largely annihilated in the various waves of revolutionary purges. A short-lived reincarnation of the *Amis des Noirs* was constituted in 1797, yet apart from a moving commemoration of the fifth anniversary of the 1794 abolition, it did little to generate popular support. In the early decades of the nineteenth century, abolitionists in France were few and far between. Perhaps the only significant figure still dedicated to antislavery was the Abbé Grégoire who had been given honorary membership in the first *Amis* on the strength of his advocacy for the Saint Domingue men of color in the National Assembly. But Grégoire, an outspoken critic of Napoleon's colonial policies, remained an isolated and, because of his involvement with the revolutionary trial of the king, divisive figure. When French antislavery was revived in the 1820s, the new generation of abolitionists came mostly from the circle of Napoleonic exiles around Madame de Staël in Coppet, Switzerland, who had been able to maintain an open channel of communication with the British antislavery network.[24]

Girondins, and the French Revolution (Princeton, NJ: Princeton University Press, 1985); Eloise Ellery, *Brissot de Warville: A Study in the History of the French Revolution* (Boston: Houghton Mifflin, 1915).
[23] Yves Bénot, *La démence coloniale sous Napoléon* (Paris: Editions La Découverte, 1992); Claude Wanquet, "Baco and Burnel's Attempt to Implement Abolition in the Mascarenes in 1796: Analysis of a Failure and Its Consequences," in *The Abolitions of Slavery: From Léger Félicité Sonthonax to Victor Schoelcher, 1793, 1794, 1848* (New York: Berghahn Books, 2003).
[24] Thomas David and Janick Marina Schaufelbuehl, "L'antiesclavagisme en Suisse," in *La Suisse et l'esclavage des noirs* (Lausanne: Editions Antipodes, 2005); Marcel Dorigny, "The Abbé Grégoire and the *Société des Amis des Noirs*," in *The Abbé Grégoire and His World*, eds. Jeremy D. Popkin and Richard H. Popkin (Dordrecht: Kluwer, 2000); Dorigny and Gainot, *Amis des Noirs*; Étienne Hofmann, "Le Groupe de Coppet," in *Vaud sous l'Acte de Médiation, 1803–1813: La naissance d'un canton confédéré*, ed. Corinne Chuard (Lausanne: Bibliothèque historique vaudoise, 2002); Lawrence C. Jennings, *French Anti-Slavery: The Movement for the Abolition of Slavery in France, 1802–1848* (Cambridge: Cambridge University Press, 2000);

THE LONDON MODEL

In the last two decades of the eighteenth century, what started as the political project of Anthony Benezet and a handful of allies grew into an international network that coordinated its activities in Britain, France, and the United States. At the same time, the center of gravity within the network shifted as London became the preeminent center of antislavery activity, while in different ways both Philadelphia, the "homeland" of antislavery, and Paris, the "late-comer," lost their significance.

The crucial development that propelled London to this preeminent position as the center of antislavery and related reform projects for more than a century afterward was the mounting of two popular campaigns for the abolition of the British slave trade between 1787 and 1792 and the related institution building in the course of which an enduring organizational structure took shape – an institutional structure that was able to reassert itself after the repressive hiatus of the wars with revolutionary and Napoleonic France. Only in Britain was the antislavery network able to recruit committed parliamentary allies: starting with William Wilberforce and then a growing number of MPs.[25] Only in Britain did an indefatigable field organizer like Thomas Clarkson emerge who – later joined by William Dickson as his counterpart in Scotland – did the methodical footwork needed for an extensive petitioning campaign. And, finally, only in Britain did various – and often overlapping – networks and organizations throw their support behind the antislavery project.

By contrast, the combination of these three elements failed to materialize in France and the United States. Although there were committed abolitionists in the French political elites, they were swept away in the turbulence of the revolutionary years. Politicians like Brissot or Robespierre, their lives tragically cut short, did not have the luxury to consistently make motions year after year, the way Wilberforce did in Britain. In the United States Congress, on the other hand, no Wilberforcean figure of national stature emerged. Neither the gout-ridden and aging Franklin, nor James Madison, whom Quakers were hoping to use as a leader in the fight against the slave trade, committed themselves to act as the congressional voice of abolition.[26] Similarly, no organizer comparable to Clarkson emerged in France or the United States – and, in fact, Clarkson himself found his effort stymied during his stay in Paris in the yearly stage of

Alyssa Goldstein Sepinwall, *The Abbé Grégoire and the French Revolution: The Making of Modern Universalism* (Berkeley: University of California Press, 2005).

[25] G. M. Ditchfield, "Repeal, Abolition, and Reform: A Study in the Interaction of Reforming Movements in the Parliament of 1790–6," in *Anti-slavery, Religion, and Reform: Essays in Memory of Roger Anstey*, eds. Christine Bolt and Seymour Drescher (Folkestone: Dawson, 1980).

[26] Ohline, "Slavery, Economics," 354. For other congressional leaders who failed to act publicly on private antislavery convictions, see Gary B. Nash, *The Forgotten Fifth: African Americans in the Age of Revolution* (Cambridge, MA: Harvard University Press, 2006), 90–122.

the revolution. Finally, the wide coalition of constituencies that gave the British mobilizations their remarkable breadth was not replicated either across the Channel or across the Atlantic.

Consider, for example, the diametrically opposed positions of manufacturers in France and Britain. From the very beginning, the French chambers of commerce and their lobbyists, the *Députés extraordinaires*, were on the side of the slave-trading interests. The English manufacturers' contribution to the early antislave-trade campaigns, on the other hand, was as significant as to be easily overestimated – as it indeed was in Seymour Drescher's important *Capitalism and Antislavery*. The book argues that it was Manchester cotton capitalists and artisans who, led by revulsion to unfree labor, created the national mobilization by forcing on timid Quakers a more aggressive campaigning style. This argument errs in minimizing the importance of the London committee. Still, it is beyond doubt that a strong reformist culture among nonaristocratic (and non-Anglican) city elites in the North of England, interest in parliamentary reform and rights for Dissenters, as well as organizational expertise acquired in earlier successful petition drives against the government's proposed cotton tax and liberalized trade with Ireland, all combined to make a strong contribution to the antislavery network.[27]

The contribution of Northern Dissenters is in line with the general contribution of English churches to the unfolding of the campaigns in the 1780s and 1790s. Only a week after the first meeting of the London Abolition Society, Northamptonshire Baptists made a pledge to support the impending parliamentary fight for abolition.[28] In North America, however, churches – apart from Friends and the New Divinity group of Congregationalists – were much more reluctant to support antislavery. Reformers who demanded that their religious organization commit to abolitionist principles were routinely silenced. In 1789, minister David Rice unsuccessfully tried to get the first General Assembly of the Presbyterian Church to make an official statement on something as uncontroversial as the religious duties of masters toward their slaves. The Synod of the Carolinas banned their ministers from mentioning emancipation from the pulpit in reaction to the antislavery sermonizing of another Presbyterian, James

[27] See Drescher, *Capitalism and Antislavery* and the correction by Oldfield, *Popular Politics*, 48–49. On reformist culture among Dissenters in Lancashire and their involvement in antislavery, see Witt Bowden, "The Influence of the Manufacturers on Some of the Early Policies of William Pitt," *The American Historical Review* 29, no. 4 (1924); Goodwin, *Friends of Liberty*, 140–42; Paul Kelly, "British and Irish Politics in 1785," *The English Historical Review* 90, no. 356 (1975); G. M. Ditchfield, "The Campaign in Lancashire and Cheshire for the Repeal of the Test and Corporation Acts, 1787–1790," *Transactions of the Historic Society of Lancashire and Cheshire* 126, nos. 109–38 (1977); Ditchfield, "Manchester College"; Turley, *Culture of English*.

[28] Baptist Church Northamptonshire Association, *The Nature and Importance of Family and Closet Religion, Considered in a Circular Letter from the Baptist Ministers and Messengers, Assembled at Leicester, May 29, 30, and 31, 1787* (Northampton: T. Dicey and Co., 1787), 8. See also Briggs, "Baptists and the Campaign."

Gilleland. Even the American Methodist Church whose early leaders were staunchly against slavery and whose ministers had organized a radical petition drive for immediate emancipation in Virginia gradually relaxed its position in the face of popular hostility in the South.[29]

The religious situation was even bleaker in France where, as Grégoire wrote to the Pennsylvania Abolition Society in 1802, "unhappily ... the number of those who are animated by the spirit of Christianity is inconsiderable; they are also scattered about and so occupied as to make it difficult to bring them together, so as to concur in doing good."[30] Grégoire himself had arrived at anti-slavery and other reform projects through his involvement with the Catholic reform movement of Richerism and through his contacts with Swiss-German Protestant reformers. Yet, even though Richerism – and the larger Jansenist movement within which it was nested – made an important contribution to the revolutionary developments, its representatives never had the chance to serve as the social carrier of a popular French antislavery. The increasingly antireligious policies of the French revolution gradually eroded the social base of religion – both for Catholics and for the small number of Protestants in France for whom the political changes had brought the first signs of freedom after almost a century of persecution with the tolerance decree of 1787. French Reformed churches were never a significant part of the early antislavery movement, while Protestants were perhaps even overrepresented among the participants in the slave trade who defended it. The only committed Protestant voice was the Swiss-born Lyon minister Benjamin-Sigismond Frossard.[31]

In sum, because of a series of factors, only in Britain was the local version of the international antislavery network institutionalized enduringly at the end of the eighteenth century. In Britain, but not in France or the United States, the antislavery project had both committed parliamentary spokespersons and organizational machinery that recruited various constituencies in a broad popular coalition. This meant that now London became the repository of a reconfigured institutional pattern of long-distance advocacy – and that at least until the early twentieth century such advocacy, even when adapted to different national contexts, had an unmistakable British and Protestant flavor. The set of practices and the organizational know-how that British abolitionists

---

[29] W. Harrison Daniel, "Southern Presbyterians and the Negro in the Early National Period," *Journal of Negro History* 58, no. 3 (1973); Mathews, *Slavery and Methodism*.

[30] Dorigny and Gainot, *Amis des Noirs*, 395–96.

[31] Robert Blanc, *Un pasteur du temps des Lumières: Benjamin-Sigismond Frossard (1754–1830)* (Paris: Champion, 2000); Ralph Gibson, *A Social History of French Catholicism, 1789–1914* (London: Routledge, 1989); Rita Hermon-Belot, *L'abbé Grégoire, la politique et la vérité* (Paris: Seuil, 2000); Norman Ravitch, "Liberalism, Catholicism, and the Abbé Grégoire," *Church History* 36, no. 4 (1967); Daniel Robert, *Les églises réformées en France (1800–1830)* (Paris: Presses universitaires de France, 1961); Dale K. Van Kley, *The Religious Origins of the French Revolution: From Calvin to the Civil Constitution, 1560–1791* (New Haven, CT: Yale University Press, 1996); Sepinwall, *Abbé Grégoire*.

were able to assemble in the course of the two first campaigns against the slave trade created an institutional pattern that was later reactivated both in Britain and elsewhere as the standard procedure of activists addressing issues related to the welfare of distant strangers.

THE DISTAL EFFECTS OF RELIGIOUS RADICALIZATION

The qualitative difference in organizational capacity and political effectiveness that established itself between London and the rest of the abolitionist network at that time was as decisive as to create the impression that the British take-off was, analytically, a nationally (or imperially) bound phenomenon that was divorced from the wider international context. Hence, British abolitionism has been researched, traditionally, as a largely self-sufficient phenomenon determined by the particulars of British social, political, and cultural realities. And Eric Williams's influential and passionate exposé of the economic calculations behind the later abolition of British colonial slavery narrowed down further the general historiographical tone after the Second World War. Although overwhelmingly critical of Williams' argument and evidence, subsequent treatments continued to start from the causal conditional that if the strongest antislavery mobilization occurred in Britain – the economic hegemon of nineteenth-century capitalism – then capitalism must be the ultimate cause. What these works attempted to do was identify the specific steps and directions in which capitalist development – and specifically British capitalist development – engendered antislavery.[32]

Yet a different set of causal forces behind the British campaigns of the last decades of the eighteenth century comes to light if we place these developments within the larger context of the international abolitionist network whose existence and work both preceded and succeeded them. Seen in itself, the British takeoff at that time changed the balance and dynamics of the network by establishing a strong institutional precedent that influenced the course of antislavery activities elsewhere. At the same time, however, the accumulated history of the abolitionist network was an important causal force contributing to the emergence of the first mass campaigns.

What made the British campaigns possible – and bestowed on the London model its prominence – was the combination of several factors, a combination

---

[32] See Eric Williams, *Capitalism and Slavery* (Chapel Hill: University of North Carolina Press, 1944). Works that sought to specify the causal role of capitalism include Howard Temperley, "Capitalism, Slavery and Ideology," *Past and Present*, no. 75 (1977); Thomas Bender, ed. *The Antislavery Debate: Capitalism and Abolitionism as a Problem in Historical Interpretation* (Berkeley: University of California Press, 1992); Drescher, *Capitalism and Antislavery*; *From Slavery to Freedom: Comparative Studies in the Rise and Fall of Atlantic Slavery*; Davis, *Age of Revolution*. Even Seymour Drescher's recent masterful comparative treatment of slavery, antislavery, and abolition treats the British popular mobilizations as largely disconnected from developments elsewhere while often discussing the international connections on the level of government policies. See Drescher, *Abolition*.

that failed to materialize in France and the United States: legislative allies, committed organizers, and a willing popular constituency. The presence of just one of these – without the other two – would not have sufficed to provide organizational cohesion and give the campaigns their wide reach. At the same time, all three elements worked together in Britain and thus mutually reinforced themselves. There was thus no single overarching factor that gave London the edge within the international abolitionist network. Capitalism, for example, whether as a set of economic conditions or as an ideology, cannot explain convincingly the specific intertwining of these three factors in the British case – and its absence in France and the United States. British preeminence was rather the historically contingent outcome of many intersecting developments.

More central to my argument is the fact that the preexisting abolitionist network with its political program and with its model of action gave an important push to the developments that produced the new extensive campaigns in Britain. As I noted earlier (see Chapter 4), the historiography of early abolitionism is still dominated by interpretations that emphasize the role of non-Quaker external allies in transforming an allegedly apolitical sectarian idiosyncrasy into a political reform movement. The effect of these influential works has been to deflect the attention from the original Quaker nucleus of antislavery and thus downgrade, if not miss entirely, the logic of religious radicalization in its origins. Thus, for Seymour Drescher, this process is eclipsed, as an explanatory factor, by capitalist development that makes a certain class of people in the industrial North susceptible to abolitionism. Christopher Brown, on the other hand, sees British mobilizations emerging out of historically contingent developments triggered by the imperial crisis. At the end, however, he credits Clarkson and Wilberforce as, respectively, the "originator" and "political sponsor" of the movement. Thus, for both the crucial contribution here comes from the non-Quaker latecomers who imparted on abolitionism its truly political character and transformed into an extensive mobilization.[33]

This contribution was substantial – yet hardly as crucial as the two historians have argued. Manchester and Lancashire reformers had important organizational expertise with petitioning after their success in repealing Pitt's cotton tax. Yet they certainly did not originate, impose, or make possible the project of nationwide petitioning. Wilberforce was a committed, if not particularly savvy, parliamentary ally. Yet he was cajoled into that role by others, including Clarkson who, himself, had developed his activist strategy in close consultation with Quaker allies.

In other words, there were causal pressures from both ends in the creation of the expansive British network. On the one hand, several important individuals and constituencies brought to the campaigns a breadth and political

---

[33] See, e.g., *Capitalism and Antislavery*, 67; Brown, *Moral Capital*, 44–45. Drescher does revisit his older causal argument in his most recent book, yet still emphasizes the importance of Manchester for the success of the campaign. See Drescher, *Abolition*, 214–15.

effectiveness that was lacking in the French and American cases. On the other hand, however, the London Quaker core – an offshoot of the initial Benezetian group in Philadelphia – actively cultivated these individuals and constituencies. The Quaker contribution was more than simply providing the "infrastructure" for more active political entrepreneurs from outside the Society of Friends. First, by 1787 the Quaker propaganda machine – initially nothing more than an individual initiative of Benezet's but then amplified by the efforts of the London Quakers – had pushed British public opinion into an antislavery direction.[34] Non-Quaker latecomers, like Clarkson, had often "recognized" their antislavery vocation after exposure to this propaganda. Second, from his very first outreach attempts in the 1760s, Benezet had set the pattern of a distinctively political activism targeting the highest imperial authorities in London: the Crown and parliament. Of course, in the interaction with various allies of various degrees of commitment, the particulars of this pattern evolved. Yet the fundamentals of this political vision never changed and, starting with the campaign of 1788, resulted in a series of popular mobilizations. And finally, from the very beginning the growing nucleus of Quaker reformers cast the net widely in a strategic search for external allies. Ever since the recruitment of Granville Sharp, the most important vector of growth in the antislavery network was the creation of alliances with non-Quakers. These alliance-building dynamics were at play in the "small world" of the abolitionist core: the relatively small set of committed activists in North America, Britain, and France. With the first petitioning campaigns, however, this logic was extended further into the wider universe of extensive public mobilization.

In contrast to earlier pro-indigenist activist networks, the antislavery network was so successful in recruiting non-Quaker members and transcending its Quaker origins as to deceive modern-day students into elevating these "external" segments of the network to the position of core contributors. While the contribution of non-Quakers was important, they were the recipients of an established body of Quaker antislavery propaganda and were strategically recruited to contribute to a vision of political intervention with political authorities. People like Clarkson and Wilberforce were clearly committed abolitionists and individuals with free wills. Yet, ironically, they ended up performing in a political script whose first draft has been composed by a poor schoolmaster in Philadelphia.[35] In this sense, the small antislavery core that crystallized in the conflicts between Quaker reformers and other imperial networks in Philadelphia exercised far-reaching if not immediately visible causal influence on the later trajectory of the growing antislavery network.

---

[34] Brown acknowledges the importance of Quaker propaganda, but only in Britain after 1783. Yet, as we saw, the Benezetian corpus had circulated at least for a decade by then. See Brown, *Moral Capital*, 427–31.

[35] See again Sword, "Remembering Dinah Nevil."

Conclusion

As I write this, there are thousands around the globe supporting and championing, in many ways, the cause of distant strangers. For the most part, what they do will remain one of those "unhistoric acts" to which George Eliot drew our attention. Although a new Clarkson or a new "saintly" Wilberforce might be creating social change right now, the majority of the people currently engaged in long-distance advocacy will not be recognized as heroes. There will not be movies and books about them and no public homage will be paid to them. Nor do they aspire for such recognition. At the same time, we, ordinary people moved by a distant issue and devoting our energy and time to it, in however miniscule allotments, have at least one thing in common with the certified heroes of the antislavery struggle. Like them, we are – unbeknownst to ourselves – enacting the script for which a poor Philadelphia schoolmaster wrote the first draft in the 1760s.

For sure, this script has been rewritten continuously through the centuries that divide us from Benezet's time. Like Hollywood remakes, our current scripts of action may appear to bear only tenuous similarities, at least on the surface, with the original: an institutional model that first crystallized enduringly in the abolitionist network of the late eighteenth century. Yet the deep structures are the same.

When we think about the plight of distant persons we do not know, say the victims of human trafficking, our thoughts are shaped and informed by the powerful stream of humanitarian ideas that has accumulated by now from different sources. Consciously or not, we evoke the principles of human dignity and human rights articulated by a series of influential thinkers at least since Locke and inscribed in national legislation, international treaties, and charters of intergovernmental organizations. We also evoke, however, the basic argument put together for the first time in early Quaker antislavery propaganda: the argument that certain ways of treating other human beings are inherently unethical and evil, even if they are sanctioned by custom and economic interest. This argument is diffuse and without clear authorship. It is not attached to either a single great philosopher or an influential political declaration of rights. Yet because of its persistent and wide distribution and because of its slow and steady infiltration into the public consciousness, it has been immeasurably more influential than the work of any single great mind. It has influenced state regimes at least since the British government's conversion to the principle of eradicating the international slave trade in the early nineteenth century. It has influenced the general moral climate internationally. And, more specifically, it shaped the international moral regime that crystallized in the twentieth century when antislavery concerns and lobbying set priorities for the League of Nations and the United Nations.[1]

Our culture is infused today with the idea that when confronted with the suffering of distant strangers, one has to intervene and do something. And in important ways, this is the historical legacy of the long-distance advocacy projects discussed on the pages of this book. A perhaps even more important and consequential part of this legacy is the institutional model of politicized action that the early abolitionist network bequeathed to us. These are the "tools" that subsequent generations of activists and grassroot supporters have consistently used for their own specific purposes: a set of roles and scripts of action that is employed whenever a distant issue is to be addressed.

We do not think of the ideas and models of action bequeathed on us by antislavery as particularly interesting or noticeable. The idea that human enslavement is inherently morally repugnant is so intuitive for us that we cannot understand how generations of our ancestors – and some of our most venerated forebears – could live with it and profit from it without batting an eyelash. But also we take it for granted that when confronted with such evil, there is a standardized set of actions that are at our disposal.

Reflecting on the scant – if any – attention we pay to electricity pylons despite our incurable reliance on what they help deliver, Alain de Botton notes that "it is rare to admire a technology which was already well established when we were children." "Histories of technology," he writes, "should usefully identify not only when a particular innovation was introduced, but also, and more interestingly, when it was forgotten – when it disappeared from collective consciousness through familiarity, becoming as commonplace and unremarkable as a pebble or a cloud."[2] In this sense, how well forgotten the early abolitionists'

[1] Chaim D. Kaufmann and Robert A. Pape, "Explaining Costly International Moral Action: Britain's Sixty-year Campaign Against the Atlantic Slave Trade," *International Organization* 53, no. 4 (1999); Suzanne Miers, *Britain and the Ending of the Slave Trade* (London: Longman, 1975); *Slavery in the Twentieth Century: The Evolution of a Global Problem* (Walnut Creek, CA: AltaMira Press, 2003); Ethan A. Nadelmann, "Global Prohibition Regimes: The Evolution of Norms in International Society," *International Organization* 44, no. 4 (1990).

[2] Alain de Botton, *The Pleasures and Sorrows of Work* (New York: Pantheon Books, 2009), 209–10.

political innovations are is only a testament to the effectiveness and persistent power of the action technologies they invented for us. When nongovernmental organizations send us their mass emails with requests that we sign a petition, they do not bother to append a historical justification for why they are following the precedent set by petition-producing abolitionist organizers in 1787.

Thus, paradoxically, the novelty – or even the noticeability – of the institutional model has "disappeared from collective consciousness" in direct proportion to the frequency of its continual reemployment. In the process, the newly assembled set of practices and roles has receded from explicit awareness and become Polanyian tacit knowledge.[3] It has been used as if instinctively, while incrementally being transformed and developed by its practitioners in each subsequent use. But still, its existence is taken for granted and rarely – if ever – discussed explicitly.

What is important here, of course, is not the strictly analytical abstraction of an institutional model of action, but rather the possibility it afforded for individuals and organizations to pursue their goals by using it in practice. It is exactly in the course of this repeated use that the model lost the crispness of its novelty. After it crystallized from within the abolitionist network in late eighteenth-century England, it was reactivated repeatedly both in Britain and in other national settings. It was applied for further mobilization and pressure on the original issue of colonial slavery and related humanitarian issues. In the process, the abolitionist network developed further. This development was not simple, linear, or always positive. It included phases of substantive and geographical expansion, and phases of deep contraction. Yet at least until the mid-twentieth century, this network – in its various manifestations – exerted an important influence on what we can now see as "global civil society." Directly or not, the enduring existence of a network of inherently imperial and international dimensions spurred the development of international nongovernmental organizations, which in turn created the conditions for the involvement of wider international constituencies in the work of long-distance advocacy.

LEGACIES

Perhaps the most lasting legacy of the late eighteenth-century developments was the enduring prominence of London as the central hub of international humanitarianism until at least the antiapartheid movement of the 1980s. Even at that late date, in a parallel to the state of affairs of antislavery in the early nineteenth century, the British branch of the movement was stronger than its North American counterpart, despite the presence of a more numerous "natural" constituency for politicized racial solidarity among African Americans. There are many reasons, of course, for this differential strength, such as British legacies of imperial links with South Africa or the

---

[3] Michael Polanyi, *The Tacit Dimension* (Garden City, NY: Doubleday, 1967).

overwhelming predominance of the civil rights struggle in the United States. Still, as Bob Skinner has argued recently, "campaigns against anti-apartheid must be understood in relation to a tradition of social protest and activism that may be traced back to the anti-slavery campaigns of the late eighteenth and early nineteenth century."[4]

This tradition is far from negligible and consisted in several iterations of the political antislavery program and a series of important institutions that further cemented the importance of London within the evolving antislavery network. The gradual revival and radicalization of the British abolitionist mobilization since the 1820s led to the parliamentary abolition of colonial slavery in 1833. Immediately after that, troubled by the abuses of the "apprenticeship system" instituted as a transition toward the full liberty of former slaves, activists launched another successful popular campaign for the abolition of apprentice-ship itself. Activism continued even after this full formal eradication of slav-ery in British colonies. In 1839, a new organization – the British and Foreign Antislavery Society – began its operations dedicated to the "universal" aboli-tion of slavery worldwide.[5]

Thus, around the 1830s, the British branch of international abolitionism continued to grow. The attention to slavery and the slave trade was expanded to include – as in the vision of the early Pennsylvania reformers – the related issues of equitable relations with non-Europeans in the colonies. Thomas Fowell Buxton, whom Wilberforce personally anointed as his antislavery heir in parliament, launched a Select Committee examining the situation of indige-nous people in the empire that again relied on the cooperation of religious fig-ures in Britain and the colonies. In 1837, Quaker physician Thomas Hodgkin founded the Aborigines Protection Society to support the rights of colonial non-Europeans.[6]

In this sense, the 1830s witnessed a continuation of the late eighteenth-century "expansionary" drive of abolitionist networks. In the process, how-ever, the composition of the British network changed. Whereas the early British takeoff was engineered mostly by Quakers, now Church of England evangeli-cals and Dissenters were firmly embedded in the network and their position was reinforced by their missionary presence in the colonies that had gained

[4] Skinner, *Foundations of Anti-Apartheid*, 2. See also Thörn, *Anti-Apartheid*, 75–76.
[5] Temperley, *British Antislavery*.
[6] J. Gallagher, "Fowell Buxton and the New African Policy, 1838–1842," *Cambridge Historical Journal* 10, no. 1 (1950); Kass and Kass, *Perfecting the World*; Lester, *Imperial Networks*; Alan Lester "Humanitarians and White Settlers in the Nineteenth Century," in *Missions and Empire*, ed. Norman Etherington (Oxford: Oxford University Press, 2005); Rainger, "Philanthropy and Science"; Swaisland, "Aborigines Protection Society"; Temperley, *British Antislavery*; Zoë Laidlaw, "'Aunt Anna's Report': The Buxton Women and the Aborigines Select Committee, 1835–37," *Journal of Imperial and Commonwealth History* 32, no. 2 (2004); Zoe Laidlaw, *Colonial Connections, 1815–45: Patronage, the Information Revolution and Colonial Government*.

strength in the interim. This changed composition certainly facilitated cooperation and strength in numbers. On the negative side, it also invited internecine conflict between different visions of humanitarian involvement.

Thus, despite the promising growth in the 1830s, the next decade brought in a period of increased setbacks for humanitarians. That was partly the result of internal disagreements that prevented the forceful concerted action of the previous decades: the tension between a predominantly Christian missionary and a non-conversionary Quaker programs of engagement with distant colonial "others," the conflict between "free-traders" and "protectionists" on the question on how to best legislate colonial sugar duties without indirectly encouraging slavery in the colonies of other states, and the intrusion into Britain of the bitter struggles between the factions of a now stronger American abolitionism, its strength itself the product of British abolitionists' support and guidance. And while British colonial planters had to accept defeat and free their slaves against financial compensations, white settlers in other colonies now mobilized much more effectively to counteract humanitarian interventions.[7]

If, as a result of these developments, by the 1870s, British antislavery and humanitarianism were a pale shadow of their buoyant configuration earlier in the century, they continued to lobby and mobilize well into the twentieth century on various issues.[8] And if, in British perspective, the later nineteenth century was a story of decline, the international context reveals different dynamics. There, the expansionary drive of the network continued at least until the 1880s when an abolitionist movement crystallized in Brazil. As I pointed out in Chapter 6, armed now with an established and working institutional model of action, British abolitionism began to influence the trajectory of a network within which it had been somewhat of a "late bloomer." First, the strengthened position and continuing energy of British abolitionists after emancipation in the colonies allowed them to reinvigorate the movements in the two other original branches of the network in the United States and France.[9] In addition, they were able to influence, through various means,

---

[7] Andrew Bank, "Losing Faith in the Civilizing Mission: The Premature Decline of Humanitarian Liberalism at the Cape, 1840–60," in *Empire and Others: British Encounters with Indigenous Peoples, 1600–1850*, eds. Martin Daunton and Rick Halpern (London: UCL Press, 1999); Julie Evans et al., *Equal Subjects, Unequal Rights: Indigenous Peoples in British Settler Colonies, 1830–1910* (Manchester, UK: Manchester University Press 2003); Fladeland, *Men and Brothers*, 257–301; Laidlaw, "Heathens, Slaves"; Lester, "Humanitarians and White Settlers"; C. Duncan Rice, "'Humanity Sold for Sugar!' The British Abolitionist Response to Free Trade in Slave-Grown Sugar," *Historical Journal* 13, no. 3 (1970); Temperley, *British Antislavery*.

[8] Grant, *Civilised Savagery*.

[9] For British influence on U.S. abolitionism in the 1830s, see Anthony J. Barker, *Captain Charles Stuart: Anglo-American Abolitionist* (Baton Rouge: Louisiana State University Press, 1986); Christine Bolt, *The Anti-Slavery Movement and Reconstruction: A Study in Anglo-American Co-Operation, 1833–77* (London: Oxford University Press, 1969); Louis Filler, *The Crusade against Slavery, 1830–1860* (New York: Harper, 1960), 48–52; Fladeland, *Men and Brothers*,

the further expansion of the network into other colonial powers that now developed their "own" antislavery movement: the Netherlands, Spain, and Brazil.[10] Through the circuits of this expanded network, antislavery initiatives were launched in states of lesser or no colonial involvement, such as Canada, Sweden, and Switzerland.[11] In the 1880s, the French cardinal Lavigerie created his own Catholic version of Protestant London antislavery, this time directed against the continuing Arab slave trade, by establishing local societies in various European states.[12]

Another important, if less easily specifiable, effect of the continuous growth and influence of the abolitionist network was that it paved the way leading to the gradual emergence of a field of international nongovernmental organizations. The key event here was the "World Antislavery Convention" held in London in 1840, the first formal international conference of civil society associations. Its participants were predominantly Anglo-American activists joined by a smattering of French abolitionists. Thus, the worldwide ambitions in the name of the convention were mostly of aspirational nature. Yet, although the Convention was hardly a mini-UN, it was the very first of a series of international nongovernmental conferences that set the initial foundation of an international "civil society." Congresses on peace, temperance, prison reform, and free trade followed in the 1840s.[13] Despite their substantively different orientation, these subsequent international gatherings were in many ways indebted to antislavery's precedent. They relied on the same international pool of reformers. Even more importantly, these movements followed closely and consciously

195–230; Gifford, "George Thompson"; Thomas F. Harwood, "British Evangelical Abolitionism and American Churches in the 1830's," *Journal of Southern History* 28, no. 3 (1962). For the French case, see Jennings, *French Anti-Slavery*.

[10] The Netherlands: M. Elisabeth Kluit, *Het Protestantse réveil in Nederland en daarbuiten, 1815–1865* (Amsterdam: Paris, 1970), 433–36. Spain: Josep M. Fradera, "Limitaciones históricas del abolicionismo catalán," in *Esclavitud y derechos humanos: La lucha por la libertad del negro en el siglo XIX*, eds. Francisco de Solano and Agustín Guimerá Ravina (Madrid: Consejo Superior de Investigaciones Científicas, 1990). Brazil: Conrad, *Destruction of Slavery*.

[11] David and Schaufelbuehl, "L'antiesclavagisme en Suisse"; David and Schaufelbuehl, "Swiss Conservatives and the Struggle for the Abolition of Slavery at the End of the Nineteenth Century," *Itinerario* 34, no. 2 (2010); Ernst Ekman, "Sweden, the Slave Trade and Slavery, 1784–1847," in *La Traite des Noirs par l'Atlantique: Nouvelles approches* (Paris: Société française d'histoire d'outre-mer, 1976), 228; Benoit Girardin, "Le mouvement anti-esclavagiste genevois de 1860 a 1900 et son echo en Suisse," *Geneve-Afrique* 22, no. 2 (1984); Fred Landon, "The Anti-Slavery Society of Canada," *The Journal of Negro History* 4, no. 1 (1919).

[12] Horst Gründer, "'Gott will es': Eine Kreuzzugsbewegung am Ende des 19. Jahrhunderts," *Geschichte in Wissenschaft und Unterricht* 28, no. 4 (1977); Miers, *Britain and the Ending*, 201–06.

[13] Steve Charnovitz, "Two Centuries of Participation: NGOs and International Governance," *Michigan Journal of International Law* 18 (1997); Douglas Maynard, "Reform and the Origin of the International Organization Movement," *Proceedings of the American Philosophical Society* 107, no. 3 (1963); "The World's Antislavery Convention of 1840," *Mississippi Valley Historical Review* 47, no. 3 (1960).

the organizational forms and models already established by abolitionists and tried out by them with remarkable effectiveness.[14]

In this sense, the trajectory of international nongovernmentalism as we know it was conditioned by the precedent of the abolitionist network and its continuous development throughout the nineteenth century. For other emerging initiatives, it offered both an action template and the example of cooperation across national borders. Clearly, all of this did not translate into a spectacular fast growth of a truly global civil society. Yet however inconclusive these developments were, they demonstrate the continuous influence of the antislavery network. Now, indirectly, it led to the exposure of a steadily growing number of constituencies in Europe and elsewhere to distant moral issues. Nor can we understand the distinct shape of the moral regime institutionalized in a series of international government organizations – the League of Nations and then the United Nations – without the direct and indirect input of the surviving and developing antislavery network. Again, the London antislavery core continued to lobby such organizations and to provide an example for other associations on how to influence their functioning.[15]

Seen in the long-term historical perspective, then, the crystallization of an abolitionist network in the eighteenth century had important and far-reaching consequences that go beyond the concrete actions and changes it produced in the last decades of the century when a new institutional model of long-distance advocacy emerged out of this network. This continuously evolving network exercised important effects on patterns of political mobilization in various settings and influenced official policies, as well as emerging international norms and practices. And an important part of the mechanics of this continuous influence the network in its changing configuration was able to exert was the repeated deployment of the same institutional model of action that first crystallized in the late eighteenth century.

There was, thus, a mutually co-constitutive relationship between the network of activists and the institutional model it was now continuously redeploying. It was in reactivating this model of action that the network developed and evolved. At the same time, a community of activists maintained the organizational skills and "know-how" of a model that had proven its effectiveness at least since the late eighteenth century. This, in turn, ensured the deep institutionalization of the model as it became taken-for-granted technology for political mobilization.

The commitment to redeploy the same institutional model was partly a matter of organizational inertia as it had become a standard organizational routine. Simultaneously, its continuous reactivation stood in a mutually reinforcing

[14] Martin Ceadel, *The Origins of War Prevention: The British Peace Movement and International Relations, 1730–1854* (Oxford: Clarendon Press, 1996); Read, *English Provinces*, 134–36.

[15] Steve Charnovitz, "The Emergence of Democratic Participation in Global Governance (Paris, 1919)," *Indiana Journal of Global Legal Studies* 10, no. 1 (2003); Miers, *Slavery in the Twentieth Century*.

relationship with the reiteration of the same conflictual dynamics that had led to its formation and emergence in the first place. The abolitionist model of long-distance advocacy emerged, by the 1780s, as the result of the radicalization of religious reformers in their contest with other imperial actors and alternative visions of empire in the 1750s. Similar instances of radicalization of religious actors continued to re-occur throughout the nineteenth and twentieth centuries in British colonies – and former colonies. Thus, missionaries in the Caribbean, Australia, Africa, and India engaged steadily in sustained confrontations with British settlers over the rights of indigenous people and former slaves.[16] For political support, they invariably connected with the organizations and individuals in London and Britain who, as heirs of the early abolitionist network, formed the humanitarian "establishment" there. In this way, the reactivation of the model of long-distance advocacy was also driven by the recurrent radicalization of religious actors. Yet at the same time, the very organizational "sedimentation" of the model in a network of individuals and enduring organizations provided subtle encouragement for such radicalization and conflict with rival networks to take place.

HISTORICAL CONTINUITIES, CHANGE, AND MODERNITY

Traversing centuries of political struggles around the rights of distant strangers, this book argues that the specific ways in which we today act around such distant issues are conditioned by deeply complex and historically contingent developments. The institutional model of long-distance advocacy that crystallized with early abolitionism, as well as its subsequent endurance, was the end-result of many intersecting and mutually reinforcing social and cultural processes. It bears repeating, too, that these processes did not arise from the advent of European modernity. They are not inherently "modern," but rather have roots that go back to at least the late Middle Ages.

   It has been a standard analytical move to explain the social origins of contemporary forms of identification and action on behalf of distant strangers by focusing on one specific feature of modernity as the ultimate determinant.

---

[16] G. A. Catherall, "Thomas Burchell, Gentle Rebel," *Baptist Quarterly* 21, no. 8 (1966); William Gervase Clarence-Smith, "Église, nation et esclavage: Angole et Mozambique portugais, 1878–1913," in *Abolir l'esclavage: Un réformisme à l'épreuve (France, Portugal, Suisse, XVIIIe-XIXe siècles)*, ed. Olivier Pétré-Grenouilleau (Rennes, France: Presses universitaires de Rennes, 2008); W. M. Freund, "The Career Of Johannes Theodorus Van Der Kemp and His Role in the History of South Africa," *Tijdschrift voor Geschiedenis* 86, no. 3 (1973); Lester, "Humanitarians and White Settlers"; Lester, "Colonial Networks, Australian Humanitarianism and the History Wars," *Geographical Research* 44, no. 3 (2006); Oddie, *Social Protest in India: British Protestant Missionaries and Social Reforms, 1850–1900*; Porter, *Religion versus Empire*, 307–10; Stanley Shaloff, "Presbyterians and Belgian Congo Exploitation: The Compagnie du Kasai v. Morrison and Sheppard," *Journal of Presbyterian History* 47, no. 2 (1969); Turner, *Slaves and Missionaries*; Edward Bean Underhill, *Life of James Mursell Phillippo, Missionary in Jamaica* (London: Yates & Alexander, 1881).

Thomas Haskell, for example, suggests that the complex cognitive models necessitated by the complex transactions of the new market economy in the eighteenth century predisposed people to more complex thinking in other, noneconomic spheres. This complex thinking accommodated and dealt with longer chains of causality, which, in turn, made people more cognitively open to the larger structures of causation accounting for the suffering of distant strangers. Luc Boltanski describes modern humanitarianism as a cultural form of "enlightened indignation" that he compares to the traditional forms of "communal indignation." According to his account, in traditional societies, sentiment was mobilized for the purpose of imposing communal standards on deviant others. In contrast, in the modern form of "enlightened" indignation, sentiment is mobilized in order to uphold more general standards of justice that abstract from the particular identity markers of the "others" concerned. Scholars working in the social-movement research tradition have explained the "transnationalization" of issues around which people mobilize, as well as the more extensive supranational scale of such mobilization, as driven by the changing scale of political authority in the recent past when the nation-state has been increasingly supplanted by intergovernmental bodies, regional blocs, and transnational corporations as the central organizing focus of collective action. Drawing on Charles Tilly's claim that consolidating nation-states transformed typically sporadic and uncoordinated local protests into movements of truly national scale in the nineteenth century, they see contemporary transnational activism as the global extension of traditional "national" social movements. And, of course, the power of "cultural" globalization is often recognized as the ultimate source for increased mobilization around distant issues in the recent past, even by those otherwise skeptical of the pervasive discourse of the powers of globalization. Thus, for Ruud Koopmans, "the main effect of globalization processes is an increasing internationalization of the themes at stake in national politics."[17]

---

[17] Ruud Koopmans, "Globalization or Still National Politics? A Comparison of Protests against the Gulf War in Germany, France and the Netherlands," in *Social Movements in a Globalizing World*, eds. Donatella Della Porta, Hanspeter Kriesi, and Dieter Rucht (New York: St. Martin's Press, 1999), 70. See also Thomas L. Haskell, "Capitalism and the Origins of the Humanitarian Sensibility, Part 1," in *The Antislavery Debate: Capitalism and Abolitionism as a Problem in Historical Interpretation*, ed. Thomas Bender (Berkeley: University of California Press, 1992); Luc Boltanski, *Distant Suffering: Morality, Media and Politics* (Cambridge: Cambridge University Press, 1999). For statements on the transnationalization of popular politics as the result of the change in scale of political authority, see Donatella Della Porta and Hanspeter Kriesi, "Social Movements in a Globalizing World: An Introduction," in *Social Movements in a Globalizing World*, eds. Donatella Della Porta, Hanspeter Kriesi, and Dieter Rucht (New York: St. Martin's Press, 1999); Lipschutz, "Reconstructing World Politics"; Dieter Rucht, "The Transnationalization of Social Movements: Trends, Causes, Problems," in *Social Movements in a Globalizing World*, eds. Donatella Della Porta, Hanspeter Kriesi, and Dieter Rucht (New York: St. Martin's Press, 1999); Jackie Smith, "Transnational Processes and Movements," in *The Blackwell Companion to Social Movements*, eds. David A. Snow, Sarah A. Soule, and Hanspeter

Expanding markets, complex societal organization, the transnationalization of political authorities, and cultural flows: these are some of the features of modernity that such arguments single out as the predominant causes for the expansion of the moral imagination and moral action. Despite their substantive, disciplinary, and methodological differences, a common thread that runs through them is the search for the single most important structural condition that made contemporary forms of action around distant issues possible. Yet my examination of the long-term developments that led to the crystallization of modern forms of distant-issue mobilization reveals their complexity and historical contingency. The causal arrows are multiple and intertwined – there is no single feature of modernity that in itself created the conditions of long-distance advocacy as we know it today.

If there is one underlying condition that opened the causal pathways toward the emergence of modern long-distance advocacy, it was the historically specific configuration of institutionally differentiated "value spheres" of European modernity that Weber identified. It is the inherent tension between these institutional sectors that afforded the initial setting for the development of a conflict out of which ideologies and practices of political action focused on the rights and well-being of distant non-Europeans developed. In this context, the decisive push toward the gradual and often halting crystallization of modern forms of long-distance advocacy came from a relatively small number of committed religious reformers who further intensified inter-sectoral tensions into outright conflict. In the process, they developed by trial and error increasingly standardized and institutionalized political strategies and technologies of mobilization.

Alongside and in spite of the important and far-reaching transformations of the global and national economic, political, and cultural contexts, it is the remarkable persistence of this structural differentiation and the religiously motivated conflicts that emerged on the interstices of competing networks that strikes the observer. The opposition between "pro-development" and pro-indigenous networks continued to fuel political struggles well into the late twentieth century, at least.[18] And religious radicalization, as we saw, provided the foundations of such powerful recent movements as antiapartheid and the movement for solidarity with Central America.

Kriesi (Malden, MA: Blackwell, 2004); Smith, Pagnucco, and Romeril, "Transnational Social Movement Organisations"; Sidney Tarrow, *The New Transnational Activism* (New York: Cambridge University Press, 2005). From among the many iterations of Tilly's argument on the formative influence of nation states, see Charles Tilly, *The Contentious French: Four Centuries of Popular Struggle* (Cambridge, MA: Harvard University Press, 1986).

[18] Sanjeev Khagram, *Dams and Development: Transnational Struggles for Water and Power* (Ithaca: Cornell University Press, 2004); Gregory M. Maney, "Rival Transnational Networks and Indigenous Rights: The San Blas Kuna in Panama and the Yanomami in Brazil," *Research in Social Movements, Conflicts and Change* 23 (2001).

Continuities and recurrences do not mean stasis, of course. Within the long-term history of a repeating religiously motivated conflict, the developments of the British abolitionist network in the late eighteenth century presented an important turning point. The formation of this network occurred in structural conditions very similar to the imperial context of earlier Iberian pro-indigenist advocacy and it was driven by the same logic of radicalization of religious reformers. Yet the model that the abolitionist network created was distinctively different. Like their Iberian predecessors, abolitionists engaged in practices of political activism with the intention of changing official policies. This nexus between political activism and pressure on political authorities was, in this sense, nothing particularly new in the eighteenth century. The initial trajectory was identical in the two cases: a relatively small group of activists engaged in enduring advocacy around a distant imperial issue. The new and consequential element that the first British campaigns added was that now a significant number of ordinary people were mobilized to express an ethical stance in regard to such an issue. And the people mobilized did not share the narrow religious identity of the Quaker originators of the networks: in fact, they came from various religious and social backgrounds. Thus, a different and distinctively modern institutional model of long-distance advocacy emerged.

Stating the differences between the two cases in such terms raises a whole set of interrelated questions. Why did the model emerge then and not at another time? Why in Britain and not elsewhere? And, finally, why did the model first employed in the late eighteenth century prove so resilient? Fully satisfactory answers to such questions will require a further careful examination of the historically contingent and complex causal processes that this book has tried to bring to attention, if often in bare outlines. Yet, in important ways, the distinctively novel shape of the long-distance advocacy introduced by British abolitionism was not simply the reflection of changing structural conditions, but a path-dependent outcome of the dynamics of network creation and main-tenance in its historically specific form.

The novelty of this model expressed itself in two interrelated features. It was socially inclusive, mobilizing people of various social and religious back-grounds. This, in turn, made possible a new larger scale of mobilization around distant issues. In fact, one could go further and argue that it was precisely this wider distribution and outreach inherent in the institutional model that ensured its survival and resilience.

What then were the causes for this inclusiveness and extended scale? As I pointed out, the standard analytical move to explain these features of the British mobilization is to see them as the surface manifestation of deeper and unrelated political and cultural processes that indirectly conspired to lend the modest pre-political Quaker project a true political expansiveness. This histo-riographical perspective conforms to the conclusions of Charles Tilly who, in what is perhaps the most systematic exploration of British popular politics of the period, documented the gradual emergence at that time of a new pattern of political mobilization. In his view, this pattern was developed by political entrepreneurs as they reacted to important structural transformations of the political context: state expansion, the parliamentarization of politics, the concentration of capital, economic polarization, and urbanization.[19] On this background, it is tempting to understand the extensive scale of British abolitionist campaigns as the natural end result of these fundamental structural changes. Abolitionists took advantage of and used for their purposes an already crystallizing new model (or "repertoire of contention") which, in turn, was conditioned by the transformation of British economy and politics.

As in other perspectives that see the rise of modern forms of long-distance advocacy as the result of important structural transformations in the course of European modernity, such approaches locate the causes for the social inclusiveness and mass appeal of early British abolitionism in factors external to the long-standing activist network that nurtured these campaigns. The presence and early history of this network is largely incidental. At best, it served to provide an issue around which various political constituencies could rally. That was, according to David Brion Davis, the main attraction of antislavery ideology. "Antislavery petitioning," he writes, "revived enthusiasm among a constituency that had become bored or disillusioned over the futile struggle to 'purify' Parliament. ...And the new movement provided the public with a safe distraction or to put it more charitably, with a mode of political participation which did not directly threaten the sources of or structure of political power."[20]

At the end, however, such explanations do not account convincingly why it was precisely slavery and the slave trade that became the magnet around which such a large coalition of constituencies gathered. Indeed, the public campaigns against the slave trade were in many ways preceded by earlier successful attempts to mobilize wider audiences around principled issues both in Britain and in the colonies: the Pennsylvania petitioning drive for royal government, the various iterations of campaigns for parliamentary reform, as well the American Revolution and the British petitions for reconciliation with the colonies. Many of the organizers and participants in these initiatives joined the abolitionist campaigns once they took off the ground in 1787.[21] Furthermore, conditions in eighteenth-century Britain were much more favorable for extensive political mobilization than anywhere in the Iberian world before or during that time. Even the fact that, in contrast to strictly Catholic Iberian states, Britain and its colonies presented a relatively hospitable environment for religious and political diversity made possible broader and socially inclusive popular coalitions.

---

[19] Tilly, *Popular Contention*.
[20] Davis, *Age of Revolution*, 363.
[21] James E. Bradley, *Popular Politics and the American Revolution in England: Petitions, the Crown, and Public Opinion* (Macon, GA: Mercer, 1986); Dickinson, *The Politics of the People in Eighteenth-Century Britain*; Hutson, *Pennsylvania Politics*.

Nevertheless, the failure of Catholic-Protestant cooperation projects in early nineteenth-century Ireland indicate the persisting confessional barriers to such broadening of popular constituencies.[22] And although the late eighteenth-century campaigns against the slave trade were in many ways indebted to earlier instances of political mobilization, they still represented something qualitatively different. First, unlike their precedents, they were oriented toward a distant imperial issue. And second, the sheer numbers of people they successfully mobilized dwarfed any earlier instances of popular campaigns.

Nor should we overestimate the antislavery "consensus" in Britain at the time. Even though by then there was indeed a general distaste for slavery, nourished in particular by the steady stream of Benezetian propaganda, there were also strong entrenched interests committed to the continuation of the slave trade: traders in ports like Liverpool, various individuals making their living from the slave trade, and absentee planters from slaveholding colonies. They mobilized to counteract abolitionist pressure.[23] Furthermore, as I pointed out, there were at the time at least two other imperial issues that attracted attention both in parliament and among the wider public: the violence against the so-called Black Caribs in the island of St. Thomas and the injustices committed by the servants of the East India Company. Yet neither of those potentially explosive imperial issues became the centerpiece of an extensive popular mobilization. One could speculate, for example, that if constituencies interested in economic and political reforms were indeed in search of a "safe" issue, they could have appropriated easily either of those.

If "outsiders" latched onto the abolitionist project, it was to a large extent because already there was a relatively coherent political program to attack slavery, a program that has been developed and nurtured by a growing network of activists. In other words, the impressive scale of early British abolitionism was not simply a question of a demand by "issue-hungry" politicized constituencies. They were responding, rather, to the "supply" provided by the preexisting abolitionist network that provided not only a compelling issue, but also a general plan of political action. And, as I pointed out in Chapter 6, what the Quaker core of the abolitionist network "supplied" consistently from the very beginning was particularly "sticky." They deliberately searched for Quaker and non-Quaker allies and provided all kinds of inducements, if not outright manipulation, for those prospective recruits.

These considerations again place in the forefront the autonomous logic of the activist network formation as an important causal force for the consolidation

---

[22] See, e.g., Irene Whelan, *The Bible War in Ireland: The "Second Reformation" and the Polarization of Protestant-Catholic Relations, 1800–1840* (Dublin: Lilliput Press, 2005).

[23] Lillian M. Penson, *The Colonial Agents of the British West Indies: A Study in Colonial Administration, Mainly in the Eighteenth Century* (London: University of London Press, 1924); James A. Rawley, "London's Defense of the Slave Trade, 1787–1807," *Slavery and Abolition* 14, no. 2 (1993); F. E. Sanderson, "The Liverpool Delegates and Sir William Dolben's Bill," *Transactions of the Historic Society of Lancashire and Cheshire* 124 (1972).

of early British abolitionism and of the modern institutional model of long distance that it created. And in turn, this draws attention to the importance of the social processes I identified for the formation of this network: the radicalization of religious reformers in the context of inter-sectoral tensions.

There is a long-standing and perhaps unresolvable debate in the social sciences over the relative importance of social structures of various kinds versus that of human agency (and "free will"). Probably the most judicious position is to acknowledge the intricate ways in which structures and agency are intertwined in practice in complex ways.[24] If anything, the various iterations of long-distance advocacy throughout several centuries give a strong sense of this complex intertwining of human actions and the larger structural contexts in which these actions occur. Still, on the background of the important, far-reaching and influential structural transformations in the early modern period, there is one human-centered "agentic" factor that stands out: the importance of religious commitment and religious reformers as the main drivers in the complex and historically contingent processes that, over the centuries, led to the crystallization of distinctively modern forms of political action focused on distant strangers. Thus, on the one hand, the Philadelphia Quaker reformers were "pushed" toward assembling a socially and denominationally inclusive network of supporters by the political realities of the British Empire. On the other hand, we cannot understand the subsequent growth of this network without taking into account the persisting deep religious commitment of the initial core of abolitionist reformers.

To paraphrase George Eliot: a historically contingent concatenation of seemingly "unhistoric" acts and their "diffusive" influence is an important reason not only for the "growing good of the world," but also that we have today at our disposal a set of idioms for understanding and interpreting the suffering and needs of distant strangers and – perhaps more importantly – standardized "technologies" for political action directed toward them. Even more generally, the acknowledgment of the historical contingency of these developments adds an interesting perspective to the larger normative debate about the relationship between morality and modernity.

Why and how we care for culturally and geographically distant strangers has been an important focus of this ongoing debate. There are those who argue that modernity and the forces of increasing political, economic, and cultural interdependence make individuals more attuned to their moral interdependence with the rest of the world. A disillusioned view argues, on the other hand, that despite these increasing interdependencies, we fail to adequately

---

[24] A position articulated, for example, in various ways in Pierre Bourdieu, *Outline of a Theory of Practice* (Cambridge: Cambridge University Press, 1977); Anthony Giddens, *The Constitution of Society: Outline of the Theory of Structuration* (Berkeley: University of California Press, 1984); William H. Sewell, Jr., "A Theory of Structure: Duality, Agency, and Transformation," *American Journal of Sociology* 98, no. 1 (1992).

care for distant strangers.[25] These debates are reiterations of a disagreement foundational of social science: the question if modernity is morally beneficial or not. Even as they worked to establish the basics of social science inquiry, the "fathers" of the canon felt compelled to deliver a normative verdict of the social transformations they witnessed and tried to understand analytically. And although, for example, Adam Smith and Émile Durkheim were attuned to the beneficial potential of modern social organization, Karl Marx and Max Weber remained deeply ambivalent about the increasing social divisions, unfairness, and oppression that modernity brought with itself.[26]

What exactly do the developments outlined in this book contribute to this debate? The history of long-distance advocacy in its "early" centuries tends to suggest a cautiously optimistic reading of the link between modernity and morality. We can see the outlines of an uneven and imperfect "moral globalization" that gradually gives more people the tools to engage with distant issues and with the fate of distant strangers. The very fact that such an institutionalized models of political engagement with their fate has been continuously available – while certainly not automatically activated or uniformly efficient – for centuries shows long-distance advocacy as an important ingredient of modernity, even if it has not attracted the scholarly attention lavished on other fundamental features of modernity, such as capitalism, nationalism, rationality, or imperialism (to name just a few). Yet these parallel trajectories of modernity and of practices of expanding moral engagement do not warrant the conclusion that modernity as such – or even a select structural feature of modernity – was the predominant force for the strengthening and expansion of moral considerability. The precarious historical contingency of the genesis of our institutionalized model of long-distance advocacy is perhaps the strongest argument for us to do our best and preserve this important yet inherently fragile legacy of our history.

---

[25] For a sample of different positions in the debates, see Jean Baudrillard, *The Illusion of the End* (Cambridge, UK: Polity Press, 1994); Boltanski, *Distant Suffering: Morality, Media and Politics*; Zygmunt Bauman, *Postmodern Ethics* (Oxford: Blackwell, 1993); de Swaan, "Widening Circles"; Arthur Kleinman and Joan Kleinman, "The Appeal of Experience; The Dismay of Images: Cultural Appropriations of Suffering in Our Times," *Daedalus* 125, no. 1 (1996); Susan D. Moeller, *Compassion Fatigue: How the Media Sell Disease, Famine, War, and Death* (New York: Routledge, 1999); John Silk, "Caring at a Distance," *Ethics, Place and Environment* 1, no. 2 (1998); Keith Tester, *Moral Culture* (London: SAGE, 1997).

[26] On the general debate of the moral valence of modernity, see Allan Silver, "Friendship in Commercial Society: Eighteenth-Century Social Theory and Modern Sociology," *American Journal of Sociology* 95, no. 6 (1990).

Bibliography

Abbott, Andrew. *Time Matters: On Theory and Method*. Chicago: University of Chicago Press, 2001.

Abernethy, David B. *The Dynamics of Global Dominance: European Overseas Empires 1415–1980*. New Haven: Yale University Press, 2000.

Alden, Dauril. "Black Robes versus White Settlers: The Struggle for 'Freedom of the Indians' in Colonial Brazil." In *Attitudes of Colonial Powers toward the American Indian*, edited by Howard Peckham and Charles Gibson. 19–45. Salt Lake City: University of Utah Press, 1969.

The Making of an Enterprise: The Society of Jesus in Portugal, Its Empire, and Beyond, 1540–1750. Stanford: Stanford University Press, 1996.

Alden, John R. "The Albany Congress and the Creation of the Indian Superintendencies." *The Mississippi Valley Historical Review* 27, no. 2 (1940): 193–210.

Allegro, James J. "'Increasing and Strengthening the Country': Law, Politics, and the Antislavery Movement in Early-Eighteenth-Century Massachusetts Bay." *New England Quarterly* 75, no. 1 (2002): 5–23.

Allen, William. *Life of William Allen, With Selections from His Correspondence*. Philadelphia: H. Longstreth, 1847.

Altamira, Rafael. "El texto de las Leyes de Burgos de 1512." *Revista de Historia de América* 4 (1938): 5–79.

Amato, Joseph A. *Victims and Values: A History and a Theory of Suffering*. New York: Praeger, 1990.

Amey, Basil. "Baptist Missionary Society Radicals." *Baptist Quarterly* 26, no. 8 (1976): 363–76.

Amussen, Susan Dwyer. *Caribbean Exchanges: Slavery and the Transformation of English Society, 1640–1700*. Chapel Hill: University of North Carolina Press, 2007.

Anderson, Fred. *The Crucible of War: The Seven Years' War and the Fate of Empire in British North America, 1754–1766*. New York: Alfred A. Knopf, 2000.

Andrés Gallego, José, and Jesús María García Añoveros. *La Iglesia y la esclavitud de los Negros*. Pamplona: Ediciones Universidad de Navarra, 2002.

Andrés Martín, Melquiades. "Evangelismo, humanismo, reforma y observancias en España (1450–1525)." *Missionalia hispanica* 23 (1966): 5–24.

Andrews, Kenneth T., and Bob Edwards. "Advocacy Organizations in the U.S. Political Process." *Annual Review of Sociology* 30, no. 1 (2004): 479–506.

Anesko, Michael. "So Discreet a Zeal: Slavery and the Anglican Church in Virginia, 1680–1730." *Virginia Magazine of History & Biography* 93, no. 3 (1985): 247–78.

Anner, Mark, and Peter Evans. "Building Bridges across a Double Divide: Alliances between US and Latin American Labour and NGOs." *Development in Practice* 14, nos. 1–2 (2004): 34–47.

Anstey, Roger. *The Atlantic Slave Trade and British Abolition, 1760–1810.* London: Macmillan, 1975.

"Religion and British Slave Emancipation." In *The Abolition of the Atlantic Slave Trade: Origins and Effects in Europe, Africa, and the Americas,* edited by David Eltis and James Walvin. 37–61. Madison: University of Wisconsin Press, 1981.

Aptheker, Herbert. "The Quakers and Negro Slavery." *The Journal of Negro History* 25, no. 3 (1940): 331–62.

Assadourian, Carlos Sempat. "Acerca del cambio en la naturaleza del dominio sobre las Indias: La mit'a minera del virrey Toledo, documentos de 1568–1571." *Anuario de Estudios Americanos* 46 (1989): 3–70.

"The Colonial Economy: The Transfer of the European System of Production to New Spain and Peru." *Journal of Latin American Studies* 24 Supplement (1992): 55–68.

"Fray Alonso de Maldonado: La política indiana, el estado de damnación del Rey Católico y la Inquisición." *Historia Mexicana* 38, no. 4 (1989): 623–61.

"Fray Bartolomé de Las Casas obispo: La naturaleza miserable de las naciones Indianas y el derecho de la iglesia. Un escrito de 1545." *Historia Mexicana* 40, no. 3 (1991): 387–451.

"Hacia la *Sublimis Deus*: Las discordias entre los dominicos indianos y el enfrentamiento del franciscano padre Tastera con el padre Betanzos." *Historia Mexicana* 47, no. 3 (1998): 465–536.

"Las rentas reales, el buen gobierno y la hacienda de Dios: El parecer de 1568 de Fray Francisco de Morales sobre la reformación de las Indias temporal y espiritual." *Historica* 9, no. 1 (1985): 75–130.

"Memoriales de Fray Gerónimo de Mendieta." *Historia Mexicana* 37, no. 3 (1988): 357–422.

Transiciones hacia el Sistema Colonial Andino. Lima: IEP, 1994.

Aznar Vallejo, Eduardo. "The Conquest of the Canary Islands." In *Implicit Understandings: Observing, Reporting, and Reflecting on the Encounters between Europeans and Other Peoples in the Early Modern Era,* edited by Stuart B. Schwartz. 134–56. Cambridge: Cambridge University Press, 1994.

Baker, Frank. "The Origins, Character, and Influence of John Wesley's Thoughts Upon Slavery." *Methodist History* 22, no. 2 (1984): 75–86.

Bakewell, Peter. "La maduración del gobierno del Perú en la década de 1560." *Historia Mexicana* 39, no. 1 (1989): 41–70.

Bank, Andrew. "Losing Faith in the Civilizing Mission: The Premature Decline of Humanitarian Liberalism at the Cape, 1840–60." In *Empire and Others: British*

Encounters with Indigenous Peoples, 1600–1850, edited by Martin Daunton and Rick Halpern. 364–83. London: UCL Press, 1999.

Baptist Church Northamptonshire Association. *The Nature and Importance of Family and Closet Religion, Considered in a Circular Letter from the Baptist Ministers and Messengers, Assembled at Leicester, May 29, 30, and 31, 1787*. Northampton: T. Dicey and Co., 1787.

Barker, Anthony J. *Captain Charles Stuart: Anglo-American Abolitionist*. Baton Rouge: Louisiana State University Press, 1986.

Bartlett, Robert. *The Making of Europe: Conquest, Colonization, and Cultural Change, 950–1350*. London: Allen Lane, 1993.

Battista, Andrew. *The Revival of Labor Liberalism*. Urbana: University of Illinois Press, 2008.

Baudot, Georges. "L'institution de la dîme pour les Indiens du Mexique. Remarques et documents." *Mélanges de la Casa de Velázquez* 1 (1965): 167–221.

Baudrillard, Jean. *The Illusion of the End*. Cambridge: Polity Press, 1994.

Bauman, Zygmunt. *Postmodern Ethics*. Oxford: Blackwell, 1993.

Bégin, Natalie. "Kontakte zwischen Gewerkschaften in Ost und West: Die Auswirkungen von 'Solidarnosc' in Deutschland und Frankreich." *Archiv für Sozialgeschichte* **45** (2005): 293–324.

Bender, Thomas, ed. *The Antislavery Debate: Capitalism and Abolitionism as a Problem in Historical Interpretation*. Berkeley: University of California Press, 1992.

Benezet, Anthony. *A Caution and Warning to Great Britain and Her Colonies, in a Short Representation of the Calamitous State of the Enslaved Negroes in the British Dominions*. Philadelphia: Henry Miller, 1766.

Observations on the Inslaving, Importing and Purchasing of Negroes. 2nd ed. Germantown Pa: Christopher Sower, 1760.

A Short Account of That Part of Africa, Inhabited by the Negroes. Philadelphia: W. Dunlap, 1762.

Bénot, Yves. *La démence coloniale sous Napoléon*. Paris: Editions La Découverte, 1992.

Benz, Ernst. *Ecclesia spiritualis: Kirchenidee und Geschichtstheologie der franziskanischen Reformation*. Stuttgart: W. Kohlhammer, 1934.

Berger, Peter L. *The Sacred Canopy: Elements of a Sociological Theory of Religion*. Garden City, NY: Doubleday, 1967.

Berlin, Ira. *Many Thousands Gone: The First Two Centuries of Slavery in North America*. Cambridge, MA: Belknap Press, 1998.

Beuchot, Mauricio. "Fray Juan Ramírez, O.P., y sus escritos en contra de la esclavitud de los Indios (1595)." In *Dominicos en Mesoamérica: 500 años*. 163–72. México, D.F.: Provincia Santiago de México, 1992.

Biermann, Benno M. "Die ersten Dominikaner in Amerika." *Missionswissenschaft und Religionswissenschaft* **32** (1947/48): 57–65, 107–21.

Bireley, Robert. *The Refashioning of Catholicism, 1450–1700: A Reassessment of the Counter Reformation*. Washington, DC: Catholic University of America Press, 1999.

Blackburn, Robin. *The Making of New World Slavery: From the Baroque to the Modern, 1492–1800*. London: Verso, 1997.

The Overthrow of Colonial Slavery, 1776–1848. London: Verso, 1988.

Blanc, Robert. *Un pasteur du temps des Lumières: Benjamin-Sigismond Frossard (1754–1830)*. Paris: Champion, 2000.

Blanck, Emily. "Seventeen Eighty-Three: The Turning Point in the Law of Slavery and Freedom in Massachusetts." *The New England Quarterly* 75, no. 1 (2002): 24–51.

Blondet, Claire. "Quand les 'terroristes' font le procès du colonialisme esclavagiste les thermidoriens organisent son oubli." In *Périssent les colonies plutôt qu'un principe! Contributions à l'histoire de l'abolition de l'esclavage, 1789–1804*, edited by Florence Gauthier. 43–65. Paris: Société des études robespierristes, 2002.

Blum, Lawrence. "Compassion." In *Explaining Emotions*, edited by Amélie Oksenberg Rorty. 507–17. Berkeley: University of California Press, 1980.

Bocchini Camaiani, Bruna. "Il papato e il nuovo mondo: A proposito di una edizione di fonti." *Cristianesimo nella Storia* 16, no. 3 (1995): 521–52.

Bockelman, Wayne L. and Owen S. Ireland. "The Internal Revolution in Pennsylvania: An Ethnic-Religious Interpretation." *Pennsylvania History* 41, no. 2 (1974): 125–59.

Bolland, O. Nigel. "Colonization and Slavery in Central America." *Slavery & Abolition* 15, no. 2 (1994): 11–25.

Bolt, Christine. *The Anti-Slavery Movement and Reconstruction: A Study in Anglo-American Co-Operation, 1833–77*. London: Oxford University Press, 1969.

Boltanski, Luc. *Distant Suffering: Morality, Media and Politics*. Cambridge: Cambridge University Press, 1999.

Boockmann, Hartmut. "Bemerkungen zu den frühen Urkunden über die Mission und Unterwerfung der Prussen." In *Die Ritterorden zwischen geistlicher und weltlicher Macht im Mittelalter*, edited by Zenon Hubert Nowak. 45–56. Torun: Uniwersytet Mikolaja Kopernika, 1990.

"Die Freiheit der Prußen im 13. Jahrhundert." In *Die Abendländische Freiheit vom 10. zum 14. Jahrhundert: Der Wirkungszusammenhang von Idee und Wirklichkeit im europäischen Vergleich*, edited by Johannes Fried. 287–306. Sigmaringen: Jan Thorbecke, 1991.

Borges, Pedro. "Posturas de los misioneros ante la duda indiana." *Corpus Hispanorum de Pace* 25 (1984): 597–630.

"Un reformador de Indias y de la Orden Franciscana bajo Felipe II: Alonso Maldonado de Buendía, O.F.M." *Archivo Ibero-Americano* 20–21, nos. 79, 80, 81 (1960/61): 281–337, 487–535, 53–97.

Bourdieu, Pierre. "Genesis and Structure of the Religious Field." *Comparative Social Research* 13 (1991): 1–44.

Outline of a Theory of Practice. Cambridge: Cambridge Univesity Press, 1977.

Bowden, Witt. "The Influence of the Manufacturers on Some of the Early Policies of William Pitt." *The American Historical Review* 29, no. 4 (1924): 655–74.

Bowen, H. V. *Revenue and Reform: The Indian Problem in British Politics, 1757–1773*. New York: Cambridge University Press, 1991.

Bradburn, Samuel. *An Address to the People Called Methodists Concerning the Evil of Encouraging the Slave Trade*. 4th ed. London: G. Paramore, 1792.

Bradley, Ian. "James Ramsay and the Slave Trade." *History Today* 22, no. 12 (1972): 866–72.

Bradley, James E. *Popular Politics and the American Revolution in England: Petitions, the Crown, and Public Opinion*. Macon, GA: Mercer, 1986.

Brady, Thomas A. Jr. "The Rise of Merchant Empires, 1400–1700: A European Counterpoint." In *The Political Economy of Merchant Empires*, edited by James D. Tracy. 117–61. Cambridge: Cambridge University Press, 1991.

Braithwaite, William C. *The Beginnings of Quakerism*. 2d ed. Cambridge: Cambridge University Press, 1955 (1912).

Breathett, George. "Religious Protectionism and the Slave in Haiti." *The Catholic Historical Review* 55, no. 1 (1969): 26–39.

Brecht, Martin, ed. *Der Pietismus vom siebzehnten bis zum frühen achtezehnten Jahrhundert*. Göttingen: Vandenhoeck and Ruprecht, 1993.

Breen, T. H. *The Marketplace of Revolution: How Consumer Politics Shaped American Independence*. Oxford: Oxford University Press, 2004.

Briggs, John H. Y. "Baptists and the Campaign to Abolish the Slave Trade." *Baptist Quarterly* 42, no. 4 (2007): 260–83.

Brookes, George S. *Friend Anthony Benezet*. Philadelphia: University of Pennsylvania Press, 1937.

Brown, Christopher Leslie. *Moral Capital: Foundations of British Abolitionism*. Chapel Hill: University of North Carolina Press, 2006.

Brown, Ira V. "Pennsylvania's Antislavery Pioneers: 1688–1776." *Pennsylvania History* 55, no. 2 (1988): 59–77.

Bruns, Roger. *Am I Not a Man and a Brother: The Antislavery Crusade of Revolutionary America, 1688–1788*. New York: Chelsea House, 1976.

Budros, Art. "Explaining the First Emancipation: Social Movements and Abolition in the U.S. North, 1776–1804." *Mobilization* 16, no. 4 (2011): 439–54.

Bullough, Donald A. "Was There a Carolingian Anti-War Movement?". *Early Medieval Europe* 12, no. 4 (2003): 365–76.

Burrus, Ernest J. "Alonso de la Vera Cruz (†1584), Pioneer Defender of the American Indians." *Catholic Historical Review* 70, no. 4 (1984): 531–46.

Bush, Jonathan A. "Free to Enslave: The Foundations of Colonial American Slave Law." *Yale Journal of Law & the Humanities* 5 (1993): 417–70.

Camenzind, Krista. "From the Holy Experiment to the Paxton Boys: Violence, Manhood, and Race in Pennsylvania during the Seven Years' War." Ph.D. Dissertation, University of California San Diego, 2003.

Campbell, Ted. *The Religion of the Heart: A Study of European Religious Life in the Seventeenth and Eighteenth Centuries*. Columbia: University of South Carolina Press, 1991.

Cantù, Francisca. "Potere vescovile, ministero pastorael ed immunità ecclesisastica in B. de Las Casas: Note per una storia dei rapporti tra stato e chiesa nel Cinquecento." *Annuario dell'Istituto Storico Italiano per l'Età Moderna e Contemporanea* 29 (1978): 534–64.

Capela, José. "Abolición y abolicionismo en Portugal y sus colonias." In *Esclavitud y derechos humanos: La lucha por la libertad del negro en el siglo XIX*, edited by Francisco de Solano and Agustín Guimerá Ravina. 577–603. Madrid: Consejo Superior de Investigaciones Científicas, 1990.

Escravatura: A empresa de saque, o abolicionismo (1810–1875). Porto: Afrontamento, 1974.

Carey, Brycchan. "Inventing a Culture of Anti-Slavery: Pennsylvanian Quakers and the Germantown Protest of 1688." In *Imagining Transatlantic Slavery*, edited by Cora

Kaplan and John Oldfield. 17–32. Basingstoke, England: Palgrave Macmillan, 2010.

"'The Power that Giveth Liberty and Freedom': The Barbadian Origins of Quaker Antislavery Rhetoric, 1657–76." *ARIEL* 38, no. 1 (2007): 27–48.

Carey, Daniel. "Sugar, Colonialism and the Critique of Slavery: Thomas Tryon in Barbados." In *Interpreting Colonialism*, edited by Bryon R. Wells and Philip Steward. 303–21. Oxford: Voltaire Foundation, 2004.

Carroll, Kenneth L. "American Quakers and Their London Lobby." *Quaker History* 70, no. 1 (1981): 22–39.

"George Fox and Slavery." *Quaker History* 86, no. 2 (1997): 16–25.

"A Look at the 'Quaker Revival of 1756'." *Quaker History* 65, no. 2 (1976): 63–80.

"William Southeby, Early Quaker Antislavery Writer." *Pennsylvania Magazine of History and Biography* 89, no. 4 (1965): 416.

Casas, Bartolomé de las. *An Account, Much Abbreviated, of the Destruction of the Indies, with Related Texts.* Indianapolis: Hackett Publishing, 2003.

Historia de las Indias. Critical ed. Madrid: Alianza, 1994 (1527).

History of the Indies. Translated by Andrée Collard. New York: Harper and Row, 1971 (1527).

Catherall, G. A. "Thomas Burchell, Gentle Rebel." *Baptist Quarterly* 21, no. 8 (1966): 349–63.

Ceadel, Martin. *The Origins of War Prevention: The British Peace Movement and International Relations, 1730–1854.* Oxford: Clarendon Press, 1996.

Chamberlain, Robert S. "Castilian Backgrounds of the Repartimiento-Encomienda." *Contributions to American Anthropology and History* 25 (1939): 19–66.

Charlton, K. "James Cropper and Liverpool's Contribution to the Anti-Slavery Movement." *Transactions of the Historic Society of Lancashire and Cheshire* 123 (1971): 57–80.

Charnovitz, Steve. "The Emergence of Democratic Participation in Global Governance (Paris, 1919)." *Indiana Journal of Global Legal Studies* 10, no. 1 (2003): 45–77.

"Two Centuries of Participation: NGOs and International Governance." *Michigan Journal of International Law* 18 (1997): 183–286.

Christiaens, Kim, Idesbald Goddeeris, and Wouter Goedertier. "Inspirées par le Sud? Les mobilisations transnationales Est-Ouest pendant la guerre froide." *Vingtième Siècle* 109 (2011): 155–68.

Churchman, John. *An Account of the Gospel Labours, and Christian Experiences of a Faithful Minister of Christ, John Churchman, Late of Nottingham, in Pennsylvania, Deceased.* London: James Phillips, 1781.

Clarence-Smith, William Gervase. "Église, nation et esclavage: Angole et Mozambique portugais, 1878–1913." In *Abolir l'esclavage: Un réformisme à l'épreuve (France, Portugal, Suisse, XVIIIe-XIXe siècles)*, edited by Olivier Pétré-Grenouilleau. 149–67. Rennes: Presses universitaires de Rennes, 2008.

Clark, Ann Marie. *Diplomacy of Conscience: Amnesty International and Changing Human Rights Norms.* Princeton, NJ: Princeton University Press, 2001.

Clarkson, Thomas. *History of the Rise, Progress, and Accomplishment of the Abolition of the African Slave Trade by the British Parliament.* London: J. W. Parker, 1839.

Clemens, Elisabeth S. "Organizational Form as Frame: Collective Identity and Political Strategy in the American Labor Movement, 1880–1920." In *Comparative*

Perspectives on Social Movements: Political Opportunities, Mobilizing Structures and Cultural Framings, edited by Doug McAdam, John D. McCarthy, and Mayer N. Zald. 205–26. Cambridge: Cambridge University Press, 1996.

Clemens, Elisabeth S. and James M. Cook. "Politics and Institutionalism: Explaining Durability and Change." *Annual Review of Sociology* 25 (1999): 441–66.

Cmiel, Kenneth. "The Emergence of Human Rights Politics in the United States." *Journal of American History* 86, no. 3 (1999): 1231–50.

"The Recent History of Human Rights." *American Historical Review* 109, no. 1 (2004): 117–35.

Cohen, Charles L. "The Colonization of British North America as an Episode in the History of Christianity." *Church History* 72, no. 3 (2003): 553–68.

Cohen, Joshua, ed. *For Love of Country: Debating the Limits of Patriotism*. Boston: Beacon Press, 1996.

Cohen, William B. *The French Encounter with Africans: White Response to Blacks, 1530–1880*. Bloomington: Indiana University Press, 1980.

Collinson, Patrick. *The Elizabethan Puritan Movement*. London: Methuen, 1967.

Colmeiro, Manuel, ed. *Cortes de los antiguos reinos de León y de Castilla*, Vol. 5. Madrid: Rivadeneyra, 1903.

Comaroff, John L. "Images of Empire, Contests of Conscience: Models of Colonial Domination in South Africa." *American Ethnologist* 16, no. 4 (1989): 661–85.

Compton, L. A. "Josiah Wedgwood and the Slave Trade: A Wider View." *Northern Ceramic Society Newsletter* 100 (1995): 50–69.

Conrad, Robert. *The Destruction of Brazilian Slavery, 1850–1888*. Berkeley: University of California Press, 1972.

Considerations Addressed to Professors of Christianity of Every Denomination on the Impropriety of Consuming West-India Sugar & Rum, As Produced by the Oppressive Labour of Slaves. s.l.: s.n., 1792.

Cook, Noble David. *Born to Die: Disease and New World Conquest, 1492–1650*. Cambridge: Cambridge University Press, 1998.

"Sickness, Starvation, and Death in Early Hispaniola." *Journal of Interdisciplinary History* 32, no. 3 (2002): 349–86.

Cooper, Frederick. *Colonialism in Question: Theory, Knowledge, History*. Berkeley: University of California Press, 2005.

Cooper, Thomas. *Considerations on the Slave Trade, and the Consumption of West Indian Produce*. London: Darton and Harvey, 1791.

Corwin, Arthur F. *Spain and the Abolition of Slavery in Cuba, 1817–1886*. Austin: University of Texas Press, 1967.

Costa, Emilia Viotti da. "The Portuguese-African Slave Trade: A Lesson in Colonialism." *Latin American Perspectives* 12, no. 1 (1985): 41–61.

Craton, Michael. *Empire, Enslavement, and Freedom in the Caribbean*. Kingston: Ian Randle, 1997.

Crawford, Michael J. *The Having of Negroes is Become a Burden: The Quaker Struggle to Free Slaves in Revolutionary North Carolina*. Gainesville: University Press of Florida, 2010.

Culverson, Donald R. *Contesting Apartheid: U.S. Activism, 1960–1987*. Westview Press, 1999.

Curtin, Philip D. *The Rise and Fall of the Plantation Complex: Essays in Atlantic History*. Cambridge: Cambridge University Press, 1990.

Cushing, John D. "The Cushing Court and the Abolition of Slavery in Massachusetts: More Notes on the 'Quock Walker Case'." *The American Journal of Legal History* 5, no. 2 (1961): 118–44.

Dagger, Richard. *Civic Virtues: Rights, Citizenship, and Republican Liberalism.* New York: Oxford University Press, 1997.

Daniel, E. Randolph. "Apocalyptic Conversion: The Joachite Alternative to the Crusades." *Traditio* 25 (1969): 127–54.

The Franciscan Concept of Mission in the High Middle Ages. Lexington: University Press of Kentucky, 1975.

Daniel, W. Harrison. "Southern Presbyterians and the Negro in the Early National Period." *Journal of Negro History* 58, no. 3 (1973): 291–312.

David, Thomas and Janick Marina Schaufelbuehl. "L'antiesclavagisme en Suisse." In *La Suisse et l'esclavage des noirs.* 107–54. Lausanne: Editions Antipodes, 2005.

"Swiss Conservatives and the Struggle for the Abolition of Slavery at the End of the Nineteenth Century." *Itinerario* 34, no. 2 (2010): 87–103.

Davis, David Brion. *From Homicide to Slavery: Studies in American Culture.* New York: Oxford University Press, 1986.

Inhuman Bondage: The Rise and Fall of Slavery in the New World. New York: Oxford University Press, 2006.

The Problem of Slavery in the Age of Revolution, 1770–1823. New York: Oxford University Press, (1975) 1999.

The Problem of Slavery in Western Culture. Ithaca, NY: Cornell University Press, 1966.

Slavery and Human Progress. New York: Oxford University Press, 1984.

De Botton, Alain. *The Pleasures and Sorrows of Work.* New York: Pantheon Books, 2009.

Debien, Gabriel. "Gens de couleur libres et colons de Saint-Domingue devant la Constituante (1789 – mars 1790)." *Revue d'histoire de l'Amérique française* 4, nos. 2, 3, 4 (1950–1951): 211–32, 398–426, 530–49.

"Le Club des Colons de La Rochelle (Septembre 1789–Octobre 1790)." *Revue d'Histoire des Colonies* 43, no. 3–4 (1956): 338–68.

Les colons de Saint-Domingue et la Révolution: Essai sur le club Massiac (août 1789-août 1792). Paris: Armand Colin, 1953.

Delgado, Mariano. "Alonso Sánchez SJ und José de Acosta SJ in der Kontroverse über die Conquista und Evangelisation Chinas am Ende des 16. Jahrhunderts." *Zeitschrift für Missionswissenschaft und Religionswissenschaft* 90, no. 3–4 (2006): 196–209.

Della Porta, Donatella and Hanspeter Kriesi. "Social Movements in a Globalizing World: An Introduction." In *Social Movements in a Globalizing World*, edited by Donatella Della Porta, Hanspeter Kriesi, and Dieter Rucht. 3–22. New York: St. Martin's Press, 1999.

Dickinson, H. T. *The Politics of the People in Eighteenth-Century Britain.* London: Macmillan, 1995.

DiGiacomantonio, William C. "'For the Gratification of a Volunteering Society': Antislavery and Pressure Group Politics in the First Federal Congress." *Journal of the Early Republic* 15, no. 2 (1995): 169–97.

Ditchfield, G. M. "The Campaign in Lancashire and Cheshire for the Repeal of the Test and Corporation Acts, 1787–1790." *Transactions of the Historic Society of Lancashire and Cheshire* 126, 109–138 (1977).

"Manchester College and Anti-Slavery." In *Truth, Liberty, Religion: Essays Celebrating Two Hundred Years of Manchester College*, edited by Barbara Smith. 185–224. Oxford: Manchester College, 1986.

"Repeal, Abolition, and Reform: A Study in the Interaction of Reforming Movements in the Parliament of 1790–6." In *Anti-slavery, Religion, and Reform: Essays in Memory of Roger Anstey*, edited by Christine Bolt and Seymour Drescher. 101–18. Folkestone: Dawson, 1980.

Dobbin, Frank R. "Cultural Models of Organization: The Social Construction of Rational Organizing Principles." In *The Sociology of Culture: Emerging Theoretical Perspectives*, edited by Diana Crane. 117–41. Oxford: Blackwell, 1994.

Dorigny, Marcel. "The Abbé Grégoire and the *Société des Amis des Noirs*." In *The Abbé Grégoire and His World*, edited by Jeremy D. Popkin and Richard H. Popkin. 27–39. Dordrecht: Kluwer, 2000.

"Mirabeau and the Société des Amis des Noirs: Which Way to Abolish Slavery?" In *The Abolitions of Slavery: From Léger Félicité Sonthonax to Victor Schoelcher, 1793, 1794, 1848*, edited by Marcel Dorigny. 121–32. New York: Berghahn Books, 2003.

Dorigny, Marcel and Bernard Gainot. *La Société des Amis des Noirs, 1788–1799: Contribution a l'histoire de l'abolition de l'esclavage*. Paris: Éditions UNESCO, 1998.

Drake, Thomas E. *Quakers and Slavery in America*. New Haven, CT: Yale University Press, 1950.

Drescher, Seymour. *Abolition: A History of Slavery and Antislavery*. Cambridge: Cambridge University Press, 2009.

Capitalism and Antislavery: British Mobilization in Comparative Perspective. New York: Oxford University Press, 1987.

From Slavery to Freedom: Comparative Studies in the Rise and Fall of Atlantic Slavery. Houndmills: Macmilllan, 1999.

"Manumission in a Society without Slave Law: Eighteenth Century England." *Slavery and Abolition* 10, no. 3 (1989): 85–101.

Dresser, Madge. *Slavery Obscured: The Social History of the Slave Trade in an English Provincial Port*. London: Continuum, 2001.

Du Bois, W. E. B. *The Suppression of the African Slave-trade to the United States of America, 1638–1870*. Longmans, Green and Company, 1904.

Dunn, Richard S. *Sugar and Slaves: The Rise of the Planter Class in the English West Indies, 1624–1713*. Chapel Hill: University of North Carolina Press, 1972.

Dussel, Enrique. *Les évêques hispano-américains: Défenseurs et évangélisateurs de l'Indien, 1504–1620*. Wiesbaden: Franz Steiner, 1970.

Eberly, Wayne J. "The Pennsylvania Abolition Society, 1775–1830." Ph.D. Dissertation, Pennsylvania State University, 1973.

Edmundson, William. *A Journal of the Life, Travels, Sufferings and Labour of Love in the Work of the Ministry of that Worthy Elder and Faithful Servant of Jesus Christ, William Edmundson*. 2nd ed. London: Mary Hinde, 1774.

Egerton, Douglas R. *Death or Liberty: African Americans and Revolutionary America*. Oxford: Oxford University Press, 2009.

Ehrman, Bart D. *God's Problem: How the Bible Fails to Answer Our Most Important Question – Why We Suffer*. HarperCollins, 2009.

Ekman, Ernst. "Sweden, the Slave Trade and Slavery, 1784–1847." In *La Traite des Noirs par l'Atlantique: Nouvelles approches*. 221–31. Paris: Société française d'histoire d'outre-mer, 1976.

Ellery, Eloise. *Brissot de Warville: A Study in the History of the French Revolution*. Boston: Houghton Mifflin, 1915.

Elliott, J. H. *Imperial Spain, 1469–1716*. New York: Penguin Books, 1963.

"The Spanish Conquest and Settlement of America." In *The Cambridge History of Latin America*, Vol. 1: *Colonial Latin America*, edited by Leslie Bethell. 149–206. Cambridge: Cambridge University Press, 1984.

Eltis, David. *The Rise of African Slavery in the Americas*. Cambridge: Cambridge University Press, 2000.

Emsley, Clive. "Repression, 'Terror' and the Rule of Law in England during the Decade of the French Revolution." *English Historical Review* 100, no. 397 (Oct. 1985): 801–25.

Evans, Julie, Patricia Grimshaw, David Philips, and Shurlee Swain. *Equal Subjects, Unequal Rights: Indigenous Peoples in British Settler Colonies, 1830–1910*. Manchester, UK: Manchester University Press, 2003.

Evans, Peter. "Fighting Marginalization with Transnational Networks: Counter-Hegemonic Globalization." *Contemporary Sociology* 29, no. 1 (2000): 230–41.

Evennett, H. Outram. "The New Orders." In *The New Cambridge Modern History*, Vol. 2: *The Reformation, 1520–1559*, edited by G. R. Elton. 313–38. Cambridge: Cambridge University Press, 1990.

The Spirit of the Counter-Reformation. Cambridge: Cambridge University Press, 1968.

Falcon, Francisco C. and Fernando A. Novais. "A extinção de escravatura africana em Portugal no quadro da política económica Pombalina." In *Anais do VI Simposio nacional dos professores universitarios de historia*. 405–31. São Paulo: [s.n.], 1973.

Fehrenbacher, Don E. *The Slaveholding Republic: An Account of the United States Government's Relations to Slavery*. Oxford: Oxford University Press, 2001.

Fernández-Armesto, Felipe. *Before Columbus: Exploration and Colonization from the Mediterranean to the Atlantic, 1229–1492*. Philadelphia: University of Pennsylvania Press, 1987.

Filler, Louis. *The Crusade against Slavery, 1830–1860*. New York: Harper, 1960.

Finkelman, Paul. *Slavery and the Founders: Race and Liberty in the Age of Jefferson*. 2nd ed. Armonk, NY: M. E. Sharpe, 2001.

Fladeland, Betty. "Abolitionist Pressures on the Concert of Europe, 1814–1822." *Journal of Modern History* 38, no. 4 (1966): 355–73.

Men and Brothers: Anglo-American Antislavery Cooperation. Urbana: University of Illinois Press, 1972.

Fogel, Robert William. *Without Consent or Contract: The Rise and Fall of American Slavery*. New York: Norton, 1989.

Fox, William. *An Address to the People of Great Britain, on the Propriety of Abstaining from West India Sugar & Rum*. Birmingham: s.n., 1791.

Fradera, Josep M. "Limitaciones históricas del abolicionismo catalán." In *Esclavitud y derechos humanos: La lucha por la libertad del negro en el siglo XIX*, edited by Francisco de Solano and Agustín Guimerá Ravina. 125–33. Madrid: Consejo Superior de Investigaciones Científicas, 1990.

Fretz, J. Herbert. "The Germantown Anti-Slavery Petition of 1688." *Mennonite Quarterly Review* 33, no. 1 (1959): 42–59.

Freund, W. M. "The Career of Johannes Theodorus Van Der Kemp and His Role in the History of South Africa." *Tijdschrift voor Geschiedenis* 86, no. 3 (1973): 376–80.

Friede, Juan. *Vida y luchas de don Juan del Valle, primer obispo de Popayán y protector de indios.* Popayán: Editorial Universidad, 1961.

Frostin, Charles. "Méthodologie missionnaire et sentiment religieux en Amérique française aux 17e et 18e siècles: Le cas de Saint-Domingue." *Cahiers d'Histoire* 24, no. 1 (1979): 19–43.

Fulbrook, Mary. *Piety and Politics: Religion and the Rise of Absolutism in England, Württemberg and Prussia.* Cambridge: Cambridge University Press, 1983.

Furneaux, Robin. *William Wilberforce.* London: Hamilton, 1974.

Gallagher, J. "Fowell Buxton and the New African Policy, 1838–1842." *Cambridge Historical Journal* 10, no. 1 (1950): 36–58.

Galston, William A. "Cosmopolitan Altruism." In *Altruism*, edited by Ellen Frankel Paul, Fred D. Miller, Jr. and Jeffrey Paul. 118–34. Cambridge: Cambridge University Press, 1993.

Gamson, William A. *The Strategy of Social Protest.* Chicago: Dorsey Press, 1975.

Garrigus, John D. "Opportunist Or Patriot? Julien Raimond (1744–1801) and the Haitian Revolution." *Slavery & Abolition* 28, no. 1 (2007): 1–21.

Gauthier, Florence. *L'aristocratie de l'épiderme: Le combat de la Société des citoyens de couleur, 1789–1791.* Paris: CNRS, 2007.

"The Role of the Saint-Domingue Deputation in the Abolition of Slavery." In *The Abolitions of Slavery: From Léger Félicité Sonthonax to Victor Schoelcher, 1793, 1794, 1848*, edited by Marcel Dorigny. 167–79. New York: Berghahn Books, 2003.

Geggus, David. "Racial Equality, Slavery, and Colonial Secession During the Constituent Assembly." *American Historical Review* 94, no. 5 (1989): 1290–308.

Gerbner, Katharine. "Antislavery in Print." *Early American Studies* 9, no. 3 (2011): 552–75.

"The Ultimate Sin: Christianising Slaves in Barbados in the Seventeenth Century." *Slavery & Abolition* 31, no. 1 (2010): 57–73.

Gerzina, Gretchen. *Black London: Life before Emancipation.* New Brunswick, NJ: Rutgers University Press, 1995.

Gibson, Charles. *The Aztecs under Spanish Rule: A History of the Indians of the Valley of Mexico, 1519–1810.* Stanford: Stanford University Press, 1964.

Gibson, Ralph. *A Social History of French Catholicism, 1789–1914.* London: Routledge, 1989.

Giddens, Anthony. *The Constitution of Society: Outline of the Theory of Structuration.* Berkeley: University of California Press, 1984.

Gifford, Ronald M., II. "George Thompson and Trans-Atlantic Antislavery, 1831–1865." Ph.D. Dissertation, Indiana University, 2000.

Giménez Fernández, Manuel. "Fray Bartolomé de Las Casas: A Biographical Sketch." In *Bartolomé de las Casas in History: Toward an Understanding of the Man and His Work*, edited by Juan Friede and Benjamin Keen. 67–125. DeKalb: Northern Illinois University Press, 1971.

Girardin, Benoit. "Le mouvement anti-esclavagiste genevois de 1860 a 1900 et son echo en Suisse." *Geneve-Afrique* 22, no. 2 (1984): 13–36.

Glasson, Travis. "'Baptism doth not bestow Freedom': Missionary Anglicanism, Slavery, and the Yorke-Talbot Opinion, 1701–30." *William & Mary Quarterly* 67, no. 2 (2010): 279–318.

Mastering Christianity: Missionary Anglicanism and Slavery in the Atlantic World. New York: Oxford University Press, 2012.

Godechot, J. "DeJoly et les gens de couleur libres." *Annales historiques de la Révolution Française* 23, no. 121 (1951): 48–61.

Godwyn, Morgan. *The Negro's & Indians Advocate, Suing for Their Admission into the Church.* London: J. D., 1680.

Goedertier, Wouter. "The Quest for Transnational Authority, the Anti-Apartheid Movements of the European Community." *Revue Belge de Philologie & d'Histoire* 89, no. 3/4 (2011): 1249–76.

Goldman, Alan H. "The Moral Significance of National Boundaries." *Midwest Studies in Philosophy* 7 (1982): 437–53.

Goldwert, Marvin. "La lucha por la perpetuidad de las encomiendas en el Perú virreinal, 1550–1600." *Revista Histórica* 22 (1955–56): 336–60.

Gómez Canedo, Lino. "Aspectos caracteristicos de la acción Franciscana en America." *Archivo Ibero-Americano* 48, no. 189–192 (1988): 441–72.

Góngora, Mario. *Studies in the Colonial History of Spanish America.* Cambridge: Cambridge University Press, 1975.

González Rodríguez, Jaime. "La Junta de Valladolid convocada por el Emperador." *Corpus Hispanorum de Pace* 25 (1984): 199–227.

"Los amigos franciscanos de Sepúlveda." *Archivo Ibero-Americano* 48, no. 189–192 (1988): 873–93.

Goodin, Robert. "What Is So Special About Our Fellow Countrymen?" *Ethics* 98 (1988): 663–86.

Goodwin, Albert. *The Friends of Liberty: The English Democratic Movement in the Age of the French Revolution.* London: Hutchinson, 1979.

Gradie, Charlotte M. "Discovering the Chichimecas." *The Americas* 51, no. 1 (1994): 67.

Gragg, Larry Dale. *The Quaker Community on Barbados: Challenging the Culture of the Planter Class.* Columbia: University of Missouri Press, 2009.

Grant, Kevin. *A Civilised Savagery: Britain and the New Slaveries in Africa, 1884–1926.* New York: Routledge, 2005.

Gray, Richard. *Black Christians and White Missionaries.* New Haven, CT: Yale University Press, 1990.

"Ingoli, the Collector of Portugal, the 'Gran Gusto' of Urban VIII and the Atlantic Slave trade." In *Ecclesiae memoria: Miscellanea in onore del R.P. Josef Metzler O.M.I., prefetto dell'Archivio segreto vaticano,* edited by Willi Henkel. 179–86. Rome: Herder, 1991.

"The Papacy and Africa in the Seventeenth Century." In *Il Cristianesimo nel mondo atlantico nel secolo XVII.* 283–305. Città del Vaticano: Libreria editrice vaticana, 1997.

Greene, Jack P. "Early Modern Southeastern North America and the Broader Atlantic and American Worlds." *Journal of Southern History* 73, no. 3 (2007): 525–38.

Imperatives, Behaviors, and Identities: Essays in Early American Cultural History. Charlottesville: University Press of Virginia, 1992.

Peripheries and Center: Constitutional Development in the Extended Polities of the British Empire and the United States, 1607–1788. Athens: University of Georgia Press, 1986.

"'A Posture of Hostility': A Reconsideration of Some Aspects of the Origins of the American Revolution." *Proceedings of the American Antiquarian Society* 87, no. 1 (1977): 27–68.

Greenleaf, Richard E. *Zumárraga and the Mexican Inquisition, 1536–1543.* Washington: Academy of American Franciscan History, 1961.

Groh, John E. "Antonio Ruíz De Montoya and the Early Reductions in the Jesuit Province of Paraguay." *Catholic Historical Review* 56, no. 3 (1970): 501–33.

Gründer, Horst. "'Gott will es': Eine Kreuzzugsbewegung am Ende des 19. Jahrhunderts." *Geschichte in Wissenschaft und Unterricht* 28, no. 4 (1977): 210–24.

Guasco, Michael. "Settling with Slavery: Human Bondage in the Early Anglo-American World." In *Envisioning an English Empire: Jamestown and the Making of the North Atlantic World*, edited by Robert Appelbaum and John Wood Sweet. 236–53. Philadelphia: University of Pennsylvania Press, 2005.

"To 'Doe Some Good upon Their Countrymen': The Paradox of Indian Slavery in Early Anglo-America." *Journal of Social History* 41, no. 2 (Winter 2007): 389–411.

Guitar, Lynne. "No More Negotiation: Slavery and the Destabilization of Colonial Hispaniola's *Encomienda* System." *Revista/Review Interamericana* 29, no. 1 (1999): http://www.sg.inter.edu/revista-ciscla/volume29/.

Gusfield, Joseph R. "Social Movements and Social Change: Perspectives of Linearity and Fluidity." *Research in Social Movements, Conflict and Change* 4 (1981): 317–39.

Gutiérrez, Lucio. *Domingo de Salazar, O.P.: First Bishop of the Philippines, 1512–1594: A Study of His Life and Work.* Manila, Philippines: University of Santo Tomas, 2001.

Hacking, Ian. *The Social Construction of What?* Cambridge, MA: Harvard University Press, 1999.

Halpern, Jean-Claude. "The Revolutionary Festivals and the Abolition in Slavery in Year II." In *The Abolitions of Slavery : From Léger Félicité Sonthonax to Victor Schoelcher, 1793, 1794, 1848.* 155–66. New York: Berghahn Books, 2003.

Hamilton, Bernice. *Political Thought in Sixteenth-Century Spain.* Oxford: Clarendon Press, 1963.

Hanke, Lewis. *All Mankind is One: A Study of the Disputation Between Bartolomé de Las Casas and Juan Ginés de Sepúlveda in 1550 on the Intellectual and Religious Capacity of the American Indians.* DeKalb: Northern Illinois University Press, 1974.

The First Social Experiments in America: A Study in the Development of Spanish Indian Policy in the Sixteenth Century. Cambridge: Harvard University Press, 1935.

"Pope Paul III and the American Indians." *Harvard Theological Review* 30, no. 2 (1937): 65–102.

The Spanish Struggle for Justice in the Conquest of America. Dallas: Southern Methodist University Press, 2002 (1949).

Hardy, Charles O. *The Negro Question in the French Revolution.* Menasha, WI: George Banta, 1919.

Harkin, Michael E. "Introduction: Revitalization as History and Theory." In *Reassessing Revitalization Movements: Perspectives from North America and the Pacific*

Islands, edited by Michael E. Harkin. xv–xxxvi. Lincoln: University of Nebraska Press, 2004.

Harper, Steven Craig. *Promised Land: Penn's Holy Experiment, the Walking Purchase, and the Dispossession of Delawares, 1600–1763*. Bethlehem, PA: Lehigh University Press, 2006.

Harwood, Thomas F. "British Evangelical Abolitionism and American Churches in the 1830's." *Journal of Southern History* 28, no. 3 (1962): 287–306.

Haskell, Thomas L. "Capitalism and the Origins of the Humanitarian Sensibility, Part 1." In *The Antislavery Debate: Capitalism and Abolitionism as a Problem in Historical Interpretation*, edited by Thomas Bender. 107–35. Berkeley: University of California Press, 1992.

Haubert, Maxime. *L'Église et la défense des "Sauvages": Le Père Antoine Vieira au Brésil*. Brussels: Académie Royale des Sciences d'Outre-Mer, 1964.

Hermon-Belot, Rita. *L'abbé Grégoire, la politique et la vérité*. Paris: Seuil, 2000.

Hidalgo Nuchera, Patricio. "Esclavitud o liberación? El fracaso de las actitudes esclavistas de los conquistadores de Filipinas." *Revista Complutense de historia de América* 20 (1994): 61–74.

Las Polémicas Iglesia-Estado en las Filipinas: La posición de la Iglesia ante la Cobranza de los Tributos en las Encomiendas sin Doctrina y las Restituciones a Fines del s. XVI. Córdoba, Spain: Universidad de Córdoba, 1993.

Higgins, A. Pearce. "International Law and the Outer World." In *The Cambridge history of the British empire*, Vol. I: *The Old Empire from the Beginnings to 1783*, edited by J. Holland Rose, A. P. Newton, and E. A. Benians. 183–206. Cambridge: Cambridge University Press, 1929.

Hoare, Prince. *Memoirs of Granville Sharp, Esq*. London: Henry Colburn, 1828.

Hochschild, Adam. *Bury the Chains: Prophets and Rebels in the Fight to Free an Empire's Slaves*. Boston: Houghton Mifflin, 2005.

King Leopold's Ghost: A Story of Greed, Terror, and Heroism in Colonial Africa. Boston: Houghton Mifflin, 1998.

Höffner, Joseph. *Kolonialismus und Evangelium: Spanische Kolonialethik im Goldenen Zeitalter*. 2nd ed. Trier: Paulinus-Verlag, 1969.

Hofmann, Étienne. "Le Groupe de Coppet." In *Vaud sous l'Acte de Médiation, 1803–1813: La naissance d'un canton confédéré*, edited by Corinne Chuard. 363–67. Lausanne: Bibliothéque historique vaudoise, 2002.

Horle, Craig W. *The Quakers and the English Legal System, 1660–1688*. Philadelphia: University of Pennsylvania Press, 1988.

Hsia, R. Po-chia. "Mission und Konfessionalisierung in Übersee." In *Die katholische Konfessionalisierung : Wissenschaftliches Symposion der Gesellschaft zur Herausgabe des Corpus Catholicorum und des Vereins für Reformationsgeschichte, 1993*, edited by Wolfgang Reinhard and Heinz Schilling. 158–65. Münster: Aschendorff, 1995.

The World of Catholic Renewal, 1540–1770. 2nd ed. Cambridge: Cambridge University Press, 2005.

Hunt, E. M. "The Anti-Slave Trade Agitation in Manchester." *Transactions of the Lancashire and Cheshire Antiquarian Society* 79 (1977): 46–72.

Hunt, N. C. *Two Early Political Associations: The Quakers and the Dissenting Deputies in the Age of Sir Robert Walpole*. Oxford: Clarendon Press, 1961.

Hurbon, Laënnec. "The Church and Slavery in Eighteenth-Century Saint-Domingue." In *The Abolitions of Slavery: From Léger Félicité Sonthonax to Victor Schoelcher, 1793, 1794, 1848*, edited by Marcel Dorigny. 55–68. New York: Berghahn Books, 2003.

Hussey, Ronald D. "Text of the Laws of Burgos (1512–1513) Concerning the Treatment of the Indians." *Hispanic American Historical Review* 12, no. 3 (August 1932): 301–26.

Hutson, James H. *Pennsylvania Politics, 1746–1770: The Movement for Royal Government and its Consequences.* Princeton, NJ: Princeton University Press, 1972.

Hyslop, Beatrice Fry. *French Nationalism in 1789 according to the General Cahiers.* New York: Columbia University Press, 1934.

Ingle, H. Larry. *First Among Friends: George Fox and the Creation of Quakerism.* New York: Oxford University Press, 1994.

Ireland, Owen S. "The Crux of Politics: Religion and Party in Pennsylvania, 1778–1789." *William & Mary Quarterly* 42, no. 4 (1985): 453–75.

"The Ethnic-Religious Dimension of Pennsylvania Politics, 1778–1779." *William & Mary Quarterly* 30, no. 3 (1973): 423–48.

"Germans against Abolition: A Minority's View of Slavery in Revolutionary Pennsylvania." *Journal of Interdisciplinary History* 3, no. 4 (Spring 1973): 685–706.

Jackson, Harvey H. "Hugh Bryan and the Evangelical Movement in Colonial South Carolina." *William & Mary Quarterly* 43, no. 4 (1986): 594–614.

Jackson, Maurice. *Let This Voice Be Heard: Anthony Benezet, Father of Atlantic Abolitionism.* Philadelphia: University of Pennsylvania Press, 2009.

James, Sydney V. *A People among Peoples: Quaker Benevolence in Eighteenth-Century America.* Cambridge: Harvard University Press, 1963.

Janin, Joseph. *La religion aux colonies françaises sous l'Ancien Régime (de 1626 à la Révolution).* Paris: D'Auteuil, 1942.

Jasper, James M. *The Art of Moral Protest: Culture, Biography, and Creativity in Social Movements.* Chicago: University of Chicago Press, 1997.

Jennings, Francis. *The Ambiguous Iroquois Empire: The Covenant Chain Confederation of Indian Tribes with English Colonies from Its Beginnings to the Lancaster Treaty of 1744.* New York: Norton, 1984.

"The Scandalous Indian Policy of William Penn's Sons: Deeds and Documents of the Walking Purchase." *Pennsylvania History* 37, no. 1 (Winter 1970): 19–39.

Jennings, Judi. *The Business of Abolishing the British Slave Trade, 1783–1807.* London: F. Cass, 1997.

"Mid-Eighteenth Century British Quakerism and the Response to the Problem of Slavery." *Quaker History* 66, no. 1 (1977): 23–40.

Jennings, Lawrence C. *French Anti-Slavery: The Movement for the Abolition of Slavery in France, 1802–1848.* Cambridge: Cambridge University Press, 2000.

Jepperson, Ronald L. "The Development and Application of Sociological Neoinstitutionalism." In *New Directions in Contemporary Sociological Theory*, edited by Joseph Berger and Morris Zelditch, Jr. 229–66. Lanham, MD: Rowman and Littlefield, 2002.

"Institutions, Institutional Effects and Institutionalism." In *The New Institutionalism in Organizational Analysis*, edited by Walter W. Powell and Paul DiMaggio. 143–63. Chicago: University of Chicago Press, 1991.

Johnston, Josee and Gordon Laxer. "Solidarity in the Age of Globalization: Lessons from the Anti-MAI and Zapatista Struggles." *Theory and Society* 32, no. 1 (2003): 39–91.

Jones, Kristine L. "Warfare, Reorganization, and Readaptation at the Margins of Spanish Rule: The Southern Margin (1573–1882)." In *The Cambridge History of the Native Peoples of the Americas*, Vol. III: *South America*, Part 2, edited by Frank Salomon and Stuart B. Schwartz. 138–87. Cambridge: Cambridge University Press, 1999.

Jones, Rufus Matthew. *The Quakers in the American Colonies*. London: Macmillan, 1911.

Kallscheuer, Otto. "'And Who Is My Neighbor?': Moral Sentiments, Proximity, Humanity." *Social Research* 62, no. 1 (1995).

Kass, Amalie M. and Edward H. Kass. *Perfecting the World: The Life and Times of Dr. Thomas Hodgkin, 1798–1866*. Boston: Harcourt Brace Jovanovich, 1988.

Kates, Gary. *The Cercle social, the Girondins, and the French Revolution*. Princeton, NJ: Princeton University Press, 1985.

Kaufmann, Chaim D. and Robert A. Pape. "Explaining Costly International Moral Action: Britain's Sixty-year Campaign against the Atlantic Slave Trade." *International Organization* 53, no. 4 (Autumn 1999): 631–68.

Keck, Margaret E. and Kathryn Sikkink. *Activists Beyond Borders: Advocacy Networks in International Politics*. Ithaca: Cornell University Press, 1998.

Kelly, Paul. "British and Irish Politics in 1785." *The English Historical Review* 90, no. 356 (1975): 536–63.

  "Constituents' Instructions to Members of Parliament in the Eighteenth Century." In *Party and Management in Parliament, 1660–1784*, edited by Clyve Jones. 169–89. New York: St. Martin's Press, 1984.

Kennedy, John Pendleton, ed. *Journals of the House of Burgesses of Virginia, 1770–1772*. Richmond, VA: Colonial Press, 1906.

Kenny, Kevin. *Peaceable Kingdom Lost: The Paxton Boys and the Destruction of William Penn's Holy Experiment*. New York: Oxford University Press, 2009.

Khagram, Sanjeev. *Dams and Development: Transnational Struggles for Water and Power*. Ithaca, NY: Cornell University Press, 2004.

Kicza, John E. "Patterns in Early Spanish Overseas Expansion." *The William and Mary Quarterly* 49, no. 2 (1992): 229–53.

Kiemen, Mathias C. *The Indian Policy of Portugal in the Amazon Region, 1614–1693*. Washington, DC: Catholic University of America Press, 1954.

Killough, Mary. "Niels Otto Tank (1800–1864): Moravian Missionary to Suriname and Wisconsin." *Transactions of the Moravian Historical Society* 29 (1996): 85–102.

Kirby, Ethyn Williams. "The Quakers' Efforts to Secure Civil and Religious Liberty, 1660–96." *The Journal of Modern History* 7, no. 4 (1935): 401–21.

Klebaner, Benjamin Joseph. "American Manumission Laws and the Responsibility for Supporting Slaves." *The Virginia Magazine of History and Biography* 63, no. 4 (1955): 443–53.

Kleinman, Arthur and Joan Kleinman. "The Appeal of Experience; The Dismay of Images: Cultural Appropriations of Suffering in Our Times." *Daedalus* 125, no. 1 (1996): 1–25.

Klotz, Audie. "Transnational Activism and Global Transformations: The Anti-Apartheid and Abolitionist Experiences." *European Journal of International Relations* 8, no. 1 (2002): 49–76.

Kluit, M. Elisabeth. *Het Protestantse réveil in Nederland en daarbuiten, 1815–1865.* Amsterdam: Paris, 1970.

Knox, Ronald A. *Enthusiasm: A Chapter in the History of Religion.* New York: Oxford University Press, 1950.

Koenigsberger, H. G. "Composite States, Representative Institutions and the American Revolution." *Historical Research* 62, no. 148 (1989): 135–53.

Koopmans, Ruud. "Globalization or Still National Politics? A Comparison of Protests against the Gulf War in Germany, France and the Netherlands." In *Social Movements in a Globalizing World*, edited by Donatella Della Porta, Hanspeter Kriesi, and Dieter Rucht. 57–70. New York: St. Martin's Press, 1999.

Korth, Eugene H. *Spanish Policy in Colonial Chile: The Struggle for Social Justice, 1535–1700.* Stanford, CA,: Stanford University Press, 1968.

Koschorke, Klaus. "Gnosis, Montanismus, Mönchtum: Zur Frage emanzipatorischer Bewegungen im Raum der Alten Kirche." *Evangelische Theologie* 53, no. 3 (1993): 216–31.

"Konfessionelle Spaltung und weltweite Ausbreitung des Christentums im Zeitalter der Reformation." *Zeitschrift für Theologie und Kirche* 91, no. 10–24 (1994).

Ladner, Gerhart B. *The Idea of Reform: Its Impact on Christian Thought and Action in the Age of the Fathers.* Cambridge: Harvard University Press, 1959.

Laidlaw, Zoë. "'Aunt Anna's Report': The Buxton Women and the Aborigines Select Committee, 1835–37." *Journal of Imperial and Commonwealth History* 32, no. 2 (2004): 1–28.

Colonial Connections, 1815–45: Patronage, the Information Revolution and Colonial Government. Manchester, UK: Manchester University Press, 2005.

"Heathens, Slaves and Aborigines: Thomas Hodgkin's Critique of Missions and Anti-slavery." *History Workshop Journal* 64, no. 1 (September 21, 2007): 133–61.

Landon, Fred. "The Anti-Slavery Society of Canada." *The Journal of Negro History* 4, no. 1 (1919): 33–40.

Larson, Rebecca. *Daughters of Light: Quaker Women Preaching and Prophesying in the Colonies and Abroad, 1700–1775.* New York: Knopf, 1999.

Latourette, Kenneth Scott. *A History of the Expansion of Christianity*, Vol. III: *Three Centuries of Advance, A.D. 1500-A.D. 1800.* New York: Harper and Brothers, 1937.

La Trobe, Christian Ignatius. *Letters to My Children; Written at Sea during a Voyage to the Cape of Good Hope, in 1815.* London: Seeleys, 1851.

Lawrence, C. H. *The Friars: The Impact of the Early Mendicant Movement on Western Society.* London: Longman, 1994.

Leclerc, Lucien. "La politique et l'influence du Club de l'Hôtel Massiac." *Annales Historiques de la Révolution Française* (1937): 342–63.

Lenhart, John M. "Capuchin Champions of Negro Emancipation in Cuba (1681–1685)." *Franciscan Studies* 6, no. 2 (1946): 195–217.

Lester, Alan. "Colonial Networks, Australian Humanitarianism and the History Wars." *Geographical Research* 44, no. 3 (2006): 229 (13).

"Humanitarians and White Settlers in the Nineteenth Century." In *Missions and Empire*, edited by Norman Etherington. 64–85. Oxford: Oxford University Press, 2005.

"Imperial Circuits and Networks: Geographies of the British Empire." *History Compass* 4, no. 1 (2006): 124–41.

Imperial Networks: Creating Identities in Nineteenth-Century South Africa and Britain. London: Routledge, 2001.

Linde, S. van der. "Der Reformierte 'Pietismus' in den Niederlanden." In *Pietismus und Reveil*, edited by J. van den Berg and J. P. van Dooren. 102–17. Leiden: E. J. Brill, 1978.

Lipschutz, Ronnie D. "Reconstructing World Politics: The Emergence of Global Civil Society." *Millennium* 21, no. 3 (1992): 389–420.

Livezey, Lowell W. "US Religious Organizations and the International Human Rights Movement." *Human Rights Quarterly* 11, no. 1 (1989): 14–81.

Lobo Cabrera, Manuel. "El clero y la trata en los siglos XVI y XVII: El ejempio de Canarias." In *De la traite à l'esclavage: Actes du colloque international sur la traite des Noirs, Nantex 1985*, Vol. 1, edited by Serge Daget. 481–96. Nantes: Centre de Recherche sur l'histoire du monde atlantique, 1988.

Lockhart, James. *Of Things of the Indies: Essays Old and New in Early Latin American History.* Stanford, CA: Stanford University Press, 1999.

Lohmann Villena, Guillermo. "La restitución por conquistadores y encomenderos: Un aspecto de la incidencia lascasiana en el Perú." *Anuario de Estudios Americanos* 23 (1966): 21–89.

López García, José Tomás. *Dos defensores de los esclavos negros en el siglo XVII (Francisco José de Jaca y Epifanio de Moirans).* Maracaibo: Biblioteca Corpozulia, 1982.

Losada, Ángel. "Diego de Avendaño S. I. moralista y jurista, defensor de la dignidad humana de indios y negros en América." *Missionalia Hispanica* 39, no. 115 (1982): 1–18.

Louis, William Roger. "The Triumph of the Congo Reform Movement, 1905–1908." *Boston University Papers on Africa* 2 (1966): 269–302.

Lovejoy, David S. *Religious Enthusiasm in the New World: Heresy to Revolution.* Cambridge, MA: Harvard University Press, 1985.

Lovejoy, Paul E. *Transformations in Slavery: A History of Slavery in Africa.* 3rd ed. New York: Cambridge University Press, 2012.

Ludwig, Frieder. "Zur 'Verteidigung und Verbreitung des Glaubens': Das Wirken der Jesuiten in Übersee und seine Rezeption in den konfessionellen Auseinandersetzungen Europas." *Zeitschrift fur Kirchengeschichte* 112, no. 1 (2001): 44–64.

Lundberg, Magnus. *Unification and Conflict: The Church Politics of Alonso de Montúfar OP, Archbishop of Mexico, 1554–1572.* Uppsala: Swedish Institute of Missionary Research, 2002.

MacLeod, Duncan. "From Gradualism to Immediatism: Another Look." *Slavery & Abolition* 3, no. 2 (1982): 141–52.

MacLeod, Murdo J. "La espada de la Iglesia: Excomunión y la evolución de la lucha por el control político y económico en Chiapas colonial, 1545–1700." *Mesoamérica* 11, no. 20 (1990): 199–213.

MacMaster, Richard K. "Arthur Lee's 'Address on Slavery': An Aspect of Virginia's Struggle to End the Slave Trade, 1765–1774." *The Virginia Magazine of History and Biography* 80, no. 2 (1972): 141–57.

"Liberty or Property? The Methodist Petition for Emancipation in Virginia, 1785." *Methodist History* 10, no. 1 (1971): 44–55.

Maney, Gregory M. "Rival Transnational Networks and Indigenous Rights: The San Blas Kuna in Panama and the Yanomami in Brazil." *Research in Social Movements, Conflicts and Change* 23 (2001): 103–44.

Mann, Michael. "Has Globalization Ended the Rise and Rise of the Nation-State?" *Review of International Political Economy* 4, no. 3 (1997): 472–96.

Maquerlot, Lucie. "Rouen et Le Havre face à la traite et à l'esclavage: Le mouvement de l'opinion (1783–1794)." In *Esclavage, résistances et abolitions*, edited by Marcel Dorigny. 165–86. Paris: Éditions du CTHS, 1999.

Marietta, Jack D. *The Reformation of American Quakerism, 1748–1783*. Philadelphia: University of Pennsylvania Press, 1984.

Marshall, P. J. *The Making and Unmaking of Empires: Britain, India, and America, c.1750–1783*. Oxford: Oxford University Press, 2005.

Marshall, Peter. "The Anti-Slave Trade Movement in Bristol." In *Bristol in the Eighteenth Century*, edited by Patrick McGrath. 185–215. Newton Abbot, UK: David and Charles, 1972.

Maschke, Erich. *Der deutsche Orden und die Preußen: Bekehrung und Unterwerfung in der preußisch-baltischen Mission des 13. Jahrhunderts*. Berlin: Emil Ebering, 1928.

Mathews, Albert. "Notes on the Proposed Abolition of Slavery in Virginia in 1785." *Publications of the Colonial Society of Massachusetts* 6 (1904): 370–80.

Mathews, Donald G. *Slavery and Methodism: A Chapter in American Morality, 1780–1845*. Princeton, NJ: Princeton University Press, 1965.

Maynard, Douglas. "Reform and the Origin of the International Organization Movement." *Proceedings of the American Philosophical Society* 107, no. 3 (1963): 220–31.

"The World's Antislavery Convention of 1840." *Mississippi Valley Historical Review* 47, no. 3 (1960): 452–71.

McAdam, Doug. "'Initiator' and 'Spin-Off' Movements: Diffusion Processes in Protest Cycles." In *Repertoires and Cycles of Collective Action*, edited by Mark Traugott. 217–39. Durham, NC: Duke University Press, 1995.

McCarthy, John D. and Mayer N. Zald. "Resource Mobilization and Social Movements: A Partial Theory." *American Journal of Sociology* 82, no. 6 (1977): 1212–41.

McCloy, Shelby T. *The Negro in France*. Lexington: University of Kentucky Press, 1961.

McDonnell, Ernest W. "The *Vita Apostolica*: Diversity or Dissent." *Church History* 24, no. 1 (1955): 15–31.

Medina, Miguel Ángel. "La primera comunidad de dominicos en Filipinas y la defensa de los derechos de los naturales (1587–1605)." *Ciencia Tomista* 80 (1989): 333–63.

Una comunidad al servicio del Indio: La obra de Fr. Pedro de Córdoba, O. P. (1482–1521). Madrid: Instituto Pontificio de Teologia, 1983.

Megged, Amos. "Accommodation and Resistance of Elites in Transition: The Case of Chiapa in Early Colonial Mesoamerica." *The Hispanic American Historical Review* 71, no. 3 (1991): 477.

Menard, Russell R. *Sweet Negotiations: Sugar, Slavery, and Plantation Agriculture in Early Barbados*. Charlottesville: University of Virginia Press, 2006.

Merluzzi, Manfredi. *Politica e governo nel Nuovo Mondo: Francisco de Toledo viceré del Perù (1569–1581)*. Rome: Carocci, 2003.

Merriman, Roger Bigelow. *The Rise of the Spanish Empire in the Old World and in the New*. New York: Macmillan, 1918.

Metcalf, Alida C. *Go-Betweens and the Colonization of Brazil, 1500–1600*. Austin: University of Texas Press, 2005.

Midgley, Clare. *Women against Slavery: The British Campaigns, 1780–1870*. London: Routledge, 1992.

Mielke, Andreas. "'What's Here to Do?' An Inquiry Concerning Sarah and Benjamin Lay, Abolitionists." *Quaker History* 86, no. 1 (1997): 22.

Miers, Suzanne. *Britain and the Ending of the Slave Trade*. London: Longman, 1975.

Slavery in the Twentieth Century: The Evolution of a Global Problem. Walnut Creek, CA: AltaMira Press, 2003.

Miller, Naomi C. "John Cartwright and Radical Parliamentary Reform, 1808–1819." *English Historical Review* 83, no. 329 (1968): 705–28.

Mira Caballos, Esteban. "La primera utopía americana: Las reducciones de indios de los jerónimos en la Española (1517–1519)." *Jahrbuch für Geschichte Lateinamerikas* 39 (2002): 9–35.

Mitterauer, Michael. *Why Europe? The Medieval Origins of its Special Path*. Chicago: University of Chicago Press, 2010.

Moeller, Susan D. *Compassion Fatigue: How the Media Sell Disease, Famine, War, and Death*. New York: Routledge, 1999.

Monteiro, John Manuel. "From Indian to Slave: Forced Native Labour and Colonial Society in São Paulo during the Seventeenth Century." *Slavery & Abolition* 9, no. 2 (1988): 105–27.

Moore, R. I. *The Formation of a Persecuting Society: Power and Deviance in Western Europe, 950–1250*. Oxford: Blackwell, 1987.

Moore, Rosemary. *The Light in Their Consciences: Early Quakers in Britain, 1646–1666*. University Park, PA: Pennsylvania State University Press, 2000.

Moulton, Phillips P., ed. *The Journal and Major Essays of John Woolman*. New York: Oxford University Press, 1971.

Moya Pons, Frank. *Después de Colón: Trabajo, sociedad y política en la economía del oro*. Madrid: Alianza, 1987.

Muldoon, James. *Empire and Order: The Concept of Empire, 800–1800*. New York: St. Martin's Press, 1999.

"John Wyclif and the Rights of the Infidels: The Requerimiento Re-Examined." *The Americas* 36, no. 3 (1980): 301–16.

Mullett, Michael A. *The Catholic Reformation*. London: Routledge, 1999.

Radical Religious Movements in Early Modern Europe. London: Allen and Unwin, 1980.

Muro Orejón, Antonio. "El Real y Supremo Consejo de las Indias." *Anuario de Estudios Americanos* 27 (1970): 195–218.

Murra, John V. "'Nos Hazen Mucha Ventaja': The Early European Perception of Andean Achievement." In *Transatlantic Encounters: Europeans and Andeans in the Sixteenth Century*, edited by Kenneth J. Andrien and Rolena Adorno. 73–89. Berkeley: University of California Press, 1991.

Mutanda, Mukuna. "L'attitude de la Sacrée Congregation de la Propagation de la Foi et des missionnaires Capucins vis-à-vis de la traite negriere au Kongo et an Angola (1645–1835)." *Revue Africaine de Théologie* 15, no. 31 (1992): 33–80.

Myers, John Lytle. "The Agency System of the Anti-Slavery Movement, 1832–1837, and Its Antecedents in Other Benevolent and Reform Societies." Ph.D. Dissertation, University of Michigan, 1961.

Nadelhaft, Jerome. "The Somersett Case and Slavery: Myth, Reality, and Repercussions." *The Journal of Negro History* 51, no. 3 (1966): 193–208.

Nadelmann, Ethan A. "Global Prohibition Regimes: The Evolution of Norms in International Society." *International Organization* 44, no. 4 (1990): 489–526.

Nader, Helen. "Desperate Men, Questionable Acts: The Moral Dilemma of Italian Merchants in the Spanish Slave Trade." *Sixteenth Century Journal* 33, no. 2 (2002): 401–22.

A Narrative of Some of the Proceedings of North Carolina Yearly Meeting on the Subject of Slavery within Its Limits Greensboro, NC: Swain and Sherwood, 1848.

Nash, Gary B. *Forging Freedom: The Formation of Philadelphia's Black Community, 1720–1840.* Cambridge, MA: Harvard University Press, 1988.

The Forgotten Fifth: African Americans in the Age of Revolution. Cambridge, MA: Harvard University Press, 2006.

"Franklin and Slavery." *Proceedings of the American Philosophical Society* 150, no. 4 (2006): 618–35.

Nash, Gary B. and Jean R. Soderlund. *Freedom by Degrees: Emancipation in Pennsylvania and Its Aftermath.* New York: Oxford University Press, 1991.

Nepstad, Sharon Erickson. *Convictions of the Soul: Religion, Culture, and Agency in the Central America Solidarity Movement.* New York: Oxford University Press, 2004.

Newman, Richard S. "Prelude to the Gag Rule: Southern Reaction to Antislavery Petitions in the First Federal Congress." *Journal of the Early Republic* 16, no. 4 (1996): 571.

The Transformation of American Abolitionism: Fighting Slavery in the Early Republic. Chapel Hill: University of North Carolina Press, 2002.

Oaks, Robert F. "Philadelphians in Exile: The Problem of Loyalty during the American Revolution." *Pennsylvania Magazine of History & Biography* 96, no. 3 (1972): 298–325.

Oddie, Geoffrey A. "'Orientalism' and British Protestant Missionary Constructions of India in the Nineteenth Century." *South Asia* 17, no. 2 (1994): 27–42.

Social Protest in India: British Protestant Missionaries and Social Reforms, 1850–1900. New Delhi: Manohar, 1979.

Ohline, Howard A. "Slavery, Economics, and Congressional Politics, 1790." *Journal of Southern History* 46, no. 3 (1980): 335–60.

Oldfield, J. R. *Popular Politics and British Anti-Slavery: The Mobilisation of Public Opinion against the Slave Trade, 1787–1807.* Manchester: Manchester University Press, 1995.

Olejniczak, Claudia. "Entwicklungspolitische Solidarität: Geschichte und Structure der Dritte Welt-Bewegung." *Forschungsjournal Neue Soziale Bewegungen* 11, no. 3 (1998): 107–12.

Oliver, Pamela E. and Gerald Marwell. "Mobilizing Technologies for Collective Action." In *Frontiers in Social Movement Theory*, edited by Aldon D. Morris and Carol McClurg Mueller. 241–72. New Haven, CT: Yale University Press, 1992.

Olsen, Glenn. "The Idea of the *Ecclesia Primitiva* in the Writings of the Twelfth-Century Canonists." *Traditio* 25 (1969): 61–86.

Olson, Alison Gilbert. "The Board of Trade and London-American Interest Groups in the Eighteenth Century." In *The British Atlantic Empire before the American Revolution*, edited by Peter Marshall and Glyndwr Williams. 33–50. London: Cass, 1980.

Making the Empire Work: London and American Interest Groups, 1690–1790. Cambridge, MA: Harvard University Press, 1992.

"Parliament, Empire, and Parliamentary Law, 1776." In *Three British Revolutions: 1641, 1688, 1776*, edited by J. G. A. Pocock. 289–322. Princeton, NJ: Princeton University Press, 1980.

Otis, James. *The Rights of the British Colonies Asserted and Proved.* Boston: Edes and Gill, 1764.

Otte, Enrique. "Un episodio desconocido de la vida de los cronistas de Indias, Bartolomé de Las Casas y Gonzalo Fernandez de Oviedo." *Ibero-Amerikanisches Archiv 3*, no. 2 (1977): 123–33.

Padden, Robert Charles. "Cultural Change and Military Resistance in Araucanian Chile, 1550–1730." *Southwestern Journal of Anthropology 13*, no. 1 (1957): 103–21.

"The Ordenanza del Patronazgo, 1574: An Interpretative Essay." *The Americas 12*, no. 4 (1956): 333–54.

Pagden, Anthony. *The Fall of Natural Man: The American Indian and the Origins of Comparative Ethnology.* Cambridge: Cambridge University Press, 1982.

"Stoicism, Cosmopolitanism, and the Legacy of European Imperialism." *Constellations 7*, no. 1 (2000): 3–22.

Parish, Helen Rand and Harold E. Weidman. "The Correct Birthdate of Bartolomé De Las Casas." *Hispanic American Historical Review 56*, no. 3 (1976): 385–403.

Las Casas en México: Historia y obras desconocidas. Mexico City: Fondo de Cultura Económica, 1992.

Park, Edwards Amasa. *Memoir of the Life and Character of Samuel Hopkins, D. D.* Boston: Doctrinal Tract and Book Society, 1854.

Parkinson, Robert G. "'Manifest Signs of Passion': The First Federal Congress, Antislavery, and Legacies of the Revolutionary War." In *Contesting Slavery: The Politics of Bondage and Freedom in the New American Nation*, edited by John Craig Hammond and Matthew Mason. 49–68. Charlottesville: University of Virginia Press, 2011.

The Parliamentary History of England, From the Earliest Period to the Year 1803. Vol. XVIII, London: T.C. Hansard, 1813.

Parrish, Samuel L. *Some Chapters in the History of the Friendly Association for Regaining and Preserving Peace with the Indians by Pacific Measures.* Philadelphia: Friends's Historical Association of Philadelphia, 1877.

Passy, Florence. "Political Altruism and the Solidarity Movement: An Introduction." In *Political Altruism? Solidarity Movements in International Perspective*, edited by Marco Giugni and Florence Passy. 3–25. Lanham, MD: Rowman and Littlefield, 2001.

Peabody, Sue. "'A Dangerous Zeal' : Catholic Missions to Slaves in the French Antilles, 1635–1800." *French Historical Studies 25*, no. 1 (2002): 53–90.

"There Are No Slaves in France": The Political Culture of Race and Slavery in the Ancien Regime. New York: Oxford University Press, 1996.

Pena González, Miguel Anxo. *Francisco José de Jaca: La primera propuesta abolicionista de la esclavitud en el pensamiento hispano.* Salamanca, Spain: Publicaciones Universidad Pontificia de Salamanca, 2003.

Pena González, Miguel Anxo, ed. *Resolución sobre la libertad de los negros y sus originarios, en estado de paganos y después ya cristianos: La primera condena de la esclavitud en el pensamiento hispano.* Madrid: Consejo Superior de Investigaciones Científicas, 2002.

Pennington, Edgar Legare. "The Reverend Francis Le Jau's Work Among Indians and Negro Slaves." *The Journal of Southern History* 1, no. 4 (1935): 442–58.

Pennington, Kenneth J., Jr. "Bartolomé de Las Casas and the Tradition of Medieval Law." *Church History* 39, no. 2 (Jun. 1970): 149–61.

Pennsylvania General Assembly. *Votes and Proceedings of the House of Representatives.* Philadelphia: Franklin, 1761.

Votes of the House of Representatives. Philadelphia: Henry Miller, 1773.

Penson, Lillian M. *The Colonial Agents of the British West Indies: A Study in Colonial Administration, Mainly in the Eighteenth Century.* London: University of London Press, 1924.

Pereña, Luciano. "La Escuela de Salamanca y la duda Indiana." *Corpus Hispanorum de Pace* 25 (1984): 291–344.

Pérez de Tudela Bueso, Juan. "La gran reforma carolina de las Indias en 1542." *Revista de Indias* 18 (1958): 463–509.

Pérez Fernández, Isacio. "Analisis extrauniversitario de la Conquista de América en los años 1534–1549." *Corpus Hispanorum de Pace* 25 (1984): 117–62.

Pérez-Prendes y Muñoz de Arraco, J. M. "La revista 'El abolicionista' (1865–1876) en la genesis de la abolición de la esclavitud en las Antillas españolas." *Anuario de Estudios Americanos* 43 (1986): 215–40.

Pérotin-Dumon, Anne. "French, English and Dutch in the Lesser Antilles: From Privateering to Planting, c. 1550–c. 1650." In *General History of the Caribbean,* Vol. II, *New Societies: The Caribbean in the Long Sixteen Century,* edited by Pieter C. Emmer. 114–58. London: Macmillan, 1997.

Pestana, Carla Gardina. *Protestant Empire: Religion and the Making of the British Atlantic World.* Philadelphia: University of Pennsylvania Press, 2009.

Peterson, Mark A. "The Selling of Joseph: Bostonians, Antislavery, and the Protestant International, 1689–1733." *Massachusetts Historical Review* 4 (2004): 1–22.

Pfister, Frederick William. "In the Cause of Freedom: American Abolition Societies, 1775–1808." Ph.D. Dissertation, Miami University, 1980.

Phelan, John Leddy. *The Millennial Kingdom of the Franciscans in the New World.* 2nd ed. Berkeley: University of California Press, 1970.

Philp, Mark. "Vulgar Conservatism, 1792–3." *English Historical Review* 110, no. 435 (1995): 42–69.

Pickering, Paul A. and Alex Tyrell. *The People's Bread: A History of the Anti-Corn Law League.* London: Leicester University Press, 2000.

Pietschmann, Horst. *Staat und staatliche Entwicklung am Beginn der spanischen Kolonisation Amerikas.* Münster: Aschendorff, 1980.

Piquet, Jean-Daniel. *L'émancipation des noirs dans la Révolution française (1789–1795).* Paris: Karthala, 2002.

Pogge, Thomas. *World Poverty and Human Rights: Cosmopolitan Responsibilities and Reforms*. 2nd ed. Cambridge: Polity Press, 2008.

Polanyi, Michael. *The Tacit Dimension*. Garden City, NY: Doubleday, 1967.

Polgar, Paul J. "'To Raise Them to an Equal Participation': Early National Abolitionism, Gradual Emancipation, and the Promise of African American Citizenship." *Journal of the Early Republic* 31, no. 2 (Summer 2011): 229–58.

Pollock, John. *Wilberforce*. New York: St. Martin's Press, 1978.

Poole, Stafford. "The Last Years of Archbishop Pedro Moya de Contreras, 1586–1591." *Americas* 47, no. 1 (1990): 1–39.

Pedro Moya de Contreras: Catholic Reform and Royal Power in New Spain, 1571–1591. Berkeley: University of California Press, 1987.

Porter, Andrew. *Religion versus Empire? British Protestant Missionaries and Overseas Expansion, 1700–1914*. Manchester, UK: Manchester University Press, 2004.

Porter, Dale H. *The Abolition of the Slave Trade in England, 1784–1807*. Hamden, CT: Archon Books, 1970.

Post, James E. "Assessing the Nestlé Boycott: Corporate Accountability and Human Rights." *California Management Review* 27, no. 2 (1985): 113–31.

Powell, Philip Wayne. *Soldiers, Indians & Silver: The Northward Advance of New Spain, 1550–1600*. Berkeley: University of California Press, 1952.

Prendes, Jorge Caceres. "Revolutionary Struggle and Church Commitment: The Case of El Salvador." *Social Compass* 30, nos. 2–3 (January 1, 1983 1983): 261–98.

Preston, David L. *The Texture of Contact: European and Indian Settler Communities on the Frontiers of Iroquoia, 1667–1783*. Lincoln: University of Nebraska Press, 2009.

Prozesky, Martin H. "The Emergence of Dutch Pietism." *Journal of Ecclesiastical History* 28, no. 1 (1977): 29–37.

Quinney, Valerie. "Decisions on Slavery, the Slave-Trade and Civil Rights for Negroes in the Early French Revolution." *Journal of Negro History* 55, no. 2 (April 1970): 117–30.

"The Problem of Civil Rights for Free Men of Color in the Early French Revolution." *French Historical Studies* 7, no. 4 (1972): 544–57.

Rainger, Ronald. "Philanthropy and Science in the 1830's: The British and Foreign Aborigines' Protection Society." *Man* 15, no. 4 (December 1980): 702–17.

Ramirez, Susan E. "The 'Dueño de Indios': Thoughts on the Consequences of the Shifting Bases of Power of the 'Curaca de los Viejos Antiguos' under the Spanish in Sixteenth-Century Peru." *The Hispanic American Historical Review* 67, no. 4 (1987): 575.

Ramos, Demetrio. "El hecho de la Conquista de América." *Corpus Hispanorum de Pace* 25 (1984): 17–63.

"El P. Córdoba y Las Casas en el plan de conquista pacifica de Tierra Firme." *Boletin americanista* 1, no. 3 (1959): 175–210.

"Las crisis indiana y la Junta Magna de 1568." *Jahrbuch für Geschichte von Staat, Wirtschaft und Gesellschaft Lateinamerikas* 23 (1986): 1–61.

Ramos Gómez, Luis J. and María Concepción Blasco. "En torno al origen del tributo indigena en la Nueva España y su evolución en la primera mitad del siglo XVI." In *Estudios sobre política indigenista española en América*, v. II. 357–91. Valladolid: Seminario de Historia de América, Universidad de Valladolid, 1975.

Rappleye, Charles. *Sons of Providence: The Brown Brothers, the Slave Trade, and the American Revolution*. New York: Simon and Schuster, 2006.

Ravitch, Norman. "Liberalism, Catholicism, and the Abbé Grégoire." *Church History* 36, no. 4 (1967): 419–39.

Rawley, James A. "London's Defense of the Slave Trade, 1787–1807." *Slavery and Abolition* 14, no. 2 (1993): 48–69.

— *The Transatlantic Slave Trade: A History*. Rev. ed. Lincoln: University of Nebraska Press, 2005.

Read, Donald. *The English Provinces, c. 1760–1960: A Study in Influence*. New York: St. Martin's Press, 1964.

Reay, Barry. *The Quakers and the English Revolution*. New York: St. Martin's Press, 1985.

Rees, Alan M. "English Friends and the Abolition of the British Slave Trade." *Bulletin of Friends Historical Association* 44, no. 2 (1955): 74–87.

Reich, Jerome. "The Slave Trade at the Congress of Vienna: A Study in English Public Opinion." *Journal of Negro History* 53, no. 2 (1968): 129–43.

Rennie, Sandra. "Virginia's Baptist Persecution, 1765–1778." *Journal of Religious History* 12, no. 1 (1982): 48–61.

Resnick, Daniel P. "The Societé des Amis des Noirs and the Abolition of Slavery." *French Historical Studies* 7, no. 4 (1972): 558–69.

Ricard, Robert. *The Spiritual Conquest of Mexico: An Essay on the Apostolate and the Evangelizing Methods of the Mendicant Orders in New Spain, 1523–1572*. Berkeley: University of California Press, 1966.

Rice, C. Duncan. "'Humanity Sold for Sugar!' The British Abolitionist Response to Free Trade in Slave-Grown Sugar." *Historical Journal* 13, no. 3 (1970): 402–18.

— "The Missionary Context of the British Anti-Slavery Movement." In *Slavery and British Society, 1776–1846*, edited by James Walvin. 150–63. London: Macmillan, 1982.

Richardson, David. "The British Empire and the Atlantic Slave Trade, 1660–1807." In *The Oxford History of the British Empire*, Vol. 2: *The Eighteenth Century*, edited by P. J. Marshall. 440–64. Oxford: Oxford University Press, 1998.

Robert, Daniel. *Les églises réformées en France (1800–1830)*. Paris: Presses universitaires de France, 1961.

Rochon, Thomas R. *Culture Moves: Ideas, Activism, and Changing Values*. Princeton, NJ: Princeton University Press, 1998.

Rogers, Nicholas. "Vagrancy, Impressment and the Regulation of Labour in Eighteenth-Century Britain." *Slavery & Abolition* 15, no. 2 (1994): 102–13.

Romano, Ruggiero. "Entre encomienda castellana y encomienda indiana: Una vez más el problema del feudalismo americano (siglos XVI–XVII)." *Anuario IEHS* 3 (1988): 11–39.

Rosenberg, Philippe. "Thomas Tryon and the Seventeenth-Century Dimensions of Antislavery." *The William and Mary Quarterly* 61, no. 4 (2004): 609–42.

Rucht, Dieter. "Distant Issue Movements in Germany: Empirical Description and Theoretical Reflections." In *Globalizations and Social Movements: Culture, Power, and the Transnational Public Sphere*, edited by John A. Guidry, Michael D. Kennedy, and Mayer N. Zald. 76–105. Ann Arbor: University of Michigan Press, 2000.

"Transnationaler politischer Protest im historischen Längsschnitt." In *Globalisierung, Partizipation, Protest,* edited by Ansgar Klein, Ruud Koopmans, and Heiko Geiling. 77–96. Opladen: Leske and Budrich, 2001.

"The Transnationalization of Social Movements: Trends, Causes, Problems." In *Social Movements in a Globalizing World,* edited by Donatella Della Porta, Hanspeter Kriesi, and Dieter Rucht. 206–22. New York: St. Martin's Press, 1999.

Rumeu de Armas, Antonio. "Los problemas derivados del contacto de razas en los albores del Renacimiento." *Cuadernos de historia* 1 (1967): 61–103.

Russell, P. E. "El descubrimiento de las Canarias y el debate medieval acerca de los derechos de los principes y pueblos paganos." *Revista de historia canaria* 36, no. 171 (1978): 9–32.

Russell-Wood, A. J. R. "Iberian Expansion and the Issue of Black Slavery: Changing Portuguese Attitudes, 1440–1770." *The American Historical Review* 83, no. 1, Supplement (February 1978): 16–42.

Saccardo, Graziano. "La schiavitù e i Cappuccini." *L'Italia Francescana* 53 (1978): 75–113.

Saillant, John. "'Some Thoughts on the Subject of Freeing the Negro Slaves in the Colony of Connecticut ...' by Levi Hart; With a Response from Samuel Hopkins." *New England Quarterly* 75, no. 1 (2002): 107–28.

Sainsbury, John A. "Indian Labor in Early Rhode Island." *New England Quarterly* 48, no. 3 (1975): 378–93.

Sanderson, F. E. "The Liverpool Delegates and Sir William Dolben's Bill." *Transactions of the Historic Society of Lancashire and Cheshire* 124 (1972): 57–84.

Sarabia, Heidy. "Organizing 'Below and to the Left': Differences in the Citizenship and Transnational Practices of Two Zapatista Groups." *Sociological Forum* 26, no. 2 (2011): 356–80.

Sassi, Jonathan D. "'This whole country have their hands full of Blood this day': Transcription and Introduction of an Antislavery Sermon Manuscript Attributed to the Reverend Samuel Hopkins." *Proceedings of the American Antiquarian Society* 112, no. 1 (2002): 29–92.

"With a Little Help from the Friends: The Quaker and Tactical Contexts of Anthony Benezet's Abolitionist Publishing." *Pennsylvania Magazine of History & Biography* 135 (2011): 33–71.

Sauer, Carl Ortwin. *The Early Spanish Main.* Berkeley: University of California Press, 1966.

Sayre, Robert Duane. "The Evolution of Early American Abolitionism: The American Convention for Promoting the Abolition of Slavery and Improving the Condition of the African Race, 1794–1837." Ph.D. Dissertation, Ohio State University, 1987.

Schmidt-Nowara, Christopher. *Empire and Antislavery: Spain, Cuba, and Puerto Rico, 1833–1874.* Pittsburgh: University of Pittsburgh Press, 1999.

Schmidt, Leigh Eric. "'The Grand Prophet,' Hugh Bryan: Early Evangelicalism's Challenge to the Establishment and Slavery in the Colonial South." *The South Carolina Historical Magazine* 87, no. 4 (1986): 238–50.

Schwartz, Stuart B. *Sugar Plantations in the Formation of Brazilian Society: Bahia, 1550–1835.* Cambridge: Cambridge University Press, 1985.

Seeber, Edward Derbyshire. *Anti-Slavery Opinion in France during the Second Half of the Eighteenth Century.* Baltimore, MD: Johns Hopkins Press, 1937.

Segal, Ronald. *Islam's Black Slaves: The Other Black Diaspora*. New York: Farrar, Straus and Giroux, 2001.

Semmes, Raphael, ed. *Proceedings and Acts of the General Assembly of Maryland, 1771 to June–July, 1773*. Baltimore: Maryland Historical Society, 1946.

Sepinwall, Alyssa Goldstein. *The Abbé Grégoire and the French Revolution: The Making of Modern Universalism*. Berkeley: University of California Press, 2005.

Sewell, William H. Jr. "A Theory of Structure: Duality, Agency, and Transformation." *American Journal of Sociology* 98, no. 1 (Jul. 1992): 1–29.

"Three Temporalities: Toward an Eventful Sociology." In *The Historic Turn in the Human Sciences*, edited by Terrence J. McDonald. 245–80. Ann Arbor: University of Michigan Press, 1996.

Shaloff, Stanley. "Presbyterians and Belgian Congo Exploitation: The Compagnie du Kasai v. Morrison and Sheppard." *Journal of Presbyterian History* 47, no. 2 (1969): 173–94.

Sherman, William L. *Forced Native Labor in Sixteenth-Century Central America*. Lincoln: University of Nebraska Press, 1979.

Shyllon, F. O. *Black Slaves in Britain*. London: Oxford University Press, 1974.

James Ramsay: The Unknown Abolitionist. Edinburgh: Canongate, 1977.

Sievernich, Michael. "Anfänge prophetischer Theologie: Antonio de Montesinos Predigt (1511) und ihre Folgen." In *Conquista und Evangelisation: 500 Jahre Orden in Lateinamerika*, edited by Michael Sievernich. 77–98. Mainz: Matthias-Grünewald-Verlag, 1992.

Sikkink, Kathryn. "Codes of Conduct for Transnational Corporations: The Case of the WHO/UNICEF Code." *International Organization* 40, no. 4 (Autumn 1986): 815–40.

Silk, John. "Caring at a Distance." *Ethics, Place and Environment* 1, no. 2 (1998): 165–82.

Silva, Maria Beatriz Nizza da. "Vieira e os conflitos com os Colonos do Pará e Maranhão." *Luso-Brazilian Review* 40, no. 1 (2003): 79–87.

Silver, Allan. "Friendship in Commercial Society: Eighteenth-Century Social Theory and Modern Sociology." *American Journal of Sociology* 95, no. 6 (1990): 1474–504.

Silver, Peter. *Our Savage Neighbors: How Indian War Transformed Early America*. New York: W. W. Norton, 2008.

Simmel, Georg. *"Conflict" and "The Web of Group-Affiliations"*. New York: Free Press, 1964 (1908).

Simpson, Lesley Byrd, ed. *The Laws of Burgos of 1512–1513: Royal Ordinances for the Good Government and Treatment of the Indians*. San Francisco: John Howell, 1960.

Skinner, Quentin. *The Foundations of Modern Political Thought, Volume Two: The Age of Reformation*. Cambridge: Cambridge University Press, 1978.

Skinner, Rob. *The Foundations of Anti-Apartheid: Liberal Humanitarians and Transnational Activists in Britain and the United States, c.1919–64*. Houndmills: Palgrave Macmillan, 2010.

Slaughter, Thomas P. *The Beautiful Soul of John Woolman, Apostle of Abolition*. New York: Hill and Wang, 2008.

Smith, Christian. "Correcting a Curious Neglect, or Bringing Religion Back In." In *Disruptive Religion: The Force of Faith in Social-Movement Activism*, edited by Christian Smith. 1–25. New York: Routledge, 1996.

Resisting Reagan: The U.S. Central America Peace Movement. Chicago: University of Chicago Press, 1996.

Smith, E. A. "The Yorkshire Elections of 1806 and 1807: A Study in Electoral Management." *Northern History* 2 (1967): 62–90.

Smith, Jackie. "Transnational Processes and Movements." In *The Blackwell Companion to Social Movements*, edited by David A. Snow, Sarah A. Soule, and Hanspeter Kriesi. 311–35. Malden, MA: Blackwell, 2004.

Smith, Jackie, Ron Pagnucco, and Winnie Romeril. "Transnational social movement organisations in the global political arena." *Voluntas* 5, no. 2 (1994): 121–54.

Smith, William. *A Brief View of the Conduct of Pennsylvania, for the Year 1755.* London: R. Griffiths, 1756.

Soderlund, Jean R. *Quakers & Slavery: A Divided Spirit.* Princeton, NJ: Princeton University Press, 1985.

Soule, Sarah A. "Situational Effects on Political Altruism: The Student Divestment Movement in the United States." In *Political Altruism? Solidarity Movements in International Perspective*, edited by Marco Giugni and Florence Passy. 161–76. Lanham, MD: Rowman and Littlefield, 2001.

Sowle, Patrick. "The North Carolina Manumission Society, 1816–1834." *North Carolina Historical Review* 42, no. 1 (1965): 47–69.

Spalding, Karen. "The Crises and Transformations of Invaded Societies: Andean Area (1500–1580)." In *The Cambridge History of the Native Peoples of the Americas South America*, Vol. III: *South America*, Part 1, edited by Frank Salomon and Stuart B. Schwartz. 904–72. Cambridge: Cambridge University Press, 1999.

Spurr, John. *English Puritanism, 1603–1689.* New York: St. Martin's Press, 1998.

Stamatov, Peter. "The Religious Field and the Path-Dependent Transformation of Popular Politics in the Anglo-American World, 1770–1840." *Theory and Society* 40 (2011): 437–73.

Stanislawski, Dan. *The Transformation of Nicaragua, 1519–1548.* Berkeley: University of California Press, 1983.

Stein, Robert. "The Free Men of Colour and the Revolution in Saint Domingue, 1789–1792." *Histoire Sociale: Social History* 14, no. 27 (1981): 7–28.

"The Revolution of 1789 and the Abolition of Slavery." *Canadian Journal of History* 17 (1982): 447–67.

Stein, Robert Louis. *The French Slave Trade in the Eighteenth Century: An Old Regime Business.* Madison: University of Wisconsin Press, 1979.

Stern, Steve J. *Peru's Indian Peoples and the Challenge of Spanish Conquest: Huamanga to 1640.* Madison: University of Wisconsin Press, 1982.

Streeck, Wolfgang and Kathleen Thelen. "Introduction: Institutional Change in Advanced Political Economies." In *Beyond Continuity: Institutional Change in Advanced Political Economies*, edited by Wolfgang Streeck and Kathleen Thelen. 1–39. Oxford Oxford University Press, 2005.

A Subject for Conversation and Reflection at the Table. London: M. Gurney, 1788.

Swaan, Abram de. "Widening Circles of Identification: Emotional Concerns in Sociogenetic Perspective." *Theory, Culture & Society* 12, no. 2 (1995): 25–39.

Swaisland, Charles. "The Aborigines Protection Society, 1837–1909." *Slavery & Abolition* 21, no. 2 (2000): 265–80.

Sweet, David G. "Black Robes and 'Black Destiny': Jesuit Views of African Slavery in 17th-Century Latin America." *Revista de historia de América* 86 (1978): 87–133.

Swift, David E. "Samuel Hopkins: Calvinist Social Concern in Eighteenth Century New England." *Journal of Presbyterian History* 47, no. 1 (1969): 31–54.

Sword, Kirsten. "Remembering Dinah Nevil: Strategic Deceptions in Eighteenth-Century Antislavery." *The Journal of American History* 97, no. 2 (September 1, 2010): 315–43.

Tarrade, Jean. "Le groupe de pression du commerce à la fin de l'Ancien régime et sous l'Assemblée Constituante." *Bulletin de la Société d'histoire moderne* 69, no. 13 (1970): 23–27.

"Les colonies et les principes de 1789: Les assemblées revolutionnaire face au problème de l'esclavage." *Revue française d'histoire d'outre-mer* 76, no. 282–83 (1989): 9–34.

Tarrow, Sidney. "Cycles of Collective Action: Between Moments of Madness and the Repertoire of Contention." In *Repertoires and Cycles of Collective Action*, edited by Mark Traugott. 89–115. Durham, NC: Duke University Press, 1995.

The New Transnational Activism. New York: Cambridge University Press, 2005.

Power in Movement: Social Movements and Contentious Politics. 2nd ed. Cambridge: Cambridge University Press, 1998.

"Studying Contentious Politics: From Event-ful History to Cycles of Collective Action." In *Acts of Dissent: New Developments in the Study of Protest*, edited by Dieter Rucht, Ruud Koopmans, and Friedhelm Neidhardt. 33–64. Lanham, MD: Rowman and Littlefield, 1999.

Temperley, Howard. *British Antislavery 1833–1870*. London: Longman, 1972.

"Capitalism, Slavery and Ideology." *Past and Present*, no. 75 (1977): 94–118.

Tester, Keith. *Moral Culture*. London: SAGE, 1997.

Thayer, Theodore. *Israel Pemberton, King of the Quakers*. Philadelphia: Historical Society of Pennsylvania, 1943.

Pennsylvania Politics and the Growth of Democracy, 1740–1776. Harrisburg: Pennsylvania Historical and Museum Commission, 1953.

Thésée, Françoise. "Autour de la Société des Amis des Noirs: Clarkson, Mirabeau et l'abolition de la traite (août 1789-mars 1790)." *Présence africaine* 125 (1983): 3–82.

Thomas, Paul. "The Caribs of St Vincent: A Study in Imperial Maladministration, 1763–73." *Journal of Caribbean History* 18, no. 2 (1983): 60–73.

"Changing Attitudes in an Expanding Empire: The Anti-Slavery Movement, 1760–1783." *Slavery & Abolition* 5, no. 1 (1984): 50–72.

Thompson, Alexander Hamilton. "The Monastic Orders." In *The Cambridge Medieval History*, Vol. V, edited by J. R. Tanner, C. W. Previté-Orton, and Z. N. Brooke. 658–96. Cambridge: Cambridge University Press, 1926.

Thompson, Mack. *Moses Brown, Reluctant Reformer*. Chapel Hill: University of North Carolina Press, 1962.

Thörn, Håkan. *Anti-Apartheid and the Emergence of a Global Civil Society*. Basingstoke: Palgrave Macmillan, 2006.

Tibesar, Antonine. "The Franciscan Province of the Holy Cross of Española, 1505–1559." *The Americas* 13, no. 4 (1957): 377.

"Instructions for the Confessors of Conquistadores Issued by the Archbishop of Lima in 1560." *The Americas* 3, no. 4 (Apr. 1947): 514–34.

Tilly, Charles. *The Contentious French: Four Centuries of Popular Struggle*. Cambridge, MA: Harvard University Press, 1986.

Popular Contention in Great Britain, 1758–1834. Cambridge, MA: Harvard University Press, 1995.

"Social Movements and National Politics." In *Statemaking and Social Movements: Essays in History and Theory*, edited by Charles Bright and Susan Harding. 297–317. Ann Arbor: University of Michigan Press, 1984.

Torre Rangel, Jesús Antonio de la. "Confesionarios: Uso del derecho canónico a favor de los Indios." In *Memoria del X congreso del Instituto Internacional de Historia del Derecho Indiano,* vol. 2. 1657–74. Mexico City: Escuela Libre de Derecho, Universidad Nacional Autónoma de México, 1995.

Torres Campos, Rafael. *Carácter de la conquista y colonización de las Islas Canarias.* Madrid: Depósito de la Guerra, 1901.

Towner, Lawrence W. "The Sewall-Saffin Dialogue on Slavery." *The William and Mary Quarterly* 21, no. 1 (1964): 40–52.

Traslosheros, Jorge E. "En derecho y en justicia: Fray Juan de Zumárraga, la administración de la justicia y el proyecto de iglesia de los primeros obispos de la Nueva España." In *Religión, poder y autoridad en la Nueva España*, edited by Alicia Mayer and Ernesto de la Torre Villar. 25–39. Mexico City: Universidad Nacional Autónoma de México, 2004.

Tully, Alan. *Forming American Politics: Ideals, Interests, and Institutions in Colonial New York and Pennsylvania.* Baltimore, MD: Johns Hopkins University Press, 1994.

Turley, David. *The Culture of English Antislavery, 1780–1860.* London: Routledge, 1991.

Turner, Mary. *Slaves and Missionaries: The Disintegration of Jamaican Slave Society, 1787–1834.* Urbana: University of Illinois Press, 1982.

Tyrell, Hartmann. "Weltgesellschaft, Weltmission und religiöse Organisationen: Einleitung." In *Weltmission und religiöse Organisationen: Protestantische Missionsgesellschaften im 19. und 20. Jahrhundert*, edited by Artur Bogner, Bernd Holtwick, and Hartmann Tyrell. 13–134. Würzburg: Ergon, 2004.

Underhill, Edward Bean. *Life of James Mursell Phillippo, Missionary in Jamaica.* London: Yates and Alexander, 1881.

Valeri, Mark. "The New Divinity and the American Revolution." *The William and Mary Quarterly* 46, no. 4 (1989): 741–69.

Van Cleve, George. *A Slaveholders' Union: Slavery, Politics, and the Constitution in the Early American Republic.* Chicago: University of Chicago Press, 2010.

"*Somerset's Case* and Its Antecedents in Imperial Perspective." *Law & History Review* 24, no. 3 (2006): 601–45.

Van Kley, Dale K. *The Religious Origins of the French Revolution: From Calvin to the Civil Constitution, 1560–1791.* New Haven, CT: Yale University Press, 1996.

Vargas, José María. *Fr. Domingo de Santo Tomás, defensor y apóstol de los indios del Perú: Su vida y sus escritos.* Quito, Ecuador: Editorial Santo Domingo, 1937.

Vaughan, Alden T. *The Roots of American Racism: Essays on the Colonial Experience.* New York: Oxford University Press, 1995.

Vaux, Roberts. *Memoirs of the Lives of Benjamin Lay and Ralph Sandiford; Two of the Earliest Public Advocates for the Emancipation of the Enslaved Africans.* London: W. Phillips, 1816.

Verter, Bradford. "Spiritual Capital: Theorizing Religion with Bourdieu Against Bourdieu." *Sociological Theory* 21, no. 2 (2003): 150–74.

Vibert, Faith. "The Society for the Propagation of the Gospel in Foreign Parts: Its Work for the Negroes in North America Before 1783." *The Journal of Negro History* 18, no. 2 (1933): 171–212.

Vigil, Ralph H. "Bartolomé de las Casas, Judge Alonso de Zorita, and the Franciscans: A Collaborative Effort for the Spiritual Conquest of the Borderlands." *The Americas* 38, no. 1 (1981): 45.

Vila Vilar, Enriqueta. "La postura de la iglesia frente a la esclavitud. Siglos XVI y XVII." In *Esclavitud y derechos humanos: La lucha por la libertad del negro en el siglo XIX*, edited by Francisco de Solano and Agustín Guimerá Ravina. 25–31. Madrid: Consejo Superior de Investigaciones Científicas, 1990.

Vila Vilar, Enriqueta and Luisa Vila Vilar, eds. *Los abolicionistas españoles: Siglo XIX*. Madrid: Ediciones de Cultura Hispánica, 1996.

Vink, Markus. "Freedom and Slavery: The Dutch Republic, the VOC World, and the Debate over the 'World's Oldest Trade'." *South African Historical Journal* 60, no. 1 (2008): 19–46.

" 'The World's Oldest Trade': Dutch Slavery and Slave Trade in the Indian Ocean in the Seventeenth Century." *Journal of World History* 14, no. 2 (2003): 131–77.

Waldstreicher, David. "The Origins of Antislavery in Pennsylvania: Early Abolitionists and Benjamin Franklin's Road Not Taken." In *Antislavery and Abolition in Philadelphia: Emancipation and the Long Struggle for Racial Justice in the City of Brotherly Love*, edited by Richard Newman and James Mueller. 45–65. Baton Rouge: Louisiana State University Press, 2011.

Wallace, Anthony F. C. "Revitalization Movements." *American Anthropologist* 58, no. 2 (1956): 264–81.

Walvin, James. *England, Slaves, and Freedom: 1776–1838*. Jackson: University Press of Mississippi, 1986.

Walzer, Michael. *Thick and Thin: Moral Argument at Home and Abroad*. South Bend, IN: University of Notre Dame Press, 1994.

Wanquet, Claude. "Baco and Burnel's Attempt to Implement Abolition in the Mascarenes in 1796: Analysis of a Failure and Its Consequences." In *The Abolitions of Slavery: From Léger Félicité Sonthonax to Victor Schoelcher, 1793, 1794, 1848*. 197–206. New York: Berghahn Books, 2003.

Ward, Matthew C. *Breaking the Backcountry: The Seven Years' War in Virginia and Pennsylvania, 1754–1765*. Pittsburgh: University of Pittsburgh Press, 2003.

Ward, W. R. *Christianity under the Ancien Régime, 1648–1789*. Cambridge: Cambridge University Press, 1999.

Watts, Michael R. *The Dissenters: From the Reformation to the French Revolution*. Oxford: Clarendon Press, 1978.

Wax, Darold D. "Negro Import Duties in Colonial Pennsylvania." *Pennsylvania Magazine of History & Biography* 97, no. 1 (1973): 22–44.

"Negro Import Duties in Colonial Virginia: A Study of British Commercial Policy and Local Public Policy." *The Virginia Magazine of History and Biography* 79, no. 1 (1971): 29–44.

"Reform and Revolution: The Movement against Slavery and the Slave Trade in Revolutionary Pennsylvania." *Western Pennsylvania Historical Magazine* 57, no. 4 (1974): 403–29.

Weber, Max. *Gesammelte Aufsätze zur Religionssoziologie*. Tübingen: Mohr, 1986.

"Religious Rejections of the World and Their Directions." In *From Max Weber: Essays in Sociology*, edited by H. H. Gerth and C. Wright Mills. 323–59. New York: Oxford University Press, (1915) 1946.

Weddle, Meredith Baldwin. *Walking in the Way of Peace: Quaker Pacifism in the Seventeenth Century*. Oxford: Oxford University Press, 2001.

West, Delno C. "Medieval Ideas of Apocalyptic Mission and the Early Franciscans in Mexico." *Americas* 45, no. 3 (1989): 293–313.

Whelan, Irene. *The Bible War in Ireland: The "Second Reformation" and the Polarization of Protestant-Catholic Relations, 1800–1840*. Dublin: Lilliput Press, 2005.

Whitehead, Neil L. "The Crises and Transformations of Invaded Societies: The Caribbean (1492–1580)." In *The Cambridge History of the Native Peoples of the Americas South America*, Vol. III: *South America*, Part 1, edited by Frank Salomon and Stuart B. Schwartz. 864–903. Cambridge: Cambridge University Press, 1999.

Whittier, Nancy. "The Consequences of Social Movements for Each Other." In *The Blackwell Companion to Social Movements*, edited by David A. Snow, Sarah A. Soule, and Hanspeter Kriesi. 531–51. Malden, MA: Blackwell, 2004.

Whyte, Iain. *Scotland and the Abolition of Black Slavery, 1756–1838*. Edinburgh: Edinburgh University Press, 2006.

Wiecek, William M. "Somerset: Lord Mansfield and the Legitimacy of Slavery in the Anglo-American World." *The University of Chicago Law Review* 42, no. 1 (1974): 86–146.

"The Statutory Law of Slavery and Race in the Thirteen Mainland Colonies of British America." *The William and Mary Quarterly* 34, no. 2 (1977): 258–80.

Williams, Eric. *Capitalism and Slavery*. Chapel Hill: University of North Carolina Press, 1944.

Wilson, Ellen Gibson. *Thomas Clarkson: A Biography*. Basingstoke: Macmillan, 1989.

Wilson, Samuel M. *Hispaniola: Caribbean Chiefdoms in the Age of Columbus*. Tuscaloosa: University of Alabama Press, 1990.

Wiltfang, Gregory L. and Doug McAdam. "The Costs and Risks of Social Activism: A Study of Sanctuary Movement Activism." *Social Forces* 69, no. 4 (1991): 987–1010.

Winter, J. M. van. "Public Opinion in the Netherlands on the Abolition of Slavery." In *Dutch Authors on West Indian History: A Historiographical Selection*, edited by M. A. P. Meilink-Roelofsz. 99–128. The Hague: M. Nijhoff, 1982.

Wise, Steven M. *Though the Heavens May Fall: The Landmark Trial that Led to the End of Human Slavery*. Cambridge, MA: Da Capo Press, 2005.

Wölfel, Dominik Josef. "La Curia Romana y la Corona de España en la defensa de los aborígenes Canarios." *Anthropos* 25 (1930): 1011–83.

Wood, Gordon S. *The Radicalism of the American Revolution*. New York: A. A. Knopf, 1992.

Wood, Marcus. "Packaging Liberty and Marketing the Gift of Freedom: 1807 and the Legacy of Clarkson's Chest." *Parliamentary History* 26 Supplement (2007): 205–23.

Woods, John A. "The Correspondence of Benjamin Rush and Granville Sharp, 1773–1809." *Journal of American Studies* 1, no. 1 (1967): 1–38.

Worrall, Arthur J. *Quakers in the Colonial Northeast*. Hanover, NH: University Press of New England, 1980.

Zald, Mayer N. and John D. McCarthy. "Social Movement Industries: Competition and Cooperation Among Movement Organizations." *Research in Social Movements, Conflict and Change* 3 (1980): 1–20.

Zavala, Silvio A. *La encomienda indiana*. 2nd ed. Mexico City: Editorial Porrúa, 1973.

Zilversmit, Arthur. *The First Emancipation: The Abolition of Slavery in the North.* Chicago: University of Chicago Press, 1967.

Zucker, Lynne G. "Organizations as Institutions." *Research in the Sociology of Organizations* 2 (1983): 1–47.

Index

Printed in the United States
By Bookmasters